Clear, Hold, and Destroy

CLEAR, HOLD, and DESTROY

Pacification in Phú Yên and the American War in Vietnam

Robert J. Thompson III

UNIVERSITY OF OKLAHOMA PRESS : NORMAN

Library of Congress Cataloging-in-Publication Data

Names: Thompson, Robert J., III, 1983– author.
Title: Clear, hold, and destroy : pacification in Phú Yên and the American war in Vietnam / Robert J. Thompson III.
Description: Norman, Oklahoma : University of Oklahoma Press, [2021] | Includes bibliographical references and index. | Summary: "Phú Yên province in Vietnam was a prominent target of American pacification, an effort to win the 'hearts and minds' of the Vietnamese. This book reviews Phú Yên's storied history with pacification before and during the French colonial period, then focuses on the American War from 1965 to 1975, exploring how the Americans advanced pacification, relying on conventional military forces, and why this effort ultimately failed"—Provided by publisher.
Identifiers: LCCN 2020058554 | ISBN 978-0-8061-6869-2 (hardcover)
Subjects: LCSH: Vietnam War, 1961–1975—Campaigns—Vietnam—Phú Yên (Province) | Vietnam War, 1961–1975—United States. | Phú Yên (Vietnam : Province)—History— 20th century.
Classification: LCC DS559.9.P5 T46 2021 | DDC 959.704/342095975—dc23
LC record available at https://lccn.loc.gov/2020058554

To Corrina and our cadre:
Anton, Lukas, Valerie, and Marcel

And to our parents:
Robert and Patricia Thompson and
David and Cynthia Clark

Contents

Acknowledgments

What began as a fledgling dissertation idea in 2011 at the University of Southern Mississippi is now my first book. After I signed my contract with the University of Oklahoma Press, I started pondering how I would write these acknowledgments; that section of a book is deceptively difficult to write. One can do the research and write the chapters, but adequately thanking all the people and institutions that have been involved is a monumental task. They are as much a part of the story as the history that unfolds in the subsequent chapters.

My interest in Phú Yên began in the office of my advisor, Andrew Wiest. Andy suggested that I examine a peculiar, seemingly nondescript province called Phú Yên and consider why the war there went so poorly for the United States. A visit to a collection of papers at the McCain Library and Archives soon filled my mind with thoughts of pacification and Phú Yên. For that conversation and the years of guidance—both academic and private—I am forever grateful to Andy. He prepared me both for the rigors of completing a PhD program and, later, for the challenges of balancing academic and family responsibilities. Assisting him with his projects on the Vietnam War afforded me invaluable opportunities to contribute to the rich discourse and prepare myself for doing so without his supervision. Again, thank you, Andy. Also at the University of Southern Mississippi, Heather Stur instilled me with confidence that I could "do" history. Through our conversations, she infused in me the need to appreciate the Vietnamese perspective and to stay focused. I sincerely hope my book makes Andy and Heather proud.

I am indebted to Adam Kane. He expressed interest in my work before I completed the dissertation. Over the years, his guidance and tolerance gave me the space and time needed to transform the dissertation into a manuscript. Adam deserves credit for coming up with the title *Clear, Hold, and Destroy*—a play on Robert W. Komer's article "Clear, Hold, and Build." When he left OU Press, Alessandra J. Tamulevich and Steven Baker took over editing responsibilities with minimal disruption. Stephanie Sykes deserves my thanks for her copyediting, and Erin Greb for creating the fantastic maps for this book. *Clear, Hold, and Destroy* would still be a dream if not for all their efforts.

One individual in particular deserves my infinite appreciation. Angela Riotto, a rising star in the realm of American Civil War scholarship, graciously edited chapters, helping me clarify and assert arguments lost in my rambling prose. Her editing skills and friendship saved me on numerous occasions. The index came together because of her. Angela undoubtably learned more about Phú Yên than she ever intended. She also proved to be a great sounding board for my map ideas. If anyone knows my book better than I, it is she.

This book would have gotten nowhere without Foreign Service Officers and U.S. Army veterans indulging me in conversation on numerous occasions. My thanks to Robert Barron, David Curtin, Steve Dike, Eugene Fluke, Courtney Frobenius, Thomas Kaulukukui, Robert C. Lafoon, Russell L. Meerdink, Rufus Phillips, Ronald Thayer, Charles S. Varnum, and Ellis Wisner for sharing their firsthand experiences in Phú Yên with me. Dave, Ellis, Ron, Steve, and Tom, thank you for sharing your stories and documents with me. Bruce Kinsey and William Stearman experienced Vietnam outside of Phú Yên, yet their knowledge proved foundational.

Clear, Hold, and Destroy exists largely because of the generosity of fellow scholars. In particular, Merle Pribbenow furnished translations of Vietnamese texts that I otherwise would never have seen, greatly improving my understanding of the People's Army of Vietnam. Thanks to Merle's generous efforts, this book sheds at least some light on the Communist perspective. Kevin Boylan and Tom Richardson answered many of my questions and provided invaluable feedback. They set the bar high with their own province studies. It is my hope that this study of Phú Yên adds to their contributions. From helping me with archival research to discussing various aspects of the war, I cannot thank Erik Villard enough. My understanding of the French experience in Phú Yên benefited greatly from Carlos Valle's translations of numerous pages of French text. Nguyễn Hồng Uyên and Lê Đức An provided tremendous assistance by ensuring the diacritic accuracy of the numerous Vietnamese terms in these pages. Jerri Bell and Aimée Fox provided formative feedback on the introduction. Martin Clemis, Greg Daddis, and Gian Gentile helped steer me in the right direction when I first began thinking about pacification's meaning. Chris Carey, Terry Peterson, and Dale Smith provided much-needed feedback on chapter one. Simon Toner's comments helped improve chapter two. On numerous occasions, Blair Tidely responded to my questions regarding Vietnam's geography and language peculiarities. Similarly, Christian Lentz graciously answered my emails about diacritics and the Vietnamese language in general. Andy Gawthorpe, too, provided insight on numerous occasions.

I am also thankful for the conversations over the years with other scholars. Many thanks to Allison Abra, Jon Askonas, Tom Bruscino, Clay Drees, Marjorie Galelli, Mike Hankins, Tavis Harris, Tim Hemmis, Alex Woo Young Kim, Ivo Komljen, Christine Leppard, Dan Margolies, Kate McGowan, Ron Milam, Ed Moïse, Amanda Nagel, Mike Neiberg, Tom Reinstein, Roger Sarty, Stuart Schrader, Susannah Ural, Jackie Whitt, Jim Willbanks, and Cameron Zinsou. Although I began my Phú Yên project long before working at Army University Press, I must nevertheless thank my fellow Films Team historians Chris Carey, Kimball Johnson, Randy Masten, Roy Parker, and Angela Riotto for their support and our numerous conversations. Also at AUP, Eric Burke, Kate Dahlstrand, and Don Wright deserve my gratitude.

The archives and the archivists maintaining precious primary sources made researching Phú Yên all the more productive. To the numerous archivists at the National Archives and Records Administration at College Park who aided me over the years, thank you. My thanks also to Jennifer Brannock at the University of Southern Mississippi's McCain Library and Archives, and to Texas Tech University's Sheon Montgomery. I commend the people at the Hoover Institution Library and Archives at Stanford University—Carol A. Leadenham, David Sun, Jill Golden, Bronweyn Coleman, Irena Czernichowska, Stephanie E. Stewart, Hsiao-ting Lin, Lisa Nguyen, and everyone else at that great facility. Without their assistance, particularly in the form of the Silas Palmer Research Fellowship and subsequent assistance on-site, chapter one would never have materialized as I envisioned. The U.S. Army Center of Military History took interest in my research, bestowing me with a dissertation fellowship from 2015 to 2016. Aided by Andrew Birtle, Thomas Boghardt, James Tobias, and Erik Villard, I acquired invaluable documents that formed the bedrock of the manuscript you are about to read.

Two other entities deserve my praise. The arguments in this book began as ideas I posed to audiences at multiple Society for Military History (SMH) meetings. I am indebted to SMH for awarding me a Russell F. Weigley Graduate Student Travel Grant for the 83rd Annual Meeting in Ottawa, Ontario. The Strategy Bridge's online journal ran a version of chapter eight's section on the Battle of Cùng Sơn. I am grateful for the editorial team's enthusiasm to bring my account of that forgotten battle to the public's attention, especially Nate Finney, Tyrell Mayfield, and Eric Michael Murphy.

I must thank my family—the most important support system I have had to aid my endeavors. *Clear, Hold, and Destroy* took shape, appropriately enough, at my parent's house, a few miles down the George Washington Parkway from Edward G. Lansdale's former home and near George Washington's Mount Vernon. My parents, Robert and Patricia Thompson, encouraged my interest in history from an early age. I cannot thank them enough for their unyielding support throughout my life. Opening up their home to my own growing family made it possible for me to complete my dissertation. From assisting with childcare to providing a quiet place to write, my parents did everything they could to help me realize my dream of earning a PhD. My parents-in-law, David and Cynthia Clark, have done a lot for me as well. First, they gave their blessing for me to marry their daughter, Corrina. Second, they organized a much-needed retreat every summer to Williamsburg, Virginia, where I could briefly escape, with family, the complexities of the world. I am also grateful for the help of my sisters, Gillian and Jocelyn. Gillian hosted me during my two weeks at the Hoover Institution. Jocelyn helped with childcare and loaned me a desk to complete my workspace. My sisters-in-law Amy Breton and Melissa Bruere, my brother-in-law Dave Clark, and their families all helped along the way. I have considered Mike Keating a brother since the eighth grade. Many thanks to Mike and his wife Christi for their support over the years. May our families always be close.

My best friend and beloved wife, Corrina, is forever deserving of my gratitude. Her companionship and unyielding support gave me the time to finish my dissertation, secure employment as a historian, and complete this book. Along the way we celebrated the Washington Capitals 2018 Stanley Cup victory and expanded our family. Our four children help us periodize that journey: comprehensive exams—baby Anton; dissertation—baby Lukas; graduation—baby Valerie; and our book baby Marcel. I thank all of them for putting up with a father glued to his laptop, writing the hours away. For the sacrifices of my family, *Clear, Hold, and Destroy* is dedicated to them.

My apologies in advance to anyone whom I forgot to thank. No work is without mistakes. Any errors and omissions herein are mine alone.

Abbreviations

AO	Area of operation
AAR	After action report
ABF	Attack by fire
AO	Area of operations
APC	Accelerated Pacification Campaign
ARVN	Army of the Republic of Vietnam
AWOL	Absent without leave
AT28	Advisory Team 28
BC	Body count
BLT	Battalion Landing Team
CIA	Central Intelligence Agency
CIDG	Civilian Irregular Defense Group
CMH	U.S. Army Center of Military History, Fort McNair, Washington, D.C.
CORDS	Civil Operations and Revolutionary Development Support (later Civil Operations and Rural Development Support)
COSVN	Central Office of South Vietnam (North Vietnamese political and military organizing body inside South Vietnam)
DPSA	Deputy Province Senior Advisor
DRVN	Democratic Republic of Vietnam
DSA	District Senior Advisor
DTIC	Defense Technical Information Center, Fort Belvoir, Va.
FFV	Field Force, Vietnam
FWMAF	Free World Military Assistance Forces

FSO	Foreign Service Officer
GVN	Government of Vietnam
HES	Hamlet Evaluation System
HIA	Hoover Institution Library and Archives, Stanford University, Stanford, Calif.
I CTZ	I Corps Tactical Zone
IFFV	I Field Force, Vietnam
JGS	Joint General Staff
JUSPAO	Joint United States Public Affairs Office
KIA	killed in action
LAW	Light Antitank Weapon
LOC	line of communication
LRRP	Long-Range Reconnaissance Platoon
LTL-6B	Liên Tỉnh Lộ 6B
LTL-7B	Liên Tỉnh Lộ 7B
LTL-9	Liên Tỉnh Lộ 9
MACCORDS	Military Assistance Command Civil Operations and Revolutionary/Rural Development Support
MACV	Military Assistance Command, Vietnam
MAT	Mobile Advisory Team
MLA	McCain Library and Archives, University of Southern Mississippi, Hattiesburg, Miss.
MR2	Military Region 2 (called II Corps by the South Vietnamese military)
MORD	Ministry of Revolutionary Development (later Ministry of Rural Development)
NARA II	National Archives and Records Administration, College Park, Md.
NLF	National Liberation Front
NPFF	National Police Field Force
NVA	North Vietnamese Army; see also PAVN
ORLL	Operational Report on Lessons Learned
OSA	Office of the Special Assistant
PAVN	People's Army of Vietnam
PF	Popular Forces
PLAF	People's Liberation Armed Forces
POL	Political Section (U.S. Embassy in Saigon)

PSA	Province Senior Advisor
PSDF	People's Self-Defense Force
PSYOP	Psychological operations
QL-1	Quốc lộ 1
RD	Revolutionary Development (later Rural Development)
RF	Regional Forces
RG	Record group
ROKA	Republic of Korea Army
ROK	Republic of Korea
ROKMC	Republic of Korea Marine Corps
RVN	Republic of Vietnam
RVNAF	Republic of Vietnam Armed Forces
SLO	Senior Liaison Office
TAOR	Tactical area of operations
TL-9B	Tỉnh Lộ 9B
TTUVA	Vietnam Center and Sam Johnson Vietnam Archive, Texas Tech University, Lubbock, Tex.
USAF	United States Air Force
USAID	United States Agency for International Development
USIS	United States Information Service
USOM	United States Operations Mission
VC	Việt Cộng; see also PLAF
VCI	Việt Cộng Infrastructure
WIA	Wounded in action

Note on Language

The Vietnamese use the Latin alphabet with diacritics to indicate different pronunciations inherent in their tonal language. When applicable in this book, Vietnamese names are rendered with diacritics. I chose to do so because Phú Yên is more than just another battlefield in what the Vietnamese call the American War. A book on Phú Yên is incomplete without diacritics. Yet Phú Yên has changed considerably since the end of the war, with borders redrawn and place names changed. Additionally, American sources from the war typically contained names without diacritics. When those factors made identifying the diacritically accurate names for certain places difficult, I selected the most accurate renderings possible. Readers will notice that I retained Americanized names when they appear in quotations. I did this to ensure historical accuracy, as not all hamlets appeared on maps from the war. Place names like Hanoi (Hà Nội), Saigon (Sài Gòn), and Vietnam (Việt Nam) are so well engrained in the minds of readers when thinking about the Vietnam War that I chose to spell such terms in Latin script without diacritics.

Language choices extend to Vietnamese names. Dissimilar from American ones, Vietnamese names go in the order of family name, middle name, then given name. To use Ngô Đình Diệm as an example, "Ngô" is the family name and "Diệm" the given name. I chose to employ the full names out of respect. Identification of the Communist actors also matters to this story. To provide clarity, this study employs neither the ambiguous and aspersing "Việt Cộng" nor its shortened form "VC" outside of quotations. Those pejorative terms, which covered anyone and anything serving the Communist cause, make it difficult to ascertain the exact entity being addressed. Thus, this book uses more accurate and specific alternatives, like the National Liberation Front and the People's Liberation Armed Forces.

Introduction

View from a Hill

Still stained with blood from a battle hours earlier, a grassy hill in Phú Yên Province glistened as the morning sun rose over the landscape. Under the silhouette of Núi Chấp Chài, the mountain that dominated the Tuy Hòa Valley, sat Hill 40, near the hamlet of Minh Đức.[1] On the night of 31 March 1970, twelve South Vietnamese troops of Regional Force 112 and seven American soldiers of the 173rd Airborne Brigade lay in wait atop that hill to ambush People's Liberation Armed Forces (PLAF) units. An hour past midnight on 1 April, the South Vietnamese and Americans instead found themselves the targets of thirty determined members of PLAF's D-96 Main Force Battalion. With B-40 rockets detonating all around them—and reluctant to die in a war being abandoned by the United States—the South Vietnamese fled after the first assault, leaving the seven Americans outnumbered. Two Americans survived the battle. U.S. resolve in Phú Yên did not.[2]

Pacification in Phú Yên nearly perished with those five American soldiers on Hill 40. Lt. Col. Frank J. McNeese, Deputy Province Senior Advisor (DPSA), later reported, "all five bodies were brought down and laid in front of the school." The grisly scene of five lifeless American bodies in front of a school briefly jolted the province from its slumber.[3] Having gone to sleep during the perceived pacification gains of the late 1960s, Phú Yên awoke in 1970 as a province largely unpacified.[4] Coupled with PLAF's abduction of scores of South Vietnamese in Phú Yên, the American deaths sowed distrust between American and South Vietnamese officials.

1

That the devastating attack of 1 April likely emanated from Núi Chấp Chài surprised no one. That jungled mountain on the periphery of the province's capital, Tuy Hòa City, functioned as a known base for Communist forces throughout the American War in the Republic of Vietnam (RVN). As McNeese surveyed the battlefield at Minh Đức, American, South Korean, and South Vietnamese authorities convened for a routine meeting in Tuy Hòa City. Although the meeting minutes do not mention Minh Đức specifically, they chronicle a dour conversation over security trends. Held on the same day as the battle—April Fools' Day no less—the meeting highlighted a grim truth: despite three years of operations conducted by I Field Force, Vietnam (IFFV) to advance pacification, the Communist presence near Tuy Hòa City remained. The enemy presence at Núi Chấp Chài embodied the failure of pacification in Phú Yên.[5] Furthermore, the hilltop disaster occurred during the Advisory Crisis, a significant yet historically forgotten part of the American War. The Advisory Crisis placed Phú Yên under scrutiny in the United States and revealed the mounting acceptance by American officials that both pacification and Vietnamization had failed.

What transpired in Phú Yên in 1970 offers damning insight into pacification. Examining Phú Yên provides a fresh perspective that observes the war across multiple levels, ranging from those making policy to those effecting policy and those affected by policy. The consequences of IFFV's abandonment of the province substantiate the effect of its operations, while addressing the confluence of causes that ultimately weakened pacification in Phú Yên. American progress was anything but seamless in Phú Yên. The North Vietnamese presence on Núi Chấp Chài was part of an extensive network used by the Communists to challenge pacification across the province. Base Areas in the province's remote tracks projected People's Army of Vietnam (PAVN) and PLAF power into the heart of Phú Yên, especially in the densely populated Tuy Hòa Valley, confining efforts by the Government of Vietnam (GVN) to expand control mostly to the province's capital. Pacification—the means by which Saigon expanded control in Phú Yên—largely depended on continuous conventional military operations. Even then, progress proved ephemeral.

The presence of American conventional military forces fostered the illusion of pacification as advancing the RVN toward permanent stability under the GVN. For American officials, in a way, the execution of more military operations meant more progress. Years of efforts to pacify Phú Yên resulted in a security situation that had gone from dangerous to uncertain. Between 1966 and 1969, operations by IFFV's maneuver battalions gave the impression of improved security. When contrasted with PAVN and PLAF nearly overrunning Phú Yên in 1965, IFFV gains appeared even more noteworthy. IFFV's operations in the province, however, left the enemy anything but beaten. Evidence slowly emerged, beginning in 1967, that PAVN and PLAF had retained sufficient strength with which to challenge pacification in the province. The 1968 Tết Offensive exposed IFFV's operations as having failed to advance pacification as much as previously thought. Events between 1969 and 1972 undoubtedly proved that PAVN and PLAF had regained *and* exercised sufficient control in Phú Yên to undermine American pacification efforts.

By the end of the American War, Phú Yên held the dubious status of being one of the least secure provinces in the RVN. Hanoi and Saigon competed in Phú Yên to establish suzerainty to extract allegiance from the people. Since the Americans and South Vietnamese consistently struggled to bring Phú Yên under Saigon's banner, examining Phú Yên offers profound insight into how the Americans advanced pacification and why pacification ultimately did not work. A province study of Phú Yên grapples with the role of conventional warfare in pacification—purposefully placing the two terms as mutually inclusive. To achieve the task of untying the pacification knot, this study reaches, albeit briefly, back into Phú Yên's storied history with pacification before and during the French colonial period to the onset of the American War in 1965, and then concludes in 1975. By focusing on the American War, it addresses how the United States physically advanced pacification with conventional military forces. Furthermore, this focus reveals the implications of the gradual drawdown of military assets focused on sustaining pacification. This work additionally offers an explanation of pacification, a term that lacked a lasting, agreed-upon definition throughout the war and continues to be debated.

How U.S. Army soldiers came to die on that hill matters. The dissolution of European empires after the Second World War offered both Moscow and Washington the opportunity to spread influence at the expense of the other. Decolonization swept the world as former colonies embraced revolution and established independent nations. "Protracted people's warfare," as practiced by Mao Zedong, influenced the Việt Nam Độc Lập Đồng Minh Hội (Vietnam Independence League)—better known as the Việt Minh. Founded by Hồ Chí Minh in 1941 to fight the French and the Japanese, the Việt Minh—and the organization it evolved into after 1951, the Liên Việt (Hội Liên hiệp Quốc dân

Việt Nam, or Vietnamese National Popular Front)—laid the nationalistic and patriotic framework for the future Democratic Republic of Vietnam (DRVN).[6] When the French lost the First Indochina War to the Việt Minh in 1954, the future of Vietnam remained anything but resolved. The Việt Minh's Communist vision did not resonate with all Vietnamese, particularly among nationalists in the south.[7] The history that followed—the presidency of Ngô Đình Diệm and the subsequent Americanization of the conflict during the Second Indochina War, as the American War in Vietnam was sometimes called—is best understood as a contest of opposing visions. Where Hanoi mandated itself with uniting all Vietnamese under its control, Saigon sought a separate existence—one free of Communist influence. The realization of both visions required control over South Vietnam's countryside. North Vietnam turned to *đấu tranh*—which translates to a struggle of the people for the benefit all—to subdue South Vietnam.

Đấu tranh targeted the people. For the North Vietnamese, đấu tranh functioned as both an ideal and a literal concept, a political and a military struggle.[8] Through an aggressive, hybrid political and military strategy centered on subversion and violence, Hanoi envisaged the infiltration of South Vietnamese society and the transformation of Saigon's dominion into an extension of the North Vietnamese state. Through đấu tranh, Hanoi backed the insurgency of the National Liberation Front (NLF) in the south. In effect, a civil war gripped South Vietnam as Saigon battled Hanoi's revolutionaries for control of the southern lands. Yet guerrillas constituted just one facet of the Politburo's strategy. PLAF received substantial support from the conventional PAVN. That force deployed many large, powerful units to the South Vietnamese countryside. In terms of military planning, the Politburo relied on *Tổng Công Kích-Tổng Khởi Nghĩa*, better known as the General Offensive and Uprising strategy. As the manifestation of đấu tranh, General Offensive and Uprising centered on Hanoi's armed forces applying pressure militarily in massive efforts to spread the revolution while fostering rebellion against Saigon among the South Vietnamese.

Đấu tranh posed a significant challenge for its opponents. Saigon therefore simultaneously combated two related yet different opponents—a conventional foe in PAVN and an unconventional opponent in PLAF. That alone made pacification in Phú Yên and elsewhere in the RVN exceedingly onerous. To that end, this study focuses on how Americans entered and operated in a Vietnamese space. Pacification is how the Saigon government and assets rendered by Washington responded to revolutionary warfare. The episode at Minh Đức—and more generally the war in Phú Yên—occurred as both Hanoi and Saigon battled one another for primacy.

The orthodox versus revisionist dichotomy that is typical of Vietnam War historiography has left an incomplete portrait of the war.[9] Warfare, pacification, and abandonment are terms hardly new to Vietnam War scholarship, but these themes remain fertile ground for further inquiry. Exactly how these themes worked together—indeed the very relationship between all three—underscores the need for a study on Phú Yên, which rectifies three prevailing errors in the historiography: the lack of American military interest in pacification until the late-war period; the mischaracterization of pacification as separate from conventional warfare; and the lack of perspective on the war at the grassroots-hamlet-to-district level. For these reasons, the history of the Vietnam War is woefully incomplete without an examination of Phú Yên.[10]

Pacification lay at the very heart of the American approach to fighting the war, yet pertinent scholarship is lacking. Some scholars have erroneously argued that pacification existed separate from the war executed by the U.S. Army.[11] Previous studies dealing with pacification never went beyond brief (if any) analysis of the term—which is not surprising, given that those who directed the war never agreed on a lasting interpretation. The constructive phase of pacification, too, is largely neglected in the literature compared with the war's far more ubiquitous destructive phase.[12] Political scientists' treatment of pacification as a mechanism of control warrants extra attention when using the term in the context of the Vietnam War.[13] Absent a detailed analysis of the word, pacification is erroneously discussed as a separate facet—rather than the foundation—of the war in the RVN. When discussed, pacification is often treated as a civilian apparatus for developing the countryside and bettering the lives of people through economic and infrastructure improvements. In reality, pacification entailed *both* destruction and construction, and thus cannot be limited merely to civilian efforts. Although pacification included peaceful, constructive methods, to be sure, it also benefited from the battles waged by conventional forces.[14] In practice, the entire conflict remained dedicated to the removal of Communist forces. To create space for the GVN to control the population, conventional military forces needed to evict PAVN and PLAF main forces from the countryside.[15] Occurring concurrently, pacification then existed as an ongoing process that lasted from the beginning to the end of the war. Wartime priorities fluctuated, too, distorting the amount of attention that American and South Vietnamese authorities placed on what one perceived as pacification.

As contentious as it was and still is, pacification happened at the barrel of a gun between 1965 and 1972. Pacification is inextricably tied to a milieu of terms, with Americans having used revolutionary development, rural construction, rural development, rural edification, counterinsurgency, and nation-building interchangeably. Pacification, or the uplifting of security conditions and the expansion of control, was the United States' modus operandi in the war for the RVN's existence. From start to finish, American civilian and military efforts to create a stable RVN rested on pacification. Indeed, pacification entailed sound security behind which allegiance to Saigon could mature, as purveyed by conventional military forces.

A province study of Phú Yên exposes that the actions of conventional military forces were indeed wedded to pacification. In 1967, for instance, Gen. William C. Westmoreland, commander of Military Assistance Command, Vietnam (MACV), declared that his military forces' first mission was "territorial security, troops in support of pacification or revolutionary development."[16] MACV fought the war with pacification front and center.[17] Both Westmoreland and his successor, Gen. Creighton Abrams, understood the importance of pacification and executed the war on its behalf. Despite a background in counterinsurgency theory, Westmoreland long suffered claims that he ignored pacification; in actuality, he placed pacification at the core of his strategy in Vietnam.[18] He also understood that the Vietnam War encompassed all facets of South Vietnamese society.[19] Westmoreland and Abrams shared an understanding of the symbiotic relationship between the big-unit war and pacification, as both generals used search and destroy to advance the latter.[20] An examination of IFFV's campaigns of 1966 and 1967 advances the argument that conventional warfare *was* pacification, as American maneuver battalions elevated—albeit temporarily—security conditions through search and destroy operations. Search and destroy created distance between Hanoi's forces and the South Vietnamese people—all to Saigon's benefit. In turn, the coexistence of both the destructive and the development aspects of pacification existed throughout the duration of the war. In that vein, this study frames pacification as ill-defined during the war, yet a strategy that the war itself posited as entailing the continued improvement of security so as to create a stable state for the GVN. Priorities changed, yet pacification remained paramount to MACV's aims throughout the war. For that reason, this study treats pacification as the overarching concept under which the entire war transpired. More recent scholarship has addressed the link between military operations and pacification, yet without decisively conjoining the two terms.[21]

Retired general and former ambassador Maxwell D. Taylor famously pronounced, "there was not just a single war to be reported by officials and the press. There were really forty-four different wars and you could have an accurate reporter in each one of those provinces and get forty-four different reports coming to Washington and all would be right in their own way. Yet none a complete picture."[22] Despite the vast array of written works on the Vietnam War, the broader discussion is limited as to date there are just seven province studies—two of which cover the same province. Further still, four of those provinces fell under III Corps, whereas I Corps, II Corps, and IV Corps each have one study apiece. Historians know little about the linkages and variations in the war from province to province. For that reason, this book adds another piece to the broader, incomplete picture. Yet a province study inherently contends with the assumption that it is hardly representative of anything outside the province. Such a perceived constraint is present in other studies of the Vietnam War. In *Working-Class War: American Combat Soldiers and Vietnam,* much of Christian G. Appy's data is from the Boston area. This limitation detracts from his broad assertion that the less privileged did most of the fighting, but it would be rather difficult to accumulate data from every major American city and insert it into a readable manuscript.[23] For the sake of a cohesive narrative, the scope of any study is constrained. In that vein, province studies are no different. A province study on pacification broadens the collective understanding of the war that raged across the RVN. Making the connection between one province out of forty-four and the rest of the Republic of Vietnam is an essential step in expanding our understanding of the Vietnam War.[24] Dictated by demography, geography, and history, multiple wars occurred across this short-lived republic. Analysis of each province advances this actuality. By concentrating on Phú Yên, this book adds another, vital piece to the puzzle. Since political and military dynamics varied from province to province, one must examine pacification at the local level and not treat it as a monolith; this study does just that by bridging the gap between thinking about pacification and its implementation.

Rarely do works on the Vietnam War focus on the middle level—the space between regional authorities and district advisors. Similarly, few studies truly reach below the province level to reveal the war among the hamlets. In that fashion, this book explores Phú Yên from the middle—looking up toward decisions emanating out of II Corps, Saigon, and Washington when necessary, and looking down to see the war unfold in the districts (*quận*), villages (*xã*), and hamlets (*ấp*) of the province (*tỉnh*). The abundance of province and district reporting made possible by the formation of Civil Operations and Revolutionary Development Support (CORDS), and its presence in Phú Yên in the form of Advisory Team 28 (AT28), permits a studying of the war at the grassroots level, or more accurately in this case, the *rice roots* level.[25] With more documentation, the 1968 Tết Offensive is correctly seen as a major blow to Saigon's pacification efforts. Similarly, province and district reports present 1969 as a year of uncertainty. A detailed month-to-month, district-to-district approach reveals the decline of pacification between 1970 and 1971, and acceptance of that reality in 1972. Since this study marks the first detailed study of the war in Phú Yên, it also stands as the first noteworthy use of AT28 reports. AT28 documents help explain the significant yet fleeting high levels of security necessary to keep pacification on track toward defeating PAVN and PLAF units in Phú Yên.

The American military executed operations to improve security in key hinterland areas of the RVN and to provide the first line of defense. Doing so relegated Saigon's forces to the patrolling of areas under pacification initiatives. For the Army of the Republic of Vietnam (ARVN), this fed the perceptions of laziness and, more significantly, did not help prepare Saigon for an existence without U.S. combat forces after the end of Vietnamization. Moreover, the advancement of Vietnamization and the subordinate Accelerated Pacification Campaign (APC) all transpired with little concern paid to the RVN's needs and limited capabilities. American decisions, not solely those of the GVN, undermined pacification's long-term success. In positing poor governance as the central cause of pacification's failure, critics of the GVN beat the proverbial horse to death. Poor political decisions emanating out of Saigon and Washington alone, however, say little about the priorities of all entities involved.[26]

Clear, Hold, and Destroy approaches the war through discussions of pacification's many meanings and its execution in Phú Yên. Chapter one offers a detailed analysis of pacification. Chapter two focuses on the province's history with pacification before the arrival of U.S. Army combat units; the third and fourth chapters cover pacification's perceived advancing by the U.S. Army in 1966 and 1967, respectively. Chapter five addresses the effect of Hanoi's Second General Offensive and Uprising on Saigon's pacification efforts. Chapter six discusses Vietnamization and the APC. The collapse of pacification unfolds across chapters seven and eight, with its death certified in chapter nine.

The previously untapped papers of former AT28 member Courtney Frobenius spurred this study of Phú Yên. Housed at the University of Southern Mississippi's McCain Library and Archives, Frobenius's collection of papers includes reports and commentary on his inspections of various hamlets in Phú Yên in 1971. Alone, Frobenius's papers do not unravel the proverbial Gordian knot that was pacification. Archival sources from the U.S. Army Center of Military History (CMH) in Washington, D.C., and the National Archives and Records Administration in College Park, Md. (NARA II) provided the bulk of evidence used throughout this study. Additional archival material came from the Hoover Institution Library and Archives at Stanford and Texas Tech's Vietnam Center and Sam Johnson Vietnam Archive. Merle Pribbenow, a preeminent expert on PAVN, furnished translations of Vietnamese documents. Interviews with CORDS personnel who served in Phú Yên provided insight into how the war transpired at the province and hamlet levels. Conversations with Russell Meerdink, a former Province Senior Advisor (PSA), and his former deputy, Col. Charles S. Varnum, shed light on the 1970–71 period. Discussions with lower-level CORDS advisors, such as Robert Barron, Courtney Frobenius, Ronald Thayer, and Ellis Wisner, revealed much about the war in Phú Yên at the district level. When woven together, the narrative of the war in Phú Yên is grounded both in contemporary reports and the lasting memories of former AT28 members.

Analyzing the American War in Phú Yên profoundly alters the collective understanding of pacification. This study places pacification in the proper context as the process under which the American War transpired. Through the lens of conventional warfare, pacification is seen as a highly mechanical, lethal process concerned with securing Saigon's legitimacy, not the hearts and minds of the South Vietnamese people. Its inability to produce an enduring RVN speaks to the mounting pressure on American authorities to save the United States from Vietnam, a point firmly accentuated by Phú Yên's late-war years. What makes Phú Yên meaningful is the province's ability to function as the ideal case study for the conventional advancement of pacification.

1

——

"What the hell does this mean?"

Understanding Pacification

"To destroy without building up would mean useless labor. To build without first destroying would be an illusion." So said Richard Holbrooke, then a staff member of the United States Operations Mission (USOM) Rural Affairs team at the U.S. Embassy in Saigon, about pacification.[1] As a mechanism of destruction, pacification included the use of force to rid the RVN countryside of Communist combat units and infrastructure. When seen as an instrument of development, pacification meant securing the loyalty of the South Vietnamese people and upgrading the nation's infrastructure to improve the relationship between the Saigon government and the people. Development, though, could only occur with the destruction of enemy infrastructure and influence. Thus, a mixture of these interpretations and others permeated the discourse during the American War in Vietnam. Pacification was an ongoing conversation. What follows in this chapter are key components of that discourse, particularly those that involved the staff at the U.S. Embassy in Saigon. Despite years of dialogue between Americans and their South Vietnamese allies, no singular understanding of pacification existed for the duration of America's involvement in the affairs of the RVN. For that reason, then, to understand pacification as it relates to the American War in Vietnam, this book begins by reassessing the very meaning of the word.

American history is replete with examples of pacification policy. The Vietnam War is just one in a list of conflicts conducted by the United States in which pacification transpired alongside conventional warfare. From the formation of the United States as a republic to the spread of American empire to maintaining the post–Second World War global order, the American military practiced pacification.[2] Throughout American history, pacification included benevolent and malevolent aspects. Local conditions dictated which version of pacification emerged. Yet pacification as a mechanism of destruction usually triumphed after the failure of the peaceful, constructive form. As the word pertained to the America's involvement in Vietnam, pacification appeared in studies before, during, and after the Vietnam War. A lasting agreement on precisely what pacification meant never fully materialized, however.[3] Instead, three assumptions emerged. The first assumption—and the most incorrect—is that pacification existed separately from the war. The second assumption is that a common definition of pacification existed. The third assumption is that pacification entailed transforming the RVN from a politically fractured state into a functioning democracy.

Even with these assumptions in place, it is difficult to understand pacification if the term itself is only vaguely defined, if at all.[4] American diplomats continuously debated the meaning of pacification during their country's involvement in Vietnamese affairs. America's foremost counterinsurgency expert, Edward G. Lansdale, was one of the many Americans working to improve pacification in the RVN. Prior to the war's escalation in 1966, Lansdale returned to Saigon in August 1965 with pacification at the heart of his mission. Lansdale had made his mark in Southeast Asia advising the French during the First Indochina War and aiding the Philippine government's defeat of the Hukbalahap Rebellion, and he was a close confidant of the RVN's first president, Ngô Đình Diệm. With Saigon's efforts to enroot its legitimacy sputtering, Lansdale returned to the South Vietnamese capital to act as a liaison between American interests and those of the GVN. Along with Lansdale, American diplomats Henry Cabot Lodge and Robert W. Komer also lent their perspectives on the continuing debate over the meaning of pacification. While not physically present in Saigon, other respected members of the counterinsurgency community, such as Briton Sir Robert Thompson and Frenchmen David Galula, Roger Trinquier, and Bernard B. Fall, influenced pacification discourse in the RVN, each expressing varying interpretations. Such views often fluctuated over time, revealing anything but a catholic understanding of the term. Unsurprisingly, a disconnect between war planning and execution later resulted in a tendency among scholars to frame the Vietnam War as comprised of two distinct wars—military operations and pacification. Yet American authorities' conceptualizations placed all the war's aims under pacification or corresponding terminology. By marrying military and civilian tasks under a single term, Americans such as Lansdale, Lodge, and Komer linked every effort to pacification.

On the South Vietnamese side, the GVN understood pacification as a mechanism with which to both defeat the growing insurgency and remain in power. Government officials including Prime Minister Nguyễn Cao Kỳ and Brig. Gen. Nguyễn Đức Thắng, head of the Ministry of Revolutionary Development (MORD), voiced their opinions on pacification, often in concert with foreigners and often at odds with one another. GVN officials wanted to build a secure state; U.S. officials who wanted to go a step further and build a nation to which the people had committed their hearts and minds. Counter to the American advisors' hopes, the GVN vision of pacification as a means of controlling the people of the RVN—not winning their hearts and minds—prevailed.

A controversial figure, Lansdale provides considerable insight into how Americans envisioned pacification. Lansdale also played a significant role in facilitating discourse. That he spent considerable time working clandestine operations on behalf of the U.S. Central Intelligence Agency (CIA) and attempting to navigate the highest political circles made Lansdale a mysterious individual, if not a problematic one. Lansdale positioned himself at the center of pacification dialogue during the formative years of the war in Vietnam. His effect on pacification matters more in terms of the conversations generated, and those he was a party to, than of actions on the ground.[5] At the behest of returning U.S. Ambassador Lodge, Lansdale also resumed residence in Saigon, where he served as chairman of the U.S. Mission Liaison Group and headed the Senior Liaison Office (SLO),[6] positions that placed him in the middle of American and South Vietnamese diplomatic relations. Furthermore, Lansdale and SLO generated discourse over the meaning of pacification as they tried to explain the complex process in the clearest manner possible. Yet none of the ongoing conversations about pacification among prominent American diplomats like Lansdale ever yielded a lasting or pervasive definition of the term. Instead, Lansdale's efforts produced just one of many definitions of pacification that emerged during the war. For him, pacification meant the GVN providing robust security to demonstrate that it cared for—and belonged to—the South Vietnamese people. Only then would they choose to support the Saigon government.[7]

Correspondence among American diplomatic corps and military support agencies always used pacification terminology when referring to the overall effort to build the RVN into a viable state.[8] It is striking that a well-established definition of pacification eluded policymakers and military planners despite contemporary efforts by Americans and South Vietnamese authorities to reach a singular understanding of what pacification entailed. Authorities preached the importance of the military phases of pacification, yet discourse tended to stress civic development, despite many explanations of pacification beginning with decisive clearing and security phases. Of perhaps the most consequence is how American authorities viewed pacification as embodying the war's entire purpose.

British and French Pacification Discourse

A mélange of related terms, including revolutionary development, rural construction, rural development, rural edification, counterinsurgency, and nation-building, pervaded during the post–Second World War decolonization period. Each approach shared a common objective—defeating communist insurgency. Yet pacification prevailed as the most widely used term. As a strategy, pacification existed before American military forces arrived in the RVN. More broadly, pacification as a concept existed at the heart of post-1945 struggles, both for the British in Malaya and the French in Indochina. The Americans, too, backed pacification in Greece and the Philippines against Communist insurgencies. In Vietnam, pacification sat at the center of the war between Hanoi and Saigon. Efforts to pacify South Vietnam occurred during the First Indochina War and again during the presidency of Ngô Đình Diệm. By 1965, American advisors, both civilian and military, used either "pacification" or "revolutionary development" to describe the stabilizing efforts in the RVN, but what either term entailed remained ill-defined.[9]

For the British in Malaya, pacification amounted to a government matter, not a military one. As Sir Robert Thompson, Great Britain's most renowned counterinsurgency expert, explained, "an insurgent movement is a war for the people. It stands to reason that government measures must be directed to restoring government authority and law and order throughout the country, so that control over the people can be regained and its support won."[10] A small and elite military, Thompson wrote, mattered only insofar as it supported the actions of the government.[11] Pacification was a governance issue, one that required military support. Essentially, Thompson posited pacification predominantly as a mechanism of development and policing.[12] Entrenching the Saigon government by way of pacification dominated his recommendations to Ngô Đình Diệm as a member of the British Advisory Mission, and his later advice to Richard Nixon's administration on its Vietnam policy.[13] But Malaya differed greatly from the war in the RVN, where priorities dictated the elevated role of American and South Vietnamese armies to advance and implement pacification programs.

France's experience also influenced American discourse on and efforts to implement pacification programs. The French counterinsurgency triumvirate of Galula, Trinquier, and Fall exposed the American public and U.S. military and civilian agencies to pacification in the age of decolonization, profoundly influencing American thinking on the subject. Galula's 1963 RAND publication, *Pacification in Algeria, 1956–1958*, in particular explained pacification efforts in Algeria. But it never defined the term.[14] Trinquier, a veteran of the First Indochina War and the Algerian War of Independence, used the tactics of these conflicts as lessons for future wars. He took the discussion of pacification further, but like Galula, he never directly explained its meaning. Instead, he indirectly conveyed pacification as meeting the needs of the people, noting that the people needed to be clear on the war's aims. "They will have to be convinced that if we call upon them to fight at our sides it can only be in defense of a just cause. And we should not deceive them. The surest means of gaining their confidence will be to crush those who want to oppress them. When we have placed the terrorists out of harm's way, the problem of pacification will be quickly resolved."[15] What is apparent is that for pacification to work, the process must gain the support of the people. Trinquier further argued against the notion of winning the hearts and minds, declaring, "we know that it is not all necessary to have the sympathy of a majority of the people in order to rule them."[16] Instead, an entity like the GVN could gain the people's loyalty by providing security that protected the people, "especially from terrorism."[17] Trinquier wrote of control—a process by which a government could extract the people's loyalty by protecting them from guerrillas, not by ideological superiority nor by catering to their every need. The idea of control at the core of pacification continued throughout the American War in Vietnam.

Fall spent most of his life amid insurgencies and counterinsurgencies. During the Second World War, he fought against the German occupation of France as a member of the French Resistance. Later, he spent considerable time studying firsthand the First Indochina War and, until his death in 1967, the Vietnam War. His academic career in the United States made him more accessible to Americans. Like his contemporaries, he also never defined pacification, despite acknowledging that "the people and the army must 'emerge on the same side of the fight.'"[18] Fall outlined his perspective on insurgency in a lecture to students at the University of Hawaii's Far East Training Center in December 1966. His lecture explained how PLAF quickly met the needs of South Vietnamese villagers, while the more bureaucratic United States Agency for International Development

(USAID) system took years to accomplish the same feat. "The point is that the VC in all likelihood will chop down two trees because the basic requirements for a Vietnamese village is that the bridge is wide enough to take two women with two carrying poles and two bags of rice, that's all. That's the average carrying requirement for a Vietnamese village—no more no less," he told the audience.[19] Conversely, he said, when a village needs a new bridge, USAID would start with a survey of a potential bridge site, with the eventual recommendation that the bridge must be able to support heavy U.S. Army vehicles. Such an aid process, contended Fall, would take years to complete, and would far exceed village's needs.[20] PLAF's approach, in all its simplicity, gained the support of the people. Indeed, "what you then find, slow but surely, is the Viet Cong cadre will come in and build up this low level organization . . . a system in which there will be constant involving of the people."[21] In short, PLAF effectively pacified a community without considerable effort.

Although Galula, Trinquier, and Fall offered valuable insight into the *goals and methods* of pacification, they did so without establishing clear *interpretations* of pacification. Therefore, an entire generation of American readers—potential students of modern warfare—matured without an established definition of pacification from which to inform U.S. decision-making in the RVN during the 1960s and 1970s. The French military, on the other hand, *did* furnish a rather profound explanation of pacification. A document translated and made available by RAND to American diplomatic and military circles referenced a statement from a 1949 report titled "General X, South Vietnam," in which pacification seemed almost beyond the purview of all but those directly affected by the Việt Minh. Accordingly, the report stated, "for a province to be considered pacified, it is necessary for the authority of the legal government to manifest itself by the restoration of normal political institutions, for the clearing of the area to have been conducted by the people themselves, and, finally, for the centers of population to have organized self-defense units capable of protecting the critical points of their province."[22]

The same 1949 report also placed pacification as a unifying strategy, one that requires clearly defining the terms "authority" and "legal government" (conditions, it noted, that the French never fully achieved in Vietnam), and "that all efforts converge toward the same goal . . . this being possible only if the same authority exercises both civil and military powers."[23] As for the effectiveness of such an approach, the report relayed that "the complete restoration of order and a return to normalcy was an undertaking which, if not actually impossible, was at the very least doomed to end in unhappy and incomplete results."[24] That dour statement epitomized the later American experience with pacification in the same places where French efforts had ultimately failed.

Pacification Discourse at the U.S. Embassy in Saigon

For the United States, a lasting interpretation of pacification never materialized, despite years of dialogue among American authorities in Saigon. The Pentagon Papers described the effect of pacification discourse on the war: "The proponents of what is called so loosely in this paper 'pacification' were often in such violent disagreement as to what pacification meant that they quarreled publicly among themselves and overlooked their common interests. At other times, people who disagreed strongly on major issues found themselves temporary allies with a common objective."[25] Achieving any meaningful definition of pacification meant overcoming the many divergent opinions—an insurmountable task. What matters, though, is how the architects of pacification discussed the term, particularly since Americans in Saigon spoke of what pacification needed to accomplish, even as they were unclear what pacification entailed. Regardless of years of pacification explanations, "the curious problem of the distance between rhetoric and reality" lasted for the duration of the war.[26]

The U.S. Army did provide a revealing doctrinal definition of pacification in 1963. The process is clearly present in Field Manual 31-22, *U.S. Army Counter-insurgency Forces*, which directed soldiers to destroy the insurgents' ability to use the population for support: "Successful pacification of subversive insurgency requires the isolation of the insurgent from internal and external support."[27] Field Manual 31-22 also called for commanders to exercise "necessary" measures to control the area of operations and the local population to diminish the guerrilla's presence, the nature and scope of which "may require actions by military commanders which impinge on the liberty and property rights of the citizens of the affected area. Such actions would normally be preceded by an announcement of a declaration of emergency by the head of the government. Application of the strictest of population controls may be required."[28]

To defeat an insurgency via destruction, with control being a significant factor, mirrored the application of pacification in the provinces. The Strategic Hamlet Program exemplified pacification as a method of control. As Edward Miller noted in his 2013 study *Misalliance*, the first concerted American and South Vietnamese effort at pacification appeared in the form of the Strategic Hamlet

Program. Based on the teachings of Roger Trinquier, whose ideas significantly influenced Ngô Đình Diệm's regime, the Strategic Hamlet Program sought to provide the Saigon government with a method to secure—and therefore control—the people. Indeed, as Trinquier argued in *Modern Warfare*, winning the hearts and minds was neither a prerequisite nor a requirement for getting the people to obey the government.[29]

Insofar as the Strategic Hamlet Program connects with this study, the failed endeavor revealed the need, at least for Americans, to define pacification thoroughly. Later released by former U.S. Mission Liaison Group member Daniel Ellsberg, the Pentagon Papers described how pacification, as a term and a policy, lacked clarity:

> A related problem arose from the uniqueness of this program in American experience—pacification by proxy. The theory of sequential phases could be variously interpreted. This is not the problem of the three blind men describing the elephant; it is the problem of men with different perspectives each moulding his own conception of a proper body to the same skeleton. If the final product were to have some semblance of coherence and mutual satisfaction it was necessary that the shapers came to agreement on substance and operational procedure, not just that they agree on the proper skeleton upon which to work.[30]

The concept of phases, more than the term "pacification" itself, caused considerable confusion as to what constituted pacification. Comprised of an undefined number of phases, what pacification specifically entailed varied depending on one's perspective. Despite efforts to reach a consensus among Americans and South Vietnamese officials in 1963, disagreement over the steps and scope of pacification persisted throughout much of the late 1960s.

The Pentagon Papers addressed how American and South Vietnamese authorities perceived pacification. Specifically, when discussing the Strategic Hamlet Program of 1963, "U.S. desires to begin an effective process of pacification had fastened onto security as a necessary precondition and slighted the historic record of rural resistance to resettlement," whereas President Ngô Đình Diệm and his brother Ngô Đình Nhu "had decided to emphasize control of the rural population as the precondition to winning loyalty."[31] Although focusing on 1963, these statements held true for subsequent years. Since security meant creating distance between the people and Communist cadres and guerrillas, doing so seemed a natural prerequisite for pacification to succeed. Even later in the war, the U.S. viewed security as the mandatory first step toward pacification, which is not to say that adequate security always existed, year after year, in every province.

When encouraging the GVN to embrace pacification, the written record left by American advisors revealed the use of a myriad of its synonyms. In helping the GVN develop a pacification plan, SLO frequently used the word itself and related terms in its written work. From the start of his 1965 appointment to the U.S. Embassy in Saigon, Lansdale used "pacification" to encapsulate into a single word the GVN's task of gaining the South Vietnamese people's loyalty. Other SLO members used similar terminology. Accordingly, pacification terminology dominated the daily vocabulary of American advisors. Nevertheless, what pacification precisely entailed varied from conversation to conversation. Whether used to denote a concept or a phase, pacification represented a joint American and South Vietnamese effort to best conceptualize the preeminent strategy for fighting the war against Hanoi and its agents south of the seventeenth parallel.

Discourse among American authorities in Saigon largely centered on what pacification meant. To guide USOM's advisory efforts, in October 1964, Ambassador Maxwell Taylor had a member of his staff, William N. Turpin, draft a memo titled "Toward an Operational Definition of Pacification."[32] Turpin opened with a tacit acknowledgment of pacification's equivocality: "Pacification, like the weather, has been discussed at great length; while it would be unfair to conclude that nobody has done anything about it, charity would not seem to require that one claim that it has yet been totally achieved in Vietnam."[33] The memo went on to explain pacification as a method of control. "Pacification is about power, it is our side of a power struggle for control of the people, the territory, the resources, and the communications lines of this country. . . . In those terms, pacification can be considered achieved where the writ of the GVN runs, over the people who obey it, over the resources it can exploit, and along the communications lines it can travel on."[34] Further, stating that "all these things can be quantified," it outlined just how to measure "the degree and the progress of GVN control" in "absolute or percentage terms."[35] Taylor agreed with Turpin's assertions in the memo, but the latter's explanations of pacification's three phases were by no means universally accepted.

Responding to Turpin's memo, Ogden Williams, acting director of USOM's Office of Rural Affairs, took issue with pacification being quantifiable. Pacification, Williams argued, "cannot be demonstrated by quantitative statistics exactly where the writ of the GVN runs, what people obey such writ, or even what communication routes are controlled."[36] He noted that statistics help with "general planning purposes" but "overlook the essence of the problem which is the feeling of the population in the area."[37] Williams pointed to the Strategic Hamlet Program to reinforce his point: "We had examples of quantified statistics showing GVN hamlets which were in fact VC hamlets surrounded by GVN barbed wire."[38]

The sequence of pacification phases mattered more in theoretical than practical terms. Turpin framed pacification based on *tâche d'huile*, or the "oil stain" (or "spot"): "The generally accepted theory of pacification defines three phases for spreading government control outward from the secure areas (the 'oil spot' technique); but it seems possibly useful to reverse the . . . order of the steps (clear, secure, build) in order to focus . . . attention on beginning where we are and proceeding to where we want to be."[39] Williams wrote that the order of phases mattered not: "Whether one conceives of pacification as clear—secure—build, or build—secure—clear, it is apparent that different priorities are applicable to each phase. Since the oil-spot concept starts at the center of the oil-spot and works outward, there is in fact nothing new about preferring the build-secure-clear terminology."[40] In practice, phase order depended on local conditions and the extent, if any, of Saigon's control. Indeed, in RVN areas under enemy control, Williams wrote, the GVN had to choose between a clear-secure-build approach—in that order—or deferring pacification altogether.[41]

Counterinsurgency expert Charles T. R. Bohannan did not entirely agree with Turpin's approach to pacification, either. Based on the comments he made on his copy of the report, Bohannan thought that pacification was anything but rigidly defined. In one instance, he took issue with Turpin's argument that during the secure phase, the military needed to maintain "an aggressive spirit and an aggressive fashion."[42] Bohannan noted that military activities ought to be "defensive i.e. defend the people."[43] Regarding the hold phase, Turpin had written, "the effort should be made to turn the 'self-help' program around so that it is responding not to the wishes and hopes, but to the felt needs, of the hamlets."[44] Bohannan wrote in the margin, "*What the hell does this mean?*"[45]

Turpin's conclusion reiterated the three pacification phases:

> The planning of pacification should assume that the three phases of pacification will proceed from building through securing to clearing areas, that building logically precedes securing and securing

clearing, though there is no reason why they should not proceed simultaneously in different areas. It suggests also that the oil spot spreads by seepage and not by jumps, but that the nicest political judgement is needed in order to determine how far it has seeped, and what needs to be done at a given spot at a given moment to make it seep faster.[46]

Bohannan remained unconvinced: "I don't get this conclusion as stated," read his note on the memo.[47] Indeed, Turpin's summation presented pacification as both rigid and malleable, slow and fast. With such uncertainty among American diplomats and military advisors, pacification remained a confusing concept. Destruction and pacification were intertwined; whereas Turpin offered a detailed, measurable explanation of pacification, Bohannan provided a simpler yet apt appraisal, recommending a more practical take on pacification in his critique of Turpin's memo. He explained pacification as a destructive process:

> The idea is to begin to break down communist rural power thus providing time and motivation for reorganization of the central government and of its rural political and administrative apparatus before undertaking the long and difficult task of replacing the communist apparatus with a government one in contested and Viet Cong zones (pacification).[48]

In other words, for Saigon to exercise any authority in contested space meant that destruction had to precede construction.

A mutual understanding of pacification had existed rather briefly among Americans before Lansdale's return to Saigon. By 2 March 1965, American advisory entities in Saigon—MACV, USOM, and the United States Information Service (USIS)—had agreed on a singular interpretation of pacification. Note that South Vietnamese ministries—MORD in particular—were not a party to this agreement. As defined by MACV, USOM, and USIS in a paper titled "The Concept of Pacification and Certain Definitions and Procedures," a pacification strategy had to coordinate all civilian, military, and police actions to eliminate organized enemy military activity, to detect and eliminate the overt and covert VC political apparatus, and to foster economic, political, and social development of a viable economy.[49] Insofar as enacting pacification, the paper specified two aspects: a military problem—"a problem of the GVN imposing its will upon the Viet Cong military establishment and those Viet Cong paramilitary forces which have been gathered in its support"; and a "constant and ever-expanding GVN effort particularly focused at the province level to effectively counter VC infiltration into, and the establishment of VC control over, the Vietnamese rural areas and the population inhabiting these areas." The latter effort, the paper explained, aimed to provide "physical security against VC guerrilla activities" in those areas through "the coordinated use of military forces and police" as well as a "socio/economic/political" focus from the household level up through villages, districts, and provinces, "arming (in the classic sense)" the population to resist enemy "encroachment and domination," aiding GVN forces in combatting such encroachment, and presenting "a hostile environment against the Viet Cong subversive effort."[50]

The above definition typified the entire American war effort. Stressing the military connection, this definition made pacification a principal problem of the American military and not just that of the RVN's. It also meant that pacification existed as anything but a peaceful process. Moreover, American authorities acknowledged that pacification had to *help* the South Vietnamese people; doing so offered the Saigon government its only true means to obtain the people's unyielding support.

The MACV, USOM, and USIS definition's enumeration of the three phases—clearing, securing, and development—presented pacification as a strategy in and of itself and not merely a component of the wider war effort. The American agencies designated the clearing and securing tasks as duties of ARVN, Regional Forces (RF), Popular Forces (PF), and National Police, reflecting the 1965 mindset of American advisors that the South Vietnamese needed to spread pacification on their own, albeit with U.S. dollars and equipment. That view changed—albeit at the displeasure of SLO and other civilian entities—as the White House increased U.S. troop levels and MACV mounted pacification-supporting operations, extending the U.S. Army's role in pacification and making it a key player in the clearing and, later, securing phases. Moreover, events varied from province to province, meaning that South Vietnamese forces no longer had a monopoly on clearing and securing.[51] These arrangements nevertheless failed to imbue coherence in discussions pertinent to pacification. Notwithstanding the detailed U.S. directive on the meaning of pacification, competing explanations of the term and its application persisted.

An undated and unauthored SLO memo, perhaps penned by Lansdale, conveyed pacification as encompassing the entire war. This memo described pacification as a process consisting of five "strategic principles"—namely, internal defense and security, economic progress "to better the standard of living," improved social services such as education and health facilities, the establishment of political institutions and "a positive ideology," and the "amelioration of the administrative system."[52] Together, these goals, which the memo noted "must be pursued with ardor," posited both military and civilian objectives for the long-term viability of the RVN.[53] With such an array of objectives, pacification did more than encompass the war; it defined it.

Pacification and permanence were two terms that rarely if ever went together. Agreements over what constituted pacification meant little insofar as those definitions lasting beyond a conversation or meeting. Richard Holbrooke, as a Foreign Service Officer (FSO) at the U.S. Embassy in Saigon, once suggested a substantial revision of pacification's components. In his undated paper filed with the U.S. Embassy in Saigon's Political Section (POL), he proposed dispensing with clearing, securing, and developing as phases of pacification, and in their place, he proposed instituting two phases, "the Destruction Phase and the Construction Phase." He called the two terms "inseparable": "To destroy without building up would mean useless labor. To build without first destroying would be an illusion."[54] Holbrooke's proposal presented pacification as a simpler concept even than Bohannan's. But his view of pacification appears not to have gained traction among other Americans advising the GVN. As pacification played out in the countryside—and in Phú Yên in particular—Holbrooke's assessment proved accurate as MACV's war hinged on destroying before constructing. What did vary, however, was the duration of the construction phase: efforts to destroy the enemy transpired again and again as Communist forces challenged the Saigon government for control of South Vietnam's contested spaces. Indeed, Holbrooke proposed two phases functioned more like a merry-go-round than anything else.

Widespread understanding as to what pacification meant remained noticeably absent among American and South Vietnamese authorities. USOM Assistant Director of Rural Affairs Rufus Phillips relayed this point to Lansdale in 1965, calling the main problem in carrying out rural construction (i.e., pacification) that "too few high echelon Americans or Vietnamese understand it."[55] Phillips hit upon leaders' inability, such as Ambassador Lodge and RVN Prime Minister Nguyễn Cao Kỳ, to articulate clear and consistent views on pacification. On more than one occasion, these two men expressed an often divergent range of interpretations of pacification. Communication within the U.S. Mission Liaison Group revealed uncertainty about the meaning of pacification, particularly when dealing with Nguyễn Cao Kỳ. The RVN leader did not grasp pacification as envisioned by Lansdale, a reality reflected in the former's public remarks: according to an October 1965 memo that Lodge sent to Lansdale, the RVN Prime Minister had stated, "once we reoccupy an area, first priority is psychological warfare and rebuilding of roads and bridges destroyed by the Communists. Once we have re-established communication with the people and roads which allow people to move freely, then we are ready for other things, like schools, dispensaries."[56] Lodge, in response, pondered in his memo, "surely pacification means: psychology, security, economic-social—in that order. General Ky's remark seems to leave out security."[57] Security being absent from Nguyễn Cao Kỳ's comments suggested either that he mistakenly omitted that facet in his remark, or that such a step fell outside the purview of pacification. In either case, the GVN's perspective on pacification did indeed include security as a key facet—if not the foundation—of gaining the support of the countryside. Notably, though, the GVN's pacification approach did not entail winning the hearts and minds of the South Vietnamese villager.

Moreover, Lodge's reaction to Nguyễn Cao Kỳ's statement conveyed additional insight into the meaning of pacification. Going against the prevailing American idea that security preceded all other pacification phases, Lodge placed security as the second stage, after "psychology"—in his view, efforts to change the opinions of the South Vietnamese peasants should begin even before friendly military forces sought to secure their hamlets. Lodge's words also demonstrate a concerted effort by American entities to find and attach a specific meaning to pacification, suggesting that the agreed-upon definition adopted by MACV, USOM, and USIS either did not last or did not permeate to other U.S. agencies.

Lansdale spent the majority of his time from 1965 to 1968 in the RVN convincing the Saigon government to embrace pacification as best serving the people's interests. Lansdale always contended that the GVN needed to embrace pacification to build a bond with the nation's villagers. In a September 1965 memo to Lodge, Lansdale recounted discussing how the Saigon government intended to spread revolutionary zeal across the country at a meeting with Nguyễn Cao Kỳ. Topics of conversation included the use of cadres at the district level to work alongside locals in bettering their communities. The prime minister and the Americans also discussed finding a "truer name for 'pacification' than 'rural construction.'"[58] Besides revealing the need for "something more inspiring,"[59] for the Vietnamese, the word "pacification" held French connotations rife with unpleasant memories of the First Indochina War. French practices and Việt Minh propaganda left South Vietnamese policymakers wanting a better term than "pacification." That legacy further complicated pacification discourse in Saigon.[60] SLO continued to influence perceptions of—and shape the RVN's inherent dependence on—pacification. In a telegram to William Bundy and Leonard Unger at the Office of the Secretary of State, Lodge forwarded an SLO paper outlining key talking points for Nguyễn Cao Kỳ's upcoming 11 October 1965 speech. Aside from demonstrating the influence that SLO held over the GVN, the paper revealed two items of note regarding the prime minister's views on pacification: that rural construction referred to the GVN's wider efforts to develop a viable country, and that pacification functioned as the means to achieve that goal. In the talking points, Nguyễn Cao Kỳ affirmed that the people "must see that you have concern for their well-being and that you are their friend," and that pacification via the rural construction program amounted to a battle for the RVN's survival: "We must hold the land liberated from the Viet Cong and patrol it so they cannot disrupt our life again with their raids and ambushes."[61] According to the document, the RVN's very survival rested on pacification. Moreover, contrary to the meeting at the end of September, Nguyễn Cao Kỳ's talking points revealed a distinction between pacification and rural construction; he placed pacification within the context of an even larger effort to modernize the nation. Rather than a peaceful process, pacification in this context meant the eradication of the Communists from South Vietnam. Pacification functioned as the method by which the GVN could eject PLAF through military means. *This* understanding of pacification permeated the ensuing discourse.

The meaning of pacification remained fluid at the end of November 1965. In a brief for Secretary of Defense Robert McNamara, Lansdale cited Lodge's summation of pacification as a means of conveying the concept. As recalled by Lansdale, Lodge defined pacification as "that part of the war which seeks to braid together all sorts of military, political, police, economic and social programs in order to root out that 65% of the Viet Cong which function as individual terrorists and in small groups."[62] Presumably, the other 35 percent operated less clandestinely as troops in PLAF's main and local battalions. Inasmuch as Lodge's definition implied that pacification only targeted the clandestine Communists, Lansdale broadened the definition to comprehend what security meant in real terms to the South Vietnamese people: "We try to give the people enough security to sleep nights," he explained. "Basically, we then ask them to choose sides. To get them to choose our side, we must give them something they can really believe in. Security that will still be there tomorrow. A government they feel is theirs, that will be there tomorrow. And, some hope of a better life, tomorrow."[63]

For Lansdale, pacification meant giving the people of the RVN a reason to resist PLAF. Democratic ideals, transplanted from America to South Vietnam, could counter the promises of change as made by the Communists. To achieve this, the South Vietnamese needed a responsible and legitimate federal government that could provide them with economic advancement and security; America's role was to provide all the necessary support while leaving the South Vietnamese to fight their own war. Lansdale proposed an idea that existed as the foundation of every perception of pacification—that only good government would win the people's loyalty and spread the GVN's authority over the whole of the nation. Essentially, both Lansdale and Lodge accentuated the development aspects while framing pacification in such a way as to include all the facets of the war in South Vietnam.

Although a vocal proponent of pacification, Lodge never revealed a concrete opinion about how the concept worked.[64] Correspondence from Lodge to Lansdale reveals a lack of clarity as the interchangeability of terms clouded the scope of pacification, and therefore the meaning. Interestingly, in the span of eight days, Lodge's opinion of pacification changed dramatically. In a memo dated 7 December 1965, Lodge used the phrase "Rural Construction-pacification effort," demonstrating the apparent interchangeability of the preferred terms.[65] Used in that manner, pacification and rural reconstruction were clearly treated as concepts that embodied subordinate phases. Yet, as understood by Lodge in a 15 December 1965 memo, revolutionary development—or the pro-GVN ideology necessary to effectively counter the NLF's promises—encompassed pacification as one of its three phases. Rather than an umbrella term as used by others, Lodge now situated pacification as the middle phase between military clearing and development.[66] This definition varied considerably from the explanation that pacification—or rural construction—embodied security and infrastructure-building phases. Moreover, the ubiquity of pacification as defined by MACV, USOM, and USIS did not resonate throughout the U.S. Embassy.

Confusion over the nature and scope of pacification remained infused in the discourse. In February 1966, Lansdale circulated Daniel Ellsberg's draft paper on GVN concepts of pacification to other members of the U.S. Mission Liaison Group.[67] Ellsberg's description of the GVN's understanding varied considerably from that posited by Lansdale. Instead of using pacification to encapsulate the larger war effort, Ellsberg referred to pacification as the last two of three phases of rural construction. First came clearing, followed by the two securing or pacification phases.[68] As referenced in the same report, Prime Minister Kỳ spoke of the pacification phases as the stage "to destroy VC political and military infrastructures, and concurrently consolidate or reconstruct our infrastructures"—that is, to liberate the people from Communist domination, and help them "realize sense of duty and rise up at will to preserve the restored security."[69] Nguyễn Cao Kỳ's understanding of pacification placed the term in a strong military context, harkening back to Ngô Đình Diệm's: to dislodge PLAF from the countryside required the use of military force.

Ellsberg's draft underscored the divide between pacification being seen as a unifying concept or merely a phase. In the same draft, Ellsberg used pacification synonyms interchangeably, such as "rural reconstruction" instead of "rural construction." Such use of various terms in place of pacification further hindered clarity. Feedback from fellow SLO members, at Lansdale's behest, resulted in a more cogent document, with the final version of Ellsberg's report using "rural construction" consistently throughout, thereby demonstrating that consistency emerged only after discourse.[70] More significantly, the concept and phases remained intact, as Ellsberg once more used a pertinent statement from the prime minister: "Rural reconstruction is a work which the military, the people and the administrative officials must unite to accomplish."[71] In addition to highlighting the problematic nature of using interchangeable terms when discussing pacification, Ellsberg's draft demonstrated the malleability of pacification as a term.

The lack of consistency extended beyond Ellsberg's draft. A SLO memo on revolutionary development—another synonym—insinuated that pacification and rural development were one in the same. Indeed, evidence for this emerged from Nguyễn Cao Kỳ officially replacing "rural construction" with "rural development" in the summer of 1965.[72] In describing this change in terminology, the SLO document treated both GVN terms as synonyms for pacification. Yet in the same report, the author continued to use the now-replaced "rural construction." Therefore, despite the phrasing selected by the GVN, the Americans continued to characterize efforts using varying terminology. Concepts and terminology mattered to those discussing pacification, but consistency thereof remained elusive.

MORD and Pacification

Brig. Gen. Nguyễn Đức Thắng, the director of MORD, held a view of pacification starkly different from Nguyễn Cao Kỳ's. In September 1966, at a II Corps conference in Đà Lạt, he expressed his frustrations over ARVN and, even more

generally, all conventional military involvement in pacification. U.S. Army
Maj. Gen. John C. F. Tillson III captured the "essence" of Nguyễn Đức Thắng's
remarks to ARVN, U.S. Army, and Republic of Korea Army (ROKA) attendees:
"Pacification is a Government function and not a military function. . . . I implore
that you fight the war and leave the pacification to us."[73] He emphasized that
the militaries did not understand the needs of the people, and that civic action
efforts did not help the people develop the skills necessary for communities to
help themselves. Instead, he asked for resources and technical assistance from
the militaries.[74] Such words startled men like Tillson, who thought that Nguyễn
Đức Thắng should know "the importance of ARVN participation."[75] Yet the
latter general did see a role for ARVN in pacification.

Months earlier, Nguyễn Đức Thắng did embrace pacification as the method to
defeat the Communist cause in the countryside. In March 1966, Lansdale relayed
to other American authorities the general's views on pacification. For Nguyễn
Đức Thắng, pacification presented an opportunity to build trust between ARVN
and the people. By providing security at all costs, ARVN could give the people
a choice as to which belligerent they supported. Doing so, according to Nguyễn
Đức Thắng, would give those residing in the nation's hamlets an alternative to the
NLF's promises of freedom. That was key to Nguyễn Đức Thắng: pacification as
giving the people a choice.[76] Local men could join the Territorial Forces (Popular
Forces and Regional Forces) instead of ARVN, thereby allowing them to operate
closer to home and see less combat.[77] Essentially, instead of forcing people to
serve in the army or otherwise controlling them, Nguyễn Đức Thắng thought that
the RVN could use ARVN as a means of spreading democracy to the people.[78]

Conversations between Lansdale and Nguyễn Đức Thắng revealed much about
contemporary views on pacification. In the private chats at Lansdale's Saigon
residence, the two men developed a common understanding of pacification as
an inclusive concept. Indeed, Nguyễn Đức Thắng shared Lansdale's ethos that
pacification should focus on improving the lot of the common villagers and
instilling the nation with a revolutionary spirit counter to that of the NLF. They
agreed that pacifying the RVN was the Saigon government's best chance for
long-term stability. Although they both appreciated the need to dislodge PLAF
influence from the countryside, they reasoned that simply killing the enemy would
not result in a better RVN. A 21 March 1966 report from Lansdale to the U.S.
Mission Council relayed Nguyễn Đức Thắng's observations of pacification at the
province level: "We must have a better measure of success than the number of
PLAF kills by a military unit. If Rural Construction/Revolutionary Development

is as important as we have decided it is, then let us use its success as the measure of military success."[79] Lansdale's statement hit on the reality that conventional military forces—particularly ARVN—could either improve or undermine relations between the Saigon government and the people in the countryside.

SLO's interactions with MORD gave rise to yet another understanding of pacification. At the Honolulu Conference in July 1966—where American and South Vietnamese officials met to address improving efforts to combat PLAF— Nguyễn Đức Thắng presented the GVN's most recent view of pacification. Here, the GVN official presented an encompassing concept quite akin to ones discussed by Lansdale and SLO. In his speech, Gen. Nguyễn Đức Thắng told the audience of "three main policies: military offensive, rural pacification, and democracy building."[80] Aside from Nguyễn Cao Kỳ's earlier use of "rural construction," the concepts behind these three objectives remained largely the same as other approaches to pacification: the military dislodges the enemy and provides immediate security, which fosters the buildup of local security networks. Accomplishing those two tasks then cultivates the growth and development of democratic institutions in the area undergoing pacification. What differed, however, was Nguyễn Đức Thắng's use of "rural pacification" and not the GVN's preferred "rural development." Of consequence, therefore, is how the fundamental ideas remained intact, while the vocabulary that pertained to the efforts to pacify South Vietnam were anything but concrete.

Heightened Intensity, Pacification Unchanged

The 1966 arrival of substantial American combat forces in the RVN marked a key shift in the intensity of the war. The May 1967 creation of Civil Operations and Revolutionary Development Support (CORDS), a new, hybrid civil-military organization under the command of MACV, entailed another significant change. Yet discussions of pacification remained largely unchanged. On balance, although its formation did represent a significant bureaucratic development, including the establishment of a new advisory entity under its purview, CORDS did not bring about a more advanced understanding of pacification or a major shift in pacification as a strategy.

Leaders of the allied nations involved in the war, including the South Vietnamese, gathered in Manila, Philippines, on 24 October 1966 for a two-day summit on the escalating war in Vietnam. Following the October 1966 Manila Conference, pacification remained a term under revision. A January 1967 publication of *Editorial Research Reports* posited pacification as a "process of pacifying the countryside" that involved military and civilian components alike: "In general, pacification means bringing a hamlet family under government control."[81] Phrasing mattered, particularly with the implication of a forced GVN takeover of the peasant population. In this context, pacification entailed neither good relations nor good government; it functioned more as a means of increasing GVN control than winning the people's loyalty and respect.

National Security Council member Robert W. Komer proved to be a key figure in shaping American understanding of pacification. In August 1966, prior to heading CORDS, Komer wrote an article titled "Giving a New Thrust to Pacification." In it, Komer posed the question "*what is pacification?*" His answer aligned with Lansdale and SLO's earlier definition: "'Pacification' can be used to encompass the whole of the military, political, and civil effort in Vietnam."[82] Like Lansdale, Komer viewed pacification as encompassing all the facets of the war. Significantly, though, he emphasized the need to narrow down the term for "operational purposes," and to separate it out as a "definable problem area."[83] Komer thus articulated the need to focus pacification on the one specific problem area where it could have the most effect—involving the people in the struggle:

> If we divide the US/GVN problem into four main components, three
> of them show encouraging progress. The campaign against the major
> VC/NVA units is in high gear, the constitutional process seems to be
> evolving favorably, and we expect to contain inflation while meeting
> most needs of the civil economy. But there is a fourth problem area,
> that of securing the country side and getting the peasant involved in
> the struggle against the Viet Cong, where we're lagging way behind.
> It is this problem area which I would term pacification.[84]

Komer went on to explain how pacification still encompassed the entire war effort: "At the risk of over-simplification, I see management of the pacification problem as involving three main sub-tasks: (1) providing local security in the countryside—essentially a military/police/cadre task; (2) breaking the hold of the VC over the people; and (3) positive programs to win the active support of the rural population."[85] Here, Komer used the versatility of the term to focus more resources on the various elements of pacification that he deemed to need extra attention.

For Komer, the villages helped define pacification. In asserting that pacification could be used to grapple with the specific problematic facet of the war effort that was the rural population, Komer further defined what he meant by pacification, directly linking pacification to events at the village level: "Chasing the large units around the boondocks still leaves intact the VC infrastructure, with its local guerrilla capability plus the weapons of terror and intimidation."[86] In chasing PAVN and PLAF, the security shield afforded by the allies also moved, leaving the people exposed to clandestine Communist interface. Indeed, Komer wrote, "winning the 'village war' which I will loosely call pacification, seems an indispensable ingredient of any high-confidence strategy and a necessary precaution to close the guerrilla option."[87] Komer envisaged pacification as dismantling the networks the Communists had forged within the RNV's communities. Komer also addressed the paradox that the U.S. Army's efforts to bring PAVN and PLAF main forces to battle adversely affected pacification at the hamlet and village level, but he was explicit in his qualification that it was not the Army hindering efforts: *"We had to go after the major VC/NVA units first. It was a matter of first things first."*[88] Priorities, not preference, dictated how pacification unfolded across the RVN.

In correspondence to President Lyndon Johnson, Komer explained the divide between military operations and rural development: "Unless we and the GVN can secure and hold the countryside cleared by military operations, we either face an ever larger and quasi-permanent military commitment or risk letting the VC infiltrate again."[89] Moreover, he foreshadowed the unified effort later provided by CORDS: "Clearly we must dovetail the military's sweep operations and civil pacification. My impression is that, since the military are moving ahead faster than the civil side we need to beef up the latter to get it in phase." But he also clarified the paramount importance of military forces' involvement in pacification: "There's little point in the military clearing areas the civil side can't pacify. On the other hand, security is the key to pacification; people won't cooperate and the cadre can't function till an area is secure."[90] The key phrase there is "security is key to pacification"—pacification revolved around security, and Komer aptly placed security at the forefront of war objectives.

With the combining of civilian and military efforts into CORDS in May 1967, pacification became the MACV's main priority. Yet during the years preceding CORDS, MACV had in fact played a pivotal role in pacification. MACV's successive operations inflicted considerable loses on PLAF, allowing the Americans to allocate more resources to the developmental phases of pacification. Chatter about pacification linked it with Vietnamization and American officials' widespread hopes that the war was nearing an acceptable end. And yet, still, in

1968 American authorities continued the dialogue over the meaning and scope of pacification. The combining of American civilian and military pacification efforts under the control of CORDS meant another explanation of pacification. L. Wade Lathram—a veteran of USAID, the Office of Civil Operations (OCO), and eventually CORDS—defined pacification broadly, like his contemporaries, but he too kept the military aspects at the forefront:

> The military, political, economic and social process of establishing or reestablishing local government responsive to and involving the participation of the people . . . includes the provision of sustained, credible territorial security, the destruction of the enemy's underground government, the assertion or reassertion of political control and involvement of the people in government, and the initiation of economic and social activity capable of self-sustenance and expansion. The economic element of pacification includes the opening of roads and waterways and the maintenance of lines of communication important to economic and military activity.[91]

Thus, over the course of three years and amid the extensive and at times ambiguous discourse, the role of the military remained that of creating the conditions necessary for pacification to last.

Pacification as a method of control entered the dialog as early as 1965. Sir Robert Thompson explained the practice of pacification as a matter of control. When addressing the RVN's state of affairs in 1965, he lamented that "all government efforts to regain control of the lost countryside (pacification) were at a stand-still and the country was in political turmoil."[92] Thompson posited pacification as encompassing every method of evicting the NLF from rural South Vietnam. Significantly, Thompson made no mention of winning the hearts and minds of the people; the operative word was "control."

Lansdale had asserted that pacification needed to focus on fostering trust between the people and the government. Yet the diminishment of Communist power became a focal point of MACV's role as it played out in the latter half of the 1960s. Despite MACV's early consensus that pacification ultimately meant improving relations between the people and the Saigon government, MACV came to perceive PAVN's eradication as vital to pacification. Throughout 1965, MACV sent a series of reports to the Defense Intelligence Agency. Under the subject heading "Monthly Report of Rural Pacification Progress and Population

Control and Area Control," these documents outlined the security status of the RVN's provinces. Omitted from these reports were any mention of improved relations between the GVN and the rural populace. Rather, attention fell on how many inhabitants and acreage were presently under GVN control.[93]

Control, again, became the operative word when discussing the purpose of pacification, especially after a U.S. Mission Liaison Group document confirmed controlling—not uplifting—the people as pacification's true aim. The undated document began by stating, "the mission of military operations is to defeat the Viet Cong in order to permit the extension of GVN control over the entire country."[94] Moreover, the document posited all allied forces as agents of pacification: "RVNAF [Republic of Vietnam Armed Forces] in coordination with International Assistance Forces should be positioned to gain military control over the installations, population centers and lines of communication."[95] Over time, allied forces would extend their areas of control, thereby permitting favorable conditions for development. Or, more clearly, "military control over areas will permit the progressive expansion of construction and vitalization within these areas."[96] Control over people and land, particularly as provided by the allied militaries, meant that from the onset, enacting pacification had little to do with fostering cordial ties between the GVN and those living in the nation's hinterlands. Furthermore, rhetoric and reality often differed. That the GVN's views of pacification often did not match its methods of executing the concept served as evidence of that disparity.

A 1968 Joint U.S. Public Affairs Office (JUSPAO) psychological operations (PSYOP) policy document, titled "PSYOP Support of Pacification," reinforced the notion of pacification as an all-inclusive undertaking: "Pacification can be described as the sum total of actions designed to win and keep the support of the rural population for the government of the Republic of Viet Nam."[97] The document disclosed more in noting that, "in the official definition, pacification is 'the military, political, economic and social process of establishing or re-establishing local government responsive to and involving the participation of the people.'"[98] The document placed "territorial security" ahead of "establishing an effective political structure at the local level," and "stimulating self-sustaining economic activity in the countryside."[99] Furthermore, it stated, effective pacification required "the provision of sustained, credible territorial security and its integral internal security" (with territorial security defined as "security from VC local forces and guerrilla units and VC/NVA main force units if any are in or threatening the area").[100] Pacification absolutely necessitated support from military entities, while focusing on improved security above all else. That pacification and revolutionary development were corresponding terms and involved all efforts to execute the war gained further credence in December 1969, when a U.S. Senate Committee on Foreign Relations staff report addressed the current situation in the RVN. The report contained the fragment "the so-called pacification program, or Revolutionary Development program."[101] These words confirmed that pacification encompassed various phases, rather than functioning as a phase unto itself.

Pacification discourse persisted well into the CORDS era. In 1970, a two-part series by Robert Komer in the magazine *Army* revisited pacification in South Vietnam. In "Clear, Hold and Rebuild," Komer described pacification as "basically those programs aimed at protecting the rural people and attempting to generate their allegiance to the government in competition with the Viet Cong."[102] This definition mirrored the evolution of the war in Vietnam, as by 1970, and considering Vietnamization, more MACV resources were being used to buttress pacification efforts. Furthermore, Komer accentuated the need to defend the lives of those living in the countryside. The implication was that security persisted as the most crucial aspect of pacification, even into the 1970s.

CORDS provided its advisors with various guides to assist them in their mission to advance pacification. District Senior Advisors (DSAs) received copies of the 1970 CORDS *Handbook for District Senior Advisor*. Here, too, was an extremely detailed definition of pacification that posited the term as encompassing the entire war:

> The Government of Vietnam is faced with the problem of building a new nation while at the same time defeating the enemy. Either of these tasks alone would be difficult, but in South Vietnam the problem is magnified by the fact that they must be accomplished simultaneously. In order to accomplish the tasks the GVN has combined the aspects of both military operations and civil nation building programs into a process which is called the "Pacification and Development Plan." It is not only a military war of opposing military forces, but a war for the allegiance of the people, a campaign to demonstrate that the Government of South Vietnam offers citizens the greatest opportunity for a free, peaceful and full life. It is not enough to defeat the enemy in the field; it is also essential to provide protection to the people of the countryside and to help meet

their aspiration for a better life. Pacification is a military, political, economic and social process.[103]

Echoing Lathram, the handbook advised that accomplishing this feat entailed "establishing, or reestablishing, local government responsive to and involving the participation of the citizens"; "providing sustained credible security"; "destroying the enemy's underground government"; "asserting, or reasserting, GVN political control"; "involvement of the people in the Central government"; and "initiating economic and social activity capable of self-sustenance and expansion."[104] Peculiarly, handbooks for advisors serving with the securers of pacification, the RF and PF, lacked any definition of the term itself. Although they did address how Saigon's security forces figured into pacification, none of the iterations of the *RF-PF Handbook for Advisors* relayed any definition such as the one found in the *Handbook for District Senior Advisor.*[105] In 1971, CORDS published *The Vietnamese Village: A Handbook for Advisors*, which also did not contain a definition of pacification, even though CORDS had one; *The Vietnamese Village* relayed the term as a solution to the PLAF insurgency without actually addressing what pacification meant.[106]

Even after the American War's end in 1973, pacification remained a term under revision. In line with what Lansdale and Komer wrote and what CORDS brought to fruition, pacification encompassed every element of Saigon's struggle against Hanoi over the future of South Vietnam. Writing after the war, ARVN General Trần Đình Thọ explained:

Pacification is the military, political, economic, and social process of establishing or reestablishing local government responsive to and involving the participation of the people. It includes the provision of sustained, credible territorial security, the destruction of the enemy's underground government, the assertion or re-assertion of political control and involvement of the people in government, and the initiation of economic and social activity capable of self-sustenance and expansion. Defined as such, pacification is a broad and complex strategic concept which encompasses many fields of national endeavor. As a program implemented jointly with the U.S. military effort in South Vietnam, pacification appears to have involved every American serviceman and civilian who served there, many of whom indeed participated in conceiving the idea and helping put it to work.[107]

At least by the fall of Saigon in 1975, the best explanation of pacification posited the term as an all-encompassing strategy. But in reality, the United States and Republic of Vietnam fought an entire war without a consistent mutual understanding of what pacification meant.

Relaying Pacification to the Public

How policymakers explained pacification to the public also matters. If articulating the meaning of pacification within political circles proved challenging, informing the average American underscored the lack of clarity around the term. Comments to the public mirrored those shared internally to other policymakers—affirming both the ambiguity of pacification as a term and a concept as well as the abstrusity of its meaning. Addressing the media at a press conference in North Dakota on 11 January 1967, U.S. Army Chief of Staff Gen. Harold K. Johnson explained revolutionary development as grassroots pacification, with security being the deciding factor for its success.[108] Aside from the explanations of pacification and revolutionary development—which ran counter to those expressed by others— Johnson's remarks conveyed the belief that the allied forces' efforts had visibly improved the military situation in the country. Security was indeed crucial to pacification's success.

When Vice President Hubert H. Humphrey appeared on NBC's *Meet the Press* on 26 November 1967, he referred to "pacification or what we call revolutionary development" as an example of progress. Humphrey contended that by the latter half of 1967, the Saigon government was making "steady progress" regarding pacification.[109] Yet his statement encapsulated the complexity of pacification. The vice president broke the war down into military, political, diplomatic, and pacification components: "I do think it is fair to say that there has been on every front in Vietnam, militarily, substantial progress, politically, very significant progress, with the Constitution and the freely-elected government, . . . diplomatically, in terms of a peace negotiation, that is the place where there has been the stalemate. There is no military stalemate. There is no pacification stalemate."[110] Coupled with Humphrey's use of pacification after qualifying it as revolutionary development, such distinctions obfuscated the central role of politics—diplomacy included—to war in general, as well as the encompassment of both military and development efforts under pacification.

In a *Stars and Stripes* story about the development side of pacification in Phú Bổn Province in 1969, Willard E. Chambers, deputy assistant director of

CORDS, framed pacification squarely as improving the relationship between the GVN and the rural populace:

> First, you must develop a government that deserves the support of the people—and demonstrate the capability of that government (to function) with reasonable honesty and efficiency. . . . If you can't do that, you won't be able to do the number two thing—assure the support of the people to that government. The government must have a dialog with the people. . . . If you can't do either of those things, there's no point in trying the third thing—to enhance the enforcement of the government to where it can deal with insurgents. Those who would suggest "get on with the fighting" don't understand the nature of the insurgency problem.[111]

Presented in this manner, pacification focused more on development than security actions. Indeed, Chambers emphasized the significance of gaining the people's trust as outweighing physically combatting PLAF. This interpretation also continued the idea that pacification meant transforming the GVN into a stable, respectworthy, government.

Development as pacification remained a point for another CORDS official. William E. Colby, who ran CORDS after Komer's tenure ended in 1968, explained his view of pacification in his memoir *Lost Victory*. A champion of improving the lives of villagers through self-help projects and benevolent actions by the GVN, Colby perceived development as the only means of South Vietnam achieving victory over the North. But he disliked the word pacification because of the violent history attached to it: "It had the drawback of suggesting that peace would be imposed on the population—reflecting the military and colonial view of what was required—and it certainly contradicted the essential element of engaging the population in a common effort to defend and develop their communities."[112] While he preferred a more peaceful tact, Colby admitted that because of widespread usage and thus familiarity, he and CORDS used the word pacification.[113] Regardless of Colby's favoring of development as the mechanism that advanced pacification, that latter term still explained the war long after the end of American participation.

The Nonexistent "Other War"

Defining pacification as being America's modus operandi for fighting the war permits the debunking of the "other war" myth. Often in quotes, the "other war" appeared as an invented concept, the ownership of which no one wanted. Notions that multiple wars took place in the RVN between 1965 and 1972 have long dogged Vietnam War discussions. For some, two distinct conflicts transpired—the so-called "big-unit war" and the mythical "other war."[114] The "other war" was code for the implication that conventional military operations often failed to secure territory and occurred at the expense of pacification. Such a fallacy emerged from the divide over whether pacification entailed improving security or was a development endeavor. Still others perceived the war as having three separate areas of attention. Regardless of the number of so-called "other" wars, the very idea presented pacification as task neglected by U.S. and RVN authorities. Only one war to pacify the Republic of Vietnam ever truly existed; priorities dictated the amount of attention MACV placed on supporting rural development.

An unpublished article by journalist Rose Kushner dismissed the notion of separate wars in the RVN: "*There is no 'other war,' separate and distinct from the military operations*," wrote the lifelong supporter of Lansdale and his vision of pacification.[115] Writing in opposition to a *Newsweek* article that had categorized pacification as merely one of many wars in the RVN, Kushner explained pacification as the war itself. With the myriad of terms used, it is not surprising that people spoke of the absence of a singular conflict. When discussing what he saw as a major lull in the GVN's attention toward pacification in *No Exit from Vietnam*, Thompson explained pacification as "all government efforts at regaining control of the lost countryside."[116] One could infer that in this context, pacification comprised any method used to expel the Communists from the RVN's villages. Thompson also roundly rejected the false narrative of three wars—military, pacification, and nation-building—as having transpired in the RVN: "There were not three wars . . . there was only one war," he wrote, noting that pacification "lip service" by American and South Vietnamese officials advanced the notion that only with the 1966 Honolulu Conference did pacification efforts gain their attention.[117]

Correspondence between Komer and Lansdale in 1971 decidedly placed pacification as the only war. Komer had sent a draft of "Was There Another Way?," a chapter in a retrospective study of counterinsurgency in the RVN for the RAND Corporation, to Lansdale for input.[118] Lansdale's comments and Komer's reply centered largely on how the U.S. Army and State Department pushed pacification, albeit differently. As noted by Lansdale, the U.S. Army did back pacification, but preferred doing much of the work for the GVN.[119] In responding to Lansdale, Komer wrote that "there was no 'other war'; it was all one ball of wax—in our case predominately military, to our cost. I brought the 'other war' concept (which I hardly invented) only as an operational device to compete more effectively with the US and ARVN military."[120] As Komer noted, after 1967, "new model pacification" brought with it the realization of Lansdale's and Komer's vision that the South Vietnamese would do the work, with America simply providing financial backing. New model pacification was the incarnation of pacification started by Komer and continued by CORDS during the 1966–69 period. Moreover, these two main influencers of pacification in the RVN placed the actions of conventional forces within the confines of pacification.

Pacification meant replacing the old with the new. In the RVN, pacification needed to destroy what opposed it—PAVN and PLAF. Those objectives, combined with conventional warfare, ensured that destruction prevailed as the lasting phase of pacification. Although development mattered, and certainly occurred, actions by all belligerents ensured the permanence of destruction. In the following chapters on Phú Yên, destruction as pacification becomes undeniable.

2

"We should not be astonished"

Phú Yên and War through 1965

"Now we are stronger than the enemy politically, we must continue to strengthen our political forces. However, we are still weaker than the enemy militarily," read the decree issued by Vietnamese Workers' Party General Secretary and Politburo head Lê Duẩn after the Ninth Plenum in December 1963. "Therefore *the key point at the present time is to make outstanding efforts to rapidly strengthen our military forces in order to create a basic change in the balance of forces between the enemy and us in South Viet-Nam.*"[1] That pronouncement from the politburo signaled the Democratic Republic of Vietnam's pursuit of a decisive military solution to unify Vietnam under its rule. To that end, the politburo embraced its General Offensive and Uprising (or *Tổng Công Kích-Tổng Khởi Nghĩa*) strategy:

> We are preparing for the General Offensive and Uprising by using military and political forces to disintegrate the pro-U.S. government's troops and provoke uprisings in the rural area and cities still under enemy occupation. . . . The process of advancing toward the General Offensive and Uprising is one marked by limited offensives and partial uprisings in a complex see-saw dispute with the enemy aimed at pushing back the enemy step by step, winning victory bit by bit and advancing toward winning total victory.[2]

Conventional warfare now superseded guerrilla warfare as Hanoi's method of choice. The Politburo's decision to intensify the war prompted a mirrored escalation by its enemies. Events in RVN provinces, particularly Phú Yên,

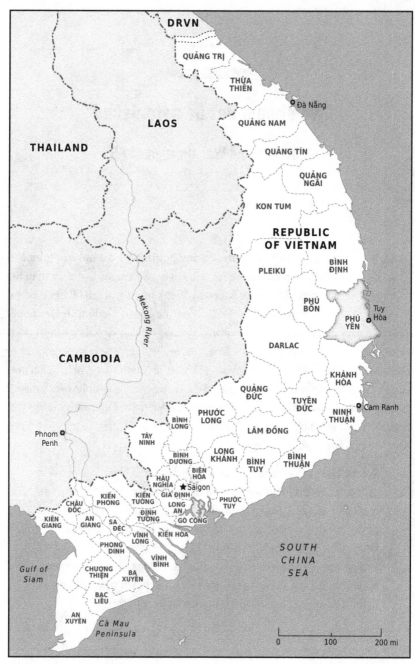

Map 1. The Republic of Vietnam, circa 1966.

Cartography by Erin Greb.

demonstrated how the ramping-up of hostilities unfolded and how the Americans responded.

Nestled between the provinces of Bình Định to the north, Khánh Hòa to the south, and Phú Bổn and Đắk Lắk to the west, Phú Yên Province sat against the South China Sea in the Republic of Vietnam's Central Highlands. Since Phú Yên translates to "endowed with tranquility," it is possible that the land gained its name from its geography. Phú Yên's jungled mountain expanses, which accounted for three-fifths of the province, gave way to agriculturally vital valleys, which in turn opened into expansive plains. These features extended across the province's districts of Đồng Xuân, Hiếu Xương, Sông Cầu, Sơn Hòa, Tuy An, and Tuy Hòa. From deep within the central highlands flowed the Sông Ba, a river that zigzagged through Sơn Hòa District, becoming the Sông Đà Rằng after a dam and entering the rice-producing valleys of Tuy Hòa and Hiếu Xương. On the Sông Đà Rằng's northern bank lay the Tuy Hòa Valley, with the Hiếu Xương Valley situated on the southern bank. The river ultimately reached the South China Sea at Tuy Hòa City. On the other side of the Hiếu Xương Valley meandered the Bàn Thạch. Another significant river, the Kỳ Lộ, flowed through a remote valley to which it gave its name in Đồng Xuân District. Prior to entering Tuy An District, the Kỳ Lộ became the Sông Cái. These rivers gave Phú Yên its rich, rice-producing lands. Yet the province's beauty beguiled its history as a land immersed in war.

Many of Phú Yên's inhabitants resided in those valleys before the American War. The Saigon government placed Phú Yên's population at 349,000 in 1966, but accessible data from the provincial government put the figure at 318,882.[3] The provincial government recorded 75,052 people living in Tuy Hòa District, including the 46,416 that lived in the economic and political center of Phú Yên, the provincial capital of Tuy Hòa City. Elsewhere in the province, 19,501 people lived in Đồng Xuân District, 94,702 in Hiếu Xương District, 53,922 in Sông Cầu District, 12,609 in Sơn Hòa District, and 63,096 in Tuy An District. By 1966, the war had displaced thousands of these inhabitants to refugee camps in the province.[4]

Phú Yên's value lay in its rice paddies. Many of the province's inhabitants made their living by harvesting rice or by catching fish; the province annually produced an average of 85,000 tons of rice and 5,000 tons of fish.[5] Rice production, although it paled in comparison to the rice-harvesting areas straddling the

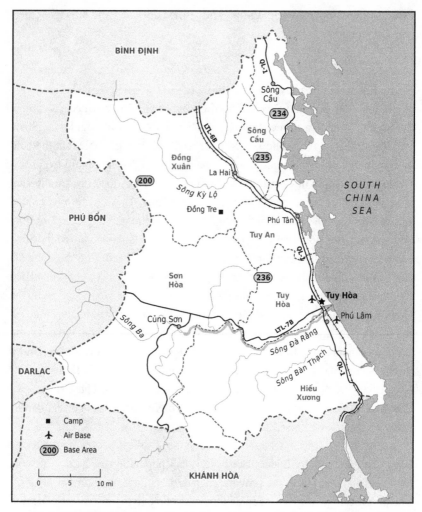

Map 2. Phú Yên Province with airbases, province and district capitals, major rivers, major roads and railroad, and PAVN and PLAF base areas, circa 1966.
Cartography by Erin Greb.

Sông Mê Kông—famously known as the Mekong River—farther south in the country, proved significant for the region. With the second-most productive rice paddies in what the South Vietnamese designated Quân đoàn II—the Americans used the identifiers II Corps, II Corps Tactical Zone (II CTZ), and later in the war, Military Region 2 (MR2)—control of Phú Yên meant access to vast sources of nourishment and revenue.[6] All participants in the war in Phú Yên understood the need to control the province's rice production. Consequently, all belligerents fought over Phú Yên's fertile rice-producing valleys, with emphasis on the Tuy Hòa Valley, so as to influence—and ultimately control—the people.

Vital road and rail networks transited Phú Yên during the Vietnam War. National Route Quốc lộ I (QL-I), the principal transportation artery for much of the RVN, stretched north to south near Phú Yên's coastline. This paved highway connected Tuy Hòa City with Nha Trang to the north and Qui Nhơn to the south. A smaller interprovincial route, Liên Tỉnh Lộ 6B (LTL-6B), linked the district capital of La Hai in Đồng Xuân District with Tuy An District. A similar road, LTL-7B, linked Tuy Hòa City on the coast with the western interior, connecting the province capital with Củng Sơn in Sơn Hòa District via a provincial road, Tỉnh Lộ 9B (TL-9B).

An Epoch of War

Phú Yên's history is one marked by numerous pacification efforts by multiple outside actors. The province's resources and geographic location had attracted various powers for hundreds of years. Long before the U.S. Army's forays into the province, other forces fought for control of the region, and a host of powers controlled what eventually became Phú Yên. Originally called Thông Xuân, the province existed under the Han Dynasty. With the end of Chinese domination of the region in 808 A.D., the Champa filled the power vacuum in what was then known as Chiêm Thành. With Champa rule came relative tranquility for the next six hundred years. Turmoil arrived with the Vietnamese invasion of 1470. Invading Vietnamese from the north swept through the region, pushing the Champa to the Đèo Cả Pass, a small area of Phú Yên to the south of what later became Tuy Hòa City. Yet the Vietnamese did not occupy all of the province; instead, they absorbed a small portion of northern Phú Yên into the province of Bình Định. Correspondingly, the Champa regained control over a large portion of the province.[7]

In 1578, the Vietnamese returned to Phú Yên. Now under the rule of Nguyễn Hoàng, Vietnamese armies conquered the area and stayed. Tension between the Champa and their Vietnamese overlords resulted in a quickly suppressed revolt in 1629.[8] Phú Yên played a significant role in 1795, when the Tây Sơn rebels conquered the province and used it as a base from which to continue their uprising against the Nguyễn lords. Peace only returned to the region in 1802.[9] Phú Yên's first brush with the United States came in January 1833 with the establishment of an American diplomatic mission, led by Edmund Roberts, at Vũng Lắm, in what later became Sông Cầu District.[10] Like the Americans in the province during the 1960s and 1970s, Roberts's party in 1833 found Phú Yên idyllic, if not tranquil, despite being contested land. Phú Yên was prized soil, as the American mission acknowledged: "The surrounding country was most beautiful, the country high, verdant, and seemingly highly cultivated—indeed, we should not be astonished, as it belongs to the Province of Phuyen, or of affluent Repose."[11] Another statement captured Phú Yên in a brief period between its resistance to and rotation of foreign rule. "We found ourselves in an extensive and secure harbor, where, I believe, the American flag has never waved before, and very rarely that of any other civilized nation," a member of Edmund's entourage remarked upon arrival. Within fifty-two years, the French would plant their flag in Southeast Asia—Phú Yên included. With the imposition of French rule in 1885, the French suppressed insurrection in the region through beheadings. Decades of French colonial rule cast a dour veil over Vietnam, interrupted only by the Second World War and the arrival of imperial Japanese forces in Indochina.[12]

After Germany's victory over France in 1940, the French retained Indochina, albeit under the Vichy government. As the war progressed, Japanese forces occupied portions of French Indochina, yet permitted French authorities to remain in power.[13] Toward the end of the war, fearing an invasion by the United States, Japanese authorities called for direct control over French Indochina. On 9 March 1945, after briefly fighting with French forces, the Japanese military claimed Indochina directly for Tokyo.[14] Japanese control proved ephemeral, as Japan surrendered to Allied forces on 15 August 1945, and Japanese troops relinquished Phú Yên to the Việt Minh.[15] Following Japan's capitulation, Phú Yên found itself once again confronting French imperialism; the presence of the Việt Minh—and later, the next generation of Communist guerrillas, PLAF—continued and reflected Phú Yên's history as a land caught up in war.

The First Indochina War

Familiar with modern warfare in the age of decolonization, Phú Yên earned a reputation for fostering capable guerrillas during the Việt Minh's struggle against French efforts to reassert rule over Indochina. Geography mattered once more as the province lay at the confluence of mountain passes used by the Việt Minh. During the First Indochina War, the Việt Minh largely controlled Phú Yên, a dilemma the French sought to rectify with conventional military forces. On 20 January 1954, during the dying days of France's war to retain Indochina, Gen. Henri Navarre launched Operation Atlante to pacify the region.[16] The French identified Phú Yên and the adjacent coastal region as being under Việt Minh control.[17] Scholar and French citizen Bernard B. Fall observed Atlante, and later mentioned the operation in his book *Street Without Joy.*[18] During the first phase, Arethuse, Navarre dispatched 25,000 men of the French Expeditionary Corps, with the majority of forces landing amphibiously at Tuy Hòa village.[19] Then just a collection of hamlets comprising a typical village, Tuy Hòa replaced Sông Cầu as the Phú Yên Province capital after the French identified the village as more defensible.[20] From the north, the French high command sent Groupement Mobile 100 (GM 100) to reopen Road 7—what the South Vietnamese later called LTL-7B—which wound along the Sông Ba from Cheo Reo deep in the Central Highlands to the coast near Tuy Hòa village. The French cleared the road of mines and rebuilt destroyed bridges, all the while encountering few enemy formations; instead, Việt Minh ambushes, mines, and snipers exacted a human toll from the French forces that slowed down the operation.[21] Near Củng Sơn, an estimated force of 2,100 Việt Minh ambushed three companies of State of Vietnam—the precursor to the RVN—army troops fighting for France, killing 200 and wounding another 100.[22] The Việt Minh ambush near Củng Sơn foreshadowed the predicament RVN troops in Phú Yên would face years later during the American War.

Operation Atlante marked the only time French forces exercised any control over Phú Yên beyond the confines of Tuy Hòa village during the First Indochina War. The operation did afford France brief control of the Tuy Hòa Valley. Yet the Việt Minh victory at Điện Biên Phủ spelled the end of both Operation Atlante and France's ambitions in Indochina. France's defeat at Điện Biên Phủ forced the premature end of Operation Atlante before the third and final phase of the campaign began, as participating forces were urgently needed elsewhere.[23]

Phú Yên existed in the middle of the ideological struggle of the Cold War. The period between the end of Operation Atlante and the rule of Ngô Đình Diệm saw the province still locked in war. USOM—an American advisory body—observed the unfolding of the entire war, Operation Atlante included. USOM worked in Vietnam long before the arrival of American combat forces, giving the agency's advisors keen insight into province matters during this formative phase between the two Indochina wars. Through USOM's reporting, the symbiotic relationship between Bình Định and Phú Yên provinces appears to have been as significant as it was during the Tây Sơn uprising. Events in either province affected conditions in the other. Bình Định Province fell under nearly unchallenged Việt Minh rule during the First Indochina War—remaining untouched by Operation Atlante; the

Việt Minh controlled much of the region—Phú Yên included—from Bình Định.[24] In 1954, Operation Atlante's failure to achieve lasting results left the coastal region in disarray. Those fearing the Việt Minh in Bình Định—landowners, wealthy farmers, and those with commercial interests—fled south to Phú Yên, a province with its own well-entrenched Việt Minh, yet a province with at least a functioning government loyal to Saigon. An estimated 1,000 Bình Định inhabitants assumed temporary refuge in Phú Yên.[25] For the first time since falling under French control in 1883, Phú Yên again existed under Vietnamese rule in February 1955.[26]

Operation Atlante left Phú Yên in comparatively better shape than Bình Định. At least in Phú Yên the operation had pushed the Việt Minh out of the urban areas, essentially ending the era of the Communists as the sole source of governance in the province. Yet the French departure after Operation Atlante severed Phú Yên from the U.S. side as well: areas "liberated"—a term used loosely by American officials because the Việt Minh remained in the province—by French forces lacked essential physical infrastructure, as the Việt Minh had destroyed government and public buildings as well as roads and bridges.[27] The "ill-fated operation Atlante" left Phú Yên with "limited relief supplies" and in need of "reconstruction of roads and bridges, school construction, rehabilitation of irrigation facilities, more effective information and assistance in Public Health such as first aid kits, medicaments, malaria control, etc."[28] According to a memo to USOM's acting assistant director for operations, Charles A. Mann, from former USOM representative William A. Dymsza, resourcefulness and anti–Việt Minh sentiment helped local Saigon government officials overcome material shortages. Saigon made "remarkable progress" in a "province controlled for over 8 years by the Viet-Minh," the memo stated, thanks to "the effective work of the Chief of Province and the District Chiefs, who have been using many Viet-Minh methods against the Viet-Minh."[29] A Việt Minh member before abandoning the cause, Phú Yên's province chief appreciated the Việt Minh's use of cadres to sway the sympathies of the common people. Fighting continued during the nebulous period between the collapse of French rule and the rise of North and South Vietnam. In using his own cadre, he took the war to the villages—forcing a delicate balance between Saigon and Việt Minh influence. Although countered, the Việt Minh survived, and thus remained a threat in Phú Yên. Tellingly, according to USOM, while many people seemed to adopt "a 'wait and see' attitude," others feared the Communists—an outlook that Phú Yên's populace maintained for the next twenty years.[30]

The memo continued that the Việt Minh had indoctrinated many, and that Việt Minh forces had only evacuated the area "temporarily," per the Geneva Accords, and would "return in two years."[31] The Việt Minh fully expected that it would regain control after elections. Since elections never occurred, the Việt Minh's promise later became that of its military successor, PLAF. Additionally, the memo noted reports that the Việt Minh, in typical Communist revolutionary fashion, were "going under cover temporarily . . . waiting for favorable opportunities to exploit against the Government. The fact that there have been incidents not long ago also shows that the Viet-Minh are not inactive."[32] Phú Yên found itself in a seemingly infinite cycle of insurgency and conventional warfare. Events in 1955 left the province a contested space, one in which both parties would look toward conventional military forces to break the stalemate.

The Second Indochina War

After the 1954 Geneva Conference, the Việt Minh largely controlled the people of Phú Yên. The "nascent Viet-Cong forces" left by the Việt Minh after the agreements made in Geneva afforded the Communists the means to exploit the GVN's meager presence in Phú Yên in 1954.[33] The formation of the Republic of Vietnam under Ngô Đình Diệm brought forth efforts to reclaim Phú Yên, and the province entered a period as a land divided between its Việt Minh history and the future envisioned by the government in Saigon. Operation Atlante's apparition lingered as ARVN launched conventional operations to pacify Phú Yên. A reputation as a Việt Minh province meant that any inroads Saigon made into Phú Yên necessitated significant military intervention.

To direct its efforts and thwart GVN expansion, the NLF established its presence in Phú Yên under the Phú Yên Province Party Committee in December 1961. As a shadow government originally headquartered in An Lĩnh, a village in Tuy An District, the Phú Yên Province Party Committee bore responsibility for all NLF operations in the province. To that end, the committee oversaw multiple subordinate organizations and maintained an active presence in the province's districts. As the war progressed, the committee decentralized to avert its annihilation.[34]

ARVN initiated Saigon's efforts to pacify Phú Yên during Ngô Đình Diệm's presidency. As cabled to Washington, the GVN approved the Delta Pacification Plan, which called for "a systematic military-political pacification of eleven provinces integrated with the strategic hamlet program," with similar plans drawn up for individual provinces elsewhere.[35] As one of six other provinces targeted for a similar pacification approach, Saigon initiated Operation Sea Swallow in Phú Yên in March 1962.[36] A follow-up effort, Operation Hải Yên II, started on 8 May 1962, with elements of the ARVN 22nd Division engaging in the process of "clear and hold." Clear and hold entailed ARVN ejecting PLAF with paramilitary forces (the clearing phase) thereby eliciting the people's loyalty to ensure that they turned toward Saigon, and not the NLF, for governance (the hold phase).[37] ARVN cleared the province capital and adjacent environs, ushering in the hold phase. The regime of Ngô Đình Diệm and its American backers promptly turned their attention to the Strategic Hamlet Program in Phú Yên. As relayed by William C. Trueheart at the U.S. Embassy in Saigon to State Department officials in Washington, "strategic hamlet construction (84 hamlets) has been initiated in most secure areas of province, especially around provincial seat of Tuy Hoa."[38] Tuy Hòa City now functioned as Saigon's bastion in Phú Yên. To better manage security, Ngô Đình Diệm's government created Phú Bổn Province from land taken from the provinces of Phú Yên and Darlac. Phú Yên's districts also took shape during this period.[39]

Phú Yên's modern history with pacification mattered, mainly because in practice, the province functioned as a test for the Strategic Hamlet Program—a truth evidenced in it being "a pilot province [for the] pacification program whose initial successes in 1962 later influenced most of the pacification planning in the country," according to a 1964 CIA report.[40] American advisors considered Phú Yên a model province with good local leadership and security.[41] Rufus Phillips, USOM's assistant director of rural affairs, observed and advised the Saigon government on matters of development and counterinsurgency, using Phú Yên as a showcase for pacification. In a cable to the U.S. Embassy in Saigon, Phillips suggested that the ambassador visit Phú Yên, "because much of our pioneer efforts in provincial rehabilitation were started there." Phillips noted that Phú Yên was "the first province in which a coordinated military and civilian pacification effort, based on the strategic hamlet concept, was started in June 1962 and where USOM placed its first Provincial Representative in October 1962."[42]

The permanence of security in Phú Yên remained questionable at best. Phillips noted the security conditions as having gone from restricting the province chief's "movements to the front yard of his house" to an improved situation where travel is "relatively free throughout most of the lowland area of the province."[43] Late November 1962 reflected a province seen by Americans as progressing toward being fully pacified.[44] Just two months later, however, in late January 1963, PLAF "completely overran a strategic hamlet in Phú Yên province that was

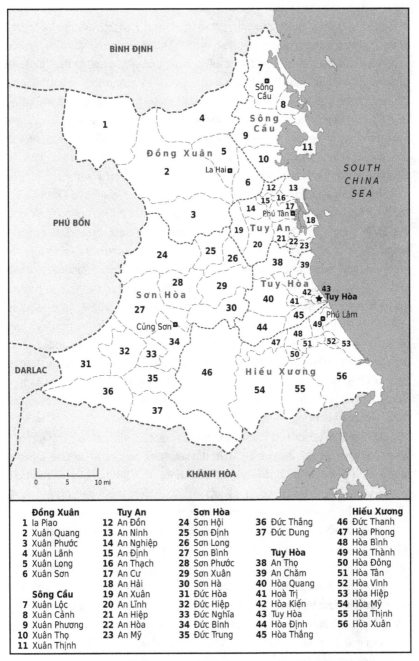

BÌNH ĐỊNH

PHÚ BỔN

DARLAC

SOUTH
CHINA
SEA

7
Sông
Cầu
8
Sông
Cầu
9
4
1
Đồng Xuân 5
2   La Hai
6
3
10
11
12 13
15 16
14   17
Phú Tân
18
19 Tuy An
20 21 22
23
38 39
24   25
26
28   29   Tuy Hòa
Sơn Hòa   40 41
27   42 43
30   Tuy Hòa
Củng Sơn   45 Phú Lâm
44 49
32 33   34   47 48 51 52 53
31   50
35   46   Hiếu Xương 56
36   54 55
37

KHÁNH HÒA

0   5   10 mi

Đồng Xuân	Tuy An	Sơn Hòa		Hiếu Xương
1 Ia Piao	12 An Đồn	24 Sơn Hội	36 Đức Thắng	46 Đức Thanh
2 Xuân Quang	13 An Ninh	25 Sơn Định	37 Đức Dung	47 Hòa Phong
3 Xuân Phước	14 An Nghiệp	26 Sơn Long		48 Hòa Bình
4 Xuân Lãnh	15 An Định	27 Sơn Bình	**Tuy Hòa**	49 Hòa Thành
5 Xuân Long	16 An Thạch	28 Sơn Phước	38 An Thọ	50 Hòa Đông
6 Xuân Sơn	17 An Cư	29 Sơn Xuân	39 An Chăm	51 Hòa Tân
	18 An Hải	30 Sơn Hà	40 Hòa Quang	52 Hòa Vinh
Sông Cầu	19 An Xuân	31 Đức Hòa	41 Hoà Trị	53 Hòa Hiệp
7 Xuân Lộc	20 An Lĩnh	32 Đức Hiệp	42 Hòa Kiến	54 Hòa Mỹ
8 Xuân Cảnh	21 An Hiệp	33 Đức Nghĩa	43 Tuy Hòa	55 Hòa Thịnh
9 Xuân Phương	22 An Hòa	34 Đức Bình	44 Hòa Định	56 Hòa Xuân
10 Xuân Thọ	23 An Mỹ	35 Đức Trung	45 Hòa Thắng	
11 Xuân Thịnh				

Map 3. Phú Yên with province and district capitals,
districts, and an index of the villages, circa 1966.

Cartography by Erin Greb.

defended by a civil guard company in addition to the village militia, killing 24 of the defenders and capturing 35 weapons."[45] Thus Saigon and Washington had expended considerable effort to establish what amounted to "a tolerable level of security by late 1963."[46] Although Tuy Hòa City remained under Saigon's banner, the rest of the province served as a de facto enemy base area, affording PLAF the means to keep pressure, overtly and covertly, on the Tuy Hòa Valley. Furthermore, progress—limited as it was—came to a sudden halt in 1963 as the coup against Ngô Đình Diệm destabilized much of South Vietnam, with the ensuing power vacuum leaving Phú Yên exposed to the NLF's plans.[47]

With the disruptions caused by the 1963 assassination of Ngô Đình Diệm, the NLF and its military arm, PLAF, made significant inroads into Phú Yên at the GVN's expense. The CIA framed the situation in starker terms. In a report prepared on 21 November 1964, the agency's Mission Province Reporting Unit reported that "security conditions in Phu Yen Province have worsened considerably in recent months."[48] The NLF and PLAF made overt moves to control the province. Targeting the fertile land, the Communists secured large tracks of Hiếu Xương District's delta and coastline, as well as areas "in the northern half of Tuy Hoa and the southern half of Tuy An districts."[49] These liberated areas underwent effective Communist counterpacification, with the construction of trenches "in the foothills of Hieu Xuong and Tuy An districts," the isolation of New Life Hamlets, the cutting of communication lines across the province, and the destruction of bridges and the interdicting of roads in Hiếu Xương District.[50] The CIA report described one of the most serious incidents, on 13 October, when trenches PLAF dug on QL-1 in the southern part of Sông Cầu District interrupted road traffic for five days.[51] Rail lines, too, fell prey to interdiction. Without a major reversal, the CIA warned, unhindered sabotage "could cut off vital links the province has with southern sources of supply."[52]

In 1964, the NLF encouraged the people themselves to foment unrest in Phú Yên. In a sign of growing Communist control over the population, a USAID briefing reported two different instances in late August when "'Buddhist' agitators in Hieu Xuong district persuaded villagers to obstruct M-113 armored personnel carriers by placing themselves in front of the vehicles during military operations." According to the briefing, Buddhist leaders in Saigon "publicly disassociated themselves from these typically Viet Cong tactics."[53] In October, the NLF "inspired demonstrations" at Hiếu Xương's district headquarters to protest "the indiscriminate use of artillery" and to call for the "release of relatives serving in the armed forces."[54] In one such demonstration, PLAF members went with villagers to the district headquarters, resulting in a firefight with the PF. Saigon found itself on the defensive because of a lack of resources, which compromised the province leadership's ability to match the NLF's ever-increasing tempo. With PLAF activity on the uptick across the RVN, ARVN dispatched most of its units elsewhere, leaving just a single unit at the province chief's disposal to challenge PLAF in Phú Yên. With momentum firmly in its metaphorical hands, PLAF effectively forced Saigon to abandon pacification efforts in the province.[55] As bemoaned by the CIA, "now, most, if not all, of this work must be redone."[56]

Decisions in North Vietnam's Politburo signaled the conflict's escalation in Phú Yên. Under the direction of Lê Duẩn, Hanoi embraced a strategy with a lineage to the First Indochina War—the General Offensive and Uprising. That strategy, as devised by Lê Duẩn, sought to replicate the successes of 1945 and 1954 in 1964 while sidestepping the three stages of Mao Zedong's protracted war. Mao's theory outlined what he termed the "strategic defensive," the "stalemate," and the "strategic offensive." Phase one involved guerrilla warfare against an opposing force on the offensive. Phase two called for the escalation of guerrilla warfare as the enemy's offensive ended and the consolidation of gains. Finally, phase three entailed a counteroffensive by conventional forces to take over the country. Instead of rigidity, the General Offensive and Uprising could adjust to any phase to meet current conditions.[57] In the August Revolution of 1945, Lê Duẩn saw a successful rural military campaign that produced a political victory by conjuring revolt in cities during the power vacuum caused by Japan's dissolution of French rule. During France's efforts to restore its control over Indochina, Lê Duẩn saw the 1954 Battle of Diện Biên Phủ as the Vietnamese having achieved a great battlefield victory against a seemingly superior foe. Looking at these two lessons together, Lê Duẩn believed that the North Vietnamese could achieve additional decisive battlefield victories that would endure widespread popular support for the Communist cause in South Vietnam.[58] In 1964, between the Politburo's control over Communists in South Vietnam through the Central Office for South Vietnam (COSVN) and PAVN sending regiments southward to bolster PLAF, the execution of the General Offensive and Uprising had begun.[59]

The General Offensive and Uprising of 1964 destroyed the remaining vestige of Ngô Đình Diệm's pacification efforts. That year, North Vietnam's Navy Group 125 ferried supplies to Vũng Rô, a bay in Phú Yên's Hiếu Xương District.[60] With such backing, PLAF seized the initiative in Phú Yên by mining the province's railroad.[61] During the rest of 1964 and well into 1965, PLAF overran Phú Yên's strategic hamlets while infiltrating others. PLAF owed its success in large part to the arrival of the PAVN 95th Regiment.[62] After infiltrating south and getting bloodied by elements of ARVN's 7th Airborne Division in March 1965, the PAVN 95th Regiment entered Phú Yên in late autumn of that year, bringing along with it conventional warfare. Although operating at two-thirds strength because of the March encounter, the PAVN 95th Regiment provided PLAF with the assistance it needed. Aside from eradicating strategic hamlets, PAVN regulars aided their PLAF comrades in securing rice production and keeping the ARVN 47th Regiment confined primarily to Tuy Hòa City.[63] The Communists effectively solidified their position in Phú Yên. Only the arrival of American and South Korean forces in late 1965 effectively countered North Vietnamese efforts, thereby thwarting the General Offensive and Uprising in Phú Yên.[64]

1965: Reversing the First General Offensive and Uprising

"Two types of warfare died in 1965–66 in Viet-Nam, in both the North and the South: Counterinsurgency was one of them, and the national war of liberation was the other. They were both killed by the sheer mass of American firepower thrown into the conflict." So said Bernard B. Fall in his essay collection *Viet-Nam Witness, 1953–66.*[65] Fall's statement captured a notion—one that persisted long after the end of the Vietnam War—that the United States ignored pacification, and thereby incorrectly fought the conflict. Such a contention presented an oversimplified view, as it ignored the conventionalization of the war for South Vietnam's future already being waged by Hanoi. As subsequent events in Phú Yên also revealed, MACV executed a war both in line with that of the Politburo and one very much concerned with pacification.

Two opposing pacification plans unfolded as the NLF challenged the GVN's efforts with its own. The NLF created "liberated areas" across Trung Bộ, the term it used to refer to South Vietnam's central region, including Phú Yên, which contained substantial agricultural production.[66] By 1965, the NLF claimed control of 75 percent of Phú Yên—a reasonable figure given that the GVN only held Tuy Hòa City. NLF figures for this time placed the province's population at 342,929, and listed 256,400 as the "liberated population,"[67] which equated to those living in an NLF "liberated area." A liberated area might amount to most if not all of a province in which the NLF exercised its own pacification process to gain control over the people; the presence of GVN forces in a liberated area did not matter.[68] For that reason, the figure of 256,400 living under the NLF is plausible. By 1966, around 46,416 lived in Tuy Hòa City, the GVN stronghold in Phú Yên. The NLF's numbers, regardless of their accuracy, thus indicated that the NLF controlled much of the remaining population.[69] Furthermore, NLF data emphasized the fact that PLAF had a considerable presence in Phú Yên.

Hanoi escalated its aide to Communist forces in the province. On 16 February 1965, American and South Vietnamese forces interdicted North Vietnamese war materiel intended for PLAF units in Phú Yên. After an American helicopter crew relayed word of having observed a well-camouflaged ship at anchor near Phú Yên's coast, South Vietnamese authorities directed RVN Air Force jets to the area. Met with considerable ground fire from the ship and the shore, the jets nonetheless sunk the vessel. Later, South Vietnamese troops successfully engaged enemy forces on the shore and secured the area, hulk included.[70] The GVN thence acquired a trove of significant documents and weapons. South Vietnamese forces discerned that China had recently built the ship.[71] Moreover, captured papers identified "several Viet Cong aboard . . . as having come from North Viet-Nam" and included a Hải Phòng newspaper dated 23 January 1965.[72] Connections to PAVN emerged as well: captured documents included soldiers' health records, which revealed that at least one passenger served with the PAVN 338th Division.[73] As for weaponry, the GVN captured an estimated one million small arms rounds, one thousand grenades, five hundred pounds of explosives, two thousand 82mm mortar shells, five hundred antitank grenades, five hundred 57mm recoilless rifle shells, at least one thousand 75mm recoilless rifle shells, one 57mm recoilless rifle, two heavy machine guns, two thousand Mauser rifles, at least one hundred carbines, one thousand submachine guns, fifteen light machine guns, five hundred rifles, and five hundred pounds of medical provisions. Supplies bore labels from China, Czechoslovakia, East Germany, North Vietnam, and the Soviet Union.[74] These discoveries verified Vũng Rô as a significant disembarkation point for PLAF supplies and served as proof positive that PLAF served Hanoi. Additionally, the sheer number of supplies demonstrated Hanoi's ability to sustain forces in remote locales via the sea.

PLAF activity increased in 1965 as the war for Vietnam's future intensified with the commitment of U.S. ground forces. A captured PLAF document disclosed an upswing in Communist activity in Phú Yên, with PLAF nearly doubling the fighting strength of its main forces. The document placed 8,214 guerrillas in the province as opposed to the 4,373 in Phú Yên at the end of 1964.[75] Comparatively, in his 1966 book *Viet Cong: The Organization and Techniques of the National Liberation Front of South Vietnam*, Douglas Pike surmised that between 55,000 and 80,000 guerrillas operated in the RVN by early 1965. The wide range in numbers, Pike noted, existed because "a characteristic of a guerrilla war is that the government side never knows how many of the enemy it faces—every cyclo driver, every Vietnamese who passes in the street could be a guerrilla."[76] Back in Phú Yên, an additional 26,630 "militiamen," or those who mobilized on a part-time basis, served in the province by the end of 1965, according to the aforementioned captured PLAF document—a sharp increase from 7,900 in the previous year.[77] With Pike's words in mind, the guerrilla numbers for Phú Yên demonstrated a noteworthy NLF presence while furthering the GVN fear that anyone could be a member of the NLF. Out of the 8,214 guerrillas, PLAF had only 2,253 individual weapons for battle—a sizable force, yet with a substantial firepower shortcoming.[78] Nevertheless, the near doubling of PLAF guerrillas in the span of a year meant that the NLF held considerably sway in the province. Moreover, to reverse such influence required more allied forces in the province.

PLAF benefited substantially from the multitude of coups that plagued the RVN after the assassination of Ngô Đình Diệm in November 1963. According to the local NLF, in Phú Yên's Tuy Hòa District, "the unstable political situation of RVN (8 coup d'état in 1964), the many great successes of the Liberation Army, the political disintegration of the enemy and the firm belief of the people in the ultimate success of our revolution were favorable factors for the development of the guerrilla movement in the district. Our cadre's enthusiasm and the considerable efforts also greatly contributed to the success of the movement."[79] The successes of 1965 certainly imbued PLAF with thoughts of superiority.

In March 1965, the deterioration of security across the whole region, not just in Phú Yên, prompted USOM to abandon its village self-help program. A USOM representative remarked to Australian embassy personnel in Saigon that "the security situation made it impossible for aid teams to operate in many parts of these provinces, but there was also concern that the village aid programme was providing direct aid to the Viet Cong."[80] A key factor in the worsening security situation, according to the same USOM representative, was the arrival of "North Vietnamese to strengthen the Viet Cong effort in the Central region."[81] Within seven months, the war in Phú Yên would enter a new, dramatic phase reliant on the efforts of conventional forces.

In a sign of the war's escalation, by October 1965, PAVN soldiers had reinforced their PLAF comrades outside of Tuy Hòa City. Falling under PAVN's B1 Front in Military Region 5 meant that the PAVN 5th Division, or Nông Trường 5, controlled Hanoi's forces in Phú Yên. Phrased differently, Hanoi controlled Nông Trường 5 and thus the war in Phú Yên. Comprised of just two regiments, the 95th and 18B, instead of the normal three, the PAVN 5th Division was a division in name only. In practice, the PAVN 5th Division amounted to a subsector of the B1 front, with the PAVN 95th Regiment, and infrequently the PAVN 18B Regiment, typically operating in and around Phú Yên.[82] A January 1967 telegram from the U.S. Embassy in Saigon to the State Department in Washington recalled that in 1965, "an estimated five NVA battalions" sweeping into Phú Yên to aid their PLAF allies, "scattering RF and PF units and twice mortaring the province capital of Tuy Hoa."[83] During its spring-summer campaign of 1965, the same five PAVN battalions isolated Tuy Hòa City, leaving the GVN stronghold in contact with a select few hamlets and largely unable to control the province's rice production. The PAVN 95th Regiment praised its 4th battalion for that unit's part in those accomplishments.[84] With conventional enemy units on the edge of Tuy Hòa City, the value of U.S. Army maneuver battalions increased dramatically and necessitated the dispatching of American and South Korean forces to Phú Yên. Seoul's military forces in the RVN fought under Korean command and operationally under MACV. Regardless of nationality, the senior commander in an area of operations would take responsibility for South Korean forces.[85]

In 1965, Defense Secretary McNamara and MACV commander Gen. Westmoreland, in concert with their South Vietnamese allies, designated Phú Yên as a priority area for the spread of the *Hợp Tác* pacification effort. First launched by the GVN in 1964 to establish a ring of pacified provinces around Saigon, Hợp Tác had faltered as Hanoi's forces increased their control over the countryside.[86] Indeed, as described in the Pentagon Papers, "the pacification program was overtaken by events of May and June. Prior to this, the II Corps, including the coastal provinces of Phu Yen and Binh Định and all of the highland provinces, was already in trouble."[87] In that vein, by July, the same American officials envisaged the infusion of U.S. Army maneuver battalions to "resume and/or expand pacification operations. Priority will be given to the Hop Tac area around Saigon, to that part of the Delta along an east-west axis from Go Cong to Chau Doc, and in the provinces of Quang Nam, Quang Tri, Quang Ngai, Binh Dinh and Phu Yen."[88] To that end, MACV put in motion plans to use American military forces to assist Hợp Tác, and thereby advance pacification through conventional warfare.

At the end of August, USOM reported an improvement in Phú Yên's political atmosphere: "Due to successful operations and air raids against VC strongholds conducted by our friendly forces, the political situation appears to have improved somewhat during the month."[89] The source of the improvement stemmed from Quyết Tháng 160, an ARVN operation "which restored security to various hamlets bordering on National Route #1 from Cu-Mong to Song-Cau and Song-Cau to Tuy-Hoa."[90] In opening the lines of communication, however limited, Tuy Hòa City experienced signs of progress. Nevertheless, such military developments did not eject PAVN and PLAF from the Tuy Hòa Valley, nor did they dramatically alter the NLF's presence in the province.

Communist troops tightened their hold in the Tuy Hòa Valley in November, and the PAVN 95th Regiment and the PLAF 3rd Regiment accordingly sought to secure the rice paddies abutting the province capital. Both regiments met stiff resistance from the ARVN 47th Regiment. According to Field Force, Vietnam (FFV)—the precursor to I Field Force, Vietnam (IFFV)—while safeguarding the rice crop, ARVN exacted "heavy casualties" from the PAVN 95th Regiment and the PLAF 3rd Regiment.[91] Nevertheless, Hanoi's forces remained in control of much of the province.

Like in Phú Yên, the rest of MR2 faced a concerted Communist effort to gain territory. After Field Force, Vietnam marshaled forces for campaigns in Phú Yên, American troops in MR2 began assisting South Vietnamese units: "Concurrently, operations continued in An Khe Base Area, Song Con River Valley (Happy Valley) and in support of ARVN operations vicinity Tuy Hoa."[92] A 1965 FFV command report spoke of using both conventional and counterinsurgency methods to help Saigon regain control—albeit *not* the hearts and minds—of the people residing in the RVN's countryside. In that vein, "the United States, Free World Military Assistance Force (FWMAF) and Republic of Vietnam Armed Forces (RNVAF) control the South China Sea, maintain air superiority in the Republic of Vietnam (RVN), conduct air strikes against enemy targets in the Democratic Republic of Vietnam (DRVN) and are actively engaged in counterinsurgency operations against the Viet Cong (VC) and the People's Army of Vietnam (PAVN) units that are located in the Republic of Vietnam."[93] In case any doubt persisted about the emphasis on control, FFV stated that "maximum effort will be made to support the GVN and its effort to extend its control over the people and the land mass of the RVN."[94] Control entailed getting the people to do what the GVN wanted, either forcibly or through more passive efforts.[95] The maneuver battalions at FFV's disposal extended the Saigon government's control over Phú Yên's inhabitants through conventional warfare. The focus on control explains why allied forces directed much of their energy toward securing Phú Yên's most populous area—the Tuy Hòa Valley.

Aside from overt challenges to the GVN through military means, as in 1964, PLAF once more sought to weaken GVN power covertly. To undermine GVN authority, PLAF encouraged demonstrations against the presence of allied forces. In Phú Yên, Brig. Gen. John F. Freund, JUSPAO assistant director for field services, recalled that "these VC themes were vividly illustrated" when the people conducted "'spontaneous' demonstrations" on 9 November. "The themes were against US airstrikes, and US artillery and that ARVN soldiers not to fight beside US soldiers," Freund stated.96 Although the demonstrations failed to derail any allied plans, they nevertheless underscored the level of influence that PLAF still held over the province's population.

As a practice, pacification—with all its development goals—seemed a task beyond the purview of conventional military forces. Yet discussions placed MACV in a pivotal role in the institution and spread of pacification. On 15 December 1965, U.S. Ambassador Henry Cabot Lodge wrote to Edward Lansdale, still head of SLO, expressing that "in the matter of the military clearing phase of rural construction, MACV's role is, of course, pre-eminent as is its liaison and advising role with the GVN's Department of Defense and the High Command."97 In practice, MACV went beyond simply advising and liaising with the Republic of Vietnam Armed Forces (RVNAF). The subordinate entities of MACV, especially IFFV, aided pacification by using American soldiers both to battle the enemy and to secure the all-important rice harvests.

Security conditions during the spring of 1965 reflected the enemy's effect on GVN pacification efforts. In the case of Phú Yên's 1965 rural construction program—the GVN's plan to advance pacification for that year—the lack of military assets hindered pacification: "Due to the unfavorable security situation in the province, the plan limits its coverage and provides priority attention to 17 selected hamlets bordering National Route No. 1. Other planned activities under this program include consolidation of the 81 hamlets which were previously pacified in 1964. This course of action was prompted by the inadequacy of troops which could provide security in the rural construction operations."98 As seen with Operation Quyết Thắng 160, ARVN's efforts improved Saigon's position in the province, yet the focus on the areas adjacent to QL-1 left most of Phú Yên under possible NLF control. Yet that operation demonstrated pacification's dependence on conventional military units. With such a restrained scope for pacification, future advancement depended on the substantial infusion of conventional military forces. Pacification undeniably existed in the realm, as did a wariness of traditional armies.

More of Phú Yên fell under the NLF banner as the year progressed. Three years removed from ARVN's Operation Sea Swallow, the province went from a GVN and USOM showpiece to an NLF stronghold. Toward the end of 1965, Gen. Westmoreland focused on the disconcerting increase of PAVN forces in MR2. Indeed, according to the Pentagon Papers, "toward the end of the year the enemy disposition of one division in Quang Ngai, one in Binh Dinh and one in Phu Yen indicated a possible intention to retain control over large population centers and LOC's and to increase his access to rice, fish, and salt. The enemy dispositions also made it possible for him to threaten to isolate the I CTZ."[99]

By the end of 1965, PAVN and PLAF had made significant gains in Phú Yên and effectively isolated Tuy Hòa City from the rest of the province. In doing so, North Vietnamese forces placed the territorial integrity—and Saigon's pacification of the countryside—of the RVN in jeopardy. As recalled in *The First Brigade in the Republic of Vietnam, July 1965–January 1968*, "USMACV considered Saigon and the coastal provinces of Binh Dinh and Phu Yen most important, the coastal provinces because they were not only heavily populated and important sources of VC support, but because there was a continuing threat of the VC in the area linking up with NVA units in the Central Highlands and thereby severing the country."[100] Furthermore, Robert Lanigan's 1971 report on Phú Yên's pre–Vietnam War history noted that PLAF "had control over 90% of all the populated areas of the province and as a result American troops were introduced into the province."[101] Such a staggering figure indicated that an entire South Vietnamese province—with most of its rural population and rice production—existed under Communist control. Moreover, any reversal of fortunes in Phú Yên entailed challenging the population's well-established PLAF sympathies.

American officials viewed events in Phú Yên with mounting consternation. Despite PLAF's shortcomings and ARVN's resilience, Communist forces remained in control of most of Phú Yên's territory. JUSPAO province representatives relayed a grim yet reversible situation befalling the province at year's end. In terms of NLF versus GVN gains, the report noted the following:

> The VC started to occupy territories which were previously under GVN control; and, however feasible, they engaged in such activities as holding of victory celebrations with exhibits of captured weapons, organization of Liberation Committees in newly occupied villages, distribution of anti-GVN propaganda leaflets, organization of training courses for new VC recruits and holding of political meetings for rural inhabitants. Although the ARVN engaged in a number of operations, it is believed that there has been no significant

accomplishment in its attempts to repel the activities of the enemy. Thus, it can be concluded that the political situation has deteriorated during the month.[102]

The security situation proved to be even worse. JUSPAO described it as follows:

Implications that can be drawn from the developments cited in the preceding paragraph strongly indicate that the security situation has also deteriorated. GVN-controlled areas have virtually decreased in size as a result of the VC-conducted activities and operations. Road travel has become more hazardous than ever due to VC roadblocks and sabotage. Moreover, the downtown area of the provincial capital (Tuy-Hoa) has been subjected to mortar attack for the second time on December 13, killing two and wounding seven inmates of the Catholic Orphanage. With the arrival of a fairly large unit of South Korean troops, however, it is predicted that some favorable changes in the overall security situation will be forthcoming.[103]

The only source of positivity emerged in the statement regarding the arrival of combat forces from South Korea. Indeed, any hope of salvaging the GVN's precarious position in Phú Yên depended on the actions of FWMAF units. For better or worse, conventional warfare *was* pacification in Phú Yên.

The Republic of Vietnam essentially emulated the French attempt at pacifying Phú Yên militarily. While strategists in Saigon and Washington debated the niceties—and definition—of pacification, in Phú Yên its reality was clear from the start. Momentary victories for pacification, though, faded with rapidity as Communist forces remained unbroken. Consistency proved to be the operative word as the war entered 1966. The Americans and South Koreans, like the South Vietnamese and the French before them, endeavored to spread pacification beyond Tuy Hòa City through warfare. Thus, to understand the war in Phú Yên is to understand pacification.

3

"Protect the rice harvest"

Search and Destroy and the Perception
of Pacification's Success, 1966

We talk in terms, and you hear the term, of revolutionary development support as opposed to search and destroy. There really isn't
much difference between searching and destroying, going out and
finding an enemy wherever you can find him, and revolutionary
development support. The only difference is that one implied going
out great distances and the other implied looking for the enemy
closer to home.[1]

As IFFV commander between 1965 and 1967, Lt. Gen. Stanley Larsen,
remarking at a 1967 White House press conference, recognized search
and destroy as part of revolutionary development, or pacification. While political
circles disagreed over the definition of pacification, IFFV established it in practice
as a matter of security and one of consequence to conventional military forces.
IFFV's campaign in Phú Yên, in particular, revealed search and destroy as an
integral part of MACV's conception of pacification. It did so by imbuing that
process with visible, quantifiable progress through the securing of rice.

Pacification destroys. Whether uplifting the people or uprooting an insurgency,
pacification destroys infrastructure—both animate and inanimate objects, friend
and foe. In the RVN, with the distinction between combatants and noncombatants often blurred, the destruction wrought by pacification frequently proved
detrimental to the country's long-term progress. Of course, hurting the enemy
often came at the expense of the civilian population, as their property often
burned after battles between the allies and the Communists.

For American conventional military forces, pacification meant improved security. How and the extent to which it improved mattered greatly; quick, displayable progress outweighed gradual, long-term progress. Search and destroy proved to be an integral part of pacification because of its visibility: American authorities could see the movement of troops and the destruction of the enemy and its assets. Otherwise pacification progressed slowly, with authorities eventually relying on statistics to support claims of success. Search and destroy brought rapid progress to pacification—regardless of quality or longevity. Search and destroy, too, offered improved security through the destruction or dispersal of enemy units away from populated areas and the all-important rice paddies of the Tuy Hòa Valley. Thus the U.S. Army's role in pacification went beyond civic action. As explained by Edward Lansdale, soldiers treating civilians kindly and executing projects on their behalf constituted civic action.[2] Inasmuch as civic action helped instill a positive image of military operations, the concept did not advance pacification as rapidly or as broadly as campaigns themselves. Yet together, both methods showed the inseparability of conventional military forces and pacification in Phú Yên. As IFFV's 1966 campaign demonstrated, operations to both protect rice harvests and annihilate enemy forces encapsulated pacification during the Vietnam War.

Operation Jefferson

Like the French before them, the Americans endeavored to pacify Phú Yên with conventional military forces. The year 1966 saw the RVN inundated with combat forces from the United States and other members of President Johnson's "Free World" coalition, or more exactly the Free World Military Assistance Forces (FWMAF). Now one of two field forces in the country, IFFV dispatched maneuver battalions to Phú Yên to assist the ARVN 47th Regiment in combatting the resilient PLAF and the PAVN 95th Regiment. IFFV organized intense operations in 1966 that involved American, South Korean, and South Vietnamese maneuver battalions engaging their Communist foes, all the while safeguarding Phú Yên's rice harvests. ROKA also executed its own series of operations in Phú Yên. Through coalition warfare, U.S. Army and Korean Army forces distanced PAVN from the populace and its major food source—rice.

ROKA units operating in Phú Yên referred to offensive combat operations and pacification as one and the same. Maj. Gen. Chung Kyu Han, commander of ROKA's 9th Division (also called the White Horse Division) later wrote, "the completion of the pacification program of Vietnam by driving out the

Communists from this land is the mission of the division."[3] ROKA understood pacification—and the intense combat operations used to achieve it—as an integral component of the war in Vietnam. Throughout the operations in Phú Yên, the Americans, too, reflected the South Korean view of pacification.

A year of continuous operations by U.S. Army maneuver battalions against the Communist forces in Phú Yên commenced with Operation Jefferson. Conducted between 1 and 16 January, Operation Jefferson was largely one of search and destroy. Jefferson entailed securing QL-1 between Tuy Hòa City and Nha Trang to the south in Khánh Hòa Province. Tasked with clearing the mountainous area south of Tuy Hòa, the Republic of Korea Marine Corps (ROKMC) 2nd Brigade and the ARVN 47th Regiment reopened the QL-1 with the help of American firepower.[4] Operation Jefferson taught IFFV of the value of long-duration operations. According to an Operational Report on Lessons Learned (ORLL) for the period of January through April, "sustained ground operations in an area permit the development of better and more precise intelligence. This in turn contributed to more effective operations." The report went on to say that longer-duration operations "provided the time needed to acquire and exploit captives, other local human sources, and documents. The immediate tactical exploitation of information thus contributed toward the acquisition of additional sources."[5]

The high tempo of operations in Phú Yên emerged from IFFV's realization. American intelligence also revealed that, despite suffering heavy losses through the II Corps as a result of ARVN and U.S./FWMAF operations, there were indications at the end of the period that PAVN and PLAF regular and irregular forces "maintained or regained their personnel strength through the absorption of replacement troops infiltrated from North Vietnam and recruitment and/or forced conscription of locals."[6] Considering the need for further intelligence and enemy resilience, IFFV planned additional operations in Phú Yên to saturate the province with friendly forces and maintain the momentum of war against the enemy.

Operation Van Buren

All of Operation Jefferson's troop movements functioned as a precursor for securing the rice harvest. Rice became the focus of—and the means by which to measure—pacification in Phú Yên in 1966. With Operation Jefferson's lessons in hand, IFFV launched a series of operations centered on safeguarding Phú Yên's rice harvests. Conducted on the heels of Operation Jefferson between 19 January and 21 February, Operation Van Buren emerged as the first of many

Troops of the 327th Infantry, 101st Airborne Division prepare to move
across a rice field in search of PAVN and PLAF during Operation
Van Buren, a combined allied operation of the military forces of the
Republic of Korea, the Republic of Vietnam, and the U.S. 101st Airborne
Division, to deny the enemy the vital rice harvest. 23 January 1966.
*Photo taken by Pfc. Robert C. Lafoon. Courtesy of National
Archives at College Park, photo no. 111-CC-33187.*

rice protection operations in the province. Van Buren functioned explicitly as a
"rice harvest protection campaign,"[7] and it demonstrated the direct correlation
between large unit sweeps and pacification. As recalled in *The Refugee Situation
in Phu-Yen Province, Viet-Nam*, the allies discovered that PLAF was supplying
units throughout the central highlands with rice from the Tuy Hòa Valley; meanwhile, the GVN was forced to import "some 600 tons of rice per month" to feed

Tuy Hòa's population. To deny the guerrillas this rice source, Korean Marines, U.S. Army units, and ARVN forces "physically guarded the paddies during the harvest."[8] The operation directed conventional coalition forces to prevent the enemy from interfering with the rice harvest in the province.

When securing Tuy Hòa's rice paddies, American forces initially faced scant if any contact with the enemy. Jack Foisie of the *Los Angeles Times* reported that on the first day of Operation Van Buren, the allies saw only "'light contact' with the enemy" south of Tuy Hòa City.[9] As American readers learned of Operation Van Buren from Foisie's article, the operation intensified: elements of the PAVN 95th Regiment engaged the ROK 2nd Marine Brigade on 31 January. Although the North Vietnamese soldiers failed to break through the South Korean marines, the PAVN 95th Regiment nevertheless rendered the ROK marines combat ineffective. To give the South Koreans a chance to recover, the 1st Brigade, 101st Airborne Division assumed duties in the ROK's area of operations. In doing so, Operation Van Buren finally provided the American paratroopers with substantial enemy contact.[10]

Contact, however, came on PAVN's terms, as the enemy constructed combat hamlets featuring networks of tunnels and bunkers, sometimes masked by civilian structures. The presence of an engineering company from the PAVN 95th Regiment indicated that the village of Mỹ Cảnh likely contained one combat hamlet.[11] During the morning of 6 February in Hiếu Xương District, a platoon from Company B, 2/502nd Infantry maneuvered near the hamlet of Mỹ Cảnh 4 and immediately drew enemy fire. The company commander dispatched two other platoons to encircle the enemy forces occupying the hamlet. When the American platoons attempted an assault, intense PAVN fire thwarted the paratroopers. Instead, thirteen airstrikes rocked the hamlet as the Americans looked on. Despite such intense aerial bombardment, the well-fortified North Vietnamese fought on until the cover of darkness, when PAVN vacated Mỹ Cảnh 4 through a network of tunnels.[12]

While the Americans secured the rubble of Mỹ Cảnh 4, PAVN soldiers in neighboring Mỹ Cảnh 2 fired on elements of the 2/502nd Infantry. The following morning, 7 February, one platoon from the 2/502nd Infantry attempted to enter Mỹ Cảnh 2 from the northeast. Another platoon moved to the northwest to act as a blocking force. Yet as the first platoon maneuvered, intense enemy fire stopped its advance. In response, the second platoon tried to relieve its comrades, but enemy fire pinned it down as well. The Americans now found themselves the prey of an enemy combat hamlet. Mỹ Cảnh 2 functioned more as a bunker complex than as a typical South Vietnamese hamlet. In need of assistance, 2/502nd Infantry requested reinforcements, with the 1/327th Infantry providing the relief force.[13]

Company B and Tiger Force, the special Long-Range Reconnaissance Platoon (LRRP) of the 327th Infantry, comprised the relief force. At this juncture of the war, Tiger Force had yet to obtain infamy as an outfit that conducted war crimes.[14] Back in 1966, under the command of Maj. David Hackworth, these troops executed the classic hammer and anvil tactic. "It was a neat, clean 'hammer and anvil,' right out of Fort Benning," Hackworth later remarked.[15] Tiger Force, the hammer, moved to the north while Company B, the anvil, moved south. Rather than attempt a breakout, PAVN soldiers held their ground—pouring withering fire against Tiger Force as the Americans' cover of tall grass unexpectedly ended. With Tiger Force's attack stymied, a Royal Australian Air Force Canberra light bomber struck the enemy bunker complex. Nevertheless, the well-entrenched PAVN soldiers continued to fight.[16] Realizing that the enemy would not break contact, Hackworth ordered Company B to attack immediately from the south. The troops of Company B, too, found themselves in the open and sustained heavy causalities, more so than Tiger Force.[17]

As Company B's attack collapsed, Tiger Force renewed its advance, only to falter once again in the face of intense enemy fire. With night approaching, Tiger Force's commander, Lt. James A. Gardner, personally destroyed three of PAVN's four machine-gun nests before being cut down by enemy fire. Despite Gardner's supreme sacrifice, for which he posthumously earned the Medal of Honor, Tiger Force remained under intense PAVN fire. To remedy the situation, Hackworth ordered Tiger Force to use the cover afforded by U.S. artillery fire to link up with Company B, after which the Americans waited until the next morning before making any further efforts to enter Mỹ Cảnh.[18] Just as in Mỹ Cảnh 4, though, PAVN soldiers had abandoned Mỹ Cảnh 2 under the cover of darkness.[19]

Aside from engaging PAVN, elements of the 101st Airborne Division served pacification in another way. Through civic action, conventional military forces reinforced their participation in pacification along less destructive lines. Encapsulating this duality of purpose, Headquarters, 5th Howitzer Battalion, 27th Artillery, reported that "in addition to rendering fire support, this battalion provided vehicles to Tuy Hoa and Hieu Xuong District to assist the local population in transporting the harvested rice."[20] Equally crucial to keeping the

Sp4. McClanton Miller, Company
A, 2nd Battalion, 327th Infantry
Regiment, 101st Airborne
Brigade, kneels in dense brush
waiting for orders to move
forward. 23 January 1966.
Photograph taken by Pfc. Robert C.
Lafoon. Courtesy of National Archives at
College Park, photo no. 111-CC-33199.

enemy away from the rice harvest, collecting the rice made for perceivable
pacification progress.

By Operation Van Buren's end, MACV deemed the paratroopers' efforts
successful, noting "over 30,000 tons of rice was gathered by local farmers while
friendly forces killed 650 enemy" as indicators of the operation's favorable
outcome.[21] Indeed, as recalled by the 10th Combat Aviation Battalion, "80%
of the rice crop had been harvested by the local farmers" because of Operation
Van Buren.[22] Whereas in 1965 the Saigon government could only claim 12,000
tons from the rice harvest, Operation Van Buren placed 30,000 tons under
its control—a drastic, measurable difference marked Van Buren a successful
operation.[23] The presence of proactive allied units played an integral role in
pacification, at least at the province level.

Operation Van Buren produced necessary destruction to advance pacification. Since pacification involved destruction in addition to construction, Van
Buren advanced the concept through the expulsion of enemy combatants from
contested areas. Conventional military forces effectively challenged PAVN for
control of hamlets and kept the province's rice out of enemy hands. Through

destruction, the GVN's presence extended beyond the confines of the province capital while robbing the enemy of assets, but success against PAVN and PLAF came at the cost of dwellings destroyed and the displacement of locals.[24] The exodus of many inhabitants to the safety of Tuy Hòa City created problems for the GVN's province administration that lasted for years. Therefore, Operation Van Buren exemplified pacification's duality as a mechanism of both destruction and construction. The inherent need to physically eject PAVN and PLAF from Phú Yên's economically vital agricultural lands meant the destruction phase would last as long as the war itself.

Operations Harrison and Reconstruction

Operation Van Buren's successor, Operation Harrison, commenced on 2 February and last until 25 March. Essentially a continuation of its predecessor, Operation Harrison expanded the area of operations to the mountains west of the Tuy Hòa Valley. Since Operation Van Buren ended with the rice harvest nearing completion, IFFV envisaged Operation Harrison as a continuation and accentuation of the search and destroy mission component. While patrolling the jungled mountains of Phú Yên, two American battalions failed to encounter any PAVN forces. Ironically, the unit left out of the offensive into the mountains—the 1/327th Infantry—brought elements of the PAVN 95th Regiment to battle, resulting in a "major fire fight."[25] On 4 March, the 1/327th Infantry located the mortar elements of the PAVN 95th Regiment headed in the direction of Thạnh Phú hamlet. Just across the Sông Đà Rằng from Tuy Hòa District in Hiếu Xương District, approaching American forces passed by Mỹ Phú hamlet, just three kilometers from the infamous Mỹ Cảnh 2 hamlet.[26] In similar fashion, the American soldiers received enemy rounds emanating from Mỹ Phú hamlet. John D. Howard, in *First In, Last Out: An American Paratrooper in Vietnam with the 101st and Vietnamese Airborne*, later recalled, "My Phu was an entrenched redoubt."[27] Like in Mỹ Cảnh 2, the American paratroopers found Mỹ Phú fortified by the PAVN 95th Regiment. Similarly, Tiger Force found itself initially caught in the open, incapable of making significant gains and taking casualties. The existence and close grouping of these combat hamlets in and near the Tuy Hòa Valley's rice paddies reflected the region's value to the Communists. Hackworth and his fellow paratroopers methodically destroyed the enemy's fighting positions. Helicopters ferried in reinforcements over the course of the night, blocking PAVN's escape route. With dawn, the Americans counted 118 enemy killed, with a possible 97 additional PAVN dead.[28]

Lt. Col. Joseph B. Rogers, commanding officer of the 1st Battalion, 327th
Infantry, 101st Airborne Division, holds a frontline briefing on his unit's situation
with Brig. Gen. Willard Pearson, commanding general of the 1st Brigade, 101st
Airborne Division, by the general's helicopter in a field near the 1st Battalion,
327th Infantry's command post area during Operation Harrison. 1966.
Photo taken by Sfc. Peter P. Ruplenas. Courtesy of National
Archives at College Park, photo no. 111-CC-33707.

Operation Harrison saw no more contact between American and North
Vietnamese forces. Captured PAVN prisoners disclosed that the PAVN 95th
Regiment had scattered in small groups to the safety of the western mountains.
Thus, attention shifted away from locating the PAVN 95th Regiment to fur-
thering security in the Tuy Hòa Valley. An aberration from the rice protection
imperative, Operation Harrison demonstrated the limits of search and destroy

Soldiers of Company C, 2nd Battalion, 502nd Infantry, 1st Brigade,
101st Airborne Division ascend a steep hill in search of PAVN and
PLAF. The company was conducting search and destroy missions
as part of Operation Harrison in the mountainous terrain around
Tuy Hòa District, Phú Yên Province. 27 February 1966.

Photo taken by Pfc. Robert C. Lafoon. Courtesy of National
Archives at College Park, photo no. 111-CC-33838.

in Phú Yên: although search and destroy kept the PAVN from the rice harvest in
Tuy Hòa Valley, PAVN's ability to elude U.S. Army forces necessitated further
IFFV operations in Phú Yên.

This period of intense, successive IFFV operations left PLAF demoralized:
"Increase in sweep operations, bombing and shelling of the enemy (Allied forces)
and their use of poisonous chemicals greatly affected the people and the guerrilla
units' moral and the development of the guerrilla force."[29] PLAF units "lacked
modern weapons" and were forced to "rely on their own initiative and war booties
to get the needed weapons."[30] Furthermore, in the face of allied firepower and a
"lack of political motivation, . . . in many instances, guerrilla men hastened to flee
the scene as soon as enemy aircraft were heard."[31] PLAF found itself confronted
with guerrillas refusing to attend faraway training courses; the effect of poorly
prepared guerrillas translated into poor upkeep of weapons, "failure to realize
the importance of primitive weapons," questionable organization of units, and
"lack of adequate military knowledge among guerrilla men and even cadre."[32] The

Sgt. Patrick L. McMullin stands guard (right) over three PAVN or PLAF
prisoners during Operation Harrison in the "rice bowl" area of Tuy Hòa
District, Phú Yên Province, approximately 250 miles from Saigon. The
mission was to search, sweep, and destroy PAVN and PLAF in an area
that had not previously been swept by American forces. 1966.

Photo taken by Sfc. Peter P. Ruplenas. Courtesy of National
Archives at College Park, photo no. 111-CC-33709.

dearth of successes compared with 1965 manifested a "lack of political acumen
and sacrifice among cadre."[33] Lastly, "no careful consideration" was given in
the "recruiting of guerrilla men. It was noted that many RVN servicemen were
present in guerrilla units and in several instances surrendered to the enemy and
disclosed the location of their guerrilla units."[34] Far from invincible, PLAF in
Phú Yên faced serious shortages of dependable personnel and matériel.

The ROKMC 2nd Brigade returned to the field after Operation Harrison. Having recovered from its earlier battle with the PAVN 95th Regiment during Operation Van Buren, the 2nd Marines resumed authority over its designated area of operations in the Tuy Hòa Valley. From 22 February to 24 March, while American paratroopers forayed into Phú Yên's interior in search of enemy main forces, the ROKMC 2nd Brigade launched Operation Reconstruction, or Operation Jaekun, as it was predominately a South Korean effort. The ROKMC 2nd Brigade, with support from the 1st Brigade, 101st Airborne Division and the ARVN 47th Regiment, once again used search and destroy to advance GVN control into the contested rice paddies outside of Tuy Hòa City. In doing so, the South Korean marines claimed 176 enemy killed.[35] Moreover, Operation Reconstruction exemplified the extent of coalition warfare in Phú Yên and the widespread use of search and destroy to advance pacification.

Operation Fillmore

With both operations Harrison and Reconstruction over, IFFV shifted its campaign to the areas north of Tuy Hòa City. Between 24 March and 21 July 1966, the 1st Brigade, 101st Airborne Division, ROKMC 2nd Brigade, and ARVN 47th Regiment safeguarded the end of the rice harvest under Operation Fillmore. IFFV Headquarters "directed that the 1st Brigade, 101st Airborne Division secure and protect the rice harvest north and northwest of Tuy Hòa while continuing to locate, fix, and destroy the remaining elements of the 95th NVA Regiment, 3d Viet Cong Main Force regiment and local Viet Cong forces."[36] With a dual focus on rice protection and engaging the enemy, Operation Fillmore's first phase called for "one battalion [to] secure and protect the rice harvest, while two battalions conducted search and destroy operations in the area."[37] With the start of Operation Fillmore, IFFV envisaged the continuation of search and destroy to boost pacification.

Operation Fillmore began with American units continuing their operations in the same areas as under Operation Harrison and with the same focus on rice protection. Accordingly, 1/327th Infantry stayed east of Sông Hòa, while 2/327th Infantry and 2/502nd Infantry remained "in the central Tuy Hoa rice area and in the mountains south of Tuy Hoa."[38] On 25 March, the 2/327th Infantry continued "saturation patrolling" of the rice paddies. Although B Company, 2/327th Infantry had "completely traversed the mountain range from south to north without enemy contact," thus far Operation Fillmore boosted security yet not to the detriment of PAVN or PLAF ranks.[39] As Operation Fillmore continued, by 2 April, the

2/327th Infantry operated north of Tuy An "to protect the rice harvest in that vicinity."[40] On the night of 2 April, 1/327th Infantry arrived at Camp Đồng Tre and began patrols the next day. Situated atop a hill in Đồng Xuân District, the camp contained a compliment of U.S. special forces and artillery as well as South Vietnamese forces. Camp Đồng Tre monitored the suspected trails used by PAVN and PLAF units to infiltrate the southern portion of Phú Yên from enemy base area 200 in the Kỳ Lộ Valley.

The pace of Operation Fillmore soon intensified. On 7 April, southeast of Đồng Tre, a company from the 1/327th Infantry encountered an "estimated" PLAF company, with helicopters landing the rest of 1/327th in an effort to encircle the enemy force. After the daylong battle, the PLAF unit "withdrew suffering heavy casualties."[41] The battle turned out to be the apogee of the first phase of Operation Fillmore as IFFV withdrew the bulk of its forces from Phú Yên to Phan Thiết, Bình Thuận Province by 9 April. By body count, the operation netted 122 PLAF killed, 57 of which were confirmed, with another 12 kills claimed through artillery fire, all the while claiming the lives of 8 Americans.[42] Headquarters, 1st Brigade, 101st Airborne Division viewed Fillmore favorably as it "was successful in protecting the rice harvest north of Tuy Hoa."[43]

For the IFFV, securing Phú Yên's rice was the principal reason that American forces were operating in the province. Midway through Operation Fillmore, IFFV Headquarters further fused the link between allied operations and pacification: as a result of IFFV's "operations . . . a sizable amount of II Corps' second most productive rice growing area [was] now under GVN control." An IFFV operational report affirmed that "In the February rice harvest, 33,303 Metric tons of an estimated crop of 50,000 tons were harvested and secured. The bulk of the reminder was destroyed to prevent its capture by the VC." The report also noted that approximately 1,500 enemy had been killed.[44] Although "most" of Phú Yên's rice production now existed under GVN control, work remained to secure it further.

In terms of civic action, Operation Fillmore did not disappoint. Medical personnel of the 1st Brigade, 101st Airborne Division treated 1,910 locals. Elsewhere, Company A, 326th Engineers repaired eighty-eight kilometers of QL-1 and LTL-7B. Other elements of the 1st Brigade transported harvest rice. Combat elements, too, participated in civic action: The 1/327th Infantry provided "food and medical treatment to approximately 100 refugees and assisted in their relocation to the District Headquarters."[45] Moreover, the 1st Brigade participated in the "'Back to the Village' campaign, designed to return refugees back to their former homes after clearing the area of Viet Cong." The 1st Brigade also assisted by "repairing roads and bridges, and by providing security for the treatment of the refugees."[46] Thus, Operation Fillmore propelled pacification both at the province and village level.

As the harbingers of pacification, IFFV's maneuver battalions made visible progress—perhaps too quickly. By the end of April, four Americans—sector advisor U.S. Army Lt. Col. Jay A. Hatch, USAID representative Daniel L. Leaty, JUSPAO representative Ross E. Petzing, and Office of the Special Assistant (OSA) representative Ray Hanchulak—noted that "the progress of the clearing phase of the Revolutionary Development Program continue to exceed the securing phase."[47] Allied troops pushed the enemy's main forces from undisclosed areas faster than local defense units could secure those locales, which meant that cleared areas remained susceptible to the enemy.

During the interlude between Operation Fillmore and the next round of U.S. military operations in Phú Yên, PLAF sought to bolster its main force units. American intelligence discerned that "*all* district mobile forces in northeastern Phu Yen have been transferred to provincial force units in order to strengthen the VC province-wide."[48] PLAF's upgrading of forces in Phú Yên indicated the pressing need for reinforcements after clashes with allied units, and the resolve to continue the war in the province. The same intelligence report revealed that PLAF's Phú Yên Province Youth Proselyting Section dispatched a letter to "all districts and villages of Phu Yen Province" urging addressees "to persuade youths to enlist in the VC Liberation Army."[49] Going into greater detail, the PLAF letter specified an amelioration plan that envisaged 30 percent of guerrilla and local unit members "upgraded to main force unit members"; 45 percent of local youths "upgraded to local force members"; 20 percent of "Vanguard Youths . . . assigned to main force units"; and 10 percent of "good prisoners" selected.[50] IFFV operations had jeopardized PLAF's fighting strength, forcing it to resort to impressment to replace it losses. PLAF also sought to replenish its ranks through the promotion of guerrillas from non–main force units, and to press for better recruitment numbers. Clearly, IFFV's 1966 campaign had drained PLAF's human resources—a sign that the U.S. Army maneuver battalions were making gains.

Operations Deckhouse I and Nathan Hale

Extensive IFFV operations in Phú Yên resumed with operations Deckhouse I and Nathan Hale. As U.S. soldiers prepared for a fresh series of search and destroy operations in the province, BLT (Battalion Landing Team) 3rd Battalion,

5th Marines executed Operation Deckhouse I. The first in a series of amphibious assaults against enemy targets along the RVN coast, Deckhouse I entailed landing U.S. Marines twelve miles north of Tuy Hòa City. In doing so, the Marines secured the northeast flank of the 1st Cavalry Division during Operation Nathan Hale. Lasting from 18 to 27 June, Deckhouse I resulted in limited enemy contact but placed "211 tons of enemy rice" in Marine hands.[51]

Unlike the Marines on the coast, the U.S. Army units involved in Operation Nathan Hale found themselves in an intense series of engagements farther south and inland.[52] Although the rice protection campaign terminated with Operation Fillmore, IFFV still focused on security improvement. Accordingly, Operation Nathan Hale represented the start of more concerted IFFV effort to crush the enemy units in Phú Yên's interior. The connection to pacification remained the crux of future American operations because of the focus on making Phú Yên a safe province. Like previous operations, Nathan Hale embodied the inseparability of search and destroy from pacification in Phú Yên. Between 19 June and 1 July, the 1st Brigade, 101st Airborne Division, with support from 3rd Brigade, 1st Air Cavalry Division, rewarded IFFV's months of intelligence gathering by bringing PAVN to battle.[53]

Accordingly, because of intelligence gathered by 20 June, IFFV moved units to the north of Tuy Hòa District. There, elements of the 2/327th Infantry found themselves in contact with an enemy battalion, while intelligence indicated the presence of more substantial enemy forces. By the afternoon of 20 July, the 1/8th Cavalry reinforced the 2/327th Infantry, yet contact with the supposed larger enemy force remained unfulfilled. That changed on 22 July, when companies B and C of the 2/327th Infantry used a "mad minute" to trick two nearby PAVN companies into an engagement. Authors of the after action report (AAR) presumed that the brief burst of intense U.S. fire caused the two PAVN companies to conclude that both had lost the element of surprise, and thus to execute an immediate assault on the Americans.[54]

The ensuing firefight was intense. The two 2/327th companies were engaged for four hours, with the attacking PAVN forces getting within six feet of the American positions.[55] With such an engagement, Operation Nathan Hale provided a boon to province security: the operation claimed at least 450 PAVN lives, with an estimated 300 more killed in action (KIA). Most significantly, IFFV figured it had wrecked the PAVN 18B Regiment—which arrived in Phú Yên to give the PAVN 95th Regiment respite—leaving that unit at 50 percent fighting strength. Such losses induced the PAVN 18B Regiment to withdrawal from Phú Yên to attempt to rebuild.[56] MACV, too, shared IFFV's opinion that the operation was a success: "Operation Nathan Hale completely disrupted the plans of an NVA regiment in Phú Yên Province," MACV noted in a weekly summary.[57] For those reasons, Operation Nathan Hale provided American officials with identifiable progress.

Operations Henry Clay and John Paul Jones

Operation Henry Clay, the follow-up operation to Nathan Hale, lasted from 2 to 20 July 1966. While Operation Nathan Hale drove the PAVN 18B Regiment from Phú Yên, Operation Henry Clay sought to hunt down and annihilate the remnants of that PAVN force. During the twenty-day operation, the 1st Cavalry Division and 2nd Battalion, 327th Airborne Infantry Regiment participated in what amounted to a fruitless pursuit that eventually took the American soldiers away from Phú Yên to the Cambodian border.[58]

With Operation Henry Clay's failure, IFFV's attention once more turned to pacification-oriented operations. Operation John Paul Jones provided another excellent example of search and destroy's value to pacification. The 2nd Brigade, 4th Infantry Division, the 1st Brigade, 101st Airborne Division, and the ROKMC 2nd Brigade executed the three-phase operation from 17 July to 30 August. As recalled in the AAR, IFFV Headquarters directed the 1st Brigade, 101st Airborne Division to "seize and hold vital terrain and installations in Vung Ro Pass and Highway 1 between Vung Ro Bay and the 2d Korean Marine Brigade AO, to provide protection for engineer work parties in the bay area along the line of communications, to relieve the 2d Korean Marine Brigade in the area south of Tuy Hoa and to be prepared to exploit B-52 strikes." Commanding officer Brig. Gen. Willard Pearson and his staff later expanded the operation to include "conducting search and destroy operations between Ky Lo Valley and Vung Ro Bay and protecting civilians during the initial stages of the rice harvest at Tuy An."[59] IFFV's instructions directly correlated search and destroy with pacification, both in forms of engineering work at the Vũng Rô Pass and in efforts to safeguard the rice harvest in Tuy An.

Heavy USAF firepower supported IFFV efforts to secure Hiếu Xương District's coastal area. Phase one of Operation John Paul Jones, from 21 to 30 July, entailed the airmobile assault of two battalions near the Vũng Rô Pass in order to secure QL-1 for engineering work. Phase two, from 30 July to 15 August, consisted of IFFV maneuver battalions returning to the field after airstrikes. One battalion executed search and destroy missions west of Sông Cầu following two

B-52 Arc Light raids in that area.[60] Similarly, two other battalions commenced search and destroy operations after four B-52 Arc Light raids west of Đồng Tre.[61] Phase three, from 15 August to 5 September, involved two American battalions relieving the ROKMC 2nd Brigade to the south of Tuy Hòa City. These two battalions also continued protecting Vũng Rô—both the bay and the pass—while "conducting search and destroy operations northwest of Tuy Hòa and providing protection to the civilians in the initial stages of the rice harvest."[62] Again, the efforts of the U.S. forces concentrated on keeping rice out of enemy stomachs.

Operation John Paul Jones entailed extensive efforts on the civic affairs and civic action fronts. Insofar as control, civic affairs efforts hastened "the return of 1,354 refugees to GVN Control" by "effecting coordination" with local Phú Yên province and district officials and GVN officials and their civilian and military advisors.[63] Through civic action, U.S. medical teams treated 4,366 Vietnamese, and on two occasions, medical teams demonstrated the use of medicine to local audiences.[64] On the engineering front, between 16 August and 5 September, American engineers regularly cleared and repaired QL-1 between Tuy Hòa City and Tuy An. Elements of the 1st Brigade transported sixty-eight refugees back to their homes from the Tuy Hòa refugee center. The 1st Brigade distributed cooking and hygiene products "to needy persons and refugees,"[65] and employed "an average of 150 laborers, per day, thus providing local refugees with a source of livelihood."[66] American troops also took 80 cows and 10 horses from PLAF controlled areas and gave them to the Tuy Hòa district chief for distribution to local South Vietnamese, and helped provide care for orphans at Tuy Hòa City's Buddhist and Catholic orphanages. Other elements participated in civic action "by replacing the roofs of 25 classrooms."[67] Indeed, Operation John Paul Jones's positive effects reverberated at the local level.

The CIA linked conventional warfare with pacification in its reporting on North Vietnamese military activity in MR2. August saw elements of the PAVN 95th Regiment attack GVN outposts in the province and strike "a revolutionary development complex less than six miles south of the provincial capital Tuy Hoa."[68] In early September, the PAVN 95th Regiment overran twenty-one hamlets, including twelve that had pacification teams working in them.[69] At this juncture, some 2,700 homes had been destroyed in the coastal districts of Phú Yên "as a result of recent enemy attacks of allied counteractions," and U.S. officials estimated that the RD program had been set back at least three months in Phu Yen.[70] For the CIA, the aforementioned viewed seemed "conservative . . . since the psychological impact on the populace of a situation wherein the government moves in to establish security and then loses it is extremely deleterious. The people are usually doubly suspicious and uncooperative in any renewed government attempt to assert control and influence."[71] Operations like those of IFFV evicted both PAVN *and* locals from contested areas, as the focus rested almost exclusively on securing rice production.

Operation Seward

Before the completion of John Paul Jones, IFFV initiated Operation Seward. Between 4 September and 25 October, the 1st Brigade of the 101st Airborne Division and 1st Battalion of the 22nd Infantry Regiment once again moved about Phú Yên, with rice protection remaining the primary interest of the operation's planners.[72] Although a search and destroy operation, Seward embodied characteristics of an effort to accomplish far more than the destruction of enemy forces. Rather, the operation used conventional forces to occupy key rice-producing areas of Phú Yên long enough to undermine PLAF influence. In doing so, IFFV endeavored to secure more of the province's littoral while furthering control of the rice paddies. The Operation Seward AAR emphasized the tactics employed and placed the effort firmly in the pacification domain: "Operation Seward was characterized by counterguerrilla tactics, primarily encompassing small unit actions and frequent contact with small enemy forces. The search and destroy tactics utilized consisted of saturation patrolling, night movement, night ambushes, raids and the use of small unit stay behind forces and small unit immediate action forces."[73] Thus, the operation demonstrated an approach by American paratroopers to more thoroughly weaken—not simply kill—PAVN and PLAF.

Accordingly, IFFV deployed its forces to cover the rice harvests in the Hiếu Xương and Tuy An districts. While Company A, 1/327th Infantry remained in Tuy Hòa District to project its power into the nearby rice paddies of Hiếu Xương District, the 2/327th Infantry continued protecting the rice harvest and conducted search and destroy operations in the Tuy An area.[74] Similarly, the 2/502nd Infantry executed search and destroy operations in the northwest of Tuy Hòa District. Farther south at the Vũng Rô Pass, the 1/22nd Infantry, which the 1st Brigade, 101st Airborne Division commanded at the time, provided "defense of critical terrain and security."[75] Such actions alone demonstrated that search and destroy served pacification well.

As Operation Seward progressed, it became a concerted effort to secure Phú Yên's rice-producing areas. Through a series of movements, American soldiers solidified their hold on the countryside outside of the province capital. Indeed, on 7 September, A Troop, 2/17th Cavalry conducted an amphibious assault with one platoon northeast of Tuy Hòa, establishing "blocking positions in support of the search and destroy operations of the remainder of the troop."[76] After shuffling forces in and out of Phú Yên, Operation Seward continued with minimal if any contact between American and enemy forces. Yet the enemy finally challenged American security efforts when, on the night of 17 September, the Company B, 2/327th Infantry command post came under attack and was overrun by an estimated one hundred enemy combatants. Ten U.S. Army soldiers were killed and twelve were wounded in the action.[77]

Two days later, on 19 September, the 2/502nd Infantry landed northwest of Tuy Hòa City near Đồng Tre via "airmobile assault."[78] After landing with the 2/502nd, an LRRP located a PLAF base camp. The find resulted in the 2/327th Infantry moving to an area southwest of the 2/502nd's area of operations. Additionally, two Civilian Irregular Defense Group (CIDG) companies left Đồng Tre to function as blocking forces for the 2/502nd and 2/327th. With allied forces now saturating the area, the 2/327th uncovered and documented "an extensive tunnel complex," which engineers then blew up.[79] On 3 October the 1/327th Infantry acted on intel acquired from an "escaped POW" and raided a PLAF prisoner of war camp in the southwest portion of its AO."[80] As a result, the American soldiers freed twenty-three South Vietnamese.[81]

Pacification expansion under IFFV continued as the Americans pushed farther into Tuy Hòa District. With attention on securing stretches of LTL-7B, the 2/327th Infantry airmobile assaulted into an area west of Tuy Hòa City on 7 October. Thereafter, the battalion "secured critical terrain" along LTL-7B and "conducted search and destroy operations in zone" until 10 October, when it returned to Tuy Hòa South. According to the Operation Seward AAR, "this operation was in conjunction with an engineering effort to repair the road and bridges along highway 7B."[82] To continue protecting the engineers working on LTL-7B, Company A, 2/327th Infantry performed an airmobile assault to the west of Tuy Hòa City on 21 October. Upon the relief of the 2/502nd Infantry in Tuy An by the 1st Brigade, 4th Infantry Division on 25 October, Operation Seward ended.[83] Once more, pacification hinged on IFFV's offensives.

The 1st Brigade, 101st Airborne Division deemed Operation Seward a success. For evidence, the AAR cited the protection of the rice harvests in the districts of Hiếu Xương and Tuy An, the securing of the Vũng Rô bay area, and the outcomes of search and destroy missions. The operation claimed to have killed 230 PAVN and PLAF soldiers, at the cost of twenty-six U.S. Army KIA. Yet the

40.5 tons of rice secured by the American soldiers proved more significant than the human toll incurred against the enemy.[84] According to the AAR, owing to Operation Seward, "the full rice harvest in Phu Yen Province was completed on 25 October 1966." The brigade had "protected and supported the accomplishment of this harvest, which yielded 17,343.5 metric tons or 89% of the Province goal of 19,500 metric tons of rice."[85] In securing such rice tonnage, Operation Seward lent the appearance of pacification working.

Concurrent with presenting Operation Seward as a success, the 101st Airborne Division noted some significant shortcomings. The operation did not cover the Kỳ Lộ Valley, a place that served as a Communist stronghold in the region. The AAR noted that the PAVN 5th Division headquarters remained situated in the vicinity of the Kỳ Lộ Valley. "This area has not been exploited by U.S. forces and is undoubtedly a well-developed safe area in which NVA/VC forces realize complete freedom of movement."[86] It also noted the Hiếu Xương District's southern portion as "another relatively rugged and unexploited area which is presently being occupied by the 18B NVA Regiment."[87] These places existed outside the Tuy Hòa Valley, thus beyond the immediate concerns of the allies to secure the land abutting Tuy Hòa City. Due to its remote location in northwestern Đồng Xuân District, the Kỳ Lộ Valley experienced few allied incursions and therefore remained a PAVN and PLAF bastion outside of Saigon's control for the duration of the war.

PLAF avoided unnecessary combat with American forces. For example, tasked with organizing hamlet cadres, the PLAF 307th Main Force evaded combat with IFFV maneuver battalions to achieve its mission in Phú Yên—to remain capable of aiding subversive activity in villages and harass any lightly armed opposition.[88] Away from the rice paddies of interest to the Americans during Operation Seward, the PLAF main force simply operated in an area of little interest to the allies; avoiding decisive battles with IFFV meant that it remained able to achieve its objectives.

Operation Seward saw the extension of the civic action initiatives started under Operation John Paul Jones. The 1st Brigade reported the completion of projects covering the aid spectra of health and sanitation (49), public work (17), transportation (15), commerce and industry (1), agriculture and natural resources (9), education and training (7), community relations (23), communication (13), and refugee assistance (14). The advancement of such projects stemmed from the network IFFV established to supply civic action efforts across its areas of responsibility in MR2.[89] Undoubtedly, civic action was a significant aspect of IFFV's pacification campaign.

Operations Adams, Geronimo I, and Geronimo II

IFFV remained dedicated to keeping the rice harvest under Saigon's control. Only successive military operations achieved that end. Thus, when Operation Seward terminated, IFFV immediately initiated Operation Adams on 26 October. Like prior efforts, Operation Adams used search and destroy and focused on rice harvest protection. It began with the 1st Brigade, 4th Infantry Division securing the rice harvest in Tuy An and Tuy Hòa districts. Concurrently, the ARVN 47th Regiment operated on the opposite side of the Sông Đà Rằng in the Hiếu Xương Valley to defend that area's rice harvest.[90] On 28 October, the Americans recovered 4,800 pounds of rice.[91]

Simultaneous with Operation Adams, the recently relieved 1st Brigade, 101st Airborne Division turned its attention elsewhere in Phú Yên. Under operations Geronimo I and Geronimo II, the 1st Brigade, 101st Airborne provided shorter, more directed efforts against enemy units in and near the Tuy Hòa Valley's western portion. Whereas Operation Adams focused on rice protection, the Geronimo operations constituted IFFV's other goal of forcing the elusive, ultimate confrontation with the PAVN 95th Regiment—a unit still lurking in the western portion of the province near Hà Roi.[92] Initially devised as a series of three operations, IFFV ultimately cancelled Geronimo's third installment. Thus the 1st Brigade, 101st Airborne Division participated in only two search and destroy operations in the interior of Phú Yên between 31 October to 4 December 1966.

Operation Geronimo I commenced without any immediate contact with the enemy. That changed on 6 November, as "the 1–327th air assaulted to the Dong Tre area, along with the 2–327th and 2–502d. There were significant contacts with the enemy as the three battalions advanced from three different directions."[93] Contact with the PAVN 95th Regiment continued with 1/327th Infantry on 8 November engaging in a "vicious fight with an estimated 100 NVA."[94] Between 10 and 11 November, the 5th Battalion, PAVN 95th Regiment found itself surrounded in the Kỳ Lộ Valley by the 2/502nd Infantry and the 1st Brigade, 4th Infantry Division, which had the express mission of "finding and destroying elements of the 95th NVA Regiment by conducting a deliberate search of all trails, streambeds and probable avenues of egress along the SONG KY LO River in northwest DONG XUAN District."[95]

The operation in this remote tract of Phú Yên featured "three companies operating in parallel areas of operation driving generally north to south; the SONG KY LO extended along the east flank of the operation."[96] American paratroopers made "light contact" with "parties of a large VC detention complex," and located "a manufacturing site containing two forges and an extensive hospital-dispensary."[97] Such physical evidence of enemy activity and infrastructure revealed the Kỳ Lộ Valley as a principal PAVN and PLAF staging area for Communist operations in the province. The American foray into the Kỳ Lộ Valley, with "relentless combat pressure and psychological warfare appeals resulted in 13 enemy killed, 35 captures, and large amounts of equipment confiscated." Yet poor weather robbed Operation Geronimo II of its predecessor's successes. As noted in the 1st Brigade, 101st Airborne Division's postwar publication, torrential rainfall inundated the 1/327th Infantry's area of operations. Weather and foot injuries forced the U.S. Army to evacuate forty-seven soldiers; those impediments harmed the Americans more than PAVN and PLAF.[98] Nevertheless, Geronimo I's outcome overshadowed any of the problems that befell Geronimo II.

Geronimo I weakened the PAVN 95th Regiment, IFFV's goal since it launched Operation Jefferson in January. Indeed, the 1st Brigade, 101st Airborne Division praised the outcome of Operation Geronimo I, stating, "For its efforts in the operation, particularly its work in decimating an NVA battalion, the 2–502d was cited in a brigade order, a practice instituted by BG Pearson to recognize superior combat performance."[99] Hackworth recalled that Operation Geronimo I rendered the PAVN 95th Regiment combat ineffective, citing the ten-to-one kill ratio and "the very high weapons-to-body count ratio (143 weapons, individual and crew-served, to 149 enemy dead)" as proof of success.[100] For Hackworth, Geronimo I revealed that the Americans could "fight the same protracted war of attrition the enemy was willing to fight, without paying the heavy, heavy price in American lives."[101] Hackworth's words proved true for Phú Yên in 1966, but events beyond IFFV's control meant that American gains were fleeting. As Hackworth himself admitted, "the enemy just went to ground and waited until the coast was clear to return and rebuild."[102] Pacification needed offensive operations by maneuver battalions to stay ahead of Communist efforts to create their own liberated areas. In Phú Yên, search and destroy advanced pacification so long as the operations continued. With demands for IFFV's assets in other provinces, its maneuver battalions' intense focus in Phú Yên could not last forever. Without such intense and prolonged American efforts, allied forces produced only momentary achievements.

American advisors in Phú Yên voiced approval of IFFV's operations and its mere presence in the province. In the "II Corps Special Joint Report on

Revolutionary Development," released on 31 October 1966, four American advisors—sector advisor U.S. Army Lt. Col. Ernest S. Ferguson, JUSPAO representative Ross E. Petzing, USAID representative Jess Snyder, and now USAID assistant province representative Ray Hanchulak—wrote that "the added military strength and expanded area of operation is creating a climate which will allow expansion of the Revolutionary Development Program into areas which were not formally considered secure enough for satisfactory progress."[103] The report added that, as perceived by the four advisors, "among the rest of the population, the feel of 'more troops' fewer VC and NVA prevails."[104] As the ARVN 47th Regiment protected the rice harvest in Tuy Hòa District, IFFV's continued use of the 1st Brigade, 101st Airborne Division to safeguard civilians in Tuy An District as they harvested rice perhaps influenced that public sentiment. Although FMWAF search and destroy operations netted meager enemy kills—seventy-three PLAF dead and thirty-four captured—the report praised search and destroy actions, noting that these operations meant that engineering projects could successfully repair the province's vital lines of communication.[105] Indeed, search and destroy operations proved essential as PLAF "placed a major emphasis on the collection of rice and other foodstuffs from the people in both GVN and Viet Cong controlled areas."[106]

The perception of progress fostered by conventional warfare resonated. With perceivably sluggish progress elsewhere in the RVN, the CIA reported that "most allied officials, nevertheless, regarded Binh Dinh and neighboring Phu Yen Province as the scene of the greatest allied successes during 1966"—a view the agency thought "was clearly justified in view of the even smaller pacification gains made is most other areas of the country."[107] The year 1966 in Phú Yên concluded with operations Geronimo I and Geronimo II, while Operation Adams continued into 1967. IFFV's intention to advance pacification using its maneuver battalions remained clear. Together, all of IFFV's Phú Yên operations constituted an intense effort to advance pacification in Phú Yên as quickly—and early—as possible. Although 1966 ended with enemy forces still operating in the province, they did so away from Tuy Hòa City. IFFV's operations represented U.S. Army efforts to create space between the local population and PLAF. Although unable to bring Communist main forces to a final battle, the actions of the U.S. Army's maneuver battalions demonstrated that search and destroy was pacification. What remained unresolved was whether or not the allies could retain the gains of 1966.

4

"We have seen our last major battle"

Perceptions of Conventional Warfare's
Pacification Gains, 1967

Many battalion-sized units are now providing security for what
is called Revolutionary development—pacification work at the
lowest levels. Security is the key to pacification and these forces
are demonstrating their determination and skill even in the face of
a stepped-up Viet Cong terror campaign. Incidentally, I view this
increased, almost desperate surge of terrorist activity as an admission in itself by the Viet Cong that our Revolutionary Development
program is working.[1]

Gen. Harold K. Johnson gave this assessment to a North Dakota audience on
13 August 1967. Aside from the explanations of pacification and revolutionary
development, the chief of staff's words encapsulated the notion that allied efforts
had visibly improved the military situation in South Vietnam. Security was
indeed "the key to pacification," as Johnson stated. For Phú Yên in particular,
IFFV's conventional military operations created the aura of improved security,
and thus progress. The perceived successes of 1966 extended into 1967, instilling
a false of continued, inevitable progress in the minds of American authorities.
Yet the gradual removal of IFFV's maneuver battalions exposed pacification
progress as transitory.

The arrival of allied forces in Phú Yên altered the balance of power in the
province, albeit temporarily, in 1966. As 1967 began, American advisors either
overtly stated or insinuated the view that recent pacification gains resulted
directly from the large unit operations of 1966. In a January 1967 memo, the

U.S. Embassy in Saigon credited the improvement of security to the previous year's operations. Whereas American officials described security in Phú Yên before 1967 as "poor," the memo informed readers that American and South Korean military forces had dramatically improved the course of the war in the province.[2] Indeed, "elements of the 1st Brigade, 101st Airborne Division, the 1st Brigade, 4th Infantry Division, and the Korean 'White Horse' Division, have neutralized the two NVA regiments and two VC main force battalions still believed to be in the province."[3] Effectively countering the Communist threat meant securing "the bulk of the 'rice bowl' harvest."[4] Of equal significance, ROKA's White Horse Division opened QL-1 in late 1966, which "established land communication between Phú Yên to Ninh Hoa in Khanh Hoa for the first time since mid-1964."[5] As of 21 January 1967, ROKA's Tiger Division moved south from Bình Định to open the northern stretch of QL-1 in Phú Yên. The U.S. Embassy noted the economic rewards for the region resulting from the opening of QL-1, as Tuy Hòa City could now trade goods with cities like Đà Lạt and Nha Trang.[6] Despite "friction" caused by the sheer number of American and South Korean soldiers in Phú Yên—specifically, the spending power of these troops inflated the local economy—the U.S. Embassy concluded that "the benefits of the increased security brought by the US and Korean troops to the people of Phu Yen far outweigh the frictions which inevitably accompany their presence."[7]

Operation Adams Continues

Continued allied operations played a similarly vital role throughout 1967 and 1968. The operations of IFFV's maneuver battalions in Phú Yên demonstrated that conventional forces were intrinsic to pacification. Like those of 1966, the operations of 1967 featured allied forces placing distance between Communist units and the province's population. Yet American maneuver battalions could only improve security, and thus advance pacification, insofar as intense and numerous military operations continued. IFFV's maneuver battalions were highly sought-after by CORDS, but they did not permanently elevate security in the province.

IFFV's offensive operations continued throughout 1967. Tasked by MACV with furthering security, IFFV received orders from Gen. Westmoreland to "expand security in the pacification priority areas of the coastal provinces" with considerable "emphasis on Phu Yen and southern Binh Dinh."[8] Those orders reflected the prevailing association between conventional military forces and the expansion of pacification. That the improvement of security rested with IFFV maneuver battalion offensive operations meant that pacification existed as a military problem. Regardless of U.S. effectiveness in furthering pacification, the top echelons of the U.S. Army in the RVN viewed the progress of military operations as affecting pacification favorably.

Even in May 1967, the military successes of 1966 remained talking points for American officials. Included in a 20 May 1967 White House memorandum by National Security Advisor Walt Rostow on one from the previous day by Defense Secretary McNamara, Gen. William E. DePuy's lined-out comments remained significant: "It is perfectly clear that progress in Revolutionary Development in large measure can be equated directly to the scope and pace of US/Free World Forces Operations against provincial VC forces."[9] As the war in the RVN's hinterland unfolded, MACV geared conventional military unit operations toward destroying Communist forces and infrastructure to spread and solidify Saigon's authority. Operations by allies in six provinces—Bình Định, Bình Thuận, Hậu Nghĩa, Phú Yên, Tây Ninh, Quảng Nam—helped DePuy make his argument. For Phú Yên, "the greatest RD progress up to November 1966 was . . . because of operations of the 101st Airborne Brigade."[10]

The improvement of security in Phú Yên proved relative. Serious security issues remained, but offensive operations instilled a perception of progress in the province. This juxtaposition meant that because Hanoi's military forces had nearly overrun Phú Yên by 1965, for Americans, all future issues in Phú Yên immediately paled in comparison. IFFV's operations in 1966 and early 1967 improved the GVN stance in Phú Yên, but the Tuy Hòa Valley remained anything but secure. Aside from the allied forces' efforts, the creation of CORDS, a civilian-military hybrid organization, offered much promise. Unsurprisingly, because of its hybrid approach and formation after the operations of allied maneuver battalions, CORDS's establishment propagated the myth that pacification transpired only during the late-war period. In practice, however, CORDS intensified pacification efforts and improved on earlier gains made by other entities.

Pacification was decidedly not a late-war manifestation. Pacification in Phú Yên simply entered a new phase with the 9 May 1967 merging of MACV and U.S. State Department advisory efforts under MACV in the form of CORDS. The subsequent activation of CORDS's Advisory Team 28 functioned as an extension of earlier efforts to pacify Phú Yên, not the start of pacification. CORDS embodied MACV's unified approach to pacification. CORDS's formation signaled a more coordinated approach to pacification in terms of both its objectives and its personnel. Composed of U.S. Army officers and State Department advisors, CORDS advisory teams dealt with both military and civil matters. Consequently,

CORDS's presence in Phú Yên produced more connections into the province's communities. Such links resulted in more reports, which in turn revealed far more about pacification in Phú Yên than ever before.

Pacification crept forward under the purview of conventional warfare in 1967. American efforts to extend security beyond the confines of the province capital continued. After the end of the rice harvest, Operation Adams shifted toward search and destroy.[11] Mid-January entailed the ARVN 47th Regiment supporting the U.S. Army's 3rd Battalion, 12th Infantry in executing search and destroy efforts in Sông Cầu District, continuing the 1966 operational emphasis on Phú Yên's northern extremities into 1967.[12] "The operation provides the shield behind which Revolutionary Development is progressing," a MACV press release claimed.[13] Yet in January, the operation produced little contact between allied and enemy forces. By month's end, contacts resulted in 282 enemy dead, and the confiscation of 129 weapons and 113 tons of rice, but that dramatic increase was temporary: February saw only 61 enemy killed and 12 weapons captured.[14]

Despite the upswing in contacts wrought by the ongoing Operation Adams, the endeavor to significantly enhance Phú Yên's long-term security nevertheless remained unrealized. In its March 1967 "Targeting Branch Revised VC/NVA Base and Operations Areas" study, MACV reported that "Operation ADAMS, currently in progress, seemingly has caused little, if any, decrease in enemy activity" in Tuy Hòa District's Base Area 236.[15] Commonly called "the Hub" by AT28, Base Area 236 was located near Núi Ông La, a mountain overlooking the Tuy Hòa Valley to the east. The study placed the base area in the middle of the province, where forested hills and numerous valleys characterized the landscape. Base Area 236 benefited from an extensive drainage system, and QL-1 formed its eastern boundary.[16] Its placement in Phú Yên mattered the most because, according to the MACV study, "the town of Tuy Hoa is 8 to 10 kilometers to the southeast. The area is a source of water and is suitable for installations; however, its suitability for defense and deployment is unknown."[17] "Numerous unidentified companies, battalions, and other elements of the 95th Regiment were reported throughout the base area during January 1967. Somewhat diminished activity within the base area was noted in February 1967," the study added.[18] Indeed, because Base Area 236 appeared relatively unaffected by the war, allied campaigns appeared even more ineffective.

PAVN's three other base camps in Phú Yên remained in use in 1967. MACV's March base area survey referenced base areas 200, 234, and 235 in addition to 236. Base Area 200 in the Kỳ Lộ Valley, noted MACV, "fails to meet the accepted criteria as a Base Area."[19] The rationale was that through "pattern analysis of unit locations and contacts; incidents, Special Agent Reports, and installation reports, in combination with terrain features," insufficient evidence of intense enemy activity existed in the Kỳ Lộ Valley.[20] That actuality proved to be temporary, as this base area remained a threat to GVN security for the duration of the war.

Elsewhere, MACV uncovered what it considered far more bustling centers of enemy activity. Located near Núi Suối Lụn, a mountain in Sông Cầu District, Base Area 234 abutted QL-1 in close proximity to inhabited hamlets. "During the period January 1966 through February 1967, the majority of enemy activity, including several scattered Special Agent Reports and several reports of unit sightings up to regimental-size, occurred within a 10 kilometer radius of the base area," the survey said.[21] "In August 1966 imagery interpretations disclosed three separate trench systems within three kilometers of the northern edge of the base area"—clear indication that Base Area 234 was a well-established and active center for Communist forces.[22] Worse yet for GVN pacification efforts, "Base Area 234 continues to be considered a base area due to the activity surrounding it. Its proximity, to the sea and reports of unit sightings near the sea during early 1966 make it likely that this area also serves as a coastal resupply point."[23]

In 1967, Base Area 235 persisted as the most disconcerting zone in all of Phú Yên. Positioned in eastern Phú Yên in Tuy An District, this base area benefited from "rugged and forested" terrain and "small streams radiat[ing] from the area."[24] Moreover, Base Area 235 sat "one to two kilometers to the west and southwest" of LTL-6B, with QL-1 just "to the east and southeast at a distance of one to two kilometers."[25] Lastly, according to the MACV study, "the area is a water source and is suitable for installations." Such assets led MACV to conclude that "this is an important VC/NVA Base Area. The VC H65 Battalion has been reported near the base area since March 1966. Furthermore, it is possible that elements, of NT 5 are using the base area. The 18B regiment has operated in the area in the past."[26]

The resilience of PAVN and its base areas precluded effective pacification in Phú Yên. PLAF offensive activity increased in March, largely owing to support PAVN and its base areas still provided. Successive extensive IFFV operations in the Tuy Hòa Valley secured the rice harvests and pushed PAVN into the mountains, but those efforts did not negate the PLAF threat. Operation Adams, still underway, produced further contact between American and PLAF units on 9 March 1967. PLAF orchestrated an assault about thirteen kilometers from Tuy Hòa City against Hill 86 (as the U.S. Army dubbed it), atop which sat A Company, 3rd Battalion, 12th Infantry. A Company found itself confronting a

Troops of A Company, 1st Squad, 10th Cavalry, 4th Infantry Division
move their M-113 APCs into a village area to pick up villagers for
questioning in Tuy Hòa District, Phú Yên Province. 10 March 1967.
*Photo taken by Pfc. Robert C Lafoon. Courtesy of National
Archives at College Park, photo no. 111-CC-41697.*

PLAF force approximately 200 soldiers strong, which overran the American
position using 60mm mortars, grenades, and satchel charges, killing twelve and
wounding twenty-six.[27] To counter the rise in enemy activity, the 2/327th Infantry
joined Operation Adams. On 17 March, A Company, 3rd Battalion, 12th Infantry
airmobile assaulted near Hill 86, producing twelve small-unit engagements that
killed twenty-two of the enemy. Three days later on 20 March, A Company
battled an enemy force in the same area, resulting in another nineteen enemy
dead with another eighteen captured. As perceived by Americans, Adams kept
the Tuy Hòa Valley and its rice production under Saigon's control: in the words

of an MACV operational report, "in effect this area was one of the worst enemy infested areas and now it is the most cleared."[28]

Operation Adams terminated on 2 April as the ROKA Capital Infantry Division and the ROKA 9th Division expanded their tactical areas of responsibility under Operation Oh Jak Kyo; the ROKA now held responsibility for securing the Tuy Hòa Valley and its rice production.[29] The implication was that IFFV now perceived the all-important Tuy Hòa Valley as secure enough to focus its attention elsewhere. Its focus largely fell on the remote Kỳ Lộ Valley—home to both the PAVN 95th Regiment and Nông Trường 5 headquarters as of March. The allies subsequently initiated the Kỳ Lộ Valley interdiction campaign on 24 April with an Arc Light raid, forcing the PAVN 95th Regiment to temporarily relocate its headquarters.[30] ROKA battered PAVN over the next few months, depleting the PAVN 95th Regiment's ranks and forcing that force's headquarters to remain on the move.

Operations Summerall and Hong Kil Dong

The war in Phú Yên did not exist in a vacuum. As evidenced by Operation Summerall, GVN control of the Tuy Hòa Valley adjacent to QL-1 factored into IFFV's larger strategy of securing the littoral of MR2. A trusted advisor to President Johnson, Walt Rostow explained that,

> In II Corps, Operation "Summerall" is aimed at expanding the area effectively covered by allied forces so that there will eventually be one continuous secure area from Qui Nhon to Tuy Hoa. This would permit the opening of Highway One and the railway along the entire coastal area of II Corps north of Phan Rang. If the hamlets along the road and railway were also durably pacified, with hard core terrorists eliminated and durable local political institutions in existence, such a continuous free area from Qui Nhon to Tuy Hoa would be very significant.[31]

On balance, Operation Summerall built on IFFV's 1966 gains. Yet the operation signified a shift from the focus on securing the Tuy Hòa Valley to firmly placing the region's principal road and rail network under GVN control. Much of the operation's action transpired in the neighboring provinces of Darlac and Khánh Hòa, but the operation affected Phú Yên in the form of resettlement. Under Operation Summerall, the 1st Battalion of the 101st Airborne Division flew forty-three civilians from a hamlet in Darlac province to Cùng Sơn village in the Sơn Hòa District of Phú Yên.[32] Cùng Sơn functioned as the district capital of Sơn Hòa and as the GVN's bastion in the western half of Phú Yên Province. As such, elements of the U.S. Army's 6th Battalion, 32nd Artillery and Special Forces camp A-221 assisted RF companies with the protection of this district capital. It thus made sense to relocate South Vietnamese civilians to Củng Sơn, well beyond PLAF's influence. Arguably, in placing these refugees in Củng Sơn, Americans officials perceived Phú Yên as a more secure province.

By this point, the war had displaced thousands of inhabitants to refugee camps. In July 1967, researchers published a study conducted in 1966, *The Refugee Situation in Phu-Yen Province, Viet-Nam.* Interviewed refugees mentioned activity by either the allies (67 percent), Communists (84 percent), or both as the primary cause behind their displacement.[33] In 1966, 29,388 refugees lived in and around Tuy Hòa City. Another 23,259 lived in Hiếu Xương District, while 21,131 more took refuge in the other districts.[34] The flight of inhabitants to refugee camps robbed the NLF of an easily exploitable population base, which hurt sustainment efforts. That gain for the GVN placed a burden on the provincial government.[35] Regaining access to the population, refugees included, became a driving force behind the Communist effort in the province.

The perceived overall success of conventional allied operations clouded American judgment. Nông Trường 5 reacted to IFFV's operations with plans of its own. Anticipating that IFFV would continue to seek out PAVN and PLAF elements, striking at the units themselves and their means of support, Nông Trường 5 stipulated engaging allied units more frequently, reoccupying the Tuy Hòa Valley, improving local forces, interdicting lines of communication used by the allies, and, most significantly, "destroy the GVN pacification program and re-settl[ing] the inhabitants."[36] To stifle pacification, elements of the PAVN 95th Regiment resumed the offensive in the Tuy Hòa Valley and occupied the very hamlets targeted by Saigon for development efforts—forcing allied troops to engage the North Vietnamese on their terms. Exacerbating the refugee crisis in Phú Yên would further strain the GVN's ability to help the local population, thereby worsening its image among the populace. PAVN was fighting a war beyond the battlefield.

Conventional warfare and pacification remained entwined. While the allies sought to advance pacification with conventional military forces, PAVN sought to use conventional warfare to derail pacification. With the PAVN 95th Regiment still operational, allied forces continued to seek its destruction. Having survived IFFV efforts to destroy it, the PAVN 95th Regiment continued to avoid American formations, yet sought conflict with South Korean and South Vietnamese troops.

In June, PAVN ended its absence from the Tuy Hòa Valley—and aversion to battle—as the PAVN 95th Regiment maneuvered toward Tuy Hòa City, engaging South Korean and South Vietnamese forces. In response, elements of ROKA's 9th and Capital divisions advanced on Base Area 236, as part of Operation Hong Kil Dong, beginning on 9 June. By the end of phase one, ROKA had dislodged the enemy from the area, claiming a high body count of over 500 enemy dead, but PAVN simply moved to where the advancing 9th and Capital divisions were not—Hiếu Xương District. There, on 9 August, the PAVN 95th Regiment struck where the allies did not expect it, raiding Phú Lâm, the district capital of Hiếu Xương, temporarily placing PAVN troops dangerously close to the valuable Americans installations at Phú Hiệp and the Tuy Hòa South Air Base. PAVN sacked an RD headquarters, killed thirteen South Vietnamese, and seized radio equipment and fifty-seven weapons.[37]

Phase two of Operation Hong Kil Dong commenced on 12 August, but despite the South Koreans pushing through the Ký Lộ Valley, they made zero contact with the enemy. On 30 August, the PAVN 95th Regiment launched a campaign against the Tuy Hòa Valley, striking the Tuy Hòa North Air Base and a JUSPAO radio station. Three weeks after embarrassing the allies with the Phú Lâm raid, two companies of the 5th Battalion, PAVN 95th Regiment occupied hamlets to the west of Tuy Hòa City. Clearly targeting pacification, PAVN entrenched itself in hamlets selected by Saigon for revolutionary development. To counter pacification progress, the PAVN 95th Regiment wanted the allies to assault the hamlets, destroying dwellings, undermining the civilian population's confidence in the GVN to protect them, and forcing Saigon to concentration on rebuilding rather than expansion. PAVN's arrival elicited a response from ROKA, which, along with ARVN, spent a week retaking the occupied hamlets with infantry to limit the collateral damage. After the allies left, PAVN reoccupied the same hamlets in early September. This time the allies blasted the hamlets with artillery and airstrikes—which left approximately 20,000 South Vietnamese homeless.[38]

IFFV considered Phú Yên pacified—an assertion largely based on the rice harvest. At a White House press conference in August, former IFFV commander Lt. Gen. Larsen, like other U.S. officials had, compared the Tuy Hòa Valley of 1966–67 to that of 1965: "The Tuy Hoa Valley a year and half ago put out 70,000 tons of rice a year. About 50,000 tons went to the Viet Cong and 20,000 tons to Tuy Hoa itself, which was under government control."[39] IFFV's operations had gained Saigon control of rice production. Larsen's statement, however, neglected the largely unaffected enemy just outside the Tuy Hòa Valley. Larsen candidly remarked that the PAVN 95th Regiment had "chosen not to fight and to avoid contact for the last year and a half"—a statement true insofar as the unit avoided the search and destroy operations of allied forces.[40] Pointing to prisoner statements that the regiment's meager supplies drove it to avoid battle, Larsen furthered the perception of progress in the province, boldly announcing, "I have made a prediction that we have seen our last major battle in the II Corps area, on the coastal area, at least, of battalion size or larger."[41] Larsen qualified his statement by adding, "We may have an attempt to put a battalion or more than a battalion in, but I don't believe that they can support a major battle—a major operation—in the coastal area in the II Corps area."[42] Tellingly, the PAVN 95th Regiment refuted Larsen's extrapolation during the same month as his press conference.

Although IFFV made some progress in improving security in Phú Yên, ROKA efforts exposed the province as still unsecured. The termination of Operation Hong Kil Dong's third phase on 26 August left Phú Yên much as it had been before. Despite MACV claims of 637 enemy dead and that the operations had "reduced a major threat posed by main force enemy units," the PAVN 95th Regiment remained a functioning military force.[43] Moreover, MACV admitted that "local force and terrorist groups remain[ed] active on the coastal plains."[44] Battered by ROKA, the PAVN 95th Regiment nonetheless achieved its task of undermining pacification, while still surviving to do so again in the future.

Operation Bolling

Events in the Tuy Hòa Valley in 1967 dictated Phú Yên's future. With province security described as having "varied from inadequate to adequate," the MACV September monthly assessment noted the return of the PAVN 95th Regiment to the Tuy Hòa Valley around 29 August.[45] Seeking to expand GVN influence, the report noted, the 3rd and 4th battalions of the ARVN 47th Regiment operated in the Tuy Hòa Valley during September. With the PAVN 95th Regiment making August and early September too eventful for the allies, IFFV launched Operation Bolling/Dân Hòa on 17 September. A long-duration, American-led operation, IFFV intended Operation Bolling to improve security—and thus advance pacification—in Phú Yên. Fresh from participation in Operation Greeley near Đắk Tô in Kon Tum Province, C and D Companies, 4th Battalion, 503rd Infantry of the 173rd Airborne Brigade now sought a conclusive battle with the PAVN 95th Regiment. Rice remained the all-important factor: according to the AAR, the operation had "a two-fold mission to seekout [sic], destroy or capture the enemy and/or his equipment [and] to deny the enemy the bountiful food

Section Sgt. Frank Dunford watches his men of C Company, 1st
Battalion, 503rd Infantry, 173rd Airborne Brigade cross a canal en
route to the site of their night camp during Operation Bolling, Tuy
Hòa District, Phú Yên Province. 21–25 September 1967.

Photo taken by Pfc. Wendell D. Garrett. Courtesy of National
Archives at College Park, photo no. 111-CC-43246.

resources available in the TUY HOA Valley."[46] Operation Bolling covered the
districts of Sơn Hòa, Tuy An, and Tuy Hòa—with the effort lasting well into
1969 and interrupted only by the 1968 Tết Offensive. Like preceding operations
ordered by IFFV, Operation Bolling represented further use of conventional
forces to advance pacification.

The Tuy Hòa Valley again teemed with activity as conventional forces sought to displace one another. On 19 September, as part of Operation Bolling, the 173rd Airborne Brigade Task Force arrived in the districts of Sơn Hòa and Tuy Hòa.[47] The 173rd dedicated its 1st and 4th battalions to the effort, with the 3rd Battalion participating after the beginning of November.[48] Together, these maneuver battalions sought to "locate and destroy the 95th NVA Regt in the high ground west of Tuy Hoa, with the 173rd Airborne Brigade subsequently "assum[ing] the mission of protecting the rice harvest from the Tuy Hoa basin."[49]

Like the American paratroopers, the 3rd and 4th battalions of the ARVN 47th Regiment operated in the Tuy Hòa Valley ostensibly to defend pacification efforts from interference by the active PAVN 95th Regiment. Accordingly, the PAVN 95th Regiment moved into the Tuy Hòa Valley on approximately 29 August, with small elements still being found by combined FWMAF/ARVN operations into September.[50] The PAVN 95th Regiment's return coincided with offensive operations of the PLAF 30th Main Force Battalion. According to AT28's 30 September progress report, the PLAF 30th Main Force Battalion "combined with local guerrilla forces in Hiếu Xương District to exert pressure in this area," which posed a challenge to the RVNAF: "In spite of these major threats and attacks on the 2d, 6th, 15th and 17th of the month, ARVN, RF, and PF forces performed in a highly creditable manner," the reported noted. Strikingly, it continued, "the decline in the degree of security is attributable not to the falling of these forces, but to the constant vigilance and alert posture required within the 1–8 September period and the heavy losses which accumulated and sapped the provincial forces of their strength and offensive capability."[51] While PAVN and PLAF units avoided contact with American paratroopers, they willingly engaged the perceivably weaker South Vietnamese forces.

Regardless of the many operations the allies executed, PAVN and PLAF units remained a direct threat to pacification in Phú Yên. AT28's September progress report reflected the adverse effects of fighting on the GVN's RD plan for Phú Yên, which it said was "estimated to be approximately three months behind schedule."[52] A cause of the delay, the report noted, stemmed from "the inaction of the service chiefs, with few exceptions, the lag in expenditures, and the actions in the Tuy Hoa Valley."[53] CORDS had yet to firmly establish itself in Phú Yên and reinvigorate the GVN approach to pacification. As American and South Vietnamese bureaucracy did its part to slow down pacification, so too did the enemy.

The Americans did acknowledge that the PAVN 95th Regiment's rekindled offensive activity had damaged pacification efforts: "Due to the enemy's aggressiveness, coupled with is effective propaganda, there was a considerable exaggeration of the enemy's posture in the province with a complementary lowering of GVN prestige during the month," American advisors reported, adding that "the time required for ROK forces to dislodge the VC during his occupation of several hamlets enhanced the image of the enemy."[54] Pacification at the lowest—and most important—level, the hamlet, suffered, too. The short-lived PAVN offensive saw "enemy occupation of several RD hamlets, coupled with the destruction which took place in several others in which VC/NVA troops infiltrated [and] increased the fear of the people for their well-being." Yet American advisors downplayed these negatives by claiming that "the general population does have a clear idea of what has happened in the hamlets that suffered the destruction and readily places blame on the VC/NVA."[55] The PAVN 95th Regiment's successful incursion into RD hamlets at the very least suggested to locals that Saigon and its allies had failed to keep the Tuy Hòa Valley safe. Indeed, AT28 deemed security as "marginally adequate," despite the continuance of warfare in the Tuy Hòa Valley.[56]

Unease consumed the Tuy Hòa Valley throughout September as the lurking PAVN 95th Regiment cast a shadow over Phú Yên. AT28 noted that the regiment retained "the capability of attacking in any area of Phú Yên with up to a reinforced battalion sized force" and the ability to "reinforce with up to a regiment in a 5–10 day period," and "used company and platoon size units frequently." During the month of September, AT28 reported one battalion, one "multi-company," three companies, two "multi-platoons," five platoons, two "multi-squads," four squads, and eighteen "unknown size contacts."[57] In these contacts, Hanoi's troops suffered 211 dead, with possibly an additional 107 killed. The Americans noted the enemy's heavy casualties in spite of receiving replacements, which they hoped would "counterbalance the infiltrations . . . from the North (as estimated 1000–1200 men in the last 4 months)."[58] Such optimism, however, meant overlooking the exhaustion of ARVN, RF, and PF units at the hands of PAVN and PLAF. Enemy offensive operations took a toll on the South Vietnamese security forces: 76 South Vietnamese troops dead, with another 230 wounded. Civilians, too, felt the effects, with 16 dead and 65 wounded due to the fighting in the Tuy Hòa Valley. In addition, two kidnappings, one mining incident, four assassinations, and two grenade attacks were reported, resulting in three civilians killed and forty-five wounded, further demonstrating the effects of Communist activity on the valley's population.[59] Arguably, the war in the Tuy Hòa Valley was one of attrition.

PAVN and PLAF units challenged allied pacification efforts to pacify Tuy Hòa District merely by existing. All parties subjected villages on the fringe of

GVN influence to intense efforts to win the war at the village and hamlet level. Villagers with crops in the contested Tuy Hòa Valley typically worked their fields during the day and slept in the far more secure Tuy Hòa City at night. The village of Phú Sen became the focal point of Operation Bolling because of its location: situated near the banks of the Sông Ba where the western mountains met the Tuy Hòa Valley, the village was a valuable entry point into the valley. Moreover, Phú Sen sat along LTL-7B between Công Sơn and Tuy Hòa City, two GVN strongholds. For that reason, Operation Bolling entailed the formation of AO Sen, with American soldiers wrestling control of this passage point from the Communists to deny PAVN and PLAF cells from using it as a possible base of operations. But even with all the efforts to interdict the enemy, the 173rd Airborne Brigade Task Force produced scant contact with enemy main forces. Between 24 August and 15 October, IFFV's maneuver battalions secured AO Sen, yet not to the detriment of PAVN and PLAF manpower. To the west of Tuy Hòa City, the 4th Battalion of the 503rd Infantry scoured for enemy formations, but "the enemy was not to be found, and though enemy bunkers, rice caches and base camps were located, few proved to be fresh."[60] In a now well-established theme in Phú Yên, "for the period the enemy had no desire to either be located or to enter contact."[61]

October in Phú Yên saw pacification remaining behind schedule for a number of reasons, as detailed in AT28's October progress report: damages inflicted by the enemy before and after the September presidential election, a lack of supplies (specifically aluminum roofing) previously pledged to support construction projects, and a "lack of aggressive action of the service chiefs."[62] As AT28's task in Phú Yên progressed, it did so under the veil of questionably adequate security. Despite being bloodied by IFFV operations in 1966 and subsequent clashes, elements of the PAVN 95th Regiment remained a threat to GVN stability in the province. Reinforcement efforts proved fruitful, particularly when combined with the unit's strategy of avoiding large-scale clashes with allied forces. "The enemy has the capability of attacking in any area of Phú Yên Province with up to reinforced battalion size forces," the report warned,[63] noting that the enemy could "reinforce with up to a regiment in a 5–10 day period," but it also noted that due to the buildup of allied forces in September and October, PAVN would "probably not risk large unit sized attacks."[64] Thus, as long as substantial conventional forces remained in the province, AT28 doubted that the enemy would commence any major combat actions. AT28's view provided further proof that search and destroy was pacification. True to form, PAVN avoided battle anyway, concentrating instead on "securing rice from the current rice harvest."[65]

Two different Tuy Hòa Valleys existed at this junction of the war in Phú Yên: the night belonged to PLAF and the daylight to the allies. Much of the Tuy Hòa Valley's population slept in or near the more secure Tuy Hòa City each night either because of their plight as refugees or to avoid PLAF. During the day, farmers returned to their hamlets to care for their crops. On 16 December, the 173rd Airborne Brigade's D Company, 16th Armor relocated from Đắk Tô in the Central Highlands to Phú Yên to participate in Operation Bolling.[66] Once in Phú Yên, D/16th provided security for those leaving the province capital to tend to their fields. On 21 October, a "typical" day, D/16th's 3rd Platoon would pick up civilian workers at Tuy Hòa North and move them to AO Sen, providing security for the rice harvesters for the remainder of the day with a platoon from the B/1/503rd Infantry, which was attached to the company.[67] After dusk, D/16th took the rice harvesters back to Tuy Hoa North, with D/16th Armor later executing "platoon size ambush patrols" in AO Sen.[68]

Operation Bolling and pacification remained linked as October progressed. Between 22 and 25 October, "the company and attached elements conducted search and destroy operations throughout AO Sen."[69] During this period, "considerable amounts of rice and other foodstuffs were found and extracted," yet without making direct contact with enemy personnel.[70] Furthermore, "Many bunkers and tunnels were found and destroyed."[71] The American forces encountered physical enemy infrastructure, although not the human networks established by PLAF, and combat with PAVN and PLAF units eluded them. Essentially, events up to the end of October had Operation Bolling as more of a rice harvest protection and enemy infrastructure dismantling endeavor than an effort to destroy enemy main forces. For those reasons, Operation Bolling represented the most concentrated effort to use American troops to pacify the Tuy Hòa Valley. Efforts by conventional allied military forces to evict PAVN and PLAF from the Tuy Hòa Valley transpired concurrently with Revolutionary/Rural Development (RD) Cadre work at the hamlet level. RD Cadre teams worked to extend pacification into individual hamlets to establish a connection between the inhabitants and Saigon. That multifaceted approach sought to eradicate Communist power over—and Communist sympathies among—Tuy Hòa District's villagers in Phú Yên.

Project Takeoff, Komer's plan to jumpstart pacification, achieved little during November.[72] AT28's monthly progress report to the MACV-staffed Military Assistance Command Civil Operations and Revolutionary Development Support (MACCORDS) balanced optimism with continued concern in addressing the state of security. The report noted that "the 1967 Province RD plan remain[ed] behind schedule because of war damage, and to a lesser degree the November Typhoon damage, arrival of roofing material and a more aggressive attitude of the service chiefs indicate that 90% completion is possible."[73] The roofing material directly affected Phú Yên's refugee situation as it stood between the dislocated populace and their return to their native hamlets. The report added that three of the five senior district advisors "clearly stated" that district security for RD was "now inadequate," citing the withdrawal of three of the 173rd Airborne Brigade's battalions.[74] Although the 3rd Battalion, 503rd Infantry arrived in Phú Yên in early November, much of the 173rd Airborne Brigade converged on Đắk Tô in Kon Tum Province when fighting erupted at that location.[75] Undeniably the U.S. advisory mission in Phú Yên perceived American combat forces as integral to pacification, and now bemoaned the loss of multiple battalion assets.

PAVN dictated the strategic situation in late 1967. To roll back pacification there, PAVN lured some of IFFV's maneuver battalions from Bình Định and Phú Yên to Kon Tum in November. As IFFV directed its gaze toward Đắk Tô during Operation MacArthur, back in Phú Yên the PAVN 95th Regiment reestablished itself in the mountains overlooking the Tuy Hòa Valley. Evidence now manifested that IFFV's operations had not improved the security situation in the Tuy Hòa Valley: In relocating the regiment, PAVN gained easier access to rice, which it obtained from Hòa Quang village. From the safety of those mountains, elements of the PAVN 95th Regiment operated within ten to fifteen kilometers of the province capital, thereby placing Tuy Hòa City in danger.[76] The 173rd Airborne Brigade intelligence suggested that the 4th, 5th, and 6th Battalions of the PAVN 95th Regiment, as well as the PLAF 30th Main Force Battalion, the PLAF 377th Local Force Company, and the PLAF 85th Local Force Battalion, "would concentrate on gathering rice and foodstuff during the rice harvest."[77] Reports placed these enemy units in or near the Tuy Hòa Valley. In so positioning the 5th Battalion, PAVN clearly intended to alter the tone of the war.

To counter the PAVN 95th Regiment's movement, the 173rd Airborne Brigade placed a battalion in the Tuy Hòa Valley. Search and destroy, which the 173rd Airborne Brigade intended, protected pacification.[78] Lack of decisive contact with the enemy nevertheless continued during Operation Bolling. PAVN remained dedicated to preparing for a nationwide offensive in early 1968. Despite intelligence placing PAVN elements in Phú Yên, a battle-reluctant enemy meant that contact with PAVN and PLAF eluded the 3rd Battalion, 503rd Infantry.[79] D/16th Armor, too, remained unable to locate sizable enemy forces in AO Sen. Instead, between 1 and 6 November, the company continued to conduct search and destroy operations in the area. In addition, the company and attached elements continued to secure the rice harvesters during the day and conduct ambushes at night.[80] For D/16th Armor, the U.S. outfit continued to support pacification by protecting the rice harvest.

Pacification remained a tedious work in progress into December. To AT28's chagrin, pacification gains for 1967 were "behind schedule"; the 1968 pacification plan would nevertheless commence on 1 January 1968. Already, AT28 already faced near-insurmountable delays. Security, too, was a source of concern: "Security for RD remains inadequate in spite of the fact that one battalion of the 173d Abn Bde (Sep) returned to the province during the reporting period," a year-end MACCORDS province report warned.[81] The battalion in question, the 3rd Battalion, 503rd Infantry, had returned in early November to participate in Operation Bolling. The security situation at the end of December practically mirrored the previous month's. Furthermore, the CORDS advisors in Phú Yên understood the American paratroopers as a source of stability, not simply purveyors of reliable security. In December, D/16th Armor continued operations in AO Sen. On 3 December, while operating in AO Sen, D/16th Armor located "a small food cache, some NVA currency and a tunnel complex."[82] Throughout the day, the American armor and attached ARVN soldiers detained numerous civilians suspected of ties to PLAF, including a *Chiêu Hồi* member and seventeen "VC wives," and six additional suspects.[83]

Operation Bolling eventually produced significant contact between allied forces and the elusive PAVN. On 27 December, away from the Tuy Hòa Valley, in Đồng Xuân District's remote Kỳ Lộ Valley, the 3rd Battalion, 503rd Infantry found well-prepared elements of the PAVN 95th Regiment. The 3rd Battalion, 503rd Infantry searched the Kỳ Lô Valley because South Vietnamese and South Korean units had recently encountered numerous ambushes in that part of the province.[84] Ironically, MACV deemed the Kỳ Lô Valley's Base Area 200 as not teeming with enough enemy activity to warrant its inclusion in the March 1967 base area study.[85] Apparently the only element absent from the base area was the PAVN 95th Regiment's 5th Battalion.

Far from inactive, the Kỳ Lô Valley was a safe zone for PAVN troops. Upon arriving in the valley, the 3rd Battalion, 503rd Infantry's scout platoon drew intense enemy fire. Suspecting that the PAVN 95th Regiment was firing on the Americans, the rest of the 3rd Battalion, 503rd Infantry landed in the Kỳ Lô Valley in hopes of bringing PAVN to battle. At Xôm Đập hamlet, well-fortified PAVN soldiers poured withering fire into landing U.S. helicopters. Eventually,

A Company cleared the PAVN bunkers one by one, with helicopters ferrying in elements of the 4th Battalion, 503rd Infantry for additional support. The fight at Xôm Đập claimed the lives of twelve Americans and wounded thirty-four, and left sixty-two PAVN dead. As the 173rd Airborne Brigade continued its sweep of the Kỳ Lô Valley, with no further contact with the enemy, the Americans uncovered vacated enemy encampments.[86]

Contrary to the U.S. intelligence reports, the Kỳ Lô Valley turned out to be a sprawling, active PAVN base area. The Kỳ Lô Valley offered the PAVN 95th Regiment a refuge just forty-four kilometers northwest of Tuy Hòa City. From there, PAVN could still support PLAF elsewhere in the province, and thereby threaten pacification across Phú Yên. The Tuy Hòa Valley mattered more than the Kỳ Lô Valley because of its rice production and population. Therefore, the focus of all the warring participants fell to Tuy Hòa City and the encompassing basin, which effectively left the Kỳ Lô Valley as NLF territory.

The positioning of the GVN's military forces in the Tuy Hòa Valley in late 1967 revealed much about the overall focus of security in that contested space by year's end. At the end of 1967, the ARVN 47th Regiment bore primary responsibility for defending the pacification efforts in the Tuy Hòa Valley. Behind the purported shield of IFFV's maneuver battalions and ROKA operated three battalions of a single ARVN regiment, just two of which operated outside of the province capital. U.S. Army advisors noted that three of the 47th's four battalions were deployed to protect the campaign area, with the fourth in Bình Định.[87] Meanwhile, the 2nd Battalion guarded against the main enemy avenue of approach into the Tuy Hòa Valley, and the 1st Battalion served as a mobile tactical reserve; only the 3rd Battalion was assigned by the ARVN 22nd Division's commanding general to direct support of RD in Tuy Hòa District.[88]

The 3rd Battalion, ARVN 47th Regiment's area of operations hardly improved security in Tuy Hòa District. Because the battalion's primary task was to safeguard RD Cadre in Tuy Hòa District, the force's placement mattered profoundly. While lacking "operation control over all the military and para-military forces within his AO," the battalion commander dealt with troublesome boundaries.[89] Furthermore, those boundaries did not contain all of the hamlets that the campaign's RD Cadre were now working in.[90] Instead, some teams were protected alternately by 2nd Battalion mobile companies, PF platoons, and ROKA units.[91] The concentration of the 3rd Battalion, ARVN 47th Regiment also reveals the part of the Tuy Hòa Valley seen as most crucial to the GVN's efforts to control that area. Indeed, this ARVN unit operated along LTL-7B to keep the lines of communication open—and thus serve as a prominent symbol of GVN strength in the province. Doing so, however, gave PAVN troops living in the western and northern tracts of the Tuy Hòa Valley, those abutting the mountains, free to move around unencumbered. In part because of location and command limitations, parts of the Tuy Hòa Valley existed in spaces removed from concentrated security. Unsurprisingly, PAVN used this open fringe zone to its advantage in 1968.

The locations of the U.S. Army units assigned to Operation Bolling, too, proved problematic. Tasked with spreading pacification farther inland, and searching for enemy units to destroy, elements of the 173rd Airborne Brigade operated away from Tuy Hòa City. Only a rapid reaction force—D Company—stood ready near the province capital.[92] Such placement mattered at the close of 1967 because of enemy intentions. As PAVN and PLAF prepared to challenge pacification head on at Tuy Hòa City, American and South Vietnamese forces remained focused on confronting ghostlike enemy elements in places the Communists avoided.

The American evaluation of the 3rd Battalion, ARVN 47th Regiment addressed enemy opposition. The PAVN 95th and the PLAF 85th, although near full strength, avoided large-scale actions, according to a draft MACCORDS evaluation report from the end of December. While those conventional forces operated near but outside the Tuy Hòa Valley, Communist infrastructure operated covertly in the area. Termed "Việt Cộng Infrastructure" (VCI), these NLF clandestine networks helped govern liberated areas while undermining any vestige of GVN authority in all but the hamlets closest to Tuy Hòa City.[93] The commander of the 3rd Battalion, ARVN 47th Regiment and his American advisors speculated that one enemy platoon, plus VCI, directly challenged ARVN efforts in the valley.[94] "During November and early December, the local enemy made light (three- and four-man teams) sporadic attacks at night while foraging for rice, medical supplies, ammunition and other military staples," the report noted.[95] Following a brief pause, enemy actions escalated after 25 December. What the Americans and South Vietnamese soldiers reported amounted to Communist efforts to recover from and work toward reversing the allied operations in Phú Yên, with attacks resuming with increased frequency by an estimated reinforced platoon.[96] Moreover, the report stated, "the enemy's most recent reaction to the RD program in Tuy Hoa has been limited to attempts to discredit and disrupt the work of the cadre. The battalion advisor believed that NVA/VC activity was entering a transitional phase."[97] While limited, such enemy efforts represented PLAF's continued ability to hit pacification at its most vital yet weakest point—the hamlet. For that reason, in direct contrast to the opinions previously voiced by American leadership, the operations of allied maneuver battalions had not significantly altered the balance of power in the province.

With the security situation as described above, it is not surprising that GVN pacification progressed slowly in Tuy Hòa Valley. American observations of the 3rd Battalion, ARVN 47th Regiment also revealed the GVN's scope of pacification in the much contested and most heavily populated of Phú Yên's lands, the Tuy Hòa Valley. At the time of the report's publication, Tuy Hòa District had ten *Ấp Đổi Mới* (ADM), or New Life Hamlets, with pacification fully realized; seven *Ấp Bình Định* (ABD), or the hamlets in the midst of pacification efforts; and five *Ấp Củng Cố* (ACC), or the hamlets about to begin the pacification process.[98] The end of 1967 also entailed the formation of pacification goals for the next year. The Saigon government's Ministry of Revolutionary Development (MORD) approved a 1968 pacification plan that called for elevating security in seventy-one hamlets in Phú Yên. Specifically, GVN officials both in Saigon and Tuy Hòa City envisaged solidifying control over twenty-eight ADM, forty-one ABD, and two ACC hamlets. Counted separately from the aforementioned seventy-one hamlets, the plan targeted fifty-three Nuôi Dưỡng hamlets for pacification efforts.[99] Considering the already troubled security situation in the Tuy Hòa Valley, the aforementioned goals marked an ambitious pacification plan. On the eve of 1968, little stood between the GVN on the Tuy Hòa Valley's eastern end and PAVN and PLAF elements in the valley's western mountains.

One revolution of the destruction-construction cycle ended in 1967. IFFV's operations kept pressure on the PAVN 95th Regiment, forcing it to operate farther away from Tuy Hòa City than it had in 1965. Yet allied operations did not preclude Communist forces from conducting offensive actions in the province. Ironically, in trying to spread GVN control farther into Phú Yên, allied operations further elevated the significance of Tuy Hòa City. Operation Bolling alone caused the destruction of 4,000 dwellings and displacement of 20,000 residents. The Tuy Hòa Valley's peasants moved to hamlets adjacent to Tuy Hòa City and away from their crops—and thus required transporting and escorting by D/16th Armor to work their lands.[100] Since allied operations created more space between the province capital and the interior, Phú Yên appeared ripe for pacification's construction phase. In truth, Phú Yên had not fundamentally changed since 1965. Indeed, PAVN remained fixated on capturing Tuy Hòa City—an objective made even more important by the provincial population's concentration there. That observation went unnoticed as IFFV curtailed operations in the province, signaling the premature end of the destruction phase.

Haste best explains America's move away from conventional warfare. Pressure to show progress in a war in which progress proved fleeting both necessitated and curtailed the use of IFFV's maneuver battalions in Phú Yên. Pacification takes an inordinate amount of time, a luxury not enjoyed by the United States. Thus, the notion of a province on the mend prevailed. For the Americans, the time seemed ripe to transition pacification from the destruction to the construction phase. Despite the 1967 emphasis placed on building, the clearing of the enemy from Phú Yên largely failed. Both PAVN and PLAF retained the ability to project their power and influence into the Tuy Hòa Valley, and they would prove it in 1968.

5

"The rural 'pacification' program has gone up in smoke"

The Second General Offensive and Uprising, 1968

The rural 'pacification' program has gone up in smoke," the Hanoi press proclaimed after the 1968 Tết Offensive.[1] On the surface, such a declaration appeared rife with embellishment. Events of 1968 in Phú Yên—never mind those across much of the RVN—revealed that Hanoi's Tết Offensive indeed had spoiled Saigon's pacification efforts. In Phú Yên, American, South Korean, and South Vietnamese conventional forces rebuffed overt PAVN and PLAF efforts to take Tuy Hòa City. Yet the PAVN and PLAF did not have to win in the traditional sense to achieve its long-term political goals. Despite failing to capture the provincial capital and incite revolt, Hanoi's forces spurned pacification by disrupting development programs. Thus, the year marked the province's entrance into the nebulous world between being perceived as pacified and, in practice, being a fertile ground for NLF activity.

Hanoi's Second General Offensive and Uprising, or the General Offensive and Uprising of Tết Mậu Thân 1968—more commonly known in American circles as the Tết Offensive—posed the greatest challenge to pacification since 1965. The 1968 offensive was the second of three attempts by Hanoi to win the war through its General Offensive and Uprising strategy, the first being the 1965 effort to take key population centers before the deployment of substantial allied forces. The third incarnation of the General Offensive and Uprising strategy would happen in 1975, nearly three years after allied forces left the RVN.

Why the General Offensive and Uprising in 1968?

The General Offensive and Uprising was Hanoi's strategy for victory. As conceived by Lê Duẩn and his Politburo in Hanoi, the General Offensive and Uprising offered North Vietnam the chance to exploit the broad lack of U.S. military progress with a massive offensive and thus hasten the end of the war in Hanoi's favor.[2] Envisioned as the vehicle with which PAVN and PLAF formations would simultaneously strike every urban center in South Vietnam—thereby igniting a popular revolt against the Saigon government—the General Offensive and Uprising in Phú Yên focused on the elimination of GVN control. The task of Front A9—the organizing body Communist officials formed to manage the offensive in the Phú Yên–Khánh Hòa Sector—devised a plan to cut QL-1 as it passed from Phú Yên into Bình Định at the Cù Mông Pass, and attack district and province capitals.[3] In execution, most of the fighting developed near or within Tuy Hòa City.

Timing mattered: the spread of Saigon's influence beyond Tuy Hòa City necessitated a massive, well-orchestrated response by Hanoi. From the American perspective, Hanoi understood the conflict as one of controlling the people. According to an April 1968 press briefing, the challenge exerted against the NLF saw its control in II Corps "rapidly deteriorating" due to the allies' RD successes of the previous two years: the Communists were "losing control of the population," "lines of communication were being opened," and they were "becoming increasingly dependent on infiltration in order to maintain [their] forces."[4] Such a view gave credence to the prevailing sense that IFFV advanced pacification in Phú Yên between 1966 and 1967. But conventional warfare as the conduit for progress also worked for PAVN.

Allied forces that remained near urban centers in the provinces—Phú Yên included—amounted to those inadequate to disrupt a large-scale enemy offensive. PAVN effectively recreated conditions in Phú Yên comparable to those of 1965—"thereby creating a situation favorable for repositioning major enemy maneuver elements in the densely populated coastal urban areas."[5] In Phú Yên, allied units operated in relatively close proximity to the province capital, hunting for the coalescing enemy force. Three battalions of the ARVN 47th Regiment and three battalions of the ROKA 26th Infantry Regiments spread out between Tuy Hòa City and Qui Nhơn to the south, while the 173rd Airborne Brigade and the 4th Battalion, 503rd Airborne Infantry—both U.S. Army entities fixated on Operation Bolling—shielded pacification in Phú Yên. Poor intelligence sharing complicated matters further: a disconnect between province officials and the 173rd Airborne hampered the latter's ability to act quickly on intelligence.[6]

Not If but When

Contrary to the mythos of the Tết Offensive, that event did not come as a surprise. IFFV reported that "GVN and ARVN authorities expected that the enemy would launch an attack either before the beginning of Tet or during the latter part of the Tet holiday season."[7] The timing, however, did surprise them, as the South Vietnamese had thought it "inconceivable . . . that the VC/NVA would attack on the most sacred night of Tet, 29 January."[8] There had been indicators of a coming PAVN offensive in the Tuy Hòa Valley—the PAVN 95th Regiment's relocation of elements to the edge of the Tuy Hòa Valley in late 1967 signaled a pending offensive—but IFFV did not know when PAVN intended to strike.[9] The enemy's disposition and timetable remained unknown to the allies. "Due to the coming TET season and threats by the VC to spend TET in Tuy Hoa, the VN and ROK forces have been conducting more patrols and ambushes," Maj. Arthur K. Wimer, DSA for Tuy Hòa District, reported.[10]

The Tết Offensive in Phú Yên required more timing and luck than surprise. With Operation Bolling underway in the province, Lt. Gen. William B. Rosson, commander of IFFV, gave explicit directives to Gen. Leo H. Schweiter, commander of the 173rd Airborne Brigade, to destroy the PAVN 95th Regiment.[11] Meanwhile, PLAF remained a comparatively underappreciated threat. While intelligence gleaned from ARVN and ROKA ambushes revealed the enemy as hungry and underequipped, PLAF enjoyed largely unhindered access to the people in the Tuy Hòa Valley.[12] AT28 reported that PLAF troops were "still capable of entering a hamlet of . . . choice without opposition."[13] That PLAF could enter any hamlet posed the gravest threat to pacification. The displacement of any South Vietnamese government force—RD Cadre especially—by PLAF meant unhindered access to the population. RD Cadre typically operated in areas cleared, at least on paper, of enemy opposition. When in a hamlet, PLAF collected rice and taxes and performed indoctrination sessions—all at the expense of Saigon's efforts to spread pacification.

On 16 January, a PLAF unit engaged and displaced an RD team consisting of fifty-nine members, including a security element of thirty-four cadres, in Tuy Hòa District's Lông Tường hamlet.[14] Instructions for RD Cadre teams stated explicitly that "a 59-man group should not be expected to face armed VC opposition of more than squad strength."[15] PAVN and PLAF activity during January in other districts hinted at the enemy's continued ability to project power at places and times of its choosing. According to AT28, in Hiếu Xương District, security was "such that VC elements infiltrate to the edges of the district-seat hamlet, itself, almost at will."[16] Before mid-January, ROKA operations achieved little. The start of the rice harvest after 13 January saw an increase in enemy efforts to obtain rice. Accordingly, ROKA operations thereafter focused on preventing the enemy from partaking in the harvest. As explained by DSA Capt. John F. McLean, "security is of course the key to progress in the pacification program. . . . The ability of the 28th ROK Regiment to provide security for the district will determine how pacification will advance."[17]

Inadequate security also plagued Sông Cầu District in January. Two years removed from the start of IFFV's operations in the province and a direct correlation between pacification and conventional warfare remained significant. DSA Maj. Frank E. Underwood reported that "the pacification effort in Song Cau remains, at most, constant."[18] He based his consistency comment on "increased enemy activity" and a lack of allied units to provide security, both of which precluded the advancement of pacification. Inadequate security meant that since November, the village of Xuân Thinh, for example, lost nearly 3,500 residents who relocated themselves to safer hamlets elsewhere in Sông Cầu District.[19]

The allied forces' focus on other areas of Phú Yên troubled Tuy An District. "The security situation in Tuy An district remains poor," remarked Maj. Charles K. Hanson, Tuy An's DSA.[20] Allied concentration elsewhere in the province left pacification in Tuy An District at risk of reversal by enemy forces. That South Vietnamese officials were unwilling to risk their lives by sleeping in the areas under their purview was a troubling sign of unabated PLAF control. In Tuy Hòa District, too, hamlet, village, and district officials sought refuge in Tuy Hòa City every evening, leaving their areas of responsibility largely leaderless. Election results from 1967 were troubling, compounding matters for the advisory team: three hamlets elected new chiefs, choosing not to keep three pro-GVN chiefs in power. Hanson noted that those three pro-GVN chiefs were proponents of self-help projects, through which the people did more to improve their lives than Saigon did. The unpopularity of that approach, coupled with PLAF propaganda, spurred the people to seek new leadership. Furthermore, Hanson noted, the new chiefs were "not known for their energy or initiative," which gave PLAF an opening to render services to the people.[21] As previously covered in chapter one, counterinsurgency expert Bernard Fall stressed that one could not underestimate PLAF's ability to easily meet the needs of the people and thereby exact their loyalty.[22] As for security in Tuy An, Hanson proposed that only the arrival of South Vietnamese troops could offset the loss of allied units and counter any enemy gains.[23]

Operation Bolling existed as a shield against failure. Only Đồng Xuân District reported improved security in January, which came as no surprise since Operation Bolling placed elements of the 173rd Airborne Brigade in Đồng Xuân. Bolling's shift in focus afforded Đồng Xuân District improved security, albeit temporarily. Đồng Xuân District DSA Maj. Alexander M. S. McColl cautioned against assumptions of sustained progress. Like Hanson in Tuy An District, McColl understood that the eventual removal of allied forces would inhibit further pacification progress unless they were replaced by adequate South Vietnamese forces. Through the movement of troops, the operation gave the appearance of improved security—feeding thoughts of progress among American advisors and officials. In Đồng Xuân District, the presence of the military component of pacification—in this case, elements of the 173rd Airborne Brigade and CIDG forces—obscured the district's problems. "The District still lacks an 'outer shield' of ARVN/FWMAF troops and [the] subsection RF and PF forces are understrength and spread very thing; in effect there is no effective ground maneuver reaction force at subsection level," McColl warned. ". . . Because of the relatively low priority of this District as to resources, especially troops, and its tactically exposed position, the major part of the overall effort will be absorbed by the program of simple military survival, and progress in all areas will be slow and uncertain."[24]

The experiences of another 173rd Airborne Brigade unit spoke to the security conditions preceding the upcoming Tết holiday. D/16th Armor of the 173rd Airborne Brigade was the primary force assigned to Phú Yên. While other IFFV units operated in Phú Yên infrequently, D/16th Armor remained in the province until the end of Operation Bolling in 1969. This American outfit supported the ARVN 47th Regiment and operated predominately in the Tuy Hòa Valley. Consisting of three platoons of M-113 armored personnel carriers, with about sixty-nine men and no tanks, D/16th Armor typically found itself tasked with convoy escort duty and kept away from IFFV maneuver battalions' offensive operations. With limited supplies and isolated from the other units of the 173rd Airborne, soldiers of D/16th Armor themselves felt unwanted by the brigade. On balance, D/16th Armor functioned as a symbolic gesture on behalf of IFFV to the GVN in Phú Yên.[25] Yet D/16th Armor's daily logs offer essential insight into the Tuy Hòa Valley's security conditions before, during, and after the Tết Offensive. Moreover, this armored unit played a significant role during PAVN's last gambit to take Tuy Hòa City in March 1968.

To thwart pacification, PAVN's top commander in Military Region 5, Maj. Gen. Chu Huy Mân, thrust his units against the sources of Saigon's influence—major urban centers—on the first night of Tết.[26] Yet the Tết Offensive's planners over-looked a crucial detail. Timing now hurt the General Offensive and Uprising as planners in Hanoi did not account for the use of two different calendars by commanders in the field: North Vietnam employed a refined calendar, making the night of 30–31 January the start of Tết, as opposed to the older traditional calendar used in South Vietnam, which placed the start of Tết on the night of 29–30 January. That oversight meant two different first nights of Tết, thus two different timetables for the offensive. Hanoi's offensive therefore unfolded over a two-day period, and not in unison as intended. In Military Region 5, where Maj. Gen. Chu Huy Mân's force relied on the traditional calendar, Tết began on the night of 29–30 January. Hanoi's awareness of this error—and efforts to inform Chu Huy Mân—came too late.[27]

The Battle of Tuy Hòa

Maj. Gen. Chu Huy Mân's plan for Phú Yên appeared relatively straightforward—seize the province's center of power, Tuy Hòa City.[28] Characterized by three separate assaults on Tuy Hòa City, the offensive rekindled conventional warfare in Phú Yên. The first effort involved a two-pronged thrust into Tuy Hòa City. Chu Huy Mân envisaged two Communist battalions executing a pincer attack and quickly enveloping the key areas of the province capital. He tasked the 5th Battalion, PAVN 95th Regiment with approaching from the northwest, seizing Tuy Hòa North Air Base—an old French airstrip updated by the Americans and from which U.S. Army helicopters and light aircraft operated—on the northwestern fringe of the city on the night of 29–30 January.[29] After the fact, the 173rd Airborne Brigade reported, "the 5–95th Regt (NVA) received orders to move down and strike the district capital of TUY HOA on the morning of Tet (30 Jan 68). They were to strike the American Artillery base at TUY HOA North, destroy the airfield there and celebrate Tet with the people of TUY HOA."[30] For the second pincer, the enemy commander planned for the PLAF 85th Local Force Battalion to infiltrate downtown Tuy Hòa City just south of the airfield along LTL-7B.[31]

The 5th Battalion, PAVN 95th Regiment positioned itself with relative ease. Originating from Base Area 236, the 5th Battalion moved freely through the valley under the cover of darkness. Composed of three companies of about fifty-five soldiers each, a fifteen-person-strong element from the PLAF K-21 Recon/Sapper Company, and a mortar platoon with two 82mm tubes from the PLAF K-17 Mortar Company, the 5th Battalion reached the edge of Tuy Hòa City intact and undetected despite the ongoing Operation Bolling and having encountered

A view of the province prison and Bình Tín hamlet, Tuy Hòa District,
Phú Yên Province, taken from the roof of subsector headquarters
facing toward C Battery 6th Battalion, 32nd Artillery. 1968.
*Photographer unknown. Courtesy of National Archives at College
Park, Record Group 472, UD 42196, box 268.*

local inhabitants. PAVN soldiers traversed the relatively ARVN-free northern extremities of the Tuy Hòa Valley from Núi Ông La to Núi Chấp Chài. Intelligence obtained after the fact by the ARVN 47th Regiment later confirmed that the 5th Battalion had traversed the Tuy Hòa Valley unopposed, that "the local people encountered on the way caused no trouble." At approximately 1800 hours, the battalion exited the mountains, arriving inside the valley at "canal No. 1" at 1900 hours. After crossing the canal, the PAVN force reached the Đông Hòa Church at 2000 hours. By 2130 hours, the entire battalion gathered at Núi Chấp Chài.[32] Aside from dominating the northwestern landscape just outside of Tuy Hòa City, Núi Chấp Chài served PAVN and PLAF as a de facto base camp on the very edge of the GVN's seat of power in the province. The PAVN battalion's unopposed movement demonstrated the tenuous security situation in the Tuy Hòa Valley.

Thereafter, the battalion took foot again. Troops moved through the rice paddies and crossed "a shallow river" before dividing into two assault forces. Both formations completed their movements by 0100 on 30 January. The 5th Battalion's 1st and 2nd companies, along with a sapper and reconnaissance force, defended the battalion headquarters positioned just south of Tuy Hòa North Air

Aerial view from subsector headquarters looking south toward
Bình Tín hamlet, Tuy Hòa District, Phú Yên Province. 1968.
*Photographer unknown. Courtesy of National Archives at College
Park, Record Group 472, UD 42196, box 268.*

Base. Meanwhile, the 3rd Company placed itself in front of the adjacent American
artillery battery. The battalion's arrival into attack positions took longer than
anticipated, as "the local guide took too long to get them there."[33] Elements of
the 5th Battalion occupied Cemetery Hill, giving PAVN an elevated field of
fire. Mortar fire signaled the start of the first phase of the offensive. Starting
at 0135 hours, the 5th Battalion's mortars bombarded the nearby ARVN 47th
Regiment's compound for twenty minutes. Alerted by the mortar fire, American
authorities placed the 173rd Airborne Brigade on high alert. Instead of advancing
immediately after the barrage, the 5th Battalion waited two hours.[34]

Matters beyond PAVN's control farther south added further delay. Concurrent
with PAVN's push to the north, PLAF intended to strike the city center, but the
reconnaissance element of the PLAF 85th Local Force Battalion suspected a
GVN ambush along the intended route of attack. PLAF thus quickly abandoned
any further effort to press on into Tuy Hòa City.[35] After waiting two hours for the
never-to-materialize PLAF assault, the 300 soldiers of the 5th Battalion, PAVN
95th Regiment commenced the Battle of Tuy Hòa.[36] The 5th Battalion tasked its
3rd Company with overrunning the U.S. artillery battery before destroying parked

aircraft at the adjacent Tuy Hòa North Air Base. Simultaneously, the 5th Battalion sent other troops to liberate the GVN prison just to south. Those PAVN troops failed to make headway as the South Vietnamese guards stymied the attack.[37]

The 3rd Company fared slightly better as it overran Battery C of the 6th Battalion, 32nd Artillery's perimeter. In penetrating the defenses—which consisted of barbed wire and four bunkers with a machine gun in each—PAVN soldiers captured the number three bunker. Consequently one of the two M-42 self-propelled antiaircraft vehicles (or Dusters) advanced "and blew the captured No. 3 bunker away."[38] With dual 40mm cannons, the Dusters provided defensive firepower for the artillery battery's compound, which helped limit PAVN's penetration to roughly thirty meters inside the perimeter. Nevertheless, PAVN soldiers damaged an artillery piece, destroyed a powder magazine, and occupied the radar site. Meanwhile men of Battery C established a new defensive perimeter and continued to hold out for reinforcements. With mortar and small arms fire engulfing the battery, its commander, 1st Lt. William Kennedy, notified the 173rd Airborne Brigade tactical command post of the situation.[39]

The 173rd Airborne Brigade reacted quickly. Elements in the Tuy Hòa Valley heard "Parablast Six" over the radio as Lt. Col. James H. Johnson indicated his pending arrival at D Company, 4/503rd Infantry's field position. Upon landing, Johnson and his commanders formulated their plan of attack. For the previous ten days, D Company had searched for PAVN and PLAF elements as part of Operation Bolling. That search promptly ended, as Johnson needed his rapid reaction force to leave the rice paddies for the battle at Tuy Hòa North Air Base. Johnson also recalled C Company from the field—but that force needed hours to reach a suitable clearing from which an extraction could occur. D Company prepared to hit the enemy alone.[40]

The distinct sound made by the twin rotators of CH-47 Chinooks signaled the imminent extraction of D Company. By 0645, a Chinook deposited the first lift near Tuy Hòa North Air Base under intense enemy fire from Cemetery Hill. PAVN machine-gun rounds raked a Chinook during its landing approach—the helicopter then slammed hard into the ground and skidded. Miraculously all of that Chinook's occupants safely disembarked.[41] As recalled by Capt. Jimmy Jackson, a member of the initial assaulting force, "when we left it the Hook was smoking."[42] The second lift diverted to Tuy Hòa South Air Base at Phú Hiệp due to enemy fire. A flight of six UH-1s transported the third lift, placing the paratroopers at the same spot where the first lift landed. The third lift then picked up the paratroopers from the second lift and rejoined them with the other two lifts.[43]

Meanwhile, D Company's spearhead entered the compound, where it exchanged small-arms fire with men of the 5th Battalion. D Company dislodged PAVN regulars from defensive positions with well-placed Light Antitank Weapons (LAWs) and retook the radar site. Only when PAVN snipers fired from an occupied prison guard tower did D Company learn of the situation at the nearby prison. After neutralizing the snipers, the paratroopers cleared the rest of the compound, pushing out remaining enemy combatants in the process. Under fire from the Dusters, 5th Battalion elements fled both the compound and the prison.[44] Jackson recalled it as follows:

> As it got light you could see that some of the die hards were still trying to come in but the others had got the message. The NVA were moving out into the rice paddies. Then we were supported by gunships firing into the rice paddies. Snoopy (C-47) sprayed right on top of the NVA. The NVA were exposed in the rice paddies. The NVA were firing back but it was sporadic.[45]

The failed PAVN assault left nineteen of its own dead in the perimeter, and an ROKA sweep found forty-three more elsewhere. Of the one hundred American soldiers present inside the compound, the attack resulted in four killed.[46] The American fatalities included Lt. Col. Robert E. Whitbeck, the officer in command of the 319th Airborne Field Artillery Battalion's radar station at the base.[47]

As the cover of darkness dissipated with dawn, elements of the 5th Battalion retrograded from the airfield toward the nearby hamlet of Bình Tín.[48] By now, Gen. Schweiter had arrived to direct the battle. Along with the 4/504rd Battalion commanding officer Lt. Col. James H. Johnson, the deputy senior providence advisor Lt. Col. Vernon Walters, and the province chief Col. Nguyễn Văn Ba, orchestrated a plan to destroy the 5th Battalion. Having arrived via helicopter, two companies from the ROKA 28th Infantry Regiment moved to the north of the U.S. artillery to establish a blocking position. A battalion of the ARVN 47th Regiment positioned itself to the west of Tuy Hòa North Air Base to thwart any possible moves by the enemy in that direction.[49]

Attention now turned to Cemetery Hill. Having already downed a Chinook, elements of the 5th Battalion dug in on Cemetery Hill could still prevent D Company from reaching Bình Tín. Initially, D Company soldiers found little trace of the enemy on Cemetery Hill, but the enemy's near-perfect concealment wreaked havoc among the assaulting Americans. Taking fire from bypassed but unseen positions, the paratroopers found themselves fighting a close-quarter battle with protection afforded only by headstones. D Company cleared the hill one enemy fighting position at a time, leaving Bình Tín as the last objective.[50]

Hemmed in by allied forces, the beleaguered 5th Battalion found itself in an ever-shrinking mass. In Bình Tín, during the interlude between the failed PAVN assault and the allied counterattack, remnants of the PAVN force replicated a tactic previously used in Hiếu Xương in 1967, where soldiers dug firing positions and used the various buildings to shield themselves from the weapons of the gathering allied forces. Such replication suggested Bình Tín's preselection should the thrust into Tuy Hòa City have failed. In occupying and entrenching in Bình Tín, PAVN guaranteed a maelstrom of responding allied firepower. Although the loss of soldiers would benefit the destruction phase of allied pacification efforts, the desolation of Bình Tín—or any hamlet for that matter—would both set back the construction phase and signal the GVN's inability to protect the people. Regardless of the outcome, PAVN provided perfect propaganda to PLAF. After a South Vietnamese psychological operation to convince the 5th Battalion to surrender failed, American aircraft blanketed the hamlet with smoke and tear gas. With the hamlet in a literal haze, D Company launched an assault. After bitter fighting, fogged-up gas masks, mounting casualties, and seemingly endless enemy resistance, D Company pulled back to higher ground.[51]

D Company then occupied positions on Cemetery Hill. The recently arrived C Company placed itself near the airstrip, where it entrenched to avoid shrapnel from imminent USAF strikes. Shoveling quickly revealed that the paratroopers sat atop the dumping ground for the hamlet's human waste. Antoine Edward Roy of C Company of the 4/503rd Infantry recalled it as follows:

> So we get our entrenching tools and we start digging in the sand and start finding these little clotted things. Then everybody realized all at once, you know with these villages and the like, they don't have plumbing. This sand hill was the toilet. So to the 4th Battalion of the 503rd 21 Parachute Infantry Regiment and of course we're talking about the Tet Offensive here, it was known to us as the Battle of Shit Hill. You talk to anybody who was there and they'll always call it the Battle of Shit Hill. But we had to dig in and I remember all these dried up little turds and everything, throwing them away.[52]

Shortly thereafter, five USAF F-100 Super Sabres delivered 250- and 500-pound bombs, as well as napalm, into the hamlet—obliterating the structures and much of what remained of the 5th Battalion.[53] Indeed, the first sortie placed bombs

Aerial view of Bình Tín hamlet, Tuy Hòa District, Phú Yên
Province, after PAVN's defeat. 31 January 1968.
Photographer unknown. Courtesy of National Archives at College
Park, Record Group 472, UD 42196, box 268.

directly into the 5th Battalion's command post.[54] Thereafter, ARVN assaults
and additional U.S. airstrikes and mortar fire battered enemy holdouts. By the
following morning, soldiers of the ARVN 47th Regiment and two RF companies attacked and cleared the cratered hamlet, ending the first phase of the Tết
Offensive in Phú Yên.[55] The fight for the U.S. Army artillery battery and the
GVN prison, as well as the resulting struggle for the nearby hamlet, cost the
5th Battalion 189 dead, with 31 captured. Having started the battle with 300
soldiers, the loss of 220 from its ranks wrecked the 5th Battalion, but replacements
allowed the battalion to partake in further fighting. The Americans suffered a
comparatively lower loss of life, with the aforementioned four artillerymen and
now fourteen men of D Company, 4/503rd.[56]

As the smoke from razed Bình Tín dissipated, American attention returned
to Operation Bolling. That shift marked a serious error, as Communist forces
remained fixated on capturing Tuy Hòa City. A captured PAVN soldier offered
prophetic words: "If we weren't successful we were to retreat, rest, then return
and hit TUY HOA again."[57] Although mauled by allied units, the PAVN 95th

Regiment, elements of the 5th Battalion included, returned to the Tuy Hòa Valley in early February. American intelligence placed significant enemy forces in the area: "Reliable agents have reported . . . units within the TUY HOA area or close enough to have influence upon the BOLLING Area of Operations."[58] The units in question revealed a sizable contingent of PAVN within striking distance of Tuy Hòa City. Indeed, the headquarters of the PAVN 5th Division (Nông Trường 5), the PAVN 95th Regiment (including its 4th, 5th, and 6th Battalions), the PAVN 18B Regiment, the 95th Artillery Regiment, the PLAF 30th Main Force Battalion, the PLAF 85th Local Force Battalion, the PLAF K-65 Engineer (Sapper) Company, and the PLAF K-76 Engineer (Sapper) Company all marked the continuation of the Tết Offensive.[59]

The second enemy assault on Tuy Hòa City transpired between 4 and 5 February. Envisaged initially as the southern pincer of the Communist's earlier effort to envelop the province capital, the abandonment of that operation by the PLAF 85th Local Force Battalion resulted in a delayed second strike against Tuy Hòa City. The PLAF unit in question, now reinforced with PAVN rifle companies, entered the city unobserved. The sound of sporadic automatic weapons fire awoke the province capital from its slumber, and alerted Saigon's forces to new trouble in Tuy Hòa District. At 0230, PLAF combatants fired on the 22nd Railroad Security Company. The district power station received incoming fire at 0415, while PLAF troops fired on the national police headquarters in Tuy Hòa City at 0650. Only with the morning light did American and South Vietnamese officials fully grasp the situation at hand: PLAF elements occupied strong points south of Tuy Hòa North Air Base in the city center—the railway station, the Catholic church, and the traffic circle.[60]

The ARVN 47th Regiment positioned two battalions to retake downtown Tuy Hòa City. At 0600, the 1st and 3rd Battalions received orders from the regimental commander to advance on the city. While the 1st Battalion entered Tuy Hòa City from the west, the 3rd Battalion did so from the north. The regiment also directed the 2nd Battalion to the western edge of the province capital late in the afternoon, but never issued it orders to attack. As the 3rd Battalion advanced southward, it made contact with PLAF. Fire from a hamlet east of QL-1 alerted the battalion of enemy resistance, which increased as the ARVN force neared the 22nd Railroad Security Company's location. The 1st Battalion, too, drew enemy fire during its advance. The 1st Battalion crossed QL-1 after 0800 hours, while simultaneously encountering enemy fire from the roofs of PLAF-occupied buildings. Elements of the PLAF 85th Local Force Battalion took two of the 1st

Aerial view of city center from Núi Nhạn, where the 106mm recoilless rifle was located during the second battle in Tuy Hòa City, Phú Yên Province. 1968.

Photographer unknown. Courtesy of National Archives at College Park, Record Group 472, UD 42196, box 268.

Picture of Tourcham, the Champa tower on Núi Nhạn, Tuy Hòa City, Phú Yên Province. 1968.

Photographer unknown. Courtesy of National Archives at College Park, Record Group 472, UD 42196, box 268.

Aerial view of the Catholic church around which the second battle
was fought. Tuy Hòa City, Phú Yên Province. 1968.
Photographer unknown. Courtesy of National Archives
at College Park, record group 472, UD 42196, box 268.

Battalion's companies under fire from the traffic circle. Similar fire thwarted
attempts by the command group and the 3rd Company from bypassing the traffic
cycle from the south. The 1st Battalion's assault failed by 0930 as the intensity
of PLAF fire made any further advance impossible.[61]

The Americans joined the fight as the 173rd Airborne Brigade dispatched
two gunships to support the 1st Battalion. U.S. Army advisors attached to the
ARVN unit directed the gunships onto enemy rooftop targets. PLAF occupi-
ers overcame the helicopter strafing runs by taking cover. With PLAF tactics
negating the gunships' effectiveness, the 173rd Airborne Brigade set up two
106mm recoilless rifles on Núi Nhạn (listed as Tourcham on wartime maps) at
1100. From Núi Nhạn, the Americans had an unobstructed view of the enemy
positions. American fire dislodged PLAF, yet the 3rd Battalion slowly resumed
the advance into Tuy Hòa City. Its 3rd Company moved southward toward the
city center as the 1st Company cleared enemy resistance in the hamlet east of
QL-1. By 1230, the 2nd Company joined the 3rd Company, with both units
pressing the attack against buildings near the traffic circle at 1530. Progress
ended there as nightfall drew nearer. The following day, 6 February, the 1st and

3rd battalions cleared downtown of the enemy, encountering scant resistance. RF/PF units patrolled the areas outside of the battalions' control. A thorough sweep began on 7 February, with the 3rd Battalion placing its command post in the city center and placing troops on seven rooftops. At 1400, the "city began to return to normal."[62]

PLAF's gambit of 4 and 5 February proved the most successful of its efforts to take Tuy Hòa City. For the first time during the Vietnam War, Communist forces occupied a portion of Tuy Hòa City proper and did so without suffering crippling casualties. Indeed, the combined enemy force temporarily controlled the portion of the province capital astride QL-1 and the Sông Đà Rằng—amounting to half the city. PLAF paid a relatively low human cost for this second endeavor to conquer Phú Yên's capital, with twenty-six of its fighters dead; the majority lived to harass the GVN another day, thus reinforcing the argument that this second attempt to take the province capital was the most successful.[63]

During the interlude between the second and third phases of the Tết Offensive in Phú Yên, American forces uncovered physical enemy infrastructure deep in the Tuy Hòa Valley. Elements of D/16th Armor identified enemy bunkers and fighting positions in Ngọc Sơn in Tuy Hòa District on 19 February.[64] Upon scouring the village for further signs of the enemy, the Americans found a tunnel complex. Never during its time in the village did elements of D/16th Armor encounter actual PAVN or PLAF soldiers, but the tunnel discovery suggested that Communist forces had positions in the contested Tuy Hòa Valley from which to execute future operations against the GVN and allied troops.[65] Three days later, on 22 February, D/16th Armor and an explosive ordnance disposal (EOD) team blew up the tunnel complex in Ngọc Sơn.[66] Whether the enemy constructed these fortifications before or after IFFV's 1966 operations mattered not; the fact that PAVN and PLAF units had these positions at all demonstrated that the enemy literally had a deeply embedded presence in the Tuy Hòa Valley.

A monthlong pause by PAVN allowed it to regroup. Intelligence acquired by the 173rd Airborne Brigade indicated that the Nông Trường 5 had received replacements and was "nearing the posture to launch offensive operations."[67] The 173rd thus surmised that PAVN had four "combat effective battalions" ready in "northern central Phú Yên Province."[68] These units included the PAVN 95th Regiment's 3rd, 4th, and 5th Battalions as well as the PLAF 85th Local Force Battalion.[69] During the break from conventional warfare, PAVN and PLAF cells instigated chaos across Phú Yên: AT28 reported that PAVN and PLAF cells "maintained pressure throughout the province by executing 34 separate

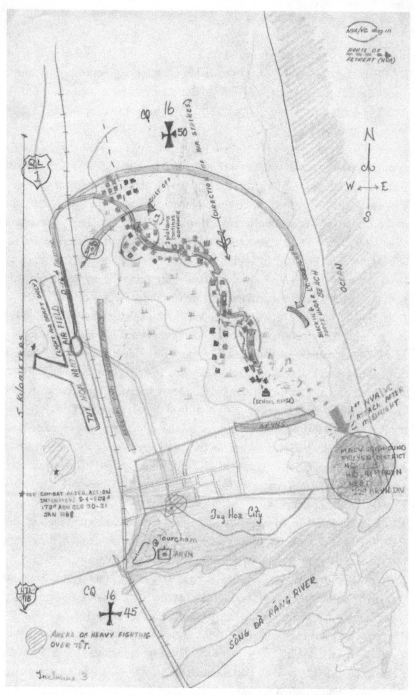

Map 4. Areas of heavy fighting in and near Tuy Hòa City during
the three attacks by PAVN and PLAF during the Second
General Uprising and Offensive, circa 1968.

Courtesy of CMH.

attacks," after which the PAVN 95th Regiment resumed its efforts to conquer the province capital between 4 and 5 March.[70]

Seizing Tuy Hòa City remained PAVN's objective. Thus Nông Trường 5 launched its third, and final, assault on Tuy Hòa City. In this effort, the PLAF 85th Local Force Battalion and the 5th Battalion, PAVN 95th Regiment, with elements of the 17th Mortar Recoilless Rifle Company and the 25th Recon Sapper Company, skirted around Tuy Hòa North Air Base and attempted to enter the city from the north along the coast. In attempting to capture the provincial head-quarters—the primary objective of the combined enemy force—the Communist troops clashed with two RF platoons and elements of the ARVN 47th Regiment near the latter unit's garrison in Tuy Hòa City. Like the two preceding assaults, this endeavor also failed. Encountering stiff resistance from South Vietnamese soldiers, PAVN's attack turned into a withdrawal. By morning, elements of the ARVN 47th Regiment had largely contained the retreating PAVN force in the hamlets of Ninh Tịnh village as it headed inland. The M-113s of the D/16 Armor provided the armor punch needed by ARVN, and led the allied efforts to crush the PAVN remnants occupying hamlets 1, 2, and 3 of Ninh Tịnh.[71] Yet the now-fortified PAVN force, equipped with B-40 rockets, proved a tough opponent. A B-40 rocket struck the second M-113 of the second platoon, 2–2, instantly killing the driver as it entered "Indian Country"—marking D/16th Armor's entrance into the battle.[72] As explained in the AAR, "when 2–2 was hit with the B-40, it was a vehicle's length off the road. The front end of it was a vehicle's length off the road. In other words, we had crossed the road and that was it. And all hell broke loose."[73] With air support from 335th Assault Helicopter Company and, from Tuy Hòa South Air Base, F-105s of the 308th and 309th Tactical Air Squadrons, American and South Vietnamese ground forces shattered what was left of the PAVN force. The confrontation resulted in at least 250 PAVN dead and seven fatalities for D/16th Armor.[74]

The Tết Offensive and Pacification

When AT28 began the process of analyzing the Tết Offensive, the Americans found significant problems bedeviling pacification in Phú Yên. Most prominently, the preceding allied operations had not improved the security situation as much as once thought. Despite suffering considerable casualties during those operations and during the Tết Offensive, PAVN and PLAF losses proved to be negligible: essentially, PAVN needed just one battalion to throw pacification off-kilter. The lasting effects of the Tết Offensive in Phú Yên, too, proved particularly noteworthy. Rather than offer an opportunity to rapidly advance pacification, the aftermath of the Tết Offensive significantly delayed pacification. AT28 surmised that the first and second enemy assaults put pacification efforts in the Tuy Hòa Valley two months behind schedule; the third attack, noted the advisory team, complicated efforts to pacify the Tuy Hòa Valley even further.[75] Between 31 January and 1 March, fighting resulted in 812 homes razed, with the 4–5 March battle leaving approximately 75 additional dwellings either "destroyed or severely damaged."[76] In other terms, "Over 3900 persons were made homeless by the three major battles and intervening clashes during the Tet Offensive."[77] By the end of March, Hanoi's offensive had locked pacification in the build phase. Across all of Phú Yên, fighting in March alone made 3,166 residents refugees while leaving 502 dwellings uninhabitable. On the whole, 8,178 people found themselves displaced as a result of the offensive.[78] If pacification truly entailed the advancement of the common people, then the destruction of whole hamlets surely worked against that end. Paltry progress defined CORDS-backed pacification during this period, producing only delays and frustration.

Enemy efforts during the Tết Offensive relied heavily on Phú Yên's history as a Việt Minh province. The Communists assumed that the people would overtly support the attacking PAVN and PLAF units. Captured PAVN and PLAF fighters revealed that they "had the mission [of] staying in Tuy Hoa [City] for 5–7 days."[79] Rather than a prolonged occupation of Phú Yên's capital, Communist intentions amounted to breaking ARVN's hold on the city, which presumably would evict the GVN and its backers from all of Phú Yên. For that plan to work, PAVN and PLAF units needed popular support. PAVN certainly had the assistance of local guides, yet as demonstrated during the first assault against Tuy Hòa City, the city itself did not rise up in support of the Communist cause. Although the citizens of Tuy Hòa City failed to rally around the Communists, that did not mean that they endorsed the GVN. Reluctance, however, played into the collective hands of PLAF as the pressure remained on the GVN to show the people that it could provide for their security.

In its wake, the General Offensive and Uprising left public confidence in the Saigon government eroded. Across MR2, the consensus among South Vietnamese civilians did not bode well for Saigon's control over the region. As explained by CORDS, "the peoples' confidence in the GVN to protect them had been greatly reduce as the VC propaganda, prior to the Tet offensive, indicated the cities would be attacked and entered, and the VC did exactly what they had promised."[80] For Phú Yên specifically, CORDS reported that "the general attitude of the populace is that the VC were defeated, but their defeat was the result of

Ground view of Bình Tín hamlet as of 19 March 1968, looking north. At this
point, the GVN had cleared the site before rebuilding efforts commenced.
Note the close proximity of Núi Chấp Chài, which is on the top left. There, the
5th Battalion, PAVN 95th Regiment gathered before attacking Battery C of
the 6th Battalion, 32nd Artillery's compound and the nearby GVN prison.
Courtesy of National Archives at College Park, record group 472, UD 42196, box 268.

U.S./ROK action and not the GVN. This attitude reflects a loss of confidence
by the people in the GVN's ability to protect them against the VC."[81] Moreover,
the Battle for Tuy Hòa turned approximately 5,500 civilians into refugees and
destroyed 752 homes.[82] AT28 acquired a better sense of Phú Yên's sympathies
from the turmoil unleashed by the offensive. Singularly, the collective sentiment
of the people placed into question the very existence of pacification. FSO Daniel
L. Leaty, formerly of USAID and now the PSA for AT28 in Phú Yên, disclosed,
"the province was under VC control as recently as 1965. The attitude of the
people now is to get along peaceably with whatever side is in power. They have
shown a curiosity about captured VC weapons on display, but little interest in
exhibits of VC bodies at the city soccer field."[83] With Communist rule a recent
memory, the neutral attitude of the people that Leaty perceived meant that
pacification had so far failed to ally the South Vietnamese peasantry with the
Saigon government. In other terms, pacification occurred around the common

people in that it did not make them feel fully, if at all, incorporated with the RVN. So long as the possibility of the NLF replacing the GVN as the sole arbiter of Phú Yên remained plausible, pacification could not permanently induce its inhabitants to favor Saigon's cause.

Anything but Beaten: PAVN and PLAF

Undeterred by their failure to topple the GVN in Tuy Hòa City, PAVN and PLAF sowed chaos elsewhere in Phú Yên. The CORDS field overview for March 1968 echoed and expanded AT28's conclusions: "In Phu Yen Province, enemy activity was primarily directed toward disrupting renewed RD efforts through the use of terror tactics and kidnapping members of the local populace," the overview stated.[84] "Of significance was the middle of the month kidnapping of approximately 500 civilians from a refugee camp in the vicinity of Dong Xuan. Subsequently 116 returned"—a sign of future troubles for pacification.[85] More immediately, however, CORDS reported that earlier in the month, the 5th Battalion, PAVN 95th Regiment and the PLAF 85th Local Force Battalion, "supported by various other local force groups, inflicted light damage on the civilian communities in the Tuy Hoa North and basin areas; while suffering heavy casualties themselves."[86]

Still, the Americans' language remained positive—if unspecific—on the security situation. In the words of AT28, "FWMAF appears to have restored some degree of security to the Tuy Hoa basin area during the past several weeks through concerted efforts at establishing more security for civilian communities."[87] The Tết Offensive did not result in a clear allied victory, in the words of Robert Komer, now head of CORDS:

> Pacification is still alive and kicking, despite the early tendency
> to many to pronounce it dead. We unquestionably suffered a real
> setback, but the enemy suffered grievous losses too. The real question
> is whether we can recover and forge ahead more quickly than he. I
> believe we can. The recovery process is already underway.[88]

Although PAVN and PLAF units failed to take Tuy Hòa City, their actions wrecked the Tuy Hòa Valley. Americans in Phú Yên could not deny that the Communist offensive successfully obstructed GVN pacification efforts. The Tết Offensive displaced many of the province's Tuy Hòa Valley residents. Ongoing warfare certainly hampered the advancement of pacification at the hamlet level in Phú Yên. Although seen as a temporary setback in 1968, that hampering of pacification eventually turned out to be an unrecoverable problem for the province.

The security situation in Phú Yên indicated that PAVN retained considerable combat power. Casualties incurred during the Tết Offensive jeopardized PAVN's combat abilities in Phú Yên but did not deter its activity. After a brief convalescence, elements of the PAVN 95th Regiment maneuvered during April. Encounters with ARVN and FWMAF forces, however, proved disastrous as the allies sapped the PAVN unit of fighting strength, causing most of the regiment to withdraw from the Tuy Hòa Valley. Tuy Hòa District DSA Wimer reported two PAVN battalions entering three hamlets—Phú Lộc, Mỹ Thành, and Mỹ Hòa—on the night of 4 April. "They entered these hamlets at approximately midnight and by daybreak were well-dispersed and dug in with excellent overhead cover and concealment." Wimer noted that hamlet residents "having experienced a similar situation in September, 1967, and knowing their homes would be destroyed, notified the 47th Regt (ARVN) of the NVA presence."[89] Ultimately, he said, elements of the USAF, the ARVN 47th Regiment, and the ROKA White Horse Division accounted for 259 PAVN KIA and 24 captured. "Since that time significant sightings and contact with the enemy has decreased sharply. This, perhaps, can be attributed to increased operations by the ARVN, ROK, and RF forces or possibly the enemy suffered a worse defeat than we realize and is now in hiding re-building and re-supplying his units," the DSA concluded.[90] Self-preservation and testing Saigon's abilities—not loyalty—were ultimately people's motivation in helping the GVN. One of the hamlets involved the 4 April battle in Tuy Hòa District, Mỹ Thành, encapsulated the recovery effort in Phú Yên: the province government listed 215 individual Mỹ Thành residents as needing GVN assistance to rebuild their dwellings.[91]

Other enemy units situated themselves away from the Tuy Hòa Valley to recover, yet remained a hindrance to the allies. Headquarters of the 173rd Airborne Brigade concluded that "the 85th LF Bn is apparently regrouping and attempting to rebuild its combat effectiveness for continuing operations in TUY AN District," while "the 30th MF Bn will probably continue to conduct limited, small scale harassing operations in eastern HIEU XUONG District."[92] With the bulk of Hanoi's main forces focused on recovery and harassing actions by the end of April, Phú Yên entered a near-seven-month period in which Saigon and Washington could perceivably advance pacification quicker than ever before.

Yet allied forces lacked sufficient military resources to truly capitalize on the Tết Offensive. Insufficient IFFV resources in Phú Yên offset PAVN's Tết Offensive losses. Notwithstanding the enemy's battered state after the three repulsed forays into Tuy Hòa City, IFFV's assets in Phú Yên proved capable of restoring the balance of power, yet not expanding it to new levels. In April, AT28 reported that, 70 percent of the recorded population resided in hamlets with "some degree of security," but that "regression of hamlets in the province since the TET offensive has occurred in Tuy Hoa, Tuy An, and Song Cau Districts. . . . This resulted from continued VC/NVA attacks, the lack of sufficient FWMAF to conduct continuous offensive operations outside the secure areas, and the insufficient number of RF companies available to the districts for inner security of the pacification effort."[93] Such sentiment reflected the emerging status quo engulfing the province.

As for D/16th Armor, the unit spent much of April near Phú Sen. On 17 April, D/16th Armor traversed the stretch of LTL-7B between Phú Sen and Cùng Sơn as a convoy escort.[94] At 1530 hours, approximately two unspecified enemy platoons ambushed the convoy. "Air strikes were called at 1545 hours and 11 500 lb bombs were dropped," in response.[95] The following morning, the D/16th Armor's 2nd and 3rd platoons "departed at 0830 hours to search the ambush site for possible KIA's and also a 500 lb bomb dud that was reported to us by air cover. Upon seeing 200–300 people in the ROK AO we were denied permission to pursue."[96] The rest of the month featured D/16th Armor keeping roads clear of enemy activity and relatively uneventful patrols near Phú Sen.

May played out no differently than April. Pacification in Phú Yên neither advanced nor regressed, yet the perspective of CORDS in Saigon perceived events differently: "Your program receives high marks. Excellent," Komer wrote in a letter dated 7 May 1968 to Leaty.[97] High praise from the head of CORDS, however, did come with two caveats—one, that AT28 in Tuy An District needed a new S-2 security officer, and two, that the District Intelligence Operations Coordinating Center in Tuy Hòa District needed "improvement," without no stipulation why, only that the local GVN should provide "pressure."[98] Such brief commentary from Komer obscured the deeper, underlying security shortcoming that affected the entire province. AT28 explained that "significant progress" had been made in May "in the execution of both the recovery and pacification programs, but that "the continued diversion of materials into recovery efforts continued to prevent the RD program from complete reinstatement during the month."[99] Moreover, security remained "inadequate. Regression of four hamlets was recorded during the month. At the same time, the security condition for eight hamlets was upgraded."[100] May demonstrated that progress on the pacification front was neither fast nor permanent. Rather, impermanence went together with pacification.

American advisors beguiled AT28 readers with a rosy June assessment. "Pacification continues to progress in a satisfactory manner especially in the heavily populated coastal area encompassing Hieu Xuong and Tuy Hoa Districts," AT28 noted for June.[101] "Satisfactory" proved an interesting word choice since in the same document, this positivity gave way to concerns about the ever-apparent trend of insufficient security and the lack of forward momentum: "security remains inadequate. Regression of ten hamlets was recorded during the month. At the same time the security condition of forty-one hamlets was upgraded."[102] Essentially, the problems detected in prior months appeared more as the new normal than aberrations. The enemy situation, however, reinforced the perception of poor security in the province. AT28 reported at the end of June that "the enemy's capabilities remain unchanged. During May there were 8 company, 4 multi-platoon, 8 platoon, 10 squad and 12 unknown size enemy attacks," this while PAVN and PLAF main and local forces focused on anything but contact with the allies.[103] Moreover, such enemy efforts equated to losing "251 KIA (BC) and 26 captured," though the more revealing figures were those of civilian loses.[104] "Guerrilla forces concentrated on terrorist activities, as shown by the large number of assassinations and kidnappings during May," with "22 assassinations reported, 100 persons kidnapped, and 12 mining incidents."[105]

The presence and actions of conventional forces still imbued a sense of progress for the allies. As a sign of some pacification progress, AT28 offered that "the attack on the infrastructure has continued to show good results."[106] Yet the only clear source of headway during May was Operation Bolling. Accordingly, the 173rd Airborne Brigade's 4th Battalion, 503rd Infantry task force continued Operation Bolling in Phú Yên Province, with the continuing mission of locating and destroying the PAVN 95th Regiment; providing security for the all-important rice harvest (in conjunction with the ROKA 28th Regiment and the ARVN 47th Regiment); providing security for the 577th Engineer Battalion and 173rd Engineer Company for their construction and minesweeping mission along Highway 436 and Routes 68 and 2D; and providing the Operation Bolling AO with an infantry rapid-reaction company.[107] Concurrent with the 4th Battalion, 503rd Infantry's efforts, U.S. Army engineers, with D/16th Armor's assistance, continued to improve the province's roads through Operation Rebuild.[108] Such a complex mission on the part of IFFV's assets in Phú Yên reinforced the bond between conventional forces and the ongoing pacification effort in the province. "But the enemy forces, after taking heavy casualties from U.S., ROK, and ARVN combat operations in middle and late April, were not easily located," meaning even Operation Bolling could only advance pacification insofar as PAVN permitted.[109] Through coalition warfare, pacification in Phú Yên appeared oriented toward progress, veiling the deeper issues that inhibited lasting success.

Between June and late July, the withdrawal of the bulk of Nông Trường 5 from the province demonstrated Operation Bolling's shortcomings. Indeed, the very departure of the majority of the PAVN 95th Regiment from Phú Yên to heal and regroup, that force left the province for Cambodia indicated the failure of the allies to destroy that particular force.[110] At best, 173rd Airborne Brigade's "intelligence data revealed that the 95th NVA Regiment has been unable to rebuild its fighting strength after its heavy losses in the month of April and, due to steady and successful allied pressure on the regiment, has also been unable to re-develop a workable supply and logistics system."[111] The CORDS overview further recounted that the PAVN 95th Regiment began withdrawing "to be able to re-equip itself with greater ease with new replacement personnel and supplies prior to returning," while leaving one of its three infantry line battalions (the 6th) in the area "to serve as a blocking force if needed."[112]

Remaining in Phú Yên, screening elements of the regiment and PLAF nonetheless retained the ability to harass pacification, as the Tết Offensive had not dramatically improved province security nor jeopardized PLAF's ability to undermine Saigon's pacification program. Before the end of 1968, PLAF demonstrated that its losses in the preceding months and years did not detract from its low-intensity warfare capabilities. It continued to launch small-unit raids precisely to counter allied claims of rendering Hanoi's forces combat ineffective during the Tết Offensive. On 6 June, the PLAF's 14th Sapper Battalion struck port facilities at Vũng Rô, a point of disembarkation for military supplies for allied forces in the province. The U.S. Army's 545th Transportation Company bore the brunt of the assault, with five American soldiers dead and eighteen trucks destroyed.[113] Toward the end of the month, on 28 June, a PLAF sapper team penetrated Tuy Hòa South Air Base, the home of the USAF's 31st Tactical Fighter Wing in the RVN. The twelve enemy sappers destroyed two C-130s while damaging five C-130s, one C-47, and one F-100 during the raid. Base security personnel intercepted the sappers before they reached the ammunition dump, thwarting what could have been a far greater psychological victory for PLAF.[114]

CORDS solidified the inseparability of the American and South Korean forces in the pacification of Phú Yên. Aside from the added security, which protected pacification, allied troops also provided resources for the development aspect of pacification. IFFV's overview for July 1968 noted that "ROK and US forces are the major participants in the Phu Yen Civic Action program. Their activities encompass the entire sphere of the pacification program."[115] That statement relayed pacification both as all-encompassing and as a major concern for conventional militaries. The overview noted a classroom construction project in Hiếu Xương District, as well as a vocational training program "designed to instruct selected Vietnamese in the skills of carpentry." It also described that

USAF personnel, working with advisors in the Đông Tác refugee camp, had "significantly improved the standard of living of camp residents," and that "US and ROK forces, concentrating in another area, youth and sports, have provided equipment, instructors and some funds for the formation of Junior RD Cadre Teams."[116] The aforementioned activities mirrored those performed by IFFV's maneuver battalions in 1966. Such a connection demonstrated that pacification continued along lines established before the arrival of CORDS, which consequently buttressed a new trend that little changed throughout the war.

The decision by PAVN to relocate did not dissuade PLAF from executing another attack. On 29 July at 0159 hours, an enemy sapper team successfully infiltrated the USAF perimeter defensive network at Tuy Hòa South Air Base and damaged two C-130 transport planes and one F-100 Super Sabre fighter with demolition charges. The PLAF attackers succumbed to retaliatory American gunfire. The 173rd Airborne Brigade warned that the attack "emphasized again the increased emphasis that the enemy is placing on sapper-type activity as a prelude or part of the expected third general offensive."[117] IFFV's concentration on annihilating PAVN had distracted American maneuver battalions, permitting small PLAF cells to execute sapper missions such as this one steeped in symbolism.

That the departure of PAVN dramatically improved security for the GVN in the Tuy Hòa Valley neglects the emergence of the area as a middle ground between all the belligerents. Notwithstanding operations to physically alter security conditions in favor of the GVN, the Tuy Hòa Valley remained a fertile ground for PLAF activity. While D/16th Armor uncovered bunkers and tunnels in the vicinity of Phú Sen earlier in the year, elements within AT28, too, noted indicators of trouble in the Tuy Hòa Valley as a whole. Local GVN officials and American advisors recognized the dangers of operating in the valley. Maj. Robert Barron, DSA in Tuy Hòa District between August 1968 and August 1969, described the Tuy Hòa Valley as a place safe in name only. Barron perceived that Capt. Nguyễn Thái Lâm, the district chief, and Ellis Wisner, a civilian advisor under Barron's command, truly understood the dangers present in the valley. As later recalled by Barron, "Dai Uy Lam would say, everything's safe, everything's safe . . . so I would ask Dai Uy Lam, I said, do you really think this is safe and Dai Uy Lam would say something and the interpreter always said oh, yes, completely safe, completely safe. And I would say, well why don't we got [sic] out there? No, it's not a good day to go out there, that kind of thing."[118]

Wisner later offered some rationale. He explained the danger in traveling to the hamlets: "Going into the more distant hamlets still in the RD area was something to do on the spur of a moment, or without much advance warning, in order to minimize chances of an ambush being set up."[119] Wisner recalled "a day when the part of the place where I had parked my vehicle in mid morning was where a command detonated mine was exploded a little later."[120] Physically and psychologically, allied operations in Phú Yên failed to transform the much-contested Tuy Hòa Valley into a GVN stronghold. Equally significant, the perception of the Tuy Hòa Valley as a dangerous place intensified during the next two years, before solidifying as fact. Other occurrences in the valley added validity to what Barron learned.

The Tết Offensive all but faded into history. Events in Phú Yên ran counter to the so-called obliteration of PLAF combat strength—a common theme during the war itself and in the ensuing historiography.[121] The longstanding argument that PLAF suffered terrible human losses, thus the sapping the Communists' abilities to counter GVN pacification efforts, did not apply to Phú Yên. The latter part of 1968 revealed the three failed Communist thrusts into the province capital as only a short-term defeat. PAVN and PLAF endured the heavy losses inflicted by allied forces to such a degree that visible signs of Communist resurgence started within six months of the last Tết Offensive assault on Tuy Hòa City. Indeed, August brought with it indicators of PLAF rebounding from the setbacks it experienced earlier in the year, but in such a manner as to make AT28 surmise that pacification had the upper hand. "Despite increased assassinations, taxation, and general harassment by VC forces during the month, pacification activities proceeded at a steady pace," began AT28's monthly province report for August.[122] AT28 downplayed the all-critical indicator of Communist plans to defeat pacification at the hamlet level; a reversion to low-intensity warfare suggested that PLAF intended to continue to challenge pacification, albeit in a manner that short-term data could not reveal. Unsurprisingly, PLAF's shift toward small-unit actions created a false sense of Communist weakness.

Events in September compounded those of August. Despite signs of the enemy's quick and growing resurgence, the correlation between PLAF losses and weakened enemy combat capability continued as truth. AT28 perceived the enemy's reversion to unconventional warfare as evidence of PLAF having little negative influence on pacification. September saw "an increase in highway and railway minings" primarily in Tuy An and Tuy Hòa districts.[123] Yet because these PLAF activities did not seriously disrupt lines of communication in the province, AT28 remained largely unconcerned. Ironically, the same province report later revealed the following:

Although enemy activity was primarily confined except for one multi-company size attack against elements of the 47th (ARVN) Regiment, to stand-off mortar attacks and small scale contacts with RD teams and PF platoons, the majority of enemy-initiated contacts has been in hamlets located well inside the perimeters of what are considered to be secure areas. The objective of these enemy attacks appears to be to undermine confidence in the ability of the GVN to provide adequate security in pacified areas. An increase in assassinations and terrorist activities was noticed concurrently with the increase in enemy attacks into secure areas.[124]

The report also cautioned that PLAF would likely continue embarrassing the Saigon government via symbolic strikes: "Reliable intelligence indicated that the primary targets for enemy attack during October will be Tuy An and Tuy Hoa District Headquarters and hamlets located close to Tuy Hoa City."[125] Moreover, it stated, "the ultimate objective of enemy forces remains population control of key areas, including Tuy Hoa City," with control of the September-October rice harvests in Tuy Hòa, Tuy An, and Hiếu Xương districts an equally important enemy objective during October.[126] Even with mounting evidence, unbeknownst to AT28, PLAF's effort to inhibit GVN pacification remained largely unaffected by the Tết Offensive.

One rather hollow victory for the Americans against the PAVN 95th Regiment occurred in October. Seen as a significant blow to physical enemy infrastructure by the 173rd Airborne Brigade, the discovery and destruction of a PAVN surgical hospital on 27 October by the 4/503rd Infantry minimally affected the regiment. Having already dispatched most of its soldiers to Cambodia, the loss of the hospital complex mattered little to the PAVN regiment.[127] The loss certainly did not affect PLAF main and local forces' abilities.

October, too, displayed omens of future pacification troubles. Unhindered movement of Communist forces demonstrated both a robust enemy and the allies' mounting inability to effectively counter its threat. Intelligence reports continued to indicate an increased enemy buildup in PLAF-controlled mountain regions of Phú Yên. The monthly province report for October mentioned the return of one U.S. and one ARVN battalion to the province, enabling several large-scale offensives into western areas of Tuy Hoa and Tuy An districts in addition to protecting the rice harvest. Those operations "served to keep the enemy off balance, although producing no concrete results."[128] Worse yet, "reliable intelligence" indicated that enemy infiltration groups were still moving into Phú Yên but were remaining in the relative security of the mountains of western Tuy An and northeastern Sơn Hòa districts. "Indications are that the enemy's primary concern will be to continue gathering rice and taxes from people in GVN controlled areas and to continue small unit harassment," the AT28 report stated.[129] Despite the "but," the enemy's avenues of concentration revealed that all was not well in Phú Yên. Regardless of the setbacks PAVN and PLAF had suffered, the remote tracts of the province remained self-sustaining communities for their forces.

Accelerating Pacification

Signs of a revived PLAF at best went unnoticed or at worst were downplayed by the higher echelons of American leadership. CORDS equated the unprecedented nationwide enemy losses as indication of PLAF's inability to effectively counter high-tempo pacification. In view of the perceived weakening of PLAF power after the Tết Offensive, American authorities sensed an opportunity to rapidly expand GVN control. For that reason, CORDS devised the Accelerated Pacification Campaign (APC). As envisaged by CORDS, the APC offered the GVN a means of simultaneously filling the political void at the hamlet level across many hamlets, signifying a major break from the previous pacification approach that featured the gradual spreading of GVN control from the cities into the countryside via *tâche d'huile*, or the oil spot technique—a process championed by the French and now by RVN President Nguyễn Văn Thiệu. Since the APC called for the quick placement of thousands of hamlets under Saigon's banner, Nguyễn Văn Thiệu expressed concern over the viability of such an audacious program. ARVN allayed fears of the strain such a program would place on South RD Cadre teams and security forces, perceiving itself as having sufficient assets to back the APC.[130] Saigon thus reluctantly adopted the APC—or *Lê Lợi* as it was called in South Vietnamese circles—with the initiative commencing on 1 November 1968. In doing so, CORDS authorities expected the APC to elevate the rankings of at least 1,000 hamlets all across the RVN to relatively secure status by the end of January 1969.[131] Specifically for Phú Yên, CORDS authorities designated an initial total of twenty-nine target hamlets for the APC, with AT28 noting that "increased physical security has been accomplished in 22 of the 29 Target Hamlets."[132] Leaty commented at the time, "while it is still too early to evaluate the degree of successes or failures of the APC in Phu Yen, the program has already produced some concrete results."[133]

PLAF again reminded the province that it had survived the Tết Offensive. On 30 November, it mortared the Vũng Rô installation; this time the results entailed only damaged buildings, no American fatalities.[134] The small attack against Vũng Rô mattered to PLAF in psychological rather than strategic terms: "The destruction of the enemy's Vung Ro base was not just of psychological value in raising our morale and confirming our army's ability to defeat the American aggressors; it also provided a living demonstration of the value of the Vietnamese military arts' concepts of 'using small forces to fight large forces,' and 'using weakness to defeat strength'" a PLAF member later wrote.[135]

With the APC very much in its infancy, the rapid nature inherent to the initiative assured a PLAF response greater than what it demonstrated after the Tết Offensive. What that response could entail went unaccounted for by American planners. "As you may have heard, I have left 'my bed of roses' at the Embassy for a 'nest of thorns' in the Pacification business at MACV," George C. Jacobson, CORDS assistance chief of staff, began a February 1969 letter to Edward Lansdale.[136] One of the architects of the APC, Jacobson recounted the start of the program:

> We moved out fast and far, and the 1969 Pacification Plan envisages more of the same. I don't pretend to know what the VC reaction will be, but it is all but certain that they must react in some way. The crux of the problem in my opinion is what our response will be to that VC reaction if and when it occurs. If we permit ourselves another "barbed-wire complex," e.g. a totally defensive attitude, the psychological impact worldwide will be much the same as Tet 1968.[137]

With all twenty-nine target hamlets in Phú Yên experiencing physical security by the end of December, evidence suggested that the APC worked. Yet like the caution Jacobson expressed, so too did Leaty note that "some evidence of political maneuvering on the part of the NLF has been evident during the month. The low level overt military activity against APC hamlets has caused some concern that this political activity may be having some success."[138] Leaty further noted that propaganda in support of APC "remained inadequate," which compounded the NLF's nascent reaction to the effort.[139] Leaty highlighted the better cooperation of GVN agencies in Phú Yên as evidence of the APC's contribution to pacification.[140] Improved GVN synergy, however, did not mean that the South Vietnamese were ready for the increased security strain that APC brought about. Moreover, PLAF's full response loomed on the horizon.

Jacobson's and Leaty's words on the possible Communist response to the APC proved prophetic. PLAF did react and, in the case of Phú Yên, a "defensive attitude" took hold with both the local GVN and later the U.S. advisory mission.

For the APC, the concept of quickly planting the RVN flag in contested villages outpaced the ability of the South Vietnamese and the allies to defend large tracks of new territory. Both these symptoms seriously jeopardized pacification for the remainder of the war. Yet for the months immediately following the failed final Communist thrust into Tuy Hòa City, the effect of the Tết Offensive appeared temporary.

A month into the APC, American and South Vietnamese forces found further evidence of enemy activity in the Tuy Hòa Valley. With Operation Bolling still underway and as the end of 1968 approached, D/16th Armor and various RF companies spent much of December patrolling near An Nghiệp, a hamlet near the western mountains that marked the end of the Tuy Hòa Valley.[141] Throughout the month, those allied forces encountered traces of the enemy in the valley. In the mountains, American and South Vietnamese troops located and swept some of the caves. In one instance, they found only "much blood was around the entrance."[142] On 12 December, D/16th Armor identified eight PLAF, calling in helicopter gunships that "fired up area around perimeter at 1945."[143] The following day, 13 December, D/16th Armor uncovered a company-sized enemy base camp, yet made no physical contact with the enemy. Indeed, PLAF continued to avoid contact with allied forces. When D/16th Armor called in artillery strikes against a group of PLAF members on 17 December, the "enemy moved into mountains."[144] Two days later, "1st platoon and RF's made contact" with PLAF, resulting in two enemy dead.[145] The unravelling of pacification between 1969 and 1970 would come from those mountains.

The 1968 Tết Offensive set in motion a chain of events that ultimately defeated Saigon's pacification efforts in Phú Yên. Although Hanoi's setbacks permitted Saigon to enact the APC and make rapid gains into contested territory, the move came as the United States sought disengagement from fighting the war with American troops. The pending removal of that shield meant that PAVN and PLAF could, again, strongly contest pacification. Moreover, despite the APC's launch, pacification in the province never achieved the permanent advances called for by planners. Ills firmly embedded in pacification remained, while the commitment of American assistance increasingly waned. The start of the APC marked a negative change in Phú Yên that brought forth far more perils that those unleashed by the Tết Offensive.

6

"Very little, if any, progress"

Vietnamization and the Accelerated
Pacification Campaign, 1969

The Americans want to withdrawal their troops but they also want to strengthen the Puppet army and Puppet government. At this, they are once again contradicting themselves. How can they prevent the Puppet army and Puppet Government from being ruined and disintegrated once they cannot increase, but have to decrease, their own troops in SVN?" the PLAF instructors asked those being indoctrinated in May 1969.[1] The Nixon administration's efforts to disengage from the war in Vietnam intensified in 1969. To preserve American credibility while extricating the nation from the grossly unpopular war required shifting more security responsibilities to the South Vietnamese government.[2] That process, called Vietnamization, included the acceleration of pacification, which in turn meant rapid improvement in security conditions at the village level. Yet America's efforts to rescue itself from the RVN manifested conditions that exposed perceived pacification gains as illusory.

Conventional armies remained as entwined with pacification into 1969 as they had in years prior, yet with diminishing intensity and longevity. The three layers of allied defense—U.S. Army operations, ARVN and ROKA operations, and RF/PF patrols—protecting the Tuy Hòa Valley remained in place, but with an ever-increasing burden on South Vietnamese shoulders. Phú Yên was itself victim of the American decision to concentrate remaining IFFV assets in Bình Định. The ROKA, too, decreased its presence in Phú Yên in favor of Bình Định. Moreover, the Accelerated Pacification Campaign in the province increasingly tasked South Vietnamese forces to secure more hamlets. The low-intensity warfare favored by Hanoi after the Tết Offensive, however, proved sufficient to negate allied military efforts to bring down PAVN and PLAF.

Events in 1969 set the stage for pacification's demise in Phú Yên as American officials embarked on a fast, risky expansion of pacification. Vietnamization, together with its subordinate APC, occurred at a time when PLAF seemed at its weakest. Yet the union of Vietnamization and the APC exacerbated the security issues already noted in prior months by AT28 documentation. The APC functioned as a mechanism to exploit the perceived decline of enemy power after Hanoi's 1968 offensive. Running out of time after President Johnson's decision not to seek reelection, and amid fervent resentment toward the war in the United States, Robert Komer and his CORDS staff pushed for accelerated pacification to make the most of what time remained.[3] Results in Phú Yên, however, presented the APC more as the legitimization of U.S. abandonment of the RVN than as an effort to improve the country's long-term stability. With the APC, Vietnamization placed a facade over the continued back-and-forth struggle between belligerents in Phú Yên. A particular metric drove perceptions of pacification's success, or lack thereof—the Hamlet Evaluation System (HES).

HES came into existence in 1967 and assumed increasing importance after the Tết Offensive. HES provided American and South Vietnamese officials with another means of measuring pacification's progress. Between 1967 and 1969, HES relied on subjective data interpretations for scoring. Imperfect from the start, HES emerged out of data collected by American district advisory teams, with results passed on to the higher echelons of the province advisory team before ultimately reaching the highest levels of CORDS, MACV, and the GVN. An "A" rating meant that a hamlet had sufficient security forces, no PLAF activity, ongoing public works initiatives, and was prospering economically. A "B" meant that a hamlet had a slight threat of PLAF meddling but a somewhat effective security force, adequate public works projects, and noticeable economic improvement. Hamlets with a "C" displayed signs of PLAF influence and infrastructure, and had limited public aid programs. A "D" meant that PLAF maintained a noteworthy presence in the hamlet—subjecting the inhabitants to taxation and threats of violence—however, a GVN administrative apparatus remained, with Saigon still viewed favorably. An "E" meant that PLAF effectively controlled the hamlet, with minuscule GVN activity. A score of "V" or "VC" meant that PLAF outright administered the hamlet. Raters used "N" to denote a hamlet not evaluated, and "X" to designate an uninhabited hamlet. By 1970, CORDS heavily revised HES, resulting in HES/70. That version relied more on objective analysis provided by experts, and ended up being more conservative in its results than the original system.[4]

HES earned little if any mention in AT28's monthly province reports during 1967 and 1968. It gained in importance in 1969, however, as a means of evaluating pacification's progress. That year, CORDS sought the rapid spread of Saigon's influence so as to support quickened American disengagement from the war. For all its flaws, HES nevertheless provided a means to track changes from afar. Daily conditions were impossible for HES to reflect, yet collections of monthly evaluations permitted one to recognize patterns. By improving HES scores and by giving the impression of increased security, the APC and HES helped justify decreased U.S. participation in the ground war. The quick placement of contested hamlets under the GVN's banner benefited American public relations, as it portrayed NLF activity in South Vietnam as little more than a nuisance. Yet stepped-up rural development intensified the need for quality security forces during a time of decreasing American ground forces. IFFV's perceived successes in 1966 had extended into 1969, instilling a false sense of continued, inevitable progress.

MACV continued to support pacification after the Tết Offensive. Although Gen. Abrams replaced Gen. Westmoreland as MACV commander—a planned move—conventional forces remained focused on defeating the enemy in battle and backing pacification. MACV rejuvenated its pacification assistance, providing more military assets to revolutionary development. Conventional forces played a role in this process with an explicit mandate to hold and clear land within their areas of operation. IFFV's operations remained central to pacification in Phú Yên. "Our mission was basically to secure the countryside and permit the so-called 'Pacification Program' to succeed," Lt. Gen. Charles A. Corcoran—commander of IFFV between 15 March 1969 and 23 February 1970, and previously MACV chief of staff—later remarked.[5] Operations Bolling, Darby March I, and Darby March II focused on expanding and solidifying pacification in the Tuy Hòa Valley and security enhancement in the same AO. As in years prior, the operations of 1969 concentrated on protecting the rice harvest and expanding GVN influence at the expense of the NLF's, all while destroying enemy units.

Supporting the APC

The first of these operations, Operation Bolling, began on 19 September 1967 and terminated on 31 January 1969. Over the course of the operation, the 1st Cavalry Division and the 173rd Airborne Brigade participated in reconnaissance in force and search and destroy maneuvers against enemy units to safeguard pacification. With a focus on rice security, Bolling demonstrated continuity in how IFFV sought to weaken enemy capabilities in 1969 the same way it had in 1966. The multiyear duration of Operation Bolling in and of itself showed how little the war had changed over time. What the operation accomplished over the years—and Bolling had certainly endured—amounted to spreading pacification and its defense. Success, however, rested on the faulty discernment that, after years of combat, and especially after the depletion of PAVN and PLAF ranks during the 1968 Tết Offensive, the enemy no longer possessed the capabilities to reverse Saigon's position in Phú Yên. Although weakened, PAVN and PLAF units were not defeated—which they demonstrated in the months following the Tết Offensive.

As between 1966 and 1968, operations in 1969 conjured perceptions of progress. The Tết Offensive had not spelled the end of conventional warfare in the province, nor had it relegated the Communists to the margins of Phú Yên's future. On 30 January 1969, D/16th Armor engaged elements of the PAVN 95th Regiment in battle near Núi Chấp Chài and Tuy Hòa North Air Base. Oddly enough, the PAVN 95th Regiment seemed to try to replicate its attack on the airfield complex from exactly a year prior. This time, however, the American armor unit and supporting fire caught PAVN soldiers traversing rice paddies and irrigation canals. "It was a real holocaust," Lt. Michael Jones of D/16th Armor said of the battle. Although elements of the PAVN regiment initially put up stiff resistance, the exposure of multiple companies of the regiment on the rice paddies worked against them. Eventually, D/16th Armor and four RF companies, as well as "massive air and artillery" support, left between twenty and twenty-eight PAVN soldiers dead.[6] James B. Engle, an FSO and Phú Yên's PSA, surmised that this battle had thwarted Communist intentions of launching an operation on Tết.[7]

Military efforts certainly provided misplaced optimism. American and South Korean military efforts in the Kỳ Lộ Valley had pushed the PAVN 95th Regiment's headquarters to the "Hub" area (Base Area 236), prompting Engle to write "the noose is drawing very tight. If that operation brings about the elimination of significant numbers of the enemy, the near-term threat to Tuy Hòa City will be nullified."[8] Executed between 1 November 1968 and 31 January 1969, these forays into Base Area 236 occurred while only a single battalion, the 6th, of the PAVN 95th Regiment operated in Phú Yên. Indeed, the 173rd Airborne Brigade later suspected—though physical proof proved elusive at the time—that other elements of the PAVN 95th Regiment were in the process of returning to Phú

Yên after months of retraining in Cambodia.[9] Allied operations into the base area therefore provided more of a psychological boost for the allies than a true disruption of PAVN's plans, as the American paratroopers recorded only ten enemy KIA.[10] The focus on PAVN, too, distracted from the continued threat posed by PLAF. As most of the PAVN 95th Regiment avoided battle, PLAF continued to disrupt pacification.

American authorities placed considerable pressure on the APC to produce signs of fast progress. The APC in Phú Yên began with CORDS authorities tasking AT28 and the provincial government with improving the ratings of twenty-nine hamlets for January.[11] As 1969 began, local GVN officials remained fixated on keeping military and civilian personnel on alert during Tết celebrations as well as preparing for upcoming elections. These factors contributed to the slow collection and dissemination of information pertinent to the APC. Despite South Vietnamese authorities giving above-mentioned target hamlets of phase one the HES ranking of "C" (i.e., relatively secure status), AT28 speculated that conditions were in fact worse. Due to "incidents or elements of adversity," some of the twenty-nine target hamlets had not met all the strict criteria to achieve "C" ratings.[12] Thus only by the end of February did AT28 consider seventeen target hamlets as having achieved relatively secure status—bringing the total of "C"-rated hamlets to twenty-seven. That total placed AT28 and the provincial government two hamlets behind the goal prescribed by the ACP for January. Seemingly good progress, those results nonetheless placed Phú Yên below the expectations of American civilian and military authorities in the RVN. In turn, CORDS head William E. Colby, IFFV commander Gen. William R. Peers, and CORDS deputy James Megellas visited Phú Yên in February to encourage better APC results.[13] Thus, 1969 began inauspiciously for AT28 and province officials as sluggish progress garnered more concern than safe hamlets, and as the province failed to meet the APC goals set for the end of January.

Province-level GVN secrecy created frustration among CORDS advisory personnel early on in 1969. Col. Nguyễn Văn Ba, the GVN province chief for Phú Yên, dismissed and then had his most able district chief arrested for exceeding his powers. The district chief had overseen Tuy An for three years, transforming the district from "solidly red" to "more than 70% relatively secure."[14] AT28 perceived him as having suppressed VCI in the district. AT28 feared that the removal might mean a reversal of fortunes in Tuy An District. As a result, the APC commenced with a disheartening start in Phú Yên. Refugee resettlement and expansion of GVN control rested ever more so on the allies' ability to keep the province secure.

Years of fighting in the province's most populous region, the Tuy Hòa Valley, had forced thousands of peasants out of their villages and into refugee
camps closer to Tuy Hòa City. Thanks in part to the Tết Offensive, the refugee
situation remained unresolved as resettlement initiatives progressed slowly.
As of 28 February, Engle estimated that 14,000–14,500 displaced persons had
"voluntarily resettled themselves." That number, he noted, included just a few
registered refugees, implying that people were returning to their communities
of their own accord.[15] Refugees were acting faster than GVN province officials
and the APC could keep up with them.

Conventional forces played a critical role in population security. Elevating
target hamlets to relatively secure status meant that these communities were
predominately in the hands of the GVN, yet not completely free from NLF
interference. Operations by conventional forces greatly increased security in the
Tuy Hòa Valley in particular. Engle argued that the "continuous operations" of
the 173rd Airborne Brigade, the ARVN 47th Regiment, and the ROKA 26th and
28th regiments against enemy forces in the mountains continue "to be a major
factor in the progress of pacification here."[16] As American, South Korean, and
South Vietnamese troops maintained the offensive and pressed Communist forces
close to their base areas, HES rankings improved for the APC target hamlets.
On paper, the allied units' creation of physical space proved essential for the
GVN and CORDS to begin rehabilitating the target hamlets.[17] Engle relayed
this point when he wrote of allied operations to protect the Tuy Hòa Valley from
occupation by PAVN and PLAF troops:

> Since I attribute major credit for the great recent improvement in
> Phu Yen to the success of spoiling operations against enemy main
> and local force units in the mountains (thus keeping them out of the
> populated areas), I would have to revise my estimate downward if
> (1) the number of US, ROK, and ARVN forces in Phú Yên were
> reduced, or if (2) these forces were kept defensively in the valleys
> with the main mission of intercepting enemy squads en route to
> hamlets, rather than attacking enemy base areas.[18]

Just as the operations of 1966 and 1967 had sought to distance PAVN and
PLAF from the South Vietnamese population, so too did operations in 1969 and
beyond. As described by Maj. Robert A. Doughty in his 1979 study of U.S. Army
doctrine, MACV adopted new phraseology in April 1968. In response to a growing
association of the phrase "search and destroy" with aimless pursuit of evasive

enemy units and wanton destruction, MACV replaced the phrase with ones not yet tainted by years of war.[19] Enter "clear and search," which denoted a closer association between military operations and pacification. On paper, search and destroy entailed the annihilation of PLAF units, while clear and search focused more on keeping the enemy off balance. Clear and search also amounted to locating and bringing to battle the enemy units bloodied by search and destroy.[20]

By providing the security required to advance the APC, conventional forces played a critical role. February began with elements of IFFV mounting operations to push the enemy away from areas targeted by the APC in the former Bolling AO. Now designated as AO Dân Phú/Wainwright, the 173rd Airborne Brigade's 4th Battalion, 503rd Infantry and D/16th Armor operated in this area to the northwest of Tuy Hòa City to enhance area security as part of Operation Darby March I. Explicitly, IFFV tasked these American units with supporting the APC objectives in Phú Yên and serving as a rapid reaction force in the province.[21] This entailed "locating and destroying enemy forces in the area of operations."[22] American paratroopers also provided security for U.S. Army's 577th Engineer Battalion as its engineers cleared highway LTL-7B from Tuy Hòa City to Cheo Reo in Phú Bổn Province. The 4/503rd left the AO temporarily to conduct operations elsewhere but returned on 22 January. Upon their return, the paratroopers furthered the appearance of progress by conducting reconnaissance in force into contested areas west of Đồng Tre.[23] Such activity marked the continuation of constant IFFV operations, beginning in 1966 with Operation Jefferson, thus ensuring that Tuy Hòa District stayed at the forefront of allied military activity.

The South Vietnamese and South Koreans also aided American-led efforts to place more of the province's population under Saigon's control. Together with the ARVN 47th Regiment and the ROKA 26th Regimental Combat Team, the 4/503rd operated in an AO that encompassed a large swath of Phú Yên—that included the mountainous regions of Đồng Xuân, Sơn Hòa, Tuy An, and Tuy Hòa.[24] An estimated 150,000 inhabitants were at stake in these parts of the province. Although only about 5,000 people lived under PLAF control, approximately 13,000 resided in contested hamlets.[25] In 1969, allied and Communist forces challenged one another directly for control of those 13,000 civilians, and indirectly for the other 137,000 inhabitants.

The APC's first major goal in Phú Yên was to improve the target hamlets' security status. One such target hamlet was An Nghiệp, a village in the southwest corner of Tuy Hòa District. Situated toward the edge of the Tuy Hòa Valley, An Nghiệp sat in contested country. As an APC target, it become a focal point of activity as D/16th Armor conducted patrols alongside RF/PF companies.[26] These allied units sought confrontation with the enemy's sizable presence in the AO. For Hanoi, Phú Yên fell under Military Region 5—territory designated for control by Nông Trường 5. Under Nông Trường 5, the PAVN 95th Regiment's 6th Battalion, the PLAF K-91st Sapper Company, the PLAF DK-7 Local Force Company, the PLAF DK-9 Local Force Company, the PLAF 30th Main Force Battalion, and the PLAF 85th Local Force Battalion all operated in AO Dân Phú/Wainwright.[27]

Nông Trường 5's forces moving in and out of AO Dân Phú/Wainwright posed a direct threat to pacification. Albeit weakened from long supply lines slow to provide new equipment and personnel, Nông Trường 5 had sufficient resources to derail the expansion of Saigon's pacification efforts. After his tour as IFFV commander, Lt. Gen. Corcoran reported that he recognized an "increased emphasis on low level activity, the fragmenting of Main Force and Local Force units to support the guerrilla units . . . on several occasions" by Communist authorities. Corcoran added that this trend had been particularly evident in Bình Định and Phú Yên provinces. "Further reinforcement of the low level effort has come through the subordination of NVA units to provincial control," he reported in February 1970.[28] The headquarters of the 173rd Airborne Brigade surmised that the units under Nông Trường 5 could undermine gains using sapper teams to harass GVN assets. Intelligence the brigade acquired offered a reminder that the enemy remained "capable of attacking population centers and allied installations in multi-battalion strength, utilizing the 4th 5th and 6th Bn, 95th NVA Regiment and the 85th LF Bn," with Tuy Hòa City district headquarters and allied airfields the principal targets.[29] The PAVN 95th Regiment remained a threat despite its setbacks during the Tết Offensive.

In operating near APC hamlets, PLAF accentuated imperfections in allied and GVN security, which undermined the public's perception of the GVN. The 173rd Airborne Brigade headquarters noted the waning public confidence in the GVN due to enemy activity, as recalled in its April ORLL:

> The enemy retains his ability to continue interdiction of commu-
> nication lines, mining of primary and secondary routes of travel,
> sabotage operations and small-scale operations against such tar-
> gets as the bridge at CQ 201351, as this is the primary crossing
> across the SONG BA River at TUY HOA City. The enemy can
> also attempt company-sized attacks, reinforced by local forces, on

weakly-defended district headquarters and outposts, as a victory for propaganda means and to harass the Government of the Republic of South Vietnam pacification efforts.[30]

Physical damage inflicted against GVN infrastructure would pale in comparison to the GVN's loss of credibility among the civilians caught between Saigon and Hanoi; the April report underscored the questionable gains of the APC in Phú Yên.

Operations Darby March I and Darby March II

Pacification remained a matter for conventional forces after Operation Bolling. Using search and clear to support the APC, Operation Darby March I commenced on 1 February 1969 with Hawk teams and companies of the 173rd Airborne Brigade maneuvering in the Tuy Hòa Valley. Concurrently, D/16th Armor's mission included securing the ever-troublesome An Nghiệp and the areas encompassing Tuy Hòa North Air Base, while also providing security to the 577th Engineer Battalion as it cleared LTL-7B. Additionally, D/16th Armor served as the rapid reaction force.[31] ROKA's 26th Regiment also participated in Darby March I.[32] Contact between the 4/503rd and its PAVN and PLAF foes was light during Darby March I, with six relatively brief engagements.[33] Albeit limited, contact with the enemy indicated the need for further engagement in the area, so Darby March II began immediately after Darby March I terminated on 8 February.

Operations Darby March I and Darby March II marked a continued allied effort to enhance province security outward from Tuy Hòa City. The 173rd's April report made the explicit point that "these operations were in conjunction with pacification programs in Phú Yên Province."[34] The major difference between these two operations was the South Koreans' involvement; concurrent operations by the ARVN 47th Regiment replaced those of ROKA during Darby March II.[35] Like Operation Bolling, Darby March I and Darby March II amounted to a concerted allied effort to solidate perceived gains in the Tuy Hòa Valley.

Like all of IFFV's preceding operations, Darby March I and Darby March II both linked the destruction of the enemy with rural security. Clear and hold operations and hunter-killer teams called Hawks played a role in both operations. Typically squad-sized, Hawks were tailored to more easily surprise and harass "small enemy squads, couriers, liaison teams, and logistical carrying parties" via night ambushes.[36] Where the larger companies of IFFV's maneuver battalions failed to fully eradicate enemy units, Hawks offered an opportunity to engage

PLAF using a small—and thus more economical—force. Although Hawks demonstrated a new approach to engaging the enemy, their purpose remained the same as that of American units in previous years: the destruction of the enemy. Specialization aside, these teams were still part of a conventional force, the 173rd Airborne Brigade. However, artillery and helicopter gunships afforded Hawks the protection of the quintessential MACV response—firepower.[37]

Darby March II saw more enemy encounters. Most engagements were brief exchanges of gunfire between elements of the 4/503rd and unspecified PAVN and PLAF units. Artillery and helicopter gunships provided the 4/503rd's companies and Hawk teams with an added layer of protection. Over the course of Darby March II, companies of the 4/503rd made fifteen contacts with the enemy, most of which involved a single company or Hawk team engaging with a squad-sized enemy force. That said, on a few occasions, larger battles erupted as the Americans brought heavy firepower to bear.[38]

The first such instance occurred on 16 February at 1635 hours, as artillery and helicopter gunships supported D Company eight kilometers west of Tuy Hòa City. On 21 February at 1700 hours, an estimated ten to twelve enemy soldiers fired on Hawk team 441. Artillery and helicopter gunships provided fire support for the Hawk team, and D Company entered the engagement. In a later firefight on 25 February at 1430 hours, A Company encountered a well-prepared foe; a 173rd Airborne operations report recalled that "17km WNW of Tuy Hoa," a "well fortified" unspecified enemy force of an undetermined size engaged A Company from a distance of 20 meters.[39] As A Company withdrew to call in artillery support, B Company moved in to act as a blocking force. Helicopter gunships also moved in to engage the enemy. At 1740 hours, the Communists broke contact, leaving seven KIAs and ten WIAs in A Company and an unknown number of enemy casualties.[40]

Darby March II minimally affected the enemy. When Darby March II terminated on 3 March 1969, its small allied units backed by heavy firepower had inflicted minor casualties among PAVN and PLAF ranks. Records indicate that U.S. forces claimed twenty-five enemy kills along with the capture of fourteen small arms and a small assortment of other equipment. The rather low number of kills and arms collected suggests that the operation did little to weaken the enemy and thus improve security in the area. The operation's biggest gain was the 1.5 tons of rice that American units captured—a meager dent in the enemy's supply network.[41] Worse, the loss of that rice likely meant that PLAF exerted more pressure on the local population by collecting rice from peasants stocks.

AT28 nevertheless viewed the operations favorably, reporting that the allied units' actions "added greatly to the overall security situation by striking at the enemy's main forces and operating bases (6th Battalion of 95th NVA Division and the 85th Local Force Battalion)."[42] Together, Bolling and the Darby March operations disrupted enemy maneuvers in AO Dân Phú/Wainwright. However, like IFFV's operations of 1966 and 1967, Darby March I and II achieved little in terms of long-term gains against the PAVN 95th Regiment and PLAF local forces. Most significantly, they did not prevent future incursions of PLAF squads into populated areas of the province.

Expanding the Accelerated Pacification Campaign

When inaugurating the APC, CORDS authorities anticipated rapid gains across the RVN. Therefore, as pacification gains in Phú Yên failed to meet the prescribed achievements, higher echelons of CORDS and the GVN mandated revised APC goals for the province. By the end of March, Phú Yên's officials reduced the APC plan from three to two phases. The revised plan targeted forty-four hamlets by 30 June, with another twenty-four hamlets by September's end. By 31 March, twenty-six of these hamlets scored a "C" for security conditions, with twenty-seven receiving an overall "C" status.[43] These gains occurred because the GVN and CORDS had spread security forces out to cover all the target hamlets. With plans revised, GVN influence expanded into target hamlets, albeit based on the ability of conventional forces to retain the tempo of war.[44] On the whole, the people of Phú Yên lived in 268 hamlets by the end of March. Based on security data, HES results for March indicated that 162 hamlets fell under either "A," "B," or "C" ratings—meaning that 87.1 percent of the province's population resided in such hamlets. However, Phú Yên seemed far away from being pacified—thirty-nine hamlets were either "D," "E," or "VC." Another fifty-six hamlets appeared as abandoned on the March HES report—an unsurprising result as Phú Yên's pacification efforts had yet to improve security across much of the province.[45] All of these numbers meant that the APC needed to move faster in Phú Yên to achieve the HES results sought by officials outside the province.

Yet expansion remained an uneasy task as the enemy challenged the APC. Regardless of plans to spread pacification rapidly, the enemy retained agency. Tuy Hòa District reported "an increasing enemy effort during the month," yet nothing of note materialized as PLAF avoided contact with conventional forces.[46] Elsewhere in Phú Yên, however, enemy activity proved more troubling. Sơn Hòa District experienced "four sniping incidents resulting in the death of two PF and two CIDG soldiers. A VC squad ambushed five civilians killing one who was a PF soldier acting as intelligence agents. A minor standoff B-40 rocket attack was conducted against the District Headquarters with negative effect."[47] Yet the most alarming news entailed PLAF interactions with civilians in the more remote areas of Sơn Hòa District. AT28's Sơn Hòa District team noted at the end of March that "food collection efforts continue in the outlying Hamlets and intelligence reports indicate the enemy is passing money to selected villagers in an effort to have them buy foodstuffs for them. The enemy has also offered to give receipts for cattle claiming they are redeemable after they win the war."[48] In Đồng Xuân District, PLAF conducted "an unsuccessful attack against the Subsector Compound on 15 March."[49] In the same district, PLAF local forces successfully mined the railroad on 15 and 27 March.[50] "Enemy initiated activity has increased considerably during the month as indicated by 13 friendly KIA and 20 WIA with only one VC soldier killed" in Tuy An District, according to the AT28 report, which noted a troubling indicator of PLAF activity in that district as "the VC have increased their normal pattern of harassing activity including booby traps, mining, sniping and small scale infiltrations."[51] For the APC, such PLAF activity meant that the Communists could reverse whatever achievements the Americans and South Vietnamese made. Nevertheless, IFFV continued to mount pacification-supporting efforts.

The 173rd Airborne Brigade's relationship with pacification was undeniable. As the bulk of the 173rd focused its attention on Bình Định, a brigade memo emphasized the American battalions' role in the South Vietnamese pacification effort: "As battalion commanders you play the essential role in that you are the principal point of contact between district and ARVN forces and are responsible for integrating and coordinate your battalion's effort with theirs in order to achieve our common goal. How well you do this will in large measure determine the success of the Brigade pacification mission, a mission that is in reality the primary mission of the IFFV."[52] Now the last U.S. maneuver force dedicated to Phú Yên, D/16th Armor's role increased. On 14 April 1969, the 173rd detached D/16th Armor, with the unit becoming the Tuy Hòa Provisional Tank Company, at least on paper.[53] Clearly, IFFV's pacification support continued after Darby March II, albeit significantly reduced.

D/16th Armor proved itself useful to pacification in Phú Yên. Still in AO Dân Phú/Wainwright, the unit operated out of An Nghiệp in concert with the 4th Battalion, ARVN 47th Regiment to advance pacification in the province. Together, the American and South Vietnamese soldiers focused on improving the security conditions of Núi Miếu and Phú Sen hamlets.[54] After Darby March II, D/16th Armor rarely found itself in direct combat with Communist forces; landmine incidents were the typical interaction between the Americans and their foes. These enemy harassment operations resulted in one deadly mining incident. On 26 April at 1850 hours, an American M-113 armored personal carrier detonated a mine, causing three U.S. fatalities. The blast hurtled the ARVN soldiers riding atop the M-113 off the vehicle and onto another mine. The detonation of that mine wounded nine ARVN soldiers. A second M-113 struck a mine as it attempted to assist the first armored personnel carrier, resulting in another five ARVN wounded.[55] Indeed, PLAF mines accounted for more loss of life and equipment damage than the Darby March operations combined.

In terms of HES, the April results revealed several points of concern. Security data indicated that thirty-four hamlets, or 64 percent, remained vulnerable to VCI interference. The same number of hamlets experienced taxation by the enemy. The April HES evaluation put Phú Yên's population at 322,500, with 286,300 residing in hamlets of either "A," "B," or "C" ratings. Such hamlets accounted for 171 out of the province's total of 249, meaning that 68.7 percent of hamlets were largely free of enemy influence. Thirty-six hamlets had either "D" or "E" ratings, or 14.5 percent.[56] Tuy Hòa District had five of those "D"-rated hamlets, which seemed fitting given the reported enemy activity.[57] Two "VC" hamlets in the province further tarnished HES results for April.[58] What happened during April—namely, hamlets' continued exposure to growing enemy activity—appeared as the new normal by the beginning of May. HES figures for May reflected the province's difficulties with accelerated pacification. For May, with the ongoing resettlement of civilians in the middle of a war, figures placed the province's population as having decreased to 318,900, with 300,700 living in "A," "B," or "C" hamlets. Yet data placed 66 percent of the province at risk of VCI control, up 2 percent from the previous month.[59] Although CORDS members could challenge the evaluation's exact numbers produced, the spread of PLAF control was undebatable.

PAVN and PLAF Respond

The mere presence of conventional and territorial forces did not solve Phú Yên's problems. Long-term security issues remained, with IFFV determining that as of 30 April 1969, Communist forces in Phú Yên remained capable of attacking "population centers and Allied installations in reinforced battalion strength."[60] Additionally, the enemy could launch standoff, terrorist, and sapper attacks against areas purportedly under GVN control. Lastly, the report noted that the enemy had the ability to interdict lines of communication.[61] AT28 confirmed such suspicions in its monthly province report for May, acknowledging heightened PAVN and PLAF activity with "the enemy launching his Summer Offensive on the morning of 12 May. During this offensive the enemy succeeded in hitting several locations with attacks by fire, and in making several small ground probes against friendly outposts, all of which were successfully repulsed."[62] Failure, noted AT28, befell PAVN because "while the enemy has increased his troop level in Phú Yên it would appear from the contacts made and from his lack of ability to mass and coordinate for any large scale offensive that the present replacements are not of the calibre of previous NVA forces."[63] Yet the enemy's shortcomings were short-lived; PAVN's May Offensive continued, and later in June PLAF embarked on its own campaign.

Sufficient security for villages remained fleeting, as substantiated in a monthly province report for June. This report confirmed that, despite a few engagements in the Tuy Hòa Valley, the remaining elements of the PAVN 95th Regiment— recently redesignated the PAVN 10th Regiment—actively avoided combat. The report suggested that PAVN were "training, regrouping and perhaps also deliberately economizing their forces for the time being."[64] The same report stated that "enemy strength is believed to be unchanged, or perhaps somewhat greater than a month ago."[65] The PAVN 10th Regiment's potential posture in Phú Yên amounted to just the 6th Battalion, which PAVN intended to relocate with the rest of the regiment to the Mekong Delta.[66] Lack of food access forced that decision, with PLAF set on intensifying efforts to regain access to the bounty of the Tuy Hòa Valley. To that end, PLAF kept pressure on pacification.

PLAF civilian abductions undermined any notion of improved security in Phú Yên. In June, PLAF cells abducted sixty-three South Vietnamese civilians—a massive increase from the five taken in May. "About 90% of the abductees were returned after less than two days, following indoctrination," AT28 noted, but the report also said that "the principal reason why the enemy manages to spirit these persons out of the hamlets untouched is that witnesses including local officials fear that a tactical response will cause injury or death to the abductees."[67] Although AT28 claimed that there was "still no evidence of a systematic enemy campaign against the 1969 target hamlets," the American advisory mission had the first indicator of a prolonged enemy abduction campaign.[68]

As PAVN's May Offensive sputtered in MR2, it nevertheless ensured that conventional warfare remained on the minds of CORDS personnel in Phú Yên. In a report dated 17 May 1969, the senior operations advisor for AT28,

Maj. Francis M. Williams, wrote that due to enemy activity, all U.S. and South Vietnamese personnel were on alert and prepared for attacks by the enemy. Williams stated that "commanders at all levels have been reminded that this offensive provides an excellent opportunity to engage and defeat possible large enemy forces."[69] Compared with the rest of the country, the May Offensive was relatively subdued in Phú Yên. Engle reported that "May was perhaps the best month in the history of pacification in Phu Yen Province,"[70] adding that "overall enemy activity was somewhat lower, and friendly forces gave a good account of themselves in the engagements that did take place. In most of the province, security improved noticeably."[71]

The APC rapidly spread GVN influence beyond Tuy Hòa City to a fault. Each month brought new numbers reflecting ever-improving security conditions in target hamlet areas. Monthly progress reports for May, June, and July extolled pacification gains and weakening enemy activity. AT28 personnel pointed to rising HES scores and the number of resettled refugees as evidence of pacification's success. In the May province report, Engle cited the return of "several thousand more displaced persons to their homes" and "somewhat lower" enemy activity as success indicators. Insofar as thirty-five of forty-four target APC hamlets earned "relatively secure status," improved HES numbers suggested that target APC hamlets were meeting prescribed security goals.[72] Adding to the improved security scores thousands of peasants returning to such hamlets, Phú Yên's hinterlands appeared to finally fall under GVN control. Out of a reported province population of 318,000 at the end of May, HES placed 300,700 inhabitants, or 94.3 percent of the population, in hamlets with a rating of "A," "B," or "C." That left 12,900 people, or 4 percent, in "D" or "E" hamlets, with another 5,300, or 1.7 percent, in "VC" hamlets. However, HES analysis revealed the perilous security predicament in Phú Yên—66 percent of the province's hamlets remained vulnerable to VCI. The presence of VCI meant that the NLF could exploit any security shortcomings and inject influence into targeted hamlets—thereby reversing the APC's gains.[73]

The rapidity with which the APC placed new hamlets under GVN governance raised questions about the permanence of their "secure" status. That the APC incurred measurable gains overlooks the program's ramifications on Phú Yên's security forces. The APC never removed the threat posed by PAVN and PLAF, nor was it ever supposed to. Indeed, PLAF frequented hamlets despite IFFV operations to advance the APC. As soon as conventional units ended operations, the enemy moved back into contested areas. The lack of large-scale enemy activity therefore reflected more of a PAVN and PLAF effort to avoid battle than a rollback of their influence caused by the APC. The all-but-guaranteed end of the American War meant preparing the battlefield for PLAF's struggle against Saigon. Understanding the pressing need for the Americans' removal of combat forces, PLAF recognized Vietnamization as the mechanism through which to reverse Saigon's gains. To PLAF, the subtraction of American maneuver battalions "would aggravate the present decaying situation of the Puppet troops and Puppet Government, and aggravate the contradictions between the U.S. and RVN, and among the various factions and groups in the Puppet Government."[74] No doubt PLAF keenly understood Vietnamization's implications for pacification's long-term durability. Indeed, as the pressure to exercise self-reliance mounted, province officials faced fighting IFFV's war of maneuver, yet without the overwhelming power projected with relative ease by IFFV. The further Vietnamization progressed, the more conditions favored PLAF.

Rather than wait for the U.S. to complete Vietnamization, the Communists actively sought to repeal accelerated pacification. For the North Vietnamese, Phú Yên fell under Nông Trường 5, which itself existed under direct control of Hanoi—the implication being that rather than take orders from COSVN's B2 Front, Communist entities in Phú Yên operated on orders expressly from Hanoi. Communist forces in Phú Yên had already begun challenging the APC in June, prior to the July 1969 release of COSVN's Resolution 9.[75] What remains unclear is Resolution 9's effect in Phú Yên. The Politburo in Hanoi had already reduced COSVN to surrogate status—meaning that southern Communists took orders from Lê Duẩn. Perhaps, then, Nông Trường 5 tested Hanoi's post-Tết strategy in Phú Yên before disseminating official guidance to COSVN.

Signs of APC success proved deceptive by June, as small PAVN and PLAF elements entered villages in the Tuy Hòa Valley. Thereafter, Phú Yên's security status appeared anything but improved. A June province report noted that the enemy did not deploy all the soldiers at its disposal. Rather, "the size of enemy forces that intelligence indicates to be present in the mountainous base areas . . . would suggest that quite a substantial proportion are not presently engaged in operations."[76] The PAVN 10th Regiment had elements of two battalions operating in the Tuy Hòa Valley, while, according to the report, "other large units" regrouped. Additionally, "enemy strength is believed to be unchanged, or perhaps somewhat greater than a month ago."[77] Essentially, allied efforts to support pacification had done nothing to improve the province's long-term security.

COSVN adapted its strategy to confront U.S. withdrawal, the APC included. Resolution 9 established how COSVN understood the war as the Americans sought quick disengagement. Such actions prompted COSVN to term the shift in

U.S. strategy as "passive" because the APC, despite initially calling for the rapid acquisition of target hamlets, ultimately surrendered the offensive to a posture of securing and holding target hamlets.[78] To offset the speed of CORDS's intensified pacification effort, COSVN sought to use the very principle of the APC—the quick spread of physical control of hamlets—against the GVN. As Saigon spread its forces to defend more communities, COSVN issued Resolution 9 in July 1969, which tasked PLAF with using the APC against the allies. Fully cognizant of Vietnamization, the resolution entailed "defeat[ing] the enemy's 'clear and hold' and 'accelerated pacification' strategies, foil[ing] the enemy's plot to end the war in a strong position and 'de-Americanize' the war."[79] Rather than the final drive to defeat COSVN with the rapid expansion of pacification, the APC provided the Communists with the opportunity to reassert itself.

COSVN's Resolution 9 helped explain why the war raged in some provinces, yet seemed to disappear in others. At the national level, Resolution 9 called for PLAF to keep pressure on key provinces so that forces could gain influence in quieter ones: "We will on one hand strive to annihilate, decimate and hold up a large U.S.-puppet force on the urban battlefront while on the other hand we will stretch enemy forces over the rural and mountainous battlefronts."[80] For Phú Yên, events in Bình Định mattered profoundly. As PAVN and PLAF created havoc across Bình Định, IFFV's mobile ground assets left Phú Yên for Bình Định, relieving the pressure on PLAF in Phú Yên. Within Phú Yên, the fast pace of the APC guaranteed gaps in security coverage, presenting PLAF with more opportunities to strike where allied forces were not.[81]

On 16 July, IFFV removed what was left of its last unit in Phú Yên, D/16th Armor, and rejoined it with the rest of the 173rd Airborne Brigade in Bình Định.[82] That force's removal from Phú Yên signaled increasing dependency on the RF/PF to cover all security issues, and the beginning of the end of U.S. interest in pacification in that troubled province. In his August report, Engle noted that "pullouts have been sudden, usually causing panic on the part of the people living in the remoter areas and temporary shifting of hundreds of homes back toward Tuy Hoa City."[83] The mere presence of conventional forces, particularly mobile ones, had a strong physical and psychological effect on pacification.

By August in Phú Yên, AT28 deemed the enemy's May Offensive a failure. "For the first time ever, an enemy offensive achieved practically nothing in Tuy Hoa Valley and Tuy Hoa City, which are always prime objectives. There is still a respectable number of enemy in the extensive mountainous areas of the Province."[84] American advisors likely did not know about Hanoi's Resolution 9. Thus, that view meant that American advisors downplayed enemy activity in the Tuy Hòa Valley during the offensive. Allied containment of PAVN and PLAF happened because the enemy chose to remain relatively quiet in Phú Yên. Moreover, the spontaneous—and often purely political—movements of ARVN battalions in and out of Phú Yên lessened the blow of the failed May Offensive on PAVN and PLAF cells. From its mountain sanctuaries, Communist cells shifted toward small-unit actions and the direct targeting of individuals and hamlets.

The Pressures of HES

A renewed emphasis on producing improved HES scores resonated differently throughout CORDS. At the province level, advisors recognized that progress occurred slowly, but at the corps headquarters, personnel expected noticeable—if not rapid—advancements with each month. Based on security data, the August HES evaluation from analysts at CORDS's corps headquarters at Nha Trang irked AT28. Aware that improving provincial security remained an ongoing process, AT28 found the gist of the August HES evaluation, absent any discernible improvements to security, comical if not insulting. In the words of one team member, "according to the HES analyst, Phu Yen has made very little, if any, progress since 31 Jan 69 in education, VC taxation, and medical facilities."[85] That assessment omitted that "30% of hamlets didn't even exist in March!"[86] Lt. Col. Thomas A. Sievers, Phú Yên's DPSA, exchanged comments with Engle on the same subject. Sievers complained how Nha Trang informed AT28 on HES progress using the very data collected by Sievers and his fellow advisors. He bemoaned to Engle, "someone distant and hemmed is using your facts to tell you how you are doing."[87] In response, Engle's explained that "they play back stuff to us all the time + present it as a discovery of theirs + a favor to us."[88] Sievers's and Engle's sentiments were warranted, as HES data spoke more to broad trends than to immediate implications for individual hamlets. Sievers and Engle undoubtably understood the realities of spreading pacification to hamlets—daily changes in security most of all, knowledge that could be acquired without studying HES metrics. Nevertheless, HES analysts identified—and made Nha Trang aware of—a truth AT28 already knew: that Phú Yên's security remained wanting.

CORDS's attention on Phú Yên was warranted. The CORDS Pacification Study Group conducted a field survey of Hòa Phong, a village in Hiếu Xương District, from 25 August to 4 September. The resettlement of the village (completed four to nine months prior depending on the specific hamlet), demographic factors, and average HES rankings of "B's" and "C's" made Hòa Phong representative in American eyes. CORDS therefore used the village to assess the quality of security provided by local RF, PF, and the People's Self-Defense Force (PSDF), the formal name for the South Vietnamese village militia forces. Each of the village's six hamlets—Lương Phước (HES-rated "C"), Tân Mỹ (HES-rated "C"), Mỹ Thạnh Tây (HES-rated "B"), Mỹ Thạnh Trung (HES-rated "B"), Mỹ Thạnh Đông (HES-rated "C"), and Phước Thạnh (HES-rated "C")—experienced PLAF activity, regardless of HES security scores. A ROKA company constituted the stable source of security in Hòa Phong, holding two hills near the middle of the village. That force, however, departed after the CORDS study was completed. The study concluded "that the enemy can enter any hamlet in Hoa Phong at nearly anytime he chooses with near impunity."[89] Significant caveats included the areas under ROKA control as being beyond PLAF's ability to take, and that PLAF had no need to seize the village "since he comes and goes pretty much at will and the area serves well for support purposes. To change his tactics in any way that might run the people out of the village would be tantamount to 'Killing the goose that lays golden eggs.'"[90] Intelligence placed anywhere from a company-sized to a platoon-sized PLAF group as completing missions in the village.[91] If anything, Hòa Phong represented a textbook example of a village undergoing PLAF pacification efforts.

Hòa Phong placed the APC in the poorest light. Yet instead of reexamining the processes behind Vietnamization, CORDS placed blame on the province's Territorial Forces—the RF and PF. Paradoxically, after reading the report, Colby wrote that "when we started the APC we said that our objective was to expand government authority 'thin and fast.' It is quite apparent that is exactly what occurred. The government presence in this area is a thin veneer indeed."[92] Both CORDS and MACV saw the Hòa Phong study as a means of applying more pressure on the provincial government. Out of shame, CORDS and MACV envisioned local officials somehow better embracing and executing President Nguyễn Văn Thiệu's upcoming plan to expand pacification outward from villages.[93] As events in Phú Yên demonstrated, however, a village system approach to pacification existed solely as an illusion.

Phú Yên's territorial security depended on the presence of quality conventional forces. Indeed, the presence of allied units made pacification possible. When operating in the Tuy Hòa Valley, American troops had improved security conditions, albeit temporarily. With U.S. Army units no longer based in the province, South Vietnamese and South Korean soldiers were a valuable source of stability—especially so since ARVN and ROKA forces constituted the second layer of defense around Tuy Hòa City. The ARVN 47th Regiment helped instill confidence among the population of Tuy Hòa District, the regiment's AO. Still, its effect on the district lasted only as long as the ARVN troops executed operations. The four battalions of the 47th Regiment never stayed on deployment for long, at times leaving their screening positions in the Tuy Hòa Valley after just a few days and without notice to CORDS officials. In September, ARVN's creation of the 220 Mobile Task Force removed two battalions of the 47th Regiment from Phú Yên, both of which were safeguarding APC target hamlets in the Tuy Hòa Valley. Engle noted that the ensuing disruption entailed "leaving vital parts of the valley exposed to the principal enemy forces in Phu Yen. There was no adequate time to readjust before a third ARVN battalion was suddenly pulled out of the Valley and airlifted to Phu Bon."[94] A solution, he noted, emerged in the form of better coordination between II Corps and the province chief, wherein the latter maintained operational control of the two remaining battalions in Phú Yên.[95]

PLAF's undermining of pacification continued throughout 1969. To lull observers into perceiving Communist activity as waning in Phú Yên, and thus adhere to Resolution 9, PLAF challenged pacification under the veil of darkness. The night of 12 September epitomized the PLAF response to accelerated pacification. In the all-important Tuy Hòa Valley, PLAF dealt a blow to the APC and the perception that the GVN could provide security when PLAF raided target hamlets. That night, PLAF demolished sixty-five homes in Ngọc Đồng hamlet and absconded with approximately eighty sheets of roofing. AT28 district team members noted that no one witnessed PLAF activity as "the RD team was staying in nearby Hanh Lam and the people, as usual, were not staying in their hamlet."[96] On the same night, a PLAF party entered Đông Phước hamlet, setting the hamlet office's document repository afire. The following night, PLAF torched a building in Đông Bình hamlet, one used by the RD Cadre.[97] As on the previous night, PLAF again escaped unseen. District advisors foresaw an increase in enemy activity because of the upcoming rice harvest "and the dark phase of the moon."[98] Thus, the events on the nights of 12 and 13 September presaged that worse lay in store for the province. If the APC was working, then hard evidence remained scarce in the Tuy Hòa Valley.

October brought with it the Tuy Hòa Valley's focus on the rice harvest. While AT28's team in Tuy Hòa District assisted with the successful relocation of Ninh Tịnh hamlet to the new Thọ Vực hamlet, visions of Ngọc Đồng likely filled the district advisors' minds. As province officials relocated South Vietnamese civilians from old to new, purportedly more secure hamlets, the GVN's timing proved poor as many peasants instead devoted to themselves to the rice harvest.

A district report noted that despite dry weather—ideal conditions for building— Ngọc Đồng "nonetheless will probably have to be considered a 'failed hamlet' as of October 31."[99] Instead of focusing on moving to a new hamlet, the coming monsoon meant families dedicated themselves to their livelihood—the rice harvest. A temporary bridge connected Ngọc Đồng with the province so long as monsoon rains did not elevate water levels. Aside from Ngọc Đồng, three other district hamlets lacked permanent bridges, which left them possible targets for Communist offers of assistance.[100]

AT28 considered the westernmost reaches of the Tuy Hòa Valley "perilous."[101] That tract of the district experienced both GVN and NLF pacification attempts. As American and South Vietnamese authorities sought to spread Saigon's control farther beyond the view of Tuy Hòa City, PLAF pushed back at the local level. *Mũi công tác*, or operations spearhead, heralded the beginning of the NLF interfacing in areas seen by local party officials as being under Saigon's control. Called "Action Arrows" by the Americans, this cadre of civilian and military personnel had a fluid composition of eight to fifteen members. Depending on the mission, an Action Arrow team included VCI members of various specialties, PLAF guerrillas and sappers, and medical personnel. Action Arrows threatened GVN control by gathering intelligence on the disposition of South Vietnamese military and security forces; identifying the individuals working covertly or overtly for Saigon; persuading families to have their loved ones stop working for the GVN; and collecting supplies purchased by other cadres on the open market.[102] In the western fringe of the Tuy Hòa Valley, Action Arrow sappers targeted allied forces while proselytizing to recruit new agents.[103]

Lullaby

Monsoon rains, beginning in October, curtailed allied activity in Phú Yên. Whatever the security condition beforehand, it remained largely the same on paper because the poor weather prevented observation. In Tuy Hòa District, HES reported "no startling changes this month. Many hamlets are still inaccessible due to the excessive rains, periodically during the month."[104] By the end of October, however, HES was providing peculiar data on Tuy Hòa District, placing the entire district population as living in either "A," "B," or "C" hamlets—meaning that all fifty-four reported hamlets either rested firmly or adequately under Saigon's control. Yet 78 percent, or thirty-nine, of the hamlets exhibited signs of vulnerability to VCI. Thirty hamlets, or 70 percent, were under enemy taxation.[105] These numbers revealed that high HES rankings did not necessarily equate to successful completion of pacification, as acquiring better HES results proved easier than keeping them. Indeed, PLAF remained able to adversely affect hamlet security. Timing could not have been worse for such a mind-set, as deteriorating weather conditions precluded any dedicated effort to sustain any momentum generated under the APC.

PLAF remained active despite the monsoon. In early November, a PLAF team destroyed the bridge at Qui Hậu in Tuy Hòa District "despite good intelligence"; AT28 reported that "the bridge was left completely unguarded. The VC were able to work on it without interference and destroy it."[106] Elsewhere in Tuy Hòa District, PLAF executed "squad size skirmishes" against ARVN and ROKA forces near the infamous Base Area 236. In other instances, PLAF deliberately targeted RF units—at Quan Triều hamlet against RF 136, then against the district's reconnaissance company RF 310, and lastly the ambushing of two RF/PF squads at Cẩm Thạch. RF 151, however, apprehended two VCI at Minh Đức—Huyền Thanh Vận, the acting secretary of the Tuy Hòa City People's Revolutionary Party and deputy chairman of the Tuy Hòa City current affairs committee; and Lê Bá Nam, a member of the security section. Huyền Thanh Vận's capture resulted in intelligence that four companies of the 96th Local Force Battalion and the 202 Sapper Company intended to strike Tuy Hòa North Air Base, AT28's compound, and the GVN's province headquarters; Huyền Thanh Vận surmised that his capture spelt an end to such plans.[107] Yet this South Vietnamese victory over VCI did not impede PLAF. As November gave way to December, the war for Phú Yên entered an irreversible stage: the Americans—even shorter on time because of Vietnamization—did not yet recognize this reality. Phú Yên remained vulnerable to NLF influence and at risk of reverting to security conditions akin to those before the IFFV campaigns began.

Monsoon rains alone inhibited any pacification progress in November. Much to AT28's dismay, "the pace of pacification progress in Phú Yên slowed still further in November."[108] HES data based on security reflects this lack of progress, as Phú Yên went from the eighteenth-most secure province in October to the nineteenth in November.[109] A cause of concern, Phú Yên's ten "D"/"E" hamlets meant NLF influence in Đồng Xuân and Tuy An. Elsewhere in the province, HES indicated that the population lived in hamlets with either "A," "B," or "C" ratings.[110] However, HES could not account for the weather and the ensuing complacency. Military operations revealed as much: "The heavy almost continuous rains not only kept the ROKs from conducting operations in the mountainous enemy base areas . . . but gave RF/PF commanders a pretext, which the Province and

District Chiefs seemed to consider sufficient, to keep under cover at night and not maintain all their ambushes."[111]

The poor weather certainly helped to explain slowed security improvement. Yet AT28 perceived that province officials' acceptance of earlier gains as permanent was the actual culprit. Engle blamed the province chief, Col. Nguyễn Văn Ba, for the slackened interest in improving pacification:

> But again, as in October, the decisive factor in stalling progress was the euphoria and overconfidence of the Province Chief, who in recent months has been living in an imaginary world. The temper of the Province and District administrations during November was one of contentment, self-congratulation and relaxation. The leadership coasted the earlier gains, and were reassured by the continued shower of compliments from Saigon and Pleiku, in part the result of false reports of achievement that they themselves sent to higher headquarters.[112]

Indeed, during a visit to Phú Yên, Prime Minister Trần Thiện Khiêm "smothered everyone with praise." In doing so, province officials regarded pacification as satisfactory if not complete.[113] Yet in Sơn Hòa District, civilians reported taxation by PLAF agents. The DSA, Maj. Robert M. Tarbet, explained pacification progress as "slow but present"—not the most convincing language one would expect after months of the APC.[114] What AT28 disclosed in its reports marked the beginning of increased scrutiny of the province administration. Perceived leadership issues aside, the American advisors' criticism neglected the South Vietnamese's participation in a form of pacification forced on them. Nevertheless, the monsoon reaffixed focus on Tuy Hòa District—where, going forward, events mattered more than ever before. Seen initially as a temporary halt of pacification, the monsoon coincided with increasing PLAF activity geared toward reversing Saigon's gains in the Tuy Hòa Valley.

The nadir for security happened in December, with AT28 bemoaning "a further slump in Pacification efforts during the month." Yet this drop did not proffer surprise: "Pacification at this time of the year when most programs are inactive is practically synonymous with security, which reached a low point just before the holidays as a result of enemy successes in Tuy An District." In that district, however, PLAF overran RF Company 735 and captured its weapons and equipment—an act PLAF would replicate against other RF units in 1970.[115] Nevertheless, true to form, AT28 retained some optimism as the year ended.

Unaware of PLAF's strategy to exploit Vietnamization, AT28 looked to the back-and-forth nature of security in the province for comfort. The advisory effort expressed optimism that security would now naturally trend upward away from further deterioration: "It is felt that the recent reversals in Pacification in Phu Yen are beginning to 'bottom out.'"[116] For evidence, the report stated that "the worst weather is believed to be over and more offensive operations should be forthcoming," along with heightened activity by South Korean and South Vietnamese troops and a decrease in oil theft from the Vũng Rô-to-Phú Hiệp pipeline.[117] Most significantly, "the attitude of Province officials has been considerably sharpened and focused regarding security. They now acknowledge that recent regressions have not been a difference of opinions on HES rankings but rather due to enemy activity. They are presently taking steps to correct the situation."[118] These developments, AT28 argued, permitted the South Vietnamese and their American advisors to concentrate more on pacification's developmental aspects.[119] Vietnamization, however, played into PLAF's intention, as events in 1970 would demonstrate.

Vietnamization and the APC did not advance pacification in Phú Yên in 1969. American advisors noted that PLAF successfully entered hamlets as it pushed back against accelerated pacification. PLAF forays into the purportedly secure areas of Tuy Hòa District suggested that the province had a long way to go before being pacified. Most strikingly, these troubling occurrences transpired alongside Vietnamization in 1969, which drove pacification forward while simultaneously reducing MACV's footprint in the RVN. The removal of U.S. forces—the vanguards of pacification—meant that Phú Yên would be pacified in name only. Years of conventional warfare fostered the view that once IFFV's units disappeared, so too did the enemy's chances for victory in the province. Problems in 1969 directly contributed the explosion of troubles that plagued Phú Yên in 1970. For that reason, the APC's perceived advancement masked the underlying issues in pacification—ones that came to the fore in early 1970. The toughest year for allied forces in the province since days of the Việt Minh occurred in 1970, because of conditions born in 1969. Unbeknownst to the Americans, their war in Phú Yên effectively ended with the November monsoon rains.

7

The Province That "Went to Sleep"

The Advisory Crisis, 1970

/ T he Vietcong have reappeared with a vengeance in central Vietnam's Phu
Yen Province," Robert G. Kaiser informed readers of the *Washington
Post* in an 18 March 1970 article.[1] "The Communists' sudden revival has been
simple, inexpensive and dramatic. Some Americans here think they may be
experimenting with a new form of protracted war in Phu Yen."[2] Its plan was
cleverly simple, PLAF struck at the heart of pacification: the people. PLAF's
response included an abduction campaign so effective that it prompted active
concealment of intelligence by Phú Yên's province administration. The decision
on the GVN province leadership's part reflected a state of accommodation
with PLAF. Whereas the Americans and South Koreans planned to depart Phú
Yên, PLAF were not leaving—a reality that left the province chief and his staff
with difficult choices. Accommodation initially caused the Advisory Crisis, a
dispute between American advisors and local South Vietnamese officials over
the latter's concealing abductions and lackluster combatting of PLAF military
activity. By March, the dispute turned into a major diplomatic issue once details
reached higher-level authorities. That momentous episode of the war revealed
Vietnamization and the Accelerated Pacification Campaign as facades, and
marked the successful countering of pacification by Hanoi. The resolution to the
crisis, which amounted to personnel changes and retraining of province security
forces, did not remedy the underlying problem that Vietnamization weakened
Saigon's ability to sustain pacification long-term.

While the war quieted down across much of the RVN, it did not in Phú
Yên. Speaking at the 1970 Annual Meeting of the American Political Science
Association, Robert Komer—now a RAND consultant and no longer head of

CORDS—noted that military forces provided "sustained territorial security," which was the "indispensable first stage of pacification."[3] He added that previous efforts to pacify the countryside had suffered from the absence of "adequate security resources," and asserted that the war was *largely localized* by 1970 across the RVN.[4] For thirty-three provinces, the intensity of the war had declined. The big-unit war continued in the sparsely inhabited regions of South Vietnam, while PLAF units conducted terrorism in select population areas. For eleven provinces—Phú Yên included—"insurgency-type activity or VC incursions into populated areas" still typified the nature of the conflict.[5] Although events across Phú Yên demonstrated the APC's failure, incidents in Tuy Hòa and Hiếu Xương districts especially raised concerns over the lasting viability of security in the province. By 1970, PLAF activity had reached the highest levels post-1968 as the Communists countered the GVN's influence in the province's villages.

What Komer spoke of, MACV had monitored throughout South Vietnam during the first two weeks of January 1970. "The spectre of 1954–55 has reared its head again in Phu Yen Province," warned a Strategic Research and Analysis (SRA) Division intelligence report.[6] The NLF sought to use Phú Yên much like its Việt Minh predecessors had by establishing the province as a nexus of political power in the region. With a long-term focus, the NLF formed a new cadre around "regroupees," whom it tasked with recruiting Phú Yên's youth for training in North Vietnam. Meanwhile, the VCI within Phú Yên had established a "military proselytizing school" in Sơn Hòa District to cultivate the next generation of GVN foes.[7] The SRA report warned that Hanoi expected these future cadres to "wear down the ARVN's strength thereby negating the positive successes of the Vietnamization and pacification programs."[8] In addition to developing new cadres, three PAVN battalions operated in Phú Yên. Most alarmingly, the report claimed that the NLF's proselytizing school in Sơn Hòa District had "58 enemy cadre and candidates," all of which were "ARVN soldiers, officers, and GVN district and village administrative cadre who have rallied to the VC ranks, some as early as 1963."[9] The province appeared dangerously close to becoming one large NLF liberated zone.

The sense that Tuy Hòa City existed in a world separate from the rest of the province—and that of accelerated pacification—permeated the discourse. Accustomed to *tâche d'huile*, GVN officials understood pacification as a slow, methodical process. Yet as the monsoon rains evaporated, the oil spot, too, dried up. The Americans, now imbued with the task of completing pacification as quickly as possible—thereby, and rather ironically, voiding the whole

Tuy Hòa City during a flood in 1970 with the Sông Đà Rằng
running left to right. Núi Chấp Chài is to the upper left.
Courtesy of Steve Dike, Advisory Team 28.

premise—found themselves at odds with GVN officials comfortable with unhur-
ried pacification advancement. Province leadership in Phú Yên, too, accepted
the continued presence of the enemy. "Less energy has been expended by GVN
officials during the last three or four months than in any period since 1967,"
PSA Engle reported. "The general attitude is that by last September the 1969
program was completed to a degree acceptable to Pleiku and Saigon, and that
the 1970 program does not have to be launched until after the beginning of the
lunar new year."[10] The promotion of an undisclosed number of Sông Cầu District
hamlets to "B" status offered the Americans a glimmer of progress. Efforts of
the 2/54 RF Group also provided some cause for optimism as it operated in the
forbidding Kỳ Lộ Valley—an area the ROKA needed considerable prodding to
sweep.[11] Yet the ROKA did operate readily in other mountains closer to Tuy Hòa
City "to the benefit of the populated areas of the valleys."[12] One such operation
entailed ROKA, with ARVN and RF/PF elements, patrolling the mountains
in Hiếu Xương District.[13] Otherwise, Phú Yên began the new year fast asleep.

A Sleepy Province

Pacification in 1970 began with a murmur in the districts of Tuy An and Tuy
Hòa. AT28 noted that six hamlets in the province held an HES/70 rating of "D,"

The Advisory Team 28 compound's main entrance with
Núi Chấp Chài in the background, circa 1970.
Courtesy of Steve Dike, Advisory Team 28.

meaning they were perilously close to becoming PLAF domain. In Tuy An
District, two hamlets hardly earned "C" ratings, while two hamlets in Tuy Hòa
District reverted to "D" status. More alarming than GVN contentment with
what the Americans saw as painfully slow progress, "slippage was mainly
due to enemy surprise clobbering of sleepy RF/PF outposts."[14] Not until April
would American advisors glean the ramifications of such overt PLAF activity.
"The new year seems to have started at the same snails [*sic*] pace with which
1969 ended," began the first district report of the year. While the 1st, 3rd,
and 4th battalions of the ARVN 47th Regiment patrolled the district, only
PLAF obtained positive results. "Despite the presence of friendly elements,
the enemy continue to move throughout Tuy Hoa Valley, indoctrinating and
taxing the populous," Phú Yên DSA Maj. Eugene E. Fluke wrote in the same
district report.[15] What Fluke hit upon marked the onset of turmoil for his
district in the year that defined pacification in Phú Yên. Trouble also existed
outside of Tuy Hòa District. For example, Đồng Xuân District experienced
a PLAF-controlled war: for January, events included minings of the railroad
that transited the district and continued PLAF attempts to collect rice from
local farmers.[16]

Security persisted as the main source of concern for Tuy Hòa District throughout 1970. That year, Tết marked a particularly active period for PLAF local forces in the province. A semimonthly report furnished by Tuy Hòa DSA Capt. Lewis R. Williams referred to the security situation as "insubstantial and worm-holed." Despite warning of PLAF movement in the district, local RF/PF forces failed to prevent PLAF from firing mortars on allied buildings at Tuy Hòa North Air Base. The report indicated that PLAF dictated the tempo of activity, adding that "the security situation in Tuy Hoa District is much more dependent on what the VC choose to do or not do—rather than what the local forces can prevent." Consequently, the report called for the reevaluation of the district's hamlets, noting that "it is clear that many rural people may in fact not live in relative security."[17] The report also addressed the contact between PLAF and the RF/PF: an aggressive PLAF force initiated nine of twelve contacts, two of which the report called "well coordinated." The presence of seven crew-served weapons during these engagements substantiated that claim. Five mining incidents along routes LTL-7B and QL-1, as well as the assassination of nine civilians by the enemy, indicated a particularly active PLAF during this reporting period.[18] Moreover, PLAF had clearly recovered from losses incurred during the war's earlier phases.

To the west of Tuy Hòa District, and on the other side of enemy Base Area 236, an upswing in enemy activity threatened the GVN presence in Sơn Hòa District. Sơn Hòa DSA Capt. Richard J. Malvesti reported that "enemy activity during this report period was greater than during any equal period over the past nine months."[19] Both PAVN and PLAF were on the prowl along the border of Sơn Hòa and Tuy Hòa districts. On 1 February, a company-sized PAVN detachment assaulted the Sơn Hòa District dispensary. Ten days later, 11 February, a PLAF squad infiltrated Vân Hòa, a hamlet that straddled the border between the two districts. The infiltrators raised a PLAF flag and "left a note stating they could attack anywhere in the district and easily capture district headquarters."[20] The report also noted "numerous sightings of VC/NVA units both north and south of the river by agents and friendly units."[21] Undoubtedly, the enemy maneuvered to quarantine the GVN presence in Củng Sơn, the Sơn Hòa District capital.

Keeping Củng Sơn linked to the outside world proved to be no easy task for the Americans. As evidenced by the mining of LTL-7B, the link between Củng Sơn and Tuy Hòa City, PLAF units exercised considerable freedom of movement in Sơn Hòa District—a point of great propaganda value for PLAF. "In addition, a report was received from a VC relative in Thanh Binh Hamlet that the VC boasted of overrunning the district in February, occupying it for 24 hours, and returning the people to their old hamlet areas," Malvesti stated in his report.[22] While a little overstated, in that PLAF had not entered Củng Sơn, PLAF were indeed "free to roam the district at will to within 2 kilometers of the populated area."[23] Nevertheless, PLAF inched closer to the district capital owing to the placement of local defenses. On 5 February, the U.S. Army's C Battery, 6/32 Artillery left Củng Sơn for Tuy Hòa City and its eventual departure from the province. To offset this substantial loss of firepower in the district, two 155mm howitzers from the ARVN 22nd Division occupied the firebase vacated by the previous American artillery unit. "Why these new howitzers occupied the old fire base is a puzzle for all personnel in the district," Malvesti wrote, elaborating as follows:

> For months before this move was made, the District Chief, RF Group Commander, and US Advisors in the district recommended that the ARVN occupy the RF Group Camp. This was the most secure base in the district and would allow for excellent coordination and economy of forces. By occupying the old fire base, however, the RF Group has been forced to deploy one company (-) to protect them. This means that all RF Companies in the district are now tied down to defense of base camps and the district headquarters. There are no company elements free to conduct offensive operations! This is a most dangerous situation and a definite regression from the plan to get as many units out on operations as possible.[24]

Enemy movement so close to the district capital and the RF troops' inability to mount offensive operations did not bode well for pacification in Sơn Hòa District.

February wore on, and conditions in Tuy Hòa District remained tenuous. Fluke summarized the situation best: "In the city all was well; in the country-side, however, the VC were able to take advantage of the GVN's weakness and undermine the people's confidence in the government's ability and will to react and protect them." Describing the GVN's security as "more sieve than shield," Fluke noted that over the course of five days, PLAF had abducted 124 civilians and marched them to the mountains without making any contact with allied or local defense forces.[25] Adjacent to Kaiser's article on Phú Yên's abduction dilemma, the *Washington Post* ran interviews with two abductees taken during February. Nguyễn Cao recounted how PLAF had entered his hamlet, Phong Niên, in the middle of the night on 10 February, announcing their presence with bullhorns. PLAF took him and other inhabitants to the mountains for indoctrination. While under PLAF supervision, he admitted to working for the GVN, something his abductors said they appreciated since "they knew he had to work to stay alive. But they told him to beware. They had already shown how easily they could enter his hamlet."[26] Despite being told to stop working for the GVN, he continued to work for the Saigon government—one he referred to with Communist phrasing as being excessively cruel, or "*ác ôn*."[27] Another abductee, a woman named Đỗ Thị Non, recalled a similar experience. She, too, found herself marched from her hamlet of Mỹ Hòa to the mountains—a journey she figured took all night and much of the next day—and underwent indoctrination. Her indoctrination featured instructions "that in the future they should give the Vietcong tax collector whatever he requested."[28] When asked during her interview with Kaiser if she and her friends would pay taxes to PLAF the next time they came around, she remarked "yes . . . they would."[29] Although just two examples of the South Vietnamese perspective of the abduction situation at the hamlet level, those experiences demonstrated PLAF's simple yet effective means of controlling the population in Phú Yên. Significantly, too, to undercut Saigon's sway in contested space, PLAF just needed peasants not to pick a side in 1970; being caught in the middle was sufficient to weaken pacification.

Future abductions seemed inevitable. The hamlets of Mỹ Hòa, Mỹ Thạnh, Phong Niên, and Phú Lộc "were left completely unguarded by any sort of force during most of this period, even after they lost abductees."[30] The only positive news in the February report for Tuy Hòa was that the ARVN 47th Regiment had engaged and killed some PLAF operating in the district.[31] But killing PLAF members only removed a symptom; the causes of the Communist incursion remained largely untouched. Moreover, PLAF proved itself capable of potentially replenishing its ranks with its unimpeded abduction efforts in Tuy Hòa District. PLAF incidents, noted the report, underscored serious problems with local defenses. The report mentioned eighteen cases in which PLAF mined local roads, ten of them intending to hamper local civilian traffic. Aside from planting mines, PLAF local forces sought to bloody their primary target—the South Vietnamese village militia forces (the PSDF). They did so with booby traps and small, unit-level firefights. The war's tempo, too, remained under PLAF control as the enemy initiated five of the eight engagements.[32] Essentially, the report's summary concluded, "none of the above bodes well for the progress of Vietnamization in this district. The troubles . . . do not augur well for much progress in the other major pacification programs either."[33]

Elsewhere in Phú Yên, security concerns dominated district reports. A litany of overt enemy activity outside of Tuy Hòa District confirmed the deterioration of security across the province. Like Tuy Hòa, Sông Cầu District experienced abductions and assassinations. Despite a quiet January, February marked a period of noteworthy enemy aggression. Capt. Joseph C. Casey, Sông Cầu DSA, wrote that "the District's defensive shield crumbled in several places during the reporting period as the VC successfully conducted several assassinations and captured eight (08) PSDF and eleven (11) weapons," and PLAF infiltrators also assassinated five civilians.[34] A subsequent district report also noted PLAF ramping up its activity. By February, PLAF was conducting raids, abducting seven civilians from the area of Triều Sơn hamlet.[35]

February in Đồng Xuân District was equally eventful. "Incidents include indirect fire, ambushes, mining of railroad, and kidnapping civilians," Đồng Xuân DSA Capt. John A. Dunn noted. Worse still, the enemy maintained "the ability to make limited attacks or probes without serious casualties to himself."[36] Furthermore, Dunn wrote, PLAF teams had twice mortared Đồng Tre and abducted four civilians, and that an emboldened PLAF had conducted daylight ambushes of RF soldiers within sight of the district compound. Although the railroad interdiction resulted in minimal damage, PLAF scored larger moral victories by planting PLAF flags on the hills overlooking nearby villages. Compounding matters for CORDS, Dunn also noted "no increase in intelligence reports" despite the clearly visible escalation of Communist audacity.[37]

Events in Tuy An District exemplified the severity and scope of the abductions occurring beyond Tuy Hòa District. As reported by Tuy An District's DSA, Maj. Jimmy R. Horn, whom PLAF abducted, revealed much about the state of security in the province. In a blow aimed at security, PLAF overran RF 151's position on 10 March after having abducted a stunning forty-four PSDF members since 1 February. In total, PLAF marched away ninety-eight individuals before mid-March. Whereas PLAF typically released abductees after proselytization, Horn noted that the PSFD members taken from his district remained absent. He and other advisors surmised that PLAF captors were using the PSDF prisoners "to harvest their vast crop of rice in the badlands,"[38] the infamous Kỳ Lộ Valley likely being the "badlands" to which Horn and fellow advisors referred.

Long the PAVN 95th Regiment's principal domain, the Kỳ Lộ Valley remained intact. Infrequent incursions into the valley—most of which transpired in 1967 by allied maneuver battalions, and a USAF bombing campaign—meant that the area helped spur the security nightmare now unfolding across Phú Yên.

That the ROKA 26th Regiment "loathed to go" into the valley, despite it often falling under their area of operations, certainly did not help Saigon's pacification efforts.[39] In late February 1970, Engle proposed another aerial response to the Kỳ Lộ Valley in a memo to USAF Col. William Yancey, commanding officer of the 31st Tactical Fighter Wing at Tuy Hòa South Air Base: "This area is a big undisturbed enemy base area. Anything that could liven up things in that area would be most helpful."[40] Livening up entailed an approach that bordered on desperation—F-100s returning to Tuy Hòa South jettisoning unused ordnance. Engle also revealed disagreement among province chiefs in 1969 over a proposed zone across the Bình Định, Phú Bổn, and Phú Yên province borders that amounted to no bombs falling on the Kỳ Lộ Valley, thus aiding PAVN and PLAF. Engle admitted to Yancey, "we probably lost hundreds of thousands of tons of ordnance by not going for the zone inside Phú Yên in the first place."[41]

By this juncture of the war in Phú Yên, two truths emerged: One, PLAF was not finished after the 1968 Tết Offensive. And two, this phase of the war was eerily reminiscent of the one waged by PLAF in Phú Yên circa 1965. During the 12–25 March reporting period, an emboldened PLAF greatly impeded pacification efforts in the countryside outside of Tuy Hòa City. Fluke disclosed that out of seven contacts between PLAF and PSDF, the Communists initiated five. With seventy-one abductions and one assassination in mid-March alone, enemy activity remained high. By this juncture, PLAF local forces conducted attacks in battalion strength and employed sapper teams. Now, going beyond abducting local civilians, PLAF routinely interdicted QL-1; CORDS recorded seven cases of PLAF mining the critical transportation artery.[42] By now, news of the events in Tuy Hòa District reached MR2 CORDS officials.

Fluke's criticism got to the heart of pacification perceptions. In his district reports, Fluke wrote of the GVN neglecting the area outside the province capital:

> The GVN needs to be shaken from its complacency—especially in regard to its control of the rural population. It is willing to tolerate VC activities in the rural areas that it would never put up with in Tuy Hoa City. The government forgets that population control is fine, but popular support must be the final goal. The security of Tuy Hoa City, containing slightly over 50% of the population, is a crutch upon which the officials lean too much. For the rural people, however, the GVN furnished security must be as illusionary as the emperor's new clothes.[43]

Arguably, with the perceived gains of the APC and the near-complete withdrawal of American assets from Phú Yên in 1969, province officials saw the American War as over. The United States, a superpower, had failed to dislodge the battered PAVN and PLAF regiments from Phú Yên. Instead of continuing the unwinnable American War, the South Vietnamese accepted reality—that the enemy remained in the province. Yet a precedent set by the Americans in 1966—when IFFV's maneuver battalions took over offensive duties from ARVN—complicated matters during Vietnamization. As much as CORDS pushed the APC and the rapid placement of recently won hamlets on maps, the act of doing that clearly rested with American-led military forays into the countryside. Moreover, Fluke's detailing of the GVN's lack of concern over PLAF activities in Tuy Hòa District troubled American and South Vietnamese officials alike.

ARVN recognized the crisis in Phú Yên. In February, Lt. Gen. Arthur S. Collins, commander of IFFV, reported to Gen. Abrams, commander of MACV, a late February surprise visit to Phú Yên by II Corps commander Lt. Gen. Lữ Mộng Lan, who initiated an ARVN investigation of the province. Lữ Mộng Lan and his staff found the Phoenix Program—the highly controversial, clandestine means of uncovering VCI—entirely ineffectual, meaning that VCI networks in the province remained unaffected by that problematic initiative. Worse, the investigation determined that the province administration provided "no effective guidance."[44] To that end, Lt. Gen. Lữ Mộng Lan's visit with the recently appointed deputy province chief, Lt. Col. Trần Đình Duyên, included tours of areas throughout Phú Yên, with the general seeking improvements to security. In response, South Vietnamese officials intended to better prepare local defense forces to fill the void.[45] In practice, however, that retraining process would prove near impossible; the plan merely allayed American concerns, because CORDS perceived the ARVN 47th Regiment's pending deployment to Kon Tum Province as necessary to Vietnamization and more important to regional pacification goals than using elements of that force in Phú Yên.[46] The value of Phú Yên seemed lost on the minds of both the Americans and the South Vietnamese.

As February turned into March, the poor security situations in the Tuy Hòa and Hiếu Xương districts remained unchanged. Abductions continued in Tuy Hòa District, thus the provincial government did not escape AT28's criticism. Fluke remained critical of the situation in the district: "The civilian side of pacification has shown no forward movement except for the growing of rice, which proceeds with or without directives."[47] U.S. advisors found the GVN's lackluster performance "a bafflement and disgrace."[48] ARVN, according to AT28, wasted valuable time doing relatively little during the reporting period. Save for operations in the Suối Trai Valley, elements of the ARVN 47th Regiment did little to improve district security. As PLAF flexed its collective muscle throughout Tuy Hòa District, neighboring Hiếu Xương District felt the effects. VCI teams assisted squad-sized PLAF elements in crossing the river from Tuy Hòa District into Hòa Bình village in Hiếu Xương. Once across, the infiltrators gathered rice and building materials and had several encounters with allied forces. The local GVN district chief viewed the low-intensity PLAF incidents as a sign that an escalation of activity loomed over Hiếu Xương.[49] The absence of offensive activity by RF troops—who were instead holed up in their compound—led FSO and DSA Alfred R. Barr to term their "operations" as "search and avoid."[50] Despite issues with the RF and the Communist infiltration of Hòa Bình, Barr reported on 25 March that unlike the rest of the province, his district remained mostly pacified, noting that HES/70 scores indicated that "one hundred percent of the district's population enjoys A or B security status."[51] Regardless of intensity, pacification had yet to end PLAF's effectiveness.

The efficacy of PLAF's local forces made the campaign successful. Throughout the course of the abduction campaign, the PLAF's 96th Local Force Battalion and its K-13 Local Force Battalion emerged as the main threats in Tuy Hòa District. There, those two PLAF units exercised considerable freedom of movement, which permitted them to aid the VCI in the district with abductions and acts of terrorism.[52] The allies recognized the need to assist the GVN in Tuy Hòa District, yet Vietnamization complicated matters.

Operational-level concerns restricted the allied response to the emerging Advisory Crisis. Gen. Collins reported the complexities to Gen. Abrams. The U.S. Army, well into its irreversible phased withdraw from the RVN, did not want to disrupt its plans by sending a maneuver battalion to Phú Yên. Withdrawal meant that ARVN found itself stretched more thinly than before as its forces assumed areas of operations once controlled by the U.S. Army. For ARVN, the RF/PF companies and the temporarily remaining ARVN 47th Regiment elements would have to suffice.[53] PLAF's abduction campaign occurred at the most inopportune time for the allies. As part of Vietnamization, ARVN command had selected the ARVN 47th Regiment to replace the departing U.S. Army's 4th Infantry Division at Pleiku. All of the 47th would have departed Phú Yên by 14 March, with the ROKA's 2nd Battalion, 28th Regiment taking over responsibilities by 20 March. Instead, ARVN reacted to PLAF, with Task Force 22 dispatched to Phú Yên to take operational control of ARVN battalions in the province and responsibility for Tuy Hòa District.[54] In Phú Yên itself, ROKA intended to direct the bulk of its operations to the mountainous interior; this preplanned move meant that ROKA would not provide any immediate assistance to the beleaguered Tuy Hòa Valley. Moreover, because of recently agreed-upon areas of operations between ARVN and ROKA, Gen. Collins surmised that South Vietnamese officials were reluctant to request a change of plans. Gen. Collins therefore offered his short-term fix: a thirty-day deployment of multiple Hawk teams from the 173rd Airborne Brigade currently operating in Bình Định. With Lt. Gen. Lữ Mộng Lan's approval, Gen. Collins implemented his plan.[55]

Reminiscent of 1966, only the arrival of American troops appeared to improve security—a pointed noted by both AT28 and the U.S. Embassy in Saigon. To combat the burgeoning PLAF influence, IFFV initiated Operation Darby Talon, which saw the deployment of six 173rd Airborne Brigade platoons to Tuy Hòa District. Under the name Task Force Talon, participating elements arrived on 13 March.[56] Darby Talon's explicit purpose was to boost security by retraining the RF/PF. On the heels of Task Force Talon's arrival, Ambassador William Colby, head of CORDS, and journalist George McArthur visited Phú Yên. McArthur reported that the 173rd Airborne Brigade's 3/503rd Infantry and ROKA forces commenced operations in the central plain area west of Tuy Hòa City.[57] Recalling Colby's 15 March inspection of Sông Cầu and Tuy An districts, Engle wrote to Willard Chambers, deputy for CORDS in MR2, "we made it clear to the Ambassador that the 173rd Airborne's assistance to us was not in the nature of a 'task force' deployed directly against the enemy but was instead a temporary training measure solely to improve the ability of the RF/PF to carry out its pacification mission more effectively."[58] The onus of completing Vietnamization meant that advisory officials were loath to reintroduce an IFFV maneuver battalion to Phú Yên, thus repeating the 1966 and 1967 operations. Engle hoped that the Hawk teams comprising the task force would have an uplifting effect on local South Vietnamese forces.[59] Task Force Talon existed to retrain RF/PF units in Tuy Hòa District to create space between PLAF and the local population.[60]

Colby's arrival, with the power of his position as head of CORDS, signaled the mounting significance of the Advisory Crisis. Improved security, the primary concern and topic of discussion, could not become—again—an American endeavor. Vietnamization proved far too monolithic; Engle noted that Task Force Talon's Hawk teams were the only means to assist the South Vietnamese militarily in Phú Yên without compromising the image of U.S. withdrawal. Instead of counterbalancing PLAF activity with U.S. Army maneuver battalions a la 1966,

American officials felt highly uncomfortable rewidening the war. Emphatically, Engle explained that the rationale behind using a fraction of IFFV's arsenal in Phú Yên "did not represent any kind of retrogression from our Vietnamization push (such as bringing in a US maneuver battalion might have involved)."[61] In that vein, a solitary, company-sized task force symbolized American interest while forcing South Vietnamese officials "to take any corrective measures under their own steam . . . to build up and encourage Vietnamese self-reliance."[62] Whereas the situation in Bình Định called for IFFV's maneuver battalions, for American officials, the equally troubling crisis unfurling in Phú Yên existed solely as a South Vietnamese problem. The conversations about the crisis talked around the very problem—PLAF resurgence. Although both provinces' suffering was in large part due to the ineffectual accelerated pacification effort pushed by CORDS, the Americans took no ownership of the Advisory Crisis.

Mandated to retrain the RF to stand ground and stop fearing PLAF, Task Force Talon's time in Phú Yên was hardly productive. Task Force Talon found its mission stymied by an apathetic province administration. As summarized by Fluke, "the much needed redeployment of troops from the overprotected Tuy Hòa City to the rural areas still did not seem to interest Sector."[63] GVN authorities' reluctance to commit troops to the troubled tracts of the district indicated an overreliance on American and South Korean soldiers. Worse still, Fluke suggested that the reduction in abductions owed more to local GVN authorities' decision to simply stop reporting the incidents—a point proven correct by a subsequent CORDS inquiry into the province's woes.[64]

American and South Vietnamese expectations now varied greatly. The Americans envisioned salvaging pacification in Phú Yên via retraining the RF and new province leadership—a lofty (if not unrealistic) expectation given the previous years spent initially training those very forces. If MACV and IFFV thought that Task Force Talon was the key to the province's salvation, they were only fooling themselves. Successive, large-scale allied operations had failed to make the province secure; the arrival of a lone task force was more of a symbolic act than one aimed at genuinely resolving Phú Yên's predicament. For the South Vietnamese, placating their American allies mattered—PLAF would remain in Phú Yên regardless of the GVN's response. Thus, the GVN found itself doing what it could to foster the appearance that Saigon was reinvigorating pacification in the province.

Meanwhile, Task Force 22's efforts failed to ameliorate the security situation. With IFFV's reluctance to deploy even one of its maneuver battalions, and in response to the rapidly deteriorating GVN presence in the Tuy Hòa Valley, ARVN executed an operation similar to those conducted by IFFV in 1966. In following the lessons learned from the Americans, Task Force 22 completed what at best amounted to a show-of-force exercise. Between 12 and 20 March, as part of Task Force 22, the ARVN's 3rd Battalion, 40th Regiment, 22nd Division moved into the depths of the Tuy Hòa Valley, commencing what AT28 viewed as a futile effort. Engle wrote that "the 'operation' into the hills represented a waste in helicopter assets—everything we had in the area was tied up—and everyone understood in advance that there was little likelihood they would see any enemy. In any case, helicopters were unnecessary; the battalion should have walked those few kilometers up hill. The 22nd Division's insistence on an 'operation' bore no relevance to the prevailing pacification requirements."[65] In a scathing statement, Engle perfectly captured the flat-footedness that defined security in the province in 1970: "We don't think the enemy paid much attention to the 3rd of the 40th, just as they seldom pay much to battalions of the 47th—they just go around them."[66] With its campaign centered on abducting civilians and harassment, direct engagement with any opposing conventional force made little sense to PLAF.

PLAF largely ignored the show of force by the ARVN 22nd Division. Engle recounted a list of issues associated with the operation:

> [Thirty-six] abductions occurred in the hamlets directly behind their positions. This was an increased number of abductions from that area. The GVN did not report all of them, but we found out about them. The exit and return routes of the abductees, according to interrogation reports, was through the so-called "bowling alley," which runs across the middle of the 3d of the 40th's AO. Enemy sapper activity continued on QL-1, along the edge of that AO. One mine exploded on that stretch of the road on March 13, damaging a truck of the 84th Engineer Battalion.[67]

Instead of reversing PLAF gains in the Tuy Hòa Valley, ARVN decisions inadvertently exacerbated the now-expansive scope of abductions. In another slight against Task Force 22, Engle added that "the enemy became more cautious when the 173rd Airborne Brigade's Hawk Teams fanned out with the RF in the valley, and infiltration became reduced when, beginning March 19, the 2nd and 3rd Battalions of the 28th ROK Regiment established a screen across the mountains rimming the valley."[68] According to Engle, rather than seeking out PLAF, Task Force 22 should have conducted a similar screening effort.[69] Regardless, pacification remained in jeopardy.

The American public, too, heard of Phú Yên's downward spiral. In a 22 March 1970 *Los Angeles Times* article, George McArthur informed the American public of the significance of events in Tuy Hòa District. He noted the province's history as a Việt Minh bastion, and wrote that prior to the PLAF abductions, Phú Yên ranked among the most secure provinces in the country; now, however, the abductions made Phú Yên as "one of three or four of the worst provinces in South Vietnam."[70] Equally startling, McArthur reported that many of those taken by PLAF were not actually abducted—rather, purported abductees willingly joined the ranks of PLAF.[71] The article hit on a vital point that the abductions indicated that the war was "going badly in Phu Yen province, a test area for the 'Vietnamization' process where the confrontation [was] largely between old-fashioned Communist guerrilla forces and militia of the Saigon government."[72] The article further noted that the U.S. government had anticipated problems with Vietnamization, and that events in Phú Yên could not be understood as a complete reversal of pacification.[73] But the enemy's ability to mount attacks against the RF/PF—as demonstrated by two successful PLAF assaults against RF/PF hilltop positions, in which the Communists killed thirty militiamen—in addition to the rash of abductions, placed Phú Yên under intense scrutiny.[74] The article noted Col. Nguyễn Văn Ba's apparent lack of concern, and claimed that after the "local disasters a South Vietnamese inspection team came down from II Corps headquarters in Pleiku," and that the province chief had "entertained the inspectors at his seaside villa and they never saw the militia outposts."[75]

Progress from 1966 through 1969—in contrast to the province's predicament in 1965—had made Phú Yên seem pacified; a relatively quiet PAVN and PLAF had furthered the myth of progress. Indeed, "the rains came and everyone went to sleep," as McArthur attributed to an undisclosed official.[76] "There was 21 inches of rain one night alone last October. Nobody wanted to fight." PLAF "had quietly change its tactics, however, adapting to the political warfare and small-unit maneuvers now called for by Hanoi's over-all strategy."[77] With its roots in the 1969 COSVN Resolution 9, this new, comparatively quiet approach toward undermining GVN pacification took effect—with spectacular results—in 1970.

The situation befalling Phú Yên besmirched the GVN, and by extension, pacification plans and the American withdrawal. Having abducted many civilians from Tuy Hòa District, PLAF's actions exposed security problems in the most politically valuable district in the province. Fallout from nearly two months of unimpeded enemy activity included a special report on the district's security situation. In the 23 March report, Douglas McCollum, the public safety division advisor for Tuy Hòa, addressed the district's vulnerability, affirming that "the area is classified as insecure and the enemy has had relatively free movement."[78] Upon investigating, the AT28 district advisors found that PLAF teams came down from the mountains and used fifteen crossing points to enter the district. The report noted the existence of underwater bridges that PLAF used to cross the canal and gain access to the district's hamlets. Besides abductions, "squad-sized" PLAF infiltrators collected food, taxes, and recruits. Summoned by letters, locals willingly responded to PLAF's orders for them to report and turned up with requested goods. The presence of five police stations near the infiltrations did nothing to halt the enemy activity. PLAF's free movement within the district and a lack of reporting on these activities exposed wider problems with the advisory effort.[79]

To assist in combatting the burgeoning PLAF abduction campaign, the ROKA 28th Regiment returned to Tuy Hòa District. Yet this redeployment created its own controversy, drawing further attention to the allies' diverging agendas. With memories of the war's widening under the Americans and South Koreans, the district's inhabitants remained suspect of allied actions and intentions. The South Koreans attempted to steer the narrative to garner public support. Two articles in *Pacific Stars and Stripes* contained accounts of supposed outpourings of support (public demonstrations and petitions) from Hòa Kiến and Hòa Thắng villagers, but all turned out to be devises of a dubious ROKA public relations campaign.[80] As worded by Engle, "the ROK public relations operation must be extremely poor if it turns out rubbish like this."[81] Engle relayed this decision as indicative of "a bad conscience" on the part of the South Korea command. Harkening back to the years of intense maneuver warfare, Engle noted that "during the early days of the ROK presence here, great battles were fought; there were several instances in which considerable numbers of innocent Vietnamese are said to have been slaughtered indiscriminately by Koreans," adding that "stories of 'massacres' at Hoa Da (Tuy An) Phu Hiep (Hieu Xuong) and Hoa Thang village (Tuy Hoa) are still current."[82] Engle acknowledged that at least the ROKA 28th Regiment appeared cognizant of the past, and keen on improving its image. The sticking point, however, amounted to the South Koreans acting without informing province officials—leaving South Vietnamese and American authorities to learn of ROKA actions secondhand.[83] Efforts to ameliorate the crisis in Tuy Hòa District ultimately undercut the already brittle relationship between the allies, much to the gain of the NLF. Actions by all three allied powers in Phú Yên to improve the coalition and province security further frayed relationships, while doing markedly little to rectify the disintegration of pacification.

A Province Jolted from Its Slumber

RF companies remained tepid to the idea of battling PLAF. Years of reliance on American soldiering and firepower, combined with questionable RF leadership, resulted in ill-prepared RF companies. Fluke noted "friction" between the 173rd and the RF/PF, writing that "the RF/PF resented being asked to perform their duties again."[84] One PLAF assault did more than kill Americans and South Vietnamese. Between the night of 31 March and 0200 on 1 April, the PLAF D-96 Main Force Battalion assaulted Hill 40 near the village of Minh Đức. Adjacent to Núi Chấp Chài and just outside the Tuy Hòa City limits, Hill 40 sat in de facto PLAF territory. Atop the hill, twelve soldiers from RF 122 and a seven-man Hawk team—3rd Squad, 2nd Platoon, C Company, 503rd Infantry, 173rd Airborne Brigade—waited as part of a larger operation to ambush PLAF units. Two other colocated units sat in wait elsewhere in the area.[85]

In 1970, PLAF regularly attacked Territorial Forces in Phú Yên, and on that night, D-96 was again on the hunt. The placement of the allies on Hill 40 offered a tantalizing target. Volleys of B-40 rockets, grenades, and small-arms fire raked the hill, causing the RF company to flee to nearby rocks for cover. Five Americans—with a wounded RF sergeant—repulsed the first assault, with two of the Americans receiving and later dying of fragmentation wounds caused by incoming B-40 rockets. When 3rd Squad, 2nd Platoon, C Company lost radio communications, one American soldier went to the hiding RF unit to use its radio. With orders for the beleaguered Americans to remain in position as two other Hawk teams maneuvered to provide relief, the American soldier returned to the ambush site. PLAF fire continued as D-96 held ground within ten to forty meters of the American position. PLAF intensified its fire, claiming a third American's life. The two surviving Americans detonated claymores and headed south to link up with the other two Hawk teams. Within five minutes, D-96 executed a third assault against the position, this time taking the hill. The tempo of the PLAF attack had outpaced the responders' ability to reach the hill in time. ROKA artillery fire, and that of U.S. Army M-42 Dusters, marked the end of the engagement. The two surviving Hawk team members assisted with the recovery and removal of their dead comrades. Elements of D-96 threw grenades, wounding another American.[86]

Controversy immediately followed the battle. The two surviving Americans claimed that the RF soldiers had fled after the first PLAF onslaught. Such accounts ran counter to those of the RF company's commander, who contended that the American fatalities all occurred away from the front line—implying that some U.S. troops had also fled. But the surviving U.S. Army sergeant found his five dead countrymen in the original positions from which they had initially repulsed PLAF attempts to clear the hill. A grisly reminder of PLAF's taking of Hill 40, every American corpse had a shot to the head—an enemy act to ensure the kill.[87] What befell the 3rd Squad, 2nd Platoon, C Company certainly added to the significant discord already developing between the Americans and South Vietnamese. Col. Nguyễn Văn Ba pinned the hilltop affair squarely on Fluke, arguing that he had refused to take command of RF 112. Without sufficient time and orders from his superiors, Fluke indeed had not accompanied the South Vietnamese troops.[88] The fallout from the Minh Đức incident was a devastating blow to the advisory effort in Phú Yên. The task force's poor results later caused Fluke to conclude that "the presence of the 173d will be of decreasing value."[89]

April Fools proved no laughing matter in Phú Yên. Hours after the disaster at Minh Đức, Col. Nguyễn Văn Ba convened the monthly meeting with allied commanders on 1 April. The province chief proposed remedies for the current ills in Phú Yên. In doing so, even without mentioning Minh Đức by name, he accentuated the grave security problems. Nguyễn Văn Ba asked for and later received ROKA support in areas that included Tuy Hòa District's Núi Chấp Chài and Tuy An District's An Ninh village, both of which had been the GVN's forces' responsibility. Even in 1970, Núi Chấp Chài functioned as "an enemy base area, swarming with VCI," which according to an April 1970 AT28 report, the GVN had "never attempted seriously to clean out."[90] An Ninh, the report continued, "has been mostly under VC control again in recent months; there have been various RF/PF/RD cadre disasters there."[91] As argued by Engle, Col. Nguyễn Văn Ba endeavored to solve a GVN dilemma with a ROKA solution.[92] Indeed, the PSA pointed toward a more recent request of Nguyễn Văn Ba that called for the ROKA to assume security of An Nghiệp, a long-troubled hamlet. Engle commented that "he called for the 28th ROKs to take over from RF/PF the valley area around An Nghiep hamlet (SW Tuy Hoa District), which enemy squads have entered and pillaged the last two nights."[93] In terms of security and the advancement of pacification, the admission of unchecked PLAF influence near the province capital meant that Phú Yên disconcertingly resembled the province on the eve of IFFV's 1966 operations.

As the center of governance and trade in the province, most of the province's ARVN assets maintained a defensive posture in Tuy Hòa City. Separated from the contested Tuy Hòa Valley by a highway, a railway, and a river, the province capital enjoyed a state of peacefulness that eluded the rest of the district. Undoubtedly the safest area in Phú Yên, security conditions in Tuy Hòa City were not representative of the province, nor even the district itself. Indeed, the district encompassing the capital reflected a province in which PLAF maintained its Việt Minh roots. Bruce W. Clark, a deputy district advisor for Tuy Hòa, substantiated perceptions of Tuy Hòa Valley as a dangerous place: "How secure the valley was at night was anybody's guess. And if you went far from the town into the woods or the jungle during the day you could be asking for trouble."[94] Decidedly, incidents in the Tuy Hòa Valley made pacification in Phú Yên seem anything but complete. The safety afforded by the city meant that on the evening of 1 April, AT28 personnel in Tuy Hòa District recorded 950 South Vietnamese entering the capital. That number included members of the National Police Field Force (NPFF), RD Cadre, the PSDF, and the RF/PF—the designated purveyors of hamlet security. The following night, 2 April, AT28 counted 887 personnel from those aforementioned RVN entities as entering Tuy Hòa City. Not to be left alone and unprotected, between 7,000 and 9,000 South Vietnamese, village officials and civilians, vacated Tuy Hòa District for the safety of the province capital every night.[95]

As allied conventional forces tried to eject PAVN and PLAF elements from the Tuy Hòa Valley, the scope of the abductions exacerbated the Advisory Crisis. The Tuy Hòa District abductions had surprised Engle and his advisors as Nguyễn Văn Ba and province officials kept to themselves the scale of problems in the district. The intelligence gathered by Fluke did more than permanently sour the relationship between AT28 and Nguyễn Văn Ba—it jeopardized Vietnamization. Upon learning that a lack of communication between AT28 district personnel and local GVN authorities was behind the slow response to PLAF incursions into Tuy Hòa District, American authorities tried to improve cooperation with the GVN. Higher echelons of CORDS, including Colby and his staff, involved themselves in events in Phú Yên.[96] On 2 April, Chambers and Gen. Collins visited Tuy Hòa District to mediate an end to the crisis. During their time in the district, they ascertained the significant discord between AT28 and Nguyễn Văn Ba. The province chief requested that Fluke, the DSA responsible for reporting on the widespread abductions across Tuy Hòa District, be removed from Phú Yên. But Chambers defended Fluke's findings, noting that relieving Fluke would amount to CORDS accepting Nguyễn Văn Ba's stance that all was well in Tuy

Hòa District.[97] In his memo to Colby, Chambers wrote that he "can't imagine a way in which things could be much worse."[98] Chambers concluded with the suggestion the Col. Nguyễn Văn Ba be replaced or that he at least permit his deputies more executive authority.[99]

The abductions had badly damaged the relationship between CORDS and GVN officials, hurting AT28's ability to work with Nguyễn Văn Ba. Neither he nor his province administration had shared information on PLAF activity, nor did they like the fallout when DSA Fluke exposed the reality. Province officials used Fluke as the scapegoat for the Tuy Hòa District crisis. As Chambers prepared his visit report, Tuy Hòa District Chief Nguyễn Thái Lâm informed Nguyễn Văn Ba and Engle on 4 April that he could not work with Fluke. Nguyễn Thái Lâm accused the DSA of trying to command his men, thus overstepping his authority as an advisor. Nguyễn Thái Lâm presented Nguyễn Văn Ba and Engle with an ultimatum: that the appropriate authorities transferred either Fluke or himself out of Tuy Hòa District.[100] Chambers inferred this as a response to his and Collins's visit and their "searching questions."[101] On 6 April, both Nguyễn Văn Ba and Nguyễn Thái Lâm publicly requested Fluke's removal from the province, in a move to make the situation about personal affronts rather than the province authorities' concealment of intelligence.[102] This distraction escalated matters profoundly. That evening, Chamber spoke with Nguyễn Văn Ba, who "expressed astonishment that I had even mentioned the Tuy Hoa advisory crisis to my higher headquarters. He had meant that it should be kept here in Phu Yen 'among friends.' I said that it was a serious business, and that [Engle] and General Collins viewed it gravely."[103] Now the Advisory Crisis transformed into a problem that jeopardized the entire premise and image of Vietnamization, and one only senior American diplomats and South Vietnamese President Nguyễn Văn Thiệu could resolve.

The U.S. Embassy in Saigon, therefore, entered the Phú Yên discussion. Information indeed made its way from Chambers to the highest levels of the American advisory apparatus in South Vietnam. On 6 April, the same day as Nguyễn Văn Ba and Nguyễn Thái Lâm requested to have Fluke removed, Theodore G. Shackley, CIA station chief and special assistant to Ambassador Ellsworth Bunker, forwarded a high-level CORDS report on Phú Yên to Gen. Abrams. Shackley prefaced the report by noting that Phú Yên faced a multitude of challenges, and wrote that although intelligence issues played a part, the "solution to Phu Yen's problems lies not in the intelligence field but in a broad Mission Council approach to the basic ills which affect Phu Yen."[104] The report itself framed events in the province in much starker terms; the data it shared shook the very foundations of pacification in the province. Between 1 June 1969 and 31 January 1970, MACV recorded 115 PLAF abductions.[105] From 1 February to 30 March 1970, PLAF abducted another 550 South Vietnamese. Most of those targeted during this period were the "families of GVN officials and relatives of ARVN and RF/PF/PSDF personnel."[106] Those taken experienced "two to five days of political indoctrination and proselytizing instructions. Political indoctrination stressed that the US is withdrawing its troops after military defeat and the people of South Vietnam must now move to VC areas."[107] After indoctrination, PLAF released most abductees, save for "some of the younger abductees" whom it kept for use as laborers and for additional indoctrination.[108] The report noted that based on the Americans' observations, the rate of abductions decreased "greatly" since March for the following reasons: the completion of the PLAF campaign, the arrival of Task Force Talon, the ROKA soldiers' return, and the "termination of reporting of abductions by GVN officials."[109] While PLAF itself played a central role, the abductions "ended" in part because local province officials simply stopped recording incidents. Unsurprisingly, the GVN's complicity and its security forces in Phú Yên bore the brunt of the blame, at least as far as CORDS was concerned.

Shackley's report also held province leadership responsible for the Advisory Crisis. The CIA man emphasized to Abrams the absence of sound GVN leadership within the province and the perceived uselessness of the South Vietnamese forces notionally responsible for security. "Lack of resistance by the RF/PF/PSDF has allowed the VC to enter villages and hamlets at night almost at will," which essentially meant that GVN security existed in name only.[110] In Tuy Hòa District, the RF and PF did not "normally conduct patrols and ambush activity at night."[111] The PSDF, too, failed to impress, as they "either bury their weapons or leave them with relatives or friends in Tuy Hoa City."[112] This was unsurprising conduct, given that PLAF targeted the families of these military forces.

The refusal to challenge PLAF confounded American authorities. In Tuy An District, the RF/PF typically avoided contact with PLAF. In one instance, RF/PF retreated to the district capital from a hamlet with an HES/70 ranking of "A"; PLAF then proceeded into the hamlet to abduct targeted residents. The report Shackley forwarded to Gen. Abrams stated that the "lack of resistance to the VC is further evidenced by the fact that there have been no casualties to GVN security forces or to the population as a result of efforts to prevent VC abductions."[113] Worse, the conventional force operating in Tuy Hòa District, the 4th Battalion, ARVN 47th Regiment, had zero effect on PLAF activity. The report noted that both the PSA and the DSA for the district regarded the ARVN unit as "worthless" as it executed "no operations and is understrength. It is being retained in province by GVN officials, although it was scheduled to join its regiment in Pleiku Province."[114] In short, PLAF encountered little resistance in a province once regarded as secure. Task Force Talon, the report noted, helped get RF and PF units out on patrols. The report also referenced the 31 March hilltop disaster at Minh Đức.[115] Task Force Talon alone could not and would not remedy Phú Yên's woes.

Shackley received a response from Abrams on 10 April. Beyond an acceptance of the information shared in the report, Abrams's reply confirmed the Advisory Crisis as more than a provincial matter. Now every U.S. entity in the RVN—the CIA, CORDS, the Embassy, IFFV, and MACV—was addressing the crisis in some fashion. These bodies would support the course of action selected by the RVN's Joint General Staff (JGS). Abrams wrote that he, Shackley, Collins, and Engle were in agreement—that "the problems in Phú Yên are directly related to a lack of leadership throughout the political and military organization of the province." The MACV commander promised support to "effect the relief of the Province Chief," ensure "maximum support of Phú Yên requirements by the JGS and RVNAF," and "strengthen our advisory effort particularly as it relates to the territorial forces." As to how to remedy the Advisory Crisis, Abrams wrote that "it would be appropriate to take action through the RVN ministerial structure and the existing advisory chain of command."[116] American diplomats took that course of action the following day.

Collins, too, received correspondence from Abrams on 10 April. Abrams's memo to Collins offered further insight: "We agree that the amount of forces assigned to the province if properly employed appears adequate to meet the threat and that the solution lies in forceful and efficient leadership."[117] The need for the American military to keep Vietnamization on track meant a restrained MACV response to events in Phú Yên. MACV only deployed Task Force Talon to the troubled province—which prevented pacification from once again becoming a task of IFFV's maneuver battalions. American officials apparently thought that the now-questionable gains of IFFV's 1966–69 operations were a sufficient foundation on which province authorities could craft a more secure Phú Yên—this despite the forced dependence of the South Vietnamese on the Americans for military assistance. Relatedly, as Abrams expressed to Collins, blame for the province's troubles fell on the province chief, Nguyễn Văn Ba.[118]

For Nguyễn Văn Ba, the mounting evidence of his province's culpability in the crisis came to the fore in a letter from Chambers to Colby. The public comments he and Nguyễn Thái Lâm had made surely prompted Chambers's written escalation. "We are aware of the hundreds of people who have been abducted from Tuy Hòa District and of the more significant fact that not one single time has one of these abduction parties been contacted by any of the thousands of troops in Tuy Hòa District," Chambers wrote. "This would seem to be far beyond the bounds of even phenomenal good luck if troops were in fact present as they are supposed to be."[119] Chambers noted that he would only seek Fluke's removal on the grounds of "harmony," for the district advisor bore no responsibility for the failings of Nguyễn Văn Ba's administration.[120] Such a stance, Engle told Chambers and now relayed to Colby, stunned Col. Nguyễn Văn Ba. The province chief affirmed his belief that nothing of consequence had transpired in Phú Yên. Chambers reiterated an earlier comment to Colby, one that perfectly summed up the Advisory Crisis: "I can't imagine a way in which things could be much worse."[121]

With the crisis going from a district to a province to a Saigon problem, U.S. officials sought to prevent it from becoming a diplomatic row. Ten days after the monthly commanders' meeting in Tuy Hòa City and the debacle at Minh Đức, on 11 April, American and South Vietnamese authorities in Saigon discussed the fate of the advisory effort in Phú Yên. The Advisory Crisis was the first and most important discussion item that Saturday morning in Prime Minister Trần Thiện Khiêm's office.[122] There, CORDS representative and Colby's chief of staff George D. Jacobson joined CORDS's chief of plans and programs Clay McManaway to discuss the dire situation in Phú Yên with the prime minister. During this meeting, the CORDS officials described events in Phú Yên "as extremely bad and deteriorating."[123] "It appears as though the enemy is carrying out COSVN Resolution #9 and doing it well," Jacobson added.[124] Print media, too, shaped the Advisory Crisis. As the meeting progressed, Jacobson and McManaway referenced the articles by Robert W. Kaiser in the *Washington Post* and George McArthur in the *Los Angeles Times* as indicators of the growing outside interest in the tumultuous events in the province. "The situation will be placed inevitably in the context of Vietnamization with the clear implication that the Vietnamese can't go it alone," Jacobson commented to Trần Thiện Khiêm, admitting that "the worst of it all is that the stories are all true."[125] Those two statements perfectly synopsized the failure of Vietnamization and, therefore, of pacification. When presented with Chambers's earlier suggestion of new province leadership, Trần Thiện Khiêm agreed with Jacobson and McManaway that Phú Yên needed a new province chief and promised to discuss the matter with President Nguyễn Văn Thiệu.[126]

Dialog in Saigon produced serious conversations back in Phú Yên. What materialized out of the discussion in Saigon on 11 April was a high-profile visit to Phú Yên by the secretary general of the Central Pacification and Development Council, Maj. Gen. Cao Hảo Hớn, on 14 April. He and his delegation of ARVN officers from II Corps asked searching questions of Nguyễn Văn Ba and Nguyễn Thái Lâm. Kaiser's article on Phú Yên drove the conversation—underscoring the significance of his role in the Advisory Crisis and the supervening effect the PLAF's abduction campaign had on the GVN and its pacification program.[127] Earlier, Kaiser's article had infuriated Nguyễn Văn Ba, with the province chief lambasting it as "a pack of lies." In private, however, Nguyễn Văn Ba admitted the article's accuracy to Engle.[128]

One phase of the meeting entailed a discussion of COSVN Resolution 9, with Gen. Cao Hảo Hớn asking Nguyễn Văn Ba and his staff if they were aware of the decree. As the chief and his staff contended that PLAF recruited some members, but not enough to offset losses, and claimed low enemy morale because lack of ammunition and food, Cao Hảo Hớn interjected. He asked of Phú Yên's Chiêu Hồi (PLAF who surrendered themselves to the GVN, receiving amnesty in exchange) numbers for March, which proved revealing with just one.[129] The implication being that if PLAF's morale was truly low, surely more members would have taken advantage of the Chiêu Hồi Program. Shortly thereafter, another member in attendance—the president of the Phú Yên Province Council, Lê Kính Huá—asserted, "Hoa Kien is all communist, they are there all day and night."[130] After some time, the conversation returned to the matter of Chiêu Hồi, which Nguyễn Văn Ba's staff quipped was a nonissue because few if any potential ralliers remained due to the program's prior success. Gen. Hớn rejected that outrageous claim, stating "there is no pressure on them—they think they are going to win, not lose."[131]

The visit eventually included a meeting with Nguyễn Thái Lâm. Like Nguyễn Văn Ba, Nguyễn Thái Lâm struggled to provide satisfactory answers—he relayed information contradicted in the very data held by Gen. Cao Hảo Hớn and his entourage. When asked about HES/70 ratings for his district, Nguyễn Thái Lâm provided rankings indicative of a rather secure Tuy Hòa: "four 'A'; six 'B'; twenty-five 'C'; and two 'D.'"[132] With PLAF's widespread infiltration of hamlets, and the ease with which it abducted inhabitants, Tuy Hòa District—the province's most populous—was far from secure. Cao Hảo Hớn subsequently asked what the district chief intended to do about the VCI at Hòa Kiến. Nguyễn Thái Lâm noted a forthcoming psychological operation effort in the village, and mentioned a proposed seven-day sweep of Núi Chấp Chài with ROKA forces. With that, Cao Hảo Hớn inquired about Hill 40—the location of the now-infamous Minh Đức debacle of 1 April.[133]

Gen. Cao Hảo Hớn wanted details from Nguyễn Thái Lâm, testing the district chief's grasp of the situation's severity and knowledge of the enemy. Nguyễn Thái Lâm provided erroneous information, claiming "the company was hit by a battalion, moving west (!)."[134] Nguyễn Thái Lâm fared no better when asked about VCI numbers in Hòa Kiến; the district chief said twelve—a figure far too low and one at odds with the data Cao Hảo Hớn held in his hands. The general, too, inquired about the province's future after Task Force Talon's departure. When Nguyễn Thái Lâm claimed that hamlet HES/70 rankings would not regress, Nguyễn Văn Ba remarked that he needed three additional RF companies plus five more PF platoons to thwart any slippage.[135] That request meant that the American troops' presence held value beyond RF retraining—Task Force Talon shielded the province from responsibility and the ramifications from the lack of pacification progress. So too did the task force's existence, however temporary, represent America's willingness to use military means, as it did before, to improve Saigon's position in Phú Yên. Symbolically, the looming end of Task Force Talon reflected the shift in priorities as dictated by Vietnamization—with the South Vietnamese unprepared for the end of the American War. Yet the answers Nguyễn Văn Ba and Nguyễn Thái Lâm offered during that day conjured "amused condescension" from those in attendance, and cemented Saigon's decision to remove both men from Phú Yên.[136]

Colby returned to Tuy Hòa City, meeting privately with Fluke. Over a bottle of Johnny Walker Red—a gift Colby said Fluke thoroughly deserved—the ambassador thanked the DSA for his work and divulged intelligence of enemy radio traffic going in and out of the province chief's residence. Moreover, Colby informed Fluke that the GVN would replace Col. Nguyễn Văn Ba only if the Americans removed Fluke from Phú Yên. Ultimately, Fluke spent the remaining few months of his tour inspecting other advisory teams. Lt. Col. Nguyễn Văn Tố would eventually replace Nguyễn Văn Ba as province chief.[137] This compromise gave both the Americans and the South Vietnamese what each wanted. Yet the resolution did little if anything to undo the immense damage already inflicted on the alliance, as the Americans remained fixated on reducing their RVN presence, while the South Vietnamese—without reassurances provided by the mere presence of U.S. combat forces—faced a resurgent NLF movement.

Events in Saigon did not produce a more secure Phú Yên. The Advisory Crisis ripped the fabric of pacification in Phú Yên, exposing the flaws in the very thread woven the by Americans to advance it. Pacification at haste with a shrinking U.S. military footprint exposed years of America's inability to properly support the South Vietnamese. Worse, in shifting away from the more familiar oil spot technique—the gradual and methodical spread of control outward from urban centers—and dramatically reducing American assets available to the GVN, the United State essentially presented PLAF with a golden opportunity to strike at the core of pacification in Phú Yên: the people. As for Col. Nguyễn Văn Ba, AT28 reported that "other than to fight a bitter action against the advisory effort aimed at proving that U.S. officials and the American press have been falsely evaluating the situation here, the province chief devoted little attention to public affairs down to April 20, the day he learned of the GVN's decision to remove him."[138] The U.S. advisory mission had bested Nguyễn Văn Ba, but only the NLF benefited.

In May, another article focused public attention on Phú Yên. Regardless of the official end to the Advisory Crisis, the episode affected the remaining years of the American War. Journalist Robert Shaplen's regular exposé on Vietnam in the *New Yorker* magazine, "Letter From Indo-China," contained a retelling of the abductions that beleaguered Phú Yên and the wider implications. Shaplen wrote, "I came away with the odd feeling that, despite some obvious changes, the situation was in many ways what it was five years ago, when American troops kept the Communists from cutting the country in two there by moving across from the coast to the Cambodian border." Continuing, he remarked "in some respects the picture was disturbingly like the one I found in 1962, when I returned to Vietnam after an absence of ten years. This was particularly true in Phú Yên, a retrograde province that a year or so ago was rated as one of the most loyal to Saigon and is now rated as one of the least so."[139] That pacification relied on IFFV's maneuver battalions, even in 1970, remained clear. The removal of American and South Korean maneuver battalions before and during 1969, Shaplen noted, had left a void in which "things have deteriorated"—one exploited by the enemy.[140]

Col. Nguyễn Văn Ba became the scapegoat the Americans needed. Like everyone else, Shaplen blamed poor leadership, especially Nguyễn Văn Ba's, for Phú Yên's downfall. While researching his article, Shaplen met with Col. Nguyễn Văn Ba, who told him the abductions ended in mid-August. A visit to the edge of the Tuy Hòa Valley on the evening of 7 April, however, took Shaplen to Thạnh Nghiệp hamlet. There, just two nights prior, PLAF had abducted nineteen individuals. When discussing Shaplen's conversation with Col. Nguyễn Văn Ba, Engle reported to his superiors, "this is one of the several instances we know of in which reporting of abductions has been suppressed."[141] Shaplen saw Phú

Yên as a test province for Hanoi's renewed emphasis on guerrilla warfare as announced in COSVN Resolution 9, and he accurately relayed the significance of the abductions to his American readership: "It seemed to me that, partly because of its Vietminh history and partly because of its hilly geographical configuration, the Communists were making a test case of Phu Yen, and that they were succeeding in undermining the whole pacification process—and also demonstrating the vulnerability of the Vietnamization process when there is a failure in leadership."[142] Vietnamization, the very process of ending the American War, proved to be the problem, more so than Nguyễn Văn Ba's leadership. Shaplen's article resonated as Congress used it to assail the Nixon administration's handling of the war.[143]

The calamity at Minh Đức persisted as an ever-present specter in the Tuy Hòa Valley. DSA Casey, previously at Sông Cầu, reported that despite the presence of allied forces, on 12 May "the VC made their presence known in Hoa Dinh Village by using cow bells, 'bull horns,' and weapons shot into the air in order to call the populace together for a propaganda rally. The RF company refused to react even though it was only 500 meters from the area."[144] PLAF had executed a successful abduction campaign and completed multiple instances like the one at Minh Đức throughout the year—significant psychological victories that improved the NLF's position in Phú Yên.

New Faces, Same Province

Before the end of May, Engle's successor, Russell Meerdink, an FSO, found himself in Phú Yên. At age 29, the new PSA faced a largely unchanged security situation. In a report to Chambers, Meerdink emphasized the lack of change: "Our problems of VC abductions are major and cannot be resolved outright by single redeployment of forces or a specific directive to subordinate units that such abductions will cease."[145] Three weeks after his arrival as new province chief, Lt. Col. Nguyễn Văn Tố posted units outside the province capital to stem the tide of South Vietnamese cadres and soldiers from taking refuge in Tuy Hòa City each night. To combat the emboldened PLAF, Nguyễn Văn Tố ordered the forces at his command to seal off and search areas around the province capital suspected of VCI use. The Phoenix Program received his attention as well, as he ordered the National Police to fully participate—meaning to resume sharing information with CORDS.[146] These alterations, however, did little to change the war in the province. The sharing of data depicting province security in a negative light remained a problem, staying unresolved because nothing could deter the United

States from its goal of complete disengagement. With Vietnamization advancing pacification on paper, regardless of events on the ground, the Americans, South Koreans, and South Vietnamese in Phú Yên embarked on diverging agendas: withdrawal, self-preservation, and accommodation, respectively. As the rest of 1970 revealed, pacification in the province suffered from allied discord, not just from PAVN and PLAF maneuvering.

The Advisory Crisis nevertheless irrevocably damaged the relationship between AT28 and GVN provincial leadership. Regardless of personnel changes, the Advisory Crisis imbedded lasting distrust among the purported partners. Province security conditions barely changed between March and the 25 April to 12 May reporting period. Resolving the discord between AT28 and the local GVN had not slowed down PLAF's activities: abductions, asserted DSA Casey, were "by no means to be taken as an indication of strengthened GVN authority in the Valley. The security of Tuy Hòa District is much more dependent on what the VC choose to do or not do than what the local forces can prevent."[147] Such sentiment echoed DSA Williams's earlier assertion that PLAF alone dictated events in the district. As noted in the report provided to Shackley, one of the reasons why the abductions ceased was simply that PLAF had achieved its goals and ended that specific campaign.

PLAF continued to move freely in Tuy Hòa District. Between 13 and 27 May, CORDS recorded that PLAF initiated two of the five contacts between friendly and enemy forces, and successfully planted two mines. The villages of Hòa Trị and Hòa Thắng found their way into a CORDS biweekly district report, after PLAF abducted seventy-two inhabitants. Despite the repositioning of forces by the district chief, "in Hoa Thang, the elusive enemy has not been hampered."[148] At the Tuy Hòa North Air Base, security concerns remained. In his report, Casey stated that "the defensive barrier along the eastern side of the air strip would not even prevent the VC from breaking stride, if he was charging at a dead run." Casey also noted that PLAF remained capable of launching battalion-sized attacks.[149]

Operation Darby Talon ultimately netted few positive results. The presence of allied units forced the RF/PF to become proactive and engage PLAF with ambushes. Although Task Force Talon retrained RF companies and pressured them to engage the enemy, these changes were neither catholic nor permeant. Rather, as contended in one report, "the RF 'relapse factor' is still high."[150] Casey reported that during the height of Operation Darby Talon, the seven RF companies in the district "averaged upwards of 60 ambush locations in any given night." This number dropped significantly after the task force departed, with nine RF companies averaging "between 35 and 45 ambush sites at night."[151] Clearly, the significant APC pressure on the RF and PF to protect pacification gains strained these units. This reality lay at the heart of Phú Yên's trouble. In turn, the protection of these gains fell on the RF/PF units as well as the CORDS personnel tasked with advising them.

Phú Yên found itself a lost cause as IFFV once more focused its attention on Bình Định. Bình Định's position as one of the most strategically vital provinces in the country—more so than Phú Yên—made the latter expendable. Bình Định owed its strategic significance to four factors: the second largest population in the RVN; one of nation's few deepwater ports at Qui Nhơn; the massive U.S. Air Force presence at Phù Cát; and the junction of QL-1 and LTL-9, which linked the nation to the central highlands.[152] Bình Định's strategic importance in the face of Vietnamization made Phú Yên expendable. The departure of remaining IFFV assets from Phú Yên to Bình Định during 1969 went unreversed, despite the Advisory Crisis. The termination of Operation Darby Talon on 21 April cemented the Advisory Crisis as the tipping point between American interest in Phú Yên and the decision to focus attention elsewhere. Without sustained IFFV operations like those of 1966, pacification in Phú Yên lost the veneer of progress provided by large American maneuver forces.

Operation Darby Talon's completion left Tuy Hòa District in the same atmosphere that existed before the task force's arrival: uncertainty. Notwithstanding the increase in firefights with the enemy, the task force provided no long-term remedies to the district's ills. Darby Talon demonstrated an underlying problem with how MACV fought the Vietnam War. The operation featured American troops on an assignment with time constraints that favored the United States and not the RVN. The RF's reluctance to perform its duties was a symptom of MACV's handling of the war and not necessarily a problem caused directly by Saigon. Local RF/PF forces remained unready for a war without American support—a problem borne out of American shortsightedness. Years of American funding had not dramatically improved the quality of local defense. RF/PF units lacked sufficient training and suffered from misuse. Rather, the reliance on conventional FWMAF meant that RF/PF platoons lacked sufficient combat experience. PLAF, realizing that it could choose between engaging well-trained forces like a ROKA contingent or a green RF company always picked the latter. Rarely did such RF troops fare well against their attackers.

By May, PLAF had ramped up its exploits in Hiếu Xương District. Moving beyond the acquisition of resources, PLAF conducted operations against allied infrastructure. Home to tactical air assets and oil reserves, Hiếu Xương District offered Communist forces a plethora of possible targets. Attackers from K-65, a PLAF local force sapper company, breached the "sieve-like" perimeter of the army airfield at Phú Hiệp on 3 May.[153] On another night, K-65 struck again, successfully mortaring the airfield and district's ROKA 26th headquarters. Shortly thereafter, the PLAF unit retreated to the safety of the nearby mountains. Tellingly, the 1 May semimonthly district report emphasized that all the attacks emanated from "HES 70 'A' hamlets."[154] The fact that PLAF used purportedly safe and secure hamlets as launching points for its attacks raises doubts about HES/70's reliability—particularly the long-term dependability of hamlet data.

The report also noted serious misgivings about ROKA security measures in Hiếu Xương District. The report stated, "the enemy is either by-passing the ROKA ambushes or ambush sites are being reported that in fact do not exist."[155] Furthermore, ROKA forces refused to respond to two previous requests to engage enemy units spotted near their positions.[156] ROKA security in the district troubled CORDS personnel. Despite the presence of the nearby ROKA 29th Regiment, local peasants pilfered fuel from a vital pipeline unhindered. Additionally, PLAF struck nine times, severing the pipeline on each occasion.[157] PSA Meerdink later remarked that the pipeline was hit so many times that one could see oil in the drinking water.[158] Compounding events in Hiếu Xương, between 7 and 8 May, PLAF infiltrators struck at five different locations in Sông Cầu District, inflicting twenty-two PSDF kills with minimal casualties. By 12 May, PLAF teams had assassinated four civilians.[159]

Local defense therefore remained a sticking point, and one the United States never solved. In June, PLAF remained in control of the situation in Tuy Hòa District. A district report covering 28 May to 14 June noted a probing attack on the night of 3–4 June by the PLAF 96th Local Force Battalion.[160] Recognizing the limitations of the RF during this time, and fearing PLAF activity, provincial authorities sought and acquired the expansion of the ROKA's AO to include much of the Tuy Hòa Valley. Initially tasked with operating in mountainous areas held by PLAF, the ROKA 2nd Battalion, 28th Regiment, found itself instead in the Tuy Hòa Valley's purportedly "pacified areas." This reality troubled CORDS personnel for two main reasons, the first being that the allies had previously agreed that ROKA should operate in the province's PLAF-infested mountains. DSA Cpt. Casey added that during its time in the new expanded AO, the battalion-sized ROKA force had little to show for its support of pacification save for fifteen PLAF KIAs—the implication being that because of its size, the ROKA battalion should have accomplished more to clear the AO of enemy combatants. That leads to point two: by widening its AO in Tuy Hòa District, the ROKA provided a "'corridor' for enemy movement" between the stronger South Korean units and the weaker RF companies.[161]

Fast-forwarding to August and September, Đồng Xuân District, like the rest of Phú Yên, experienced activity by resurgent enemy forces. Elements of PLAF's Phú Yên Provincial Unit had established themselves in the outreaches of Đồng Xuân along the western border between the provinces of Phú Yên and Phú Bổn. In late August, Communist forces wrecked Camp Đồng Tre and Phú Tân hamlet. September entailed "minings, abductions, and assassinations" at higher rates than in August.[162] AT28 district advisors noted that "enemy sightings have increased in number as well as in unit sizes." Worse, those forces interdicted the railroad and roads "under ROK guard."[163] "Abductions and assassinations of PSDF and families who have sons in the territorial forces have occurred when friendly forces were supposedly in the immediate vicinity," meaning that security in Đồng Xuân existed in theory, not practice.[164] To advance pacification, IFFV dispatched the 1st Brigade, 4th Infantry Division and the 2nd Battalion, 35th Infantry Division to this border area. The recently arrived 1st Brigade, 4th Infantry Division aided in the rebuilding of the camp and "the upgrading of Province Road 2d."[165]

Similarly, efforts to combat PLAF provided no progress indicators in Tuy An District. An area once targeted by IFFV for the retraining of RF units and a district beset by PLAF activity, Tuy An remained unpacified. There, too, ROKA efforts to bolster South Vietnamese security forces effected little security improvement. AT28 advisors in Tuy An District reported that "no significant damage to the VC Infrastructure or military units has been noticed."[166] Long-term security conditions therefore remained unaltered in the district.

On the whole, "September was a month which found both the American advisors and ranking Vietnamese officials in Phu Yen doing a great amount of 'soul-searching' as to the reasons for continuing GVN failures on numerous fronts," Meerdink wrote in his 30 September district report.[167] If HES/70 alone functioned as the sole metric for progress in Phú Yên, then security seemed better in September than during the past few months. HES/70 indicated that 88 percent of the population was "once again in A B C hamlets," suggesting "steady improvement in the realm of security."[168] These figures were deceptive, however, as Meerdink emphasized that "security in many hamlets in the Tuy Hoa Valley is a fragile thing which can be broken at any moment with the slightest bit of enemy initiative"—a point rather emblematic of the American War in Phú Yên.[169] Enemy power, or course, remained relatively unscathed, as "the RF/PF maintain a kill ration if their favor but the enemy's ranks are quickly replenished in the absence of an aggressive campaign."[170] Yet, like Engle observed on the heels of the 1968 Tết Offensive, the province inhabitants' interest in the war remained questionable—both civilian and military officials performed their duties "in a generally perfunctory manner."[171] In Tuy Hòa District, PLAF had resumed rice collection and abductions in the outermost western reaches of Tuy Hòa District in the Cẩm Sơn, Mậu Lâm, and Phú Thạnh hamlets.[172] Again, as in previous district reports, the lack of adequate security undermined the effectiveness of pacification in the district. With his frustration palpable, DSA Maj. Jesse H. Denton wrote that "last week this District had four (4) night combat patrols, but they were all conducted by the VC."[173] Denton's report explained that within the ROKA AO, it appeared as if no war was being fought by allied forces. With one ROKA company responsible for 9,000 meters of territory, it lacked sufficient manpower to thwart PLAF infiltrators, and PLAF units took ready advantage of the situation, moving through the gaps in the ROKA AO. Only "the complete application of all principles of war," Denton stated, would remedy the dire security situation.[174] More specifically, he called for allied units in the area to adopt economy of force, noting the that proper use of assets would offset personnel shortages.[175]

September affirmed the Advisory Crisis as the defining episode of the war in Phú Yên, in that it validated American suspicions of ubiquitous public apathy after the 1968 Tết Offensive. AT28 perceived the public as largely disinterested in advancing any cause—Hanoi's or Saigon's. In that vein, "government programs go on without any evidence of popular involvement as the local population appears to be more content nidificating for themselves rather than getting involved with either the GVN or the VC."[176] Indifference had emerged from a war that, for the Vietnamese, began decades before the one presently waged by the Americans, and with no foreseeable end. Peace, like HES/70, was a deceptive indicator, as Meerdink explained:

> Peace has already come to much of that valley. For those living in the valley who are not of draft age, the law of survival is to avoid involve-ment with either antagonist. Phu Yen's much publicized abductions by the enemy clearly supports this thesis. Despite the fact that over 1,000 individuals have been abducted during 1970 and taken to the

hills for indoctrination (most return after less than a week) there is no public outcry against this practice. The hamleteers apparently view this practice as a necessary annoyance not unlike similar 'training' programs carried out by the GVN's PSDF cadre and the like. But the practice also underscored the theme "don't get involved." For draft age males, the problem is much more basic—avoiding GVN or VC conscription requires an equal amount of agility. The population owes its allegiance to the force that has the upper hand at any given point. Accommodation? It appears so.[177]

Peace in the context of the Tuy Hòa Valley meant the continuance of war, but at a level that inhabitants found acceptable. "The 'endless war syndrome' is a malady which appears to have permeated all levels of the GVN and its constituents and is a matter which can only be dealt with by the Vietnamese leadership at the highest levels," Meerdink lamented.[178]

For public relations purposes, Phú Yên held some value for Hanoi. In August, news of the NLF's gains in Phú Yên spurred former chairman of the Phú Yên Resistance and Administrative Committee, Võ Học, to issue a radio address from the North Vietnamese capital. He recalled the Việt Minh's victories in Phú Yên during Operation Atlante and, more significantly, celebrated his compatriots current struggle back in the province. Albeit propaganda, his words nonetheless reflected the aftermath of the Advisory Crisis period as reported by American sources: "as the brothers and sons of Phu Yen now living in the North, we are very happy to hear of the repeated victories of the native province during the first six months of the year."[179] Võ Học referenced the PLAF campaign against the APC: "Tens of thousands of compatriots . . . won back the right to be masters. Guerrillas tracked down diehards and punished reconnaissance agents and spies. The revolutionary spirit seethed everywhere in the province. Even the U.S. military spokesman [sic] in Saigon had to admit the obvious failure of the pacification program."[180] Võ Học also noted how ARVN still needed U.S. Army assistance in Phú Yên.[181] Since it is unlikely that anyone would speak on the war without the approval of Lê Duẩn and the Party, Võ Hoc's words suggest that Hanoi perceived PLAF efforts to challenge Saigon's pacification of Phú Yên as successful.

Conventional warfare as pacification remained in effect in 1970. Between 8 September and 1 October 1970, the 1st Brigade, 4th Infantry Division and the 2nd Battalion, 35th Infantry Division participated in Operation Wayne Forge.

Transpiring along the border between Phú Yên and Phú Bổn, U.S. Army soldiers engaged in small actions against enemy forces. According to the AAR, "as predicted, elements of the Phu Yen Provincial Unit were discovered in this area. This was shown by documents and personal letters taken from hootches and enemy KIA's. One detainee, captured by C Co, stated that a large number of the Phu Yen Provincial Unit was located not far from his place of capture."[182] Although a small operation, as reflected in the number of captured PLAF weapons and supplies, Wayne Forge was by no means insignificant. Rather, "contacts during this period were numerous and were made with groups of 2–3 individuals. The enemy was more aggressive in this area of operations than the enemy contacted by this battalion previously."[183] Thus, after the height of CORDS's support of pacification in Phú Yên, conventional forces continued to play a central role in creating the space necessary for the GVN and AT28 to conduct developmental initiatives. In the grand scheme of the Vietnam War, Operation Wayne Forge paled in comparison to larger operations that transpired elsewhere in the RVN. But what Wayne Forge lacked in intensity it made up for in demonstrating the threat still posed by PLAF. Able to project power, Phú Yên's PLAF demonstrated that the sparsely populated hinterlands of the province were essentially NLF domain.

The disintegration of security continued in Phú Yên. MACV's higher echelons were nonetheless aware of the dangers in the province's more populated locales. Phú Yên appeared in the fourteenth revision of MACV's "VC/NVA Base Study Area Study" as Communist forces maintained a noteworthy presence in the province. Compiled from data collected between 1 April and 1 October 1970, the MACV study detailed the status of enemy base areas and corresponding PAVN and PLAF activity. Situated in the mountains overlooking the western extremity of the Tuy Hòa Valley, the Communists still operated out of Base Area 236. From there, the PLAF K-13 Local Force Battalion orchestrated its operations into Tuy An District. Also from 236, the PLAF 96th Local Force Battalion launched forays into the nearby districts of Tuy Hòa and Hiếu Xương. Noting a slight upswing in enemy activity between April and June, the study reported the presence of "30 Confirmed and 34 Unconfirmed Intelligence Reports, 3 ground-to-air fire incidents, 450 foxholes, 6 contacts, 1 mine incident, and 1 unit sighting . . . compared to 48 Unconfirmed Intelligence Reports, 3 ground-to-air fire incidents, 1 AA/AW position, and 30 foxholes during the first quarter" noted by intelligence in April.[184] By June, intelligence confirmed increased activity and indicated expansion of the base area, with "13 Confirmed and 28 Unconfirmed Intelligence Reports, 1373 foxholes, 8 AA/AA positions, 13 mortar positions,

8 ground-to-air fire incidents, and 3 secondary explosions."[185] This upswing in base area activity reflected the Communist resurgence in Phú Yên, which continued to take direct aim at stymieing allied pacification in Tuy Hòa Valley.

The Recurring Nightmare

Even after the Advisory Crisis officially ended in the minds of senior American and South Vietnamese leadership, PSA Meerdink found himself in charge of an American advisory effort fixated on completing Vietnamization while still dealing with the breakdown of relations between his team and local officials. Meerdink advised a province not markedly different than the one his predecessor had inherited. GVN resistance to fully battling the Communists still plagued the province despite the arrival of Province Chief Lt. Col. Nguyễn Văn Tố. Despite the best efforts of CORDS personnel and abundant U.S. funding, pacification remained undermined by security lapses—as evidenced by the plight of Hiếu Xương District. The lack of intelligence sharing between the GVN and CORDS, as seen during the Advisory Crisis, proved to be a province-wide problem and one not limited to Tuy Hòa District. Reliable reporting existed as a problem in Hiếu Xương District as HES/70—the increasingly relied-upon metric that MACV used to gauge pacification progress—produced ratings from incomplete data. In a September monthly district progress report on Hiếu Xương District, DSA Maj. Walter Kyle emphasized the questionable intelligence reporting: "It appears as though we (advisors) don't get information on all the assassinations, abductions and collections of the V.C. This could account for the high ratings of some hamlets that actually have VC in them every night."[186] MACV used such data when computing HES/70 rankings, so the absence of complete intelligence surely undermined CORDS understandings of certain hamlet conditions.

The Advisory Crisis was anything but over. Never fundamentally resolved, it existed as a condition emblematic of the growing discord caused by the looming end of the American War and the return to a solely Vietnamese conflict. One that transcended individuals, and spoke more to diverging geopolitical needs, the continuance of the Advisory Crisis encapsulated the American War. Although considered over after personnel changes and resumed reporting by South Vietnamese sources in Tuy Hòa District, all was not well elsewhere in Phú Yên. Into November, the Advisory Crisis lingered in Hiếu Xương District. Pacification in that district continued to suffer from PLAF activity and the ensuing GVN cover-up. "Again the Vietnamese are not reporting all the assassinations, taxation and abductions by the V.C.," Kyle wrote at the end of

November. "During the period 1 thru 18 Nov 70 we have uncovered evidence of 12 non reported incidents."[187] During that same period, he continued, "the VC entered a hamlet approximately 3 miles from District Headquarters and routed a PF platoon."[188] The lack of communication between AT28 and GVN province officials compounded the incidents committed by the emboldened PLAF, much as it had in Tuy Hòa District.

Kyle also wrote to Meerdink, informing the PSA of the severity of the situation in Hiếu Xương. The DSA began his strongly worded letter by stating, "I feel the time has come for all of us to make a crucial decision."[189] Next, Kyle asked Meerdink a question that spoke to the decision-making processes that made pacification in Phú Yên a strategy focused on Tuy Hòa City: "What shall it profit us if we gain Tuy Hoa and Tuy An District and lose Hieu Xuong?"[190] Inasmuch as the Advisory Crisis exposed the flaws in pacification, the occurrence of a similar situation in Hiếu Xương toward the end of the year revealed it as the harbinger of the new normal—pacification as a facade. The lack of reporting by local GVN authorities hid from CORDS's view all PLAF activities in the Hiếu Xương District, just as it had in Tuy Hòa District early in 1970. Kyle noted that "few hamlet officials actually live in their hamlets and many hamlet residents, RD Cadre and even PF sleep in Phu Lam and Dong Tao."[191] The reason why became apparent as Mobile Advisory Teams (MATs) questioned villagers: in an all-too-familiar story, the American advisors learned that PLAF cells frequented many hamlets at night and taxed inhabitants. Kyle reported that with the onset of darkness, the enemy "virtually controlled" the three villages of Hòa Tân, Hòa Vinh, and Hòa Xuân. More alarmingly, platoon-sized PLAF formations entered villages during the daylight hours. Kyle recounted to Meerdink one instance in which "the PF platoons knew a VC unit occupied a village office, however, they made no effort to intervene. The VC proceeded to burn records and furniture in the building. It's significant that the District did not inform me or my teams of the incident."[192] Kyle found himself in a situation painfully similar to Fluke's months earlier as the poor security conditions synonymous with Tuy Hòa replicated in Hiếu Xương.

Equally damaging were reports about how PLAF interacted with civilians in Hiếu Xương District and the ensuing ramifications that held for HES/70. Local GVN authorities released captured VCI members as quickly as they were apprehended, since "a sum of money can easily gain their release," Kyle wrote. Moreover, local GVN officials "are quick to claim a KIA as a VCI," the implications being that bribery and distortion of the Phoenix Program posited a false representation of the district's security situation.[193] Deeper still, contended Kyle,

PLAF's success resulted from its interactions with district residents. PLAF taxed and collected supplies from district inhabitants working at American military installations around Tuy Hòa City. Such conduct meant that the loyalty of the people rested not with Saigon, but rather with whichever entity forcibly elicited their assistance. Without the people's clear allegiance to the RVN, the GVN was losing regardless of the citizenry's ideological views. Local authorities found few people willing to speak about enemy activities, thus leaving the GVN with little to report to CORDS. Considering that district authorities collected pacification measurement data, Kyle surmised that HES/70 results were untrustworthy.[194] In that vein, pacification itself rested on a bed of fabrications and lies borne out of a lack of regular communication and, more significantly, high expectations on the part of the United States. HES/70, a system designed to measure progress, was doing just that, albeit with information pleasing to American eyes. In the grand scheme of the war, Phú Yên's situation appeared an inconvenient truth that the province mattered little, if at all.

Meerdink echoed Kyle's misgivings in his November monthly progress report:

> The previously suspected concealment of incidents and abductions in "pacified" Hieu Xuong District is becoming more of a fact than a suspicion. The efforts of local officials to keep the District looking good in HES rating by report all incidents has long been suspect. . . . Between 1–18 November 1970, 12 persons were found to be abducted but had not been reported. In addition, the increased activity in this District indicate that the District may be is as much trouble as Tuy Hoa and an honest report may well find this District slipping in its overall pacification rating.[195]

Amid the pressure of Vietnamization and the demand for rapid pacification gains, South Vietnamese authorities likely withheld damning information so as to please the Americans. That concealment of negative information from American advisors also revealed a major breakdown in the relationship between them and their South Vietnamese allies. Worse, the relationship, now strained at best, meant that pacification appeared as far from complete as ever.

Events in Phú Yên troubled American authorities. As 1970 closed, the news of a resurgent PLAF reached II Corps headquarters and even the U.S. Congress. On 30 December, Congressman John G. Schmitz made remarks on the instances of PLAF violence as reported by South Vietnam's National Police.[196] Schmitz listed the PLAF actions that transpired in November and December 1970 in the *Congressional Record*, which included attacks on hamlets, abductions, and murders throughout Phú Yên.

Attacks by the enemy against South Vietnamese forces, too, undermined perceived pacification gains. In Đồng Xuân District, PLAF members hurled grenades at a PSDF position in Phước Hòa hamlet on 27 November.[197] On 28 November in Sơn Hòa District, one PSDF soldier and one civilian were abducted from Xuân Phong village.[198] A late November district report for Sông Cầu noted that "the VC still make their presence known and felt" with interdictions of QL-1 and efforts to enter hamlets.[199] One such incident occurred on 29 November, when, as recalled in Representative Schmitz's remarks, PLAF infiltrated Khoan Hậu hamlet and killed the hamlet chief and two members of the RD Cadre.[200]

December was also eventful as the enemy maintained its harassment campaign against GVN infrastructure. In Sơn Hòa District on 1 December, PLAF abducted one civilian.[201] In Hiếu Xương District, PLAF kidnapped six 15-year-old boys and one 14-year-old girl from Phước Mỹ hamlet on 1 December.[202] On 1 December, PLAF took a civilian from Đồng Xuân's Triều Sơn hamlet.[203] The next day, 2 December, PLAF fired mortars that wounded five civilians in Sông Cầu District. Assassinations resumed when a PLAF platoon moved into Chanh Tục hamlet and killed one civilian on 11 December.[204] Then, on 14 December, a PLAF platoon entered Từ Nham hamlet, assassinating a civilian and leaving another wounded.[205]

Representative Schmitz's remarks also noted events in Tuy Hòa District. On 2 December, PLAF mortared Chí Thạnh hamlet, and a PLAF mine detonated near Vĩnh Phú hamlet. On 5 December, two female PLAF members assassinated the Chi Duc hamlet chief. Also on 5 December, PLAF abducted a civilian from An Nghiệp hamlet in Tuy Hòa District, as well as one from Phước Huệ hamlet in Đồng Xuân District. On 9 December in Tuy Hòa District, PLAF abducted a PSFD member from Bình Chánh hamlet, and, on 11 December, four civilians from Tân Long hamlet.[206] Clearly, troubling events in Tuy Hòa District dominated the information relayed to Congress.

"It was a strange month," opened Meerdink's December report.[207] On top of all the PLAF activity in Tuy Hòa, Đồng Xuân, and Hiếu Xương districts, enemy forces executed successful "major operations" in the districts of Sông Cầu and Tuy An. "On the night of 1–2 December, the defenses of the district compound at Tuy An were breached by sappers, who, utilizing the darkness and extreme weather conditions, kept in contact for nearly four hours," Meerdink recounted.[208] The results of that raid left fifteen RF and PF personnel dead and ten members of AT28 wounded, in addition to damaging the district compound.[209] Seventeen days later, on 19 December, PLAF struck Từ Nham hamlet in Sông Cầu in an "an amphibious operation" from the sea, resulting in seven PF and five PSDF dead.[210] "The walls are crumbling around us and the Deputy Province Chief's orders are to retreat to your forts and pray," Sông Cầu DSA Maj. Donald M. Scher asserted in his end-of-December report.[211] Scher wrote that PLAF "chopped off 1/3 of XUAN THINH Village by dispossession of TU NHAM Hamlet while apparently controlling TUY LUAT and VINH CUU AN."[212] Moreover, he said, "if the above is even close to factual, the VC are steadily realizing their stated objectives of control of the countryside while pinning sub-sector forces in defense of the District Headquarters."[213] Meerdink noted in his December report that the operations in those two districts "constituted 2/3 of the fatalities suffered by RF/PF during the month."[214] Yet other incidents also happened in December in Sông Cầu: PLAF ambushed two American conveys using captured claymores; elsewhere in the district, PLAF teams obtained supplies from villages, while other teams mortared GVN assets, targeting the district headquarters on two occasions.[215] In total, Scher identified six "indirect fire attacks" and three "coordinated ground attacks."[216] Even before the intensified PLAF activity, as of 1 December, HES/70 indicated that Sông Cầu District went from one "D"-rated hamlet to six.[217] Only the movement of C/75 Ranger Company in the Hub "may have well disrupted enemy plans" for additional operations.[218]

What transpired in 1970 defined the war in Phú Yên. Regardless of allied efforts to push PAVN and PLAF forces away from the province's communities, the enemy remained capable of undermining GVN legitimacy. The intensity of the Communists' resolve amplified as they infiltrated and harassed the Accelerated Pacification Campaign on multiple levels—physically and psychologically. Indeed, by the close of 1970, the NLF had rebuilt much of its political infrastructure and effectively challenged pacification efforts in the province.[219]

8

"Like reeds in the wind"

The War in the Hamlets, 1971

"The central Vietnam coastal provinces—Binh Dinh, Quang Ngai to the north, and Phu Yen to the south—represent the last heavily populated areas not under government control," Rowland Evans and Robert Novak reported in their 16 September 1971 *Los Angeles Times* article.[1] "If control could be imposed here, Saigon's hand would be strengthened immeasurably in any future negotiations with Hanoi."[2] Their point encapsulated 1971 in Phú Yên: "control" was the operative word, for much of Phú Yên existed in contested space at this point in the war. That space, however, increasingly fell under NLF control—even if HES/70 data reflected otherwise. In Phú Yên, this period revealed Vietnamization and a resurgent PLAF as heavily restricting the GVN's ability to advance pacification.

Vietnamization at any price undermined pacification in Phú Yên. As much as 1969 and 1970 illuminated clear problems with pacification's expansion in the form of the APC, 1971 affirmed that such issues were more than momentary. Pacification at haste created a scenario in Phú Yên in which measurement data suggested progress, but in fact conditions in 1971 remained little changed from 1969–70. Although HES/70 portrayed favorable hamlet ratings, PLAF remained markedly intact and continued to make inroads into APC target hamlets—a fact well known to CORDS personnel in the province. Ironically, American authorities, either knowingly or unwittingly, adopted the GVN's stance of accepting the Communist's continued presence in the South Vietnamese countryside.

Bình Định continued to divert attention away from Phú Yên. Still seen as strategically more significant than its neighbor to the south, IFFV continued to focus more on Bình Định. In September 1971, pacification in Bình Định floundered further, and it became the least pacified of the RVN's forty-four provinces.[3] For this reason, IFFV and ARVN devoted more time and resources to pacifying Bình Định as Vietnamization's completion loomed closer. Phú Yên looked less troubled by comparison, and therefore everything that transpired in that province paled in the shadow of events in Bình Định. More than a sideshow, however, Phú Yên persisted as a prime example of how a low-intensity conflict could endure despite abundant U.S. economic and military assets. To offset the departure of U.S. maneuver battalions from Phú Yên, American advisors sought an increase in offensive activity by South Korean and South Vietnamese forces. Progress remained fixed on the execution of operations against the enemy, albeit by allied units. Conventional warfare as an indicator of advancement toward victory remained intact, regardless of American involvement. All the major military events of 1971 in Phú Yên involved allied units destroying highly visible enemy forces in battle. Notably, these engagements did not entail evicting PLAF or VCI from the province. Consequently, acts of terrorism persisted in the province as the emboldened enemy gained ground well into 1972.[4] In reality, conditions in Phú Yên were not much better than those in Bình Định.

Well-Placed Optimism

In Phú Yên, 1971 commenced the same way as 1970 ended. "The Phu Yen advisory effort has had little to cheer about over the past year and has learned to deftly move from crisis to crisis," PSA Meerdink wrote in his 31 January 1971 province report.[5] Despite his dour opening line, Meerdink injected a sense of positivity in referencing the South Vietnamese: "For the first time in many months, friendly units were in the enemy strongholds for extended periods," Meerdink said of South Vietnamese security forces.[6] Outpacing ROKA, RF units "combat assaulted" into areas such as the "Hub," Kỳ Lộ Valley, and the Hà Roi Secret Zone—places once deemed "too dangerous for such forces to venture into."[7] Even ARVN, often criticized for its lack of urgency, brought battle to those three PLAF strongholds. Operation Bãi Đông I, which launched on 16 January and saw RF units inserted into PLAF sanctuaries, quickly improved the GVN's image in Phú Yên. With an offensive spirit not normally associated with the RF in the province, the South Vietnamese outpaced the ROKA 26th and 28th—South Korean forces once noted for their effectiveness. Meerdink asserted that the province chief sought to make Bãi Đông I the benchmark for future operations.[8] The follow-up operation, Bãi Đông II, however, faltered due to coordination problems between allied forces. Poor communication between

South Korean and South Vietnamese officials meant those forces stumbling into the other's ambushes. Moreover, ROKA denied RF units access to South Korean AOs.[9]

South Korean and South Vietnamese spoiling operations were indeed helpful in maintaining pressure on PLAF. Distracting PLAF's attention from interfering in hamlet affairs provided only a fleeting advantage, though, as the rewards of those spoiling operations lasted only as long as their forces maintained the offensive. Furthermore, allied activity in enemy base areas did not necessarily mean removing the Communist threat from the district, let alone the province. Rather, it dispersed PLAF and disrupted its plans, but did nothing to prevent the enemy from regrouping. Allied operations near enemy strongholds in 1969 did not prevent the occurrence of the Advisory Crisis, nor did later allied actions alter the province's future. Simply because South Korean and South Vietnamese soldiers found themselves fighting deep into PLAF territory did not spell an end to PLAF in Phú Yên. Nor did allied victories against PLAF stop Hanoi's conventional forces from probing Phú Yên's defenses and discrediting GVN assurances of security.

Abductions dropped to low levels by the end of January. Meerdink referenced a sharp decrease in abductions—just seven for the month—which he credited to MAT efforts in the Tuy Hòa Valley. MATs orchestrated successful ambushes of the PLAF K-13 Battalion. In southern Hiếu Xương District and the Hà Roi Secret Zone, the C/75 Rangers killed six PLAF soldiers in limited contact with the enemy. However, communication mishaps involving the Rangers, the province chief, and ROKA prevented the Rangers from exploiting one particular contact with the enemy. Living among the rural population, the MAT anti-abduction campaign was somewhat successful, as PLAF abducted just five civilians in a seventy-five-day period. The end of January also marked the conclusion of the anti-abduction campaign in Tuy Hòa District as attention shifted toward Tuy An District.[10]

All of January's perceived accomplishments did not mean that pacification was working. Like allied units on the offensive, HES/70, too, uplifted the perception of pacification in Phú Yên. With overly optimistic ratings, HES/70 proved troublesome to both the PSA and the province chief. "The HES reacted favorably (perhaps, in fact, over-reacted) to the GVN success and Viet Cong failures and startlingly declared that 91 percent of Phu Yen's population now resides in secure areas and 72 percent in A and B hamlets," Meerdink reported.[11] "This headquarters believes," he continued, "that the Viet Cong are presently placing great emphasis on the development of their infrastructure and the GVN has not yet demonstrated a capacity or willingness to meaningfully cope with this threat."[12] Despite alterations to HES/70 to better account for VCI, which pleased Advisory Team 28, the province chief, Lt. Col. Nguyễn Văn Tố, did "not share this enthusiasm for the change," Meerdink said.[13] Rather, "he declared that as a man of few vices, 'the HES is the only lottery' in which he participates!"[14] For Meerdink, HES/70 scores better reflected a moment in time than dependable long-term identifiers of a hamlet's progress or decline.[15] In the case of Phú Yên, high HES/70 scores did not necessarily translate into stellar security. As before, what PLAF chose to do and not do played the deciding role in Phú Yên's future.

Nor did January's successes drastically alter the prevailing sense of skepticism in Phú Yên. The January province report underscored that tone: "At month's end, the most startling of all pronouncements was made: 'We will open Highway 7-B in February or March!' One's knees begin to tremble at the heady thought that after losing the previous rounds to points, the local GVN may be going for a knockout in the closing minutes!"[16] Evidently, doubt remained regarding the GVN's capabilities. Indeed, save for brief moments, the highway in question remained predominately under the control of local PLAF units for much of the reminder of the war.

In February, the *New York Times* reported that on 1 February, "ten mortar rounds struck the military advisors' compound at Tuy Hoa air base."[17] Also that month, on at least two occasions, enemy forces challenged GVN resolve in Sông Cầu District. Each time, RF/PF and U.S. Army helicopter gunships thwarted Communist advances, continuing into February the image of a revitalized province. Efforts by GVN forces to improve province security received a major boost on 3 February, as allied forces trapped elements of the PAVN 9th Battalion on a small peninsula in Sông Cầu District. "Early on the morning of 3 February, elements of the 9th NVA Battalion (Gold Star Division) made another of its amphibious assaults in the rocky coves adjacent to Vinh Hoa hamlet, Song Cau District," Meerdink recounted in the monthly progress report for February. Adding that the PAVN unit probably intended to take up positions in the nearby hills before launching an attack the following evening, the PSA wrote, "a PF platoon operating (we'll give them the benefit of the doubt) in the hills discovered the NVA presence and radioed the district for help."[18] Subsequently, and unfortunately for this PAVN force, solid communication resulted in the quick arrival of 134th Assault Helicopter Company gunships. With helicopters inserting two RF companies and providing fire support, allied forces trapped the PAVN contingent on the peninsula. Americans and South Vietnamese killed somewhere between fifty-seven and ninety-eight North Vietnamese regulars; the large discrepancy came from two different body counts, with U.S. figures placing the number of enemy killed at fifty-seven, while the GVN claimed ninety-eight.[19]

A second, similar incident occurred on 12 February, when a PLAF company tried to cross a sand bar near Vĩnh Cửu Phú village, approximately one mile northeast of the town of Sông Cầu. As recounted in a history of the 134th Assault Helicopter Company, the "Song Cau massacre" (as they called it) entailed American helicopters and South Vietnamese troops entrapping the PLAF company. At Vĩnh Cửu Phú, helicopters from the 134th inserted ARVN soldiers on the northern end of the peninsula. Effectively blocked by ARVN, the PLAF company attempted to retreat to the nearby hills. Machine-gun and rocket fire from the helicopters thwarted the enemy's retreat, thereby forcing PLAF to dig in and fight. After an hour and ten minutes, the Americans and South Vietnamese counted forty-one PLAF dead.[20]

Phú Yên remained a troubled province. MACV data for March 1971 indicated noteworthy VCI strength clustered strategically throughout the RVN, including Phú Yên. Thomas C. Thayer, director of the U.S. Department of Defense's Southeast Asia Division between 1967 and 1972, wrote that according to MACV numbers, "estimated communist clandestine strength" was 2,183 individuals, therefore 3.3% of the national total.[21] Worse, Phú Yên found itself in a group of five abutting provinces teaming with PLAF activity. "The grouping suggests pockets of strength and the ability to provide mutual support and operating flexibility," Thayer deduced.[22] For AT28, these numbers meant that pacification in Phú Yên faced a well-devised late-war Communist insurgency. This larger enemy effort sought to undermine the GVN's legitimacy and consolidate NLF gains. Thus, in early 1971, pacification seemed as far from complete as ever before.

PLAF defied GVN pacification efforts as February turned into March. "The Phu Yen Viet Cong leadership certainly must be composed of some of the most thoroughly inspired officers ever to have engaged in warfare," the monthly province report ominously began. "Their tenacity in the face of overwhelming odds is truly remarkable. As the reader might surmise, from the GVN point of view, it was another bad month in Phu Yen," which, for Phú Yên during the Vietnam War, was dismally normal.[23] Although ROKA operations in the "Hub" exacted a heavy toll on PLAF, they did so at the civilian population's expense. ROKA forces claimed 450 PLAF killed; AT28 figured that most of the dead were rear support personnel, since the South Koreans confiscated only 100 weapons. Of PLAF's response, Meerdink wrote, "it is possible the enemy's actions are

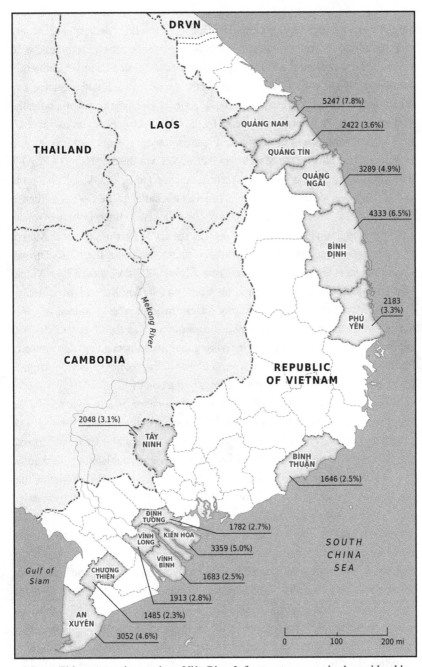

DRVN

LAOS

THAILAND

5247 (7.8%)

QUẢNG NAM

2422 (3.6%)

QUẢNG TÍN

QUẢNG
NGÃI

3289 (4.9%)

4333 (6.5%)

BÌNH
ĐỊNH

2183
(3.3%)

PHÚ
YÊN

CAMBODIA

Mekong River

REPUBLIC
OF VIETNAM

2048 (3.1%)

TÂY
NINH

BÌNH
THUẬN

1646 (2.5%)

ĐỊNH
TƯỜNG

1782 (2.7%)

VĨNH
LONG

KIẾN HÒA

3359 (5.0%)

VĨNH
BÌNH

Gulf of
Siam

CHƯƠNG
THIỆN

1683 (2.5%)

1913 (2.8%)

AN
XUYÊN

1485 (2.3%)

3052 (4.6%)

SOUTH
CHINA
SEA

0   100   200 mi

Map 5. Thirteen provinces where Việt Cộng Infrastructure exercised considerable
strength as of March 1971. Data from Thomas C. Thayer, *War Without Fronts:
The American Experience in Vietnam* (Annapolis, Md.: Naval Institute Press, 2016).

Cartography by Erin Greb.

based on seasonal change or perhaps he has been reading Shakespeare. At any rate, the Ides of March signaled the start of another abduction campaign."[24] To replace its losses from the ROKA operation, PLAF initiated another abduction campaign. By the end of the March reporting period, PLAF had abducted 107 inhabitants from the western portions of the Tuy Hòa Valley. Unsurprisingly, the area targeted by PLAF was not covered by the GVN's anti-abduction campaign.[25] In Phú Yên, solutions to problems propagated more problems.

Equally revealing in the March province report was the discussion of PLAF's reversion to its phase I of guerrilla warfare. As directed by COSVN, PLAF units in Phú Yên reverted to harassment techniques to challenge the GVN's influence in the province. Abductions, disruption of communication lines, mining of roads, and snipers typified PLAF's interactions with the GVN. On the night of 28 March, PLAF launched a series of highly symbolic attacks, mortaring the "GVN District Headquarters at Song Cau, Tuy Hoa Army Airfield, ROKA bases in Hieu Xuong District, and a combined sapper-mortar attack on the Hieu Xuong District Head-quarters."[26] Although the Hiếu Xương district headquarters remained in GVN hands, the structure "was virtually destroyed as well as the three vehicles and approximately 100 M-16 rifles."[27] In striking multiple targets across the province, PLAF sent the clear message that it remained an active participant in the struggle for Phú Yên, despite years of allied efforts to the contrary.

Ironically, it was Phú Yên's RF/PF units that appeared to adhere to COSVN's avoid battle directive. According to the March province report, "the spur of enemy activity was matched by virtual cessation of activities by RF/PF forces. Citing lack of air assets as the most common excuse for not leaving the shadow of the flagpole, Territorial Forces made only one foray into the highlands that resulted in no contacts." The RF and PF evidently preferred defending themselves and their own individual futures than fighting the GVN's enemy. Attrition-like numbers reflected a decreased will to fight on the part of the RF and PF: "As could be expected, the favorable kill and weapons ratio of previous months dropped to a 1:1 on kills and an adverse 1:2 on weapons."[28] Thus, the best source of gauging enemy activity—and therefore the health of the province—were the MATs. Indeed, "much of the enemy activity in the areas that MAT habitually visited would not be reported except for these teams. Since they only occupy a small portion of the province, one conjectures as to how much enemy activity is taking place in our supposedly secure areas that is not reported."[29]

April—never a good month in Phú Yên—featured deteriorating security conditions in Hiếu Xương and especially in Tuy Hòa. If any criticism from

AT28 damned the situation in Phú Yên, surely it was Meerdink's commentary: "'Disaster' is the only word which can be used to describe the situation in Phú Yên during the month of April," began the monthly province report for April.[30] According to the report, PLAF initiated eighty-five incidents versus forty-six in the month prior.[31] Task Force Talon's efforts in 1970 now surely looked to have been in vain. AT28 blamed the Tuy Hòa district chief, Lt. Đỗ Thể Tấn, for not matching PLAF's aggressiveness. Despite calls from Nguyễn Văn Tố requesting Đỗ Thể Tấn's removal, the GVN did nothing. As leadership faltered, GVN security forces refused to engage PLAF. In western Tuy Hòa District, "on four separate occasions Vietnamese units broke and ran after establishing contact with the enemy (twice leaving their American advisors behind to fend for themselves)."[32] Moreover, "on these same four occasions, the enemy's position was well fixed at nightfall only to have the GVN forces call off the war for the day and return home."[33] In one case, a single PLAF unit "stood off 3 RF companies, 4 sets of gunships and 2 airstrikes in western Tuy Hoa, with the last sound of battle being the enemy machine gun that initiated the contact at 0830 firing at the last RF company returning to Tuy Hoa at 1600 (0830–1600 being the normal working hours for the RF in Phu Yen). The machine gun and operator are still there as of this writing."[34] With instances like this, all the conventional military power wielded by the allies could not overcome the low-level insurgency waged by PLAF. Alarmingly, "within one month, most of the hard fought for improvements in Tuy Hoa over the past year have been lost."[35]

Yet the trouble extended beyond Tuy Hòa District. Events elsewhere in Phú Yên compounded those in Tuy Hòa. In Hiểu Xương District, "virtually no military facility escaped some kind of enemy attack."[36] Here, Meerdink reported that "the enemy launched attacks by fire and/or ground against nearly every major Vietnamese, Korean, and American military installation in the area."[37] His choice of the word "disaster" indeed epitomized the month of April in Phú Yên as pacification problems solidified as the new normal. Moreover, IFFV's deactivation on 30 April as part of Vietnamization meant no forthcoming military solution from the Americans.

May saw unabated, intense PLAF activity. While a new district chief made a positive impact on Sông Cầu using air assets to resupply the district, PLAF intensified its efforts to interdict the GVN's lines of communication in Phú Yên. PLAF devoted considerable attention toward mining the province's high-ways.[38] On one occasion, a convoy encountered enemy ambushes and mines on LTL-7B, resulting in seven vehicles destroyed, leaving the GVN's promise to open LTL-7B by February or March largely unfulfilled by April. Phú Yên's principal highway, QL-1, also felt PLAF's wrath as the enemy attacked three bridges, destroying one and using snipers to harass traffic over another two. But for AT28, the enemy's attacks on LTL-6B amounted to the most serious. Previously considered a safe and secure road, multiple ambushes and mining incidents morphed LTL-6B into a particularly dangerous stretch of asphalt. In the most severe incident during the reporting period, the Đồng Xuân District medical advisor died and a district senior advisor, severely injured, left Phú Yên via medical evacuation. Enemy activity peaked on 24 May, as PLAF launched seven major attacks throughout Đồng Xuân. On 26 May, two civilians died when a mine exploded at the Phụng Tường market.[39]

Closer Inspection

AT28's observations at the hamlet, village, and district levels offer valuable insight into the deteriorating situation unfolding in Phú Yên in 1971. Sent to Phú Yên in 1971, during the height of Vietnamization, U.S. Army Capt. Courtney L. Frobenius found himself attached to AT28. Tasked with advising the PSDF and later the RF/PF, Frobenius's duties had him visiting the province's hamlets and evaluating security conditions. During his inspections of local defense units, Frobenius found numerous pacification shortcomings. His reports called attention to PLAF activities and the enemy's continued hold on the province. Noted in his statements were the GVN's deficiencies, limited use of allied troops, and unchecked enemy activity. These three factors portrayed the U.S. Army's withdrawal from the RVN in an extremely negative light. Essentially, Frobenius's findings harkened back to Fluke's during the Advisory Crisis.

Even in 1971, keeping the province capital physically linked to the rest of the province remained a challenge. As LTL-6B linked the inland district of Đồng Xuân to Tuy Hòa City, whoever controlled this artery essentially ruled the district. Frobenius detailed LTL-6B's significance to Đồng Xuân District's existence under the GVN. "All supplies, both in and out of the District must flow over this route," he noted.[40] Indeed, as a landlocked district, Đồng Xuân relied solely on LTL-6B as a connection to the rest of the province. "A 20% rice deficiency in Dong Xuan District makes overland route even more zenith in importance," Frobenius continued.[41] The psychological value of the GVN maintaining full control of this artery mattered even more. "If 6B were to be closed by the enemy, a psychological blow of hurricane proportions would not settle easy on the population of Dong Xuan," he warned. "If 6B were closed the population could not travel either in or out of Dong Xuan, but would be forced to remain immobile. The closing would also represent a drastic blow to the GVN in the eyes of the populace."[42] Vietnamization, too, complicated matters, since any sustained enemy interdiction of LTL-6B would test the GVN's ability to maximize its limited assets in Phú Yên. Frobenius surmised that "all supplies would have to be carried in by air, something that the GVN can ill afford with the evaporation of American withdrawal."[43] Conversely, Frobenius suggested that the GVN could force convoys through LTL-6B, a method he noted as being employed on LTL-7B. Yet doing so would come at a price, as Frobenius noted that each time the GVN reopened LTL-7B, it lost equipment. "The last time 7B was opened to Song Hoa District, a total of 13 vehicles were destroyed along with a bulldozer," he reminded his superiors—a steep price for a temporary reopening.[44]

Frobenius pondered the future of LTL-6B because, as he saw it, the enemy had realized the route's value. Essentially, PLAF's "whole plan in Dong Xuan depends upon the closure of this road."[45] To support such a claim, Frobenius referenced the plight of Xuân Sơn, one of five villages in the district but the only one adjacent to LTL-6B. Xuân Sơn's "infrastructure has tremendous depth and width," Frobenius reported.[46] Worse still for the future of the GVN in Đồng Xuân District, the enemy maintained a visible presence in each of the village's hamlets—Phư Hoa, Phú Long, Phú Vang, and Hà Bằng. With Xuân Sơn almost entirely under its control, PLAF had "a vital base of intelligence, supplies, food, rice, labor, and money, and men."[47] PLAF's possession of Xuân Sơn did not bode well for the GVN's prospects of keeping LTL-6B safe from enemy activity.

Deeper still, Frobenius wrote of the current state the railway that traversed Đồng Xuân District. He reported the railway as "nominally open thru the District. But this is at great risk to the traveler. Railroad cars can be seen among the twisted track laying alongside of the railroad lines."[48] After each successful enemy mining, "the track is repaired and the next train is rolling thru at the next scheduled time. A type of Russian roulette."[49] Furthermore, Frobenius accentuated the effect of the enemy interdiction of the lines of communication in the district. In that vein, he commented that the reports of mine detonations typically read, "Victor Charlie mine was detonated at Grid coordinates Bravo Quebec 003755, killing 12 civilians, 3 soldiers, wounding 16 civilians and 4 soldiers. The mine was believed to be command detonated. The railroad is impassable until repairs can be made. 1 railroad car totally destroyed. . . . Not exactly Union Pacific travel brochure material," he quipped.[50] LTL-6B, Frobenius remarked, "reads the same. Hulls of vehicles can be seen resting upside down, shattered, and burnt out, over craters that were obviously made by an anti-tank mine."[51] Although not referring a specific incident, Frobenius nonetheless relayed the new normal for those traveling on LTL-6B.

Placement of local security compounded the situation in Đồng Xuân. Indeed, Frobenius reported that the bridges received the bulk of attention, with bunkers astride both sides of the approaching track. Although such security made sense, it occurred at the expense of the rest of the railway. "Sweeps are made daily of the track to find mines, but often this proves to no avail. While the troops huddle inside of their bunkers, the Viet Cong have freedom to roam at will where the troops are not located. Because of the enemy's domination of the hamlets, he has excellent intelligence as to where the mobile government troops are at night. He can easily skirt these positions and plant his mines on the road and on the railroad."[52] On a slightly more positive note, Frobenius recalled the following:

> [One] Korean company, one RF Group Headquarters along with two of its companies and two PF platoons are situated along 6B and given the mission of its defense. They have artillery support located just outside of the village boundaries to the West. A total of 8 Kilometers of road must be defended by these troops, not a bad batting average. The troops seek to evade the civilian population at night and generally move away from them. If they didn't the enemy would have exceptionally correct intelligence and could remove them.[53]

Movement of friendly forces appeared to be the main factor in keeping the area even marginally under GVN control. Ending his report, Frobenius bemoaned the continued hindrance of Đồng Xuân's transportation arteries. "The minings continue. The people continue to use 6B. People die from minings, and equipment is destroyed. How long can it continue? How long will it continue? If the enemy were to insure [sic] that each time a vehicle traveling 6B and the railroad were mined, the game of Russian Roulette just wouldn't be any fun anymore and it wouldn't be worth the chance."[54]

Back in Tuy Hòa District, events remained far too similar to those of 1970. There, both ROKA and ARVN 2nd Company, 44th Battalion concluded operations. ROKA's regimental-sized operation netted 264 KIA, capturing just 50 weapons. Worse still for long-term district security, ROKA commenced to close all its platoon-sized firebases. Confidence in the district's future under the GVN shook further as reports circulated on the "VC's entry into fringe hamlets without being engaged." Accordingly, the enemy had "the same freedom of movement he enjoyed in the latter part of 1970."[55] As for ARVN, the 2nd Company's sweep of LTL-7B ended with poor results, as evidenced by PLAF's continued interdiction of the road.[56] Like LTL-6B, LTL-7B remained under the constant threat of enemy interdiction.

The Battle of Củng Sơn

Pacification in Phú Yên seemed on the cusp of ruin. Two events demonstrated that the province existed in the nebulous world between GVN and NLF control: the Battle of Củng Sơn and the dropping of the Sông Đà Rằng bridges. Roughly 56 kilometers inland from Tuy Hòa City, Củng Sơn sat near two enemy base areas, a point not missed by the Communists themselves. Here, 15,000 South Vietnamese lived along the riverbanks of the Sông Ba with LTL-7B on the other side of the hills to the north. Roughly two kilometers to the northwest of the Sơn Hòa district headquarters sat Hòn Ngang, a piece of high ground that dominated the terrain near Cùng Sơn. Complicating matters for PLAF, the district capital sat amid a defensive ring formed by four strategic hamlets: Bắc Lý, Đông Hòa, Mả Vôi, and Tây Hòa. Sr. Col. Trần Văn Mười, K-13 Local Force Battalion commander, recalled that the Province Party Current Affairs Committee and the Phú Yên Province Military Unit viewed Sơn Hòa District as a liberated area, with only Cùng Sơn beyond their control. To remedy this predicament and turn Sơn Hòa District into a true liberated area, PLAF received orders to take the district capital.[57]

By 1 June, PLAF elements grouped for the Cùng Sơn operation to the northwest of the enclave. Intelligence obtained by the GVN indicated the maneuvering of an enemy company or battalion near Cùng Sơn. To spoil PLAF intentions, RF Group 53 launched recon operations that killed fifty-two PLAF soldiers. Additionally, on 15 June, Nguyễn Văn Tố authorized Đại Bàng Campaign 7 "to break down VC High Point."[58] An American AAR noted the lack of "intelligence of an impending attack, however the units were alert due to the number of contacts that they had prior to this time."[59] GVN spoiling efforts delayed PLAF preparations, yet an estimated enemy force of 500 soldiers ultimately descended on the environs of Cùng Sơn.[60] PLAF units organic to Sơn Hòa—the 167th Artillery Company, the 202 Sapper Unit, the 96th Local Force Battalion, and C-25 Sapper Unit—constituted the bulk of the attacking force. Only Tuy An's K-13 Local Force Battalion came from outside the district.[61]

Despite GVN harassment efforts, three days later, on 18 June, the biggest engagement between allied and Communist forces in Phú Yên since 1968 transpired in Sơn Hòa District. At 0230, the PLAF 167th Artillery Company fired mortar rounds and B-40 rockets against Hòn Ngang and the nearby airfield. That barrage marked the start of PLAF's gambit to take Củng Sơn.[62] The explosions awoke the DSA, Capt. Ronald Thayer, all too prematurely. He had been on the job, and asleep, for just a few hours. Thayer found himself in Sơn Hòa District after the last DSA vacated via medical evacuation in May. With just two weeks remaining on his tour, Thayer filled in as Sơn Hòa DSA for approximately five days, because of his familiarity with the area and his friendship with the South Vietnamese district chief, Maj. Nguyễn Phú Hiếu. As the enemy launched its attack, both Thayer and Nguyễn Phú Hiếu quickly rallied South Vietnamese forces.[63]

At 0300, PLAF launched its two-pronged ground assault. To take Củng Sơn, PLAF targeted the Sơn Hòa district headquarters and airstrip as well as the nearby RF Group 53 headquarters and the firebase atop Hòn Ngang. The 202 Sapper Unit assailed Hòn Ngang and engaged two RF companies defending the RF headquarters.[64] As the fight for Hòn Ngang unfolded, the K-13 Local Force Battalion's 13th Company engaged RF troops at the airfield before withdrawing to rejoin the battalion. Meanwhile, the rest of the K-13 Local Force Battalion attacked Đông Hòa and Bắc Lý to position itself east of Củng Sơn to block possible RF reinforcements from relieving the district headquarters via TL-9B (see map 2 in chapter 2).[65] Elements of the K-13 Local Force Battalion also attacked the district headquarters. On the opposite side of Củng Sơn, the 96th Local Force Battalion placed itself to thwart possible RF attempts to relieve the RF Group 53 headquarters from the southwest.[66] From the south, PLAF command tasked the C-25 Sapper Unit with crossing the Sông Ba and seizing the district capital. Yet the swollen river, with its strong current, kept the C-25 Sapper Unit on the wrong bank.[67]

PLAF's plans went further awry. Thayer's experience as an artillery officer during two previous tours paid dividends: he helped direct precise mortar fire, breaking up the enemy attack against the GVN assets.[68] The ardent RF defenders, too, slowed the PLAF advance. Nevertheless, the enemy retained the advantage. Upon realizing the precariousness of the situation, Maj. Nguyễn Phú Hiếu radioed for immediate assistance. He had much at stake: being North Vietnamese by birth and choosing to fight for Saigon almost assuredly meant his demise should he fall into PLAF hands.[69] Assistance materialized in the form of the U.S. Army 134th Assault Helicopter Company's Huey gunships. With the company on standby, the fully loaded helicopters of the 134th sat ready on a tarmac at Tuy Hòa North Air Base. Alerted to the crisis unfolding in Sơn Hòa, the gunships set out to Củng Sơn. Arriving on station within minutes, the gunships provided much-needed fire support.[70] As the gunships engaged targets near the RF headquarters, the RF repositioned its troops and established defensive lines to contain the PLAF battalions by 0400. At 0515, a helicopter carrying Meerdink and the GVN's deputy for security arrived overhead and the pair assessed the unfolding battle below.[71]

Back on Hòn Ngang, PLAF's assault continued at 0600. There, the RF's one 50-caliber machine gun mounted in a gun tower and three 105mm howitzers made life difficult for PLAF sappers. RF artillery fired at zero elevation with "bee-hive" and high-explosive shells that "greatly deterred the enemy access to the artillery positions."[72] According to the American AAR, "although close to being overran during the engagement," RF artillery crews "met the enemy face on and used their artillery pieces in the most outstanding defensive role."[73] Additional gunships arrived on scene at 0700, as those already engaging the enemy expended their munitions. Two platoons of RF 996 relocated to the RF headquarters, while the RF 994 moved to reinforce the RF headquarters by taking up positions overlooking the hill to the east. RF reconnaissance elements spread out to better access the placement of the opposing PLAF troops. At 0730, Meerdink and the GVN's deputy for security landed at the district compound. The forward air controller (FAC) observed substantial enemy movement to the north of the RF headquarters, at which point Nguyễn Phú Hiếu and Thayer requested airstrikes. The subsequent airstrike hit the enemy just north of Hòn Ngang, causing a secondary explosion. The American AAR noted that two days after the battle, thirty-one PLAF bodies from the 96th Local Force Battalion were found near the crater caused by that airstrike.[74] The presence of so many enemy dead was testament to the engagement's ferocity.

As the morning hours passed, the tide of the battle turned in favor of the RF. Between 0900 and 0930 hours, while American gunships continued to engage PLAF with machine-gun and rocket fire, other American helicopters inserted the RF Mobile Battalion 206 to the north of Củng Sơn. Thirty minutes later, two RF Mobile Battalion 206 companies, 389 and 988, simultaneously engaged the enemy on Hòn Ngang.[75] These two companies' actions resulted in five PLAF kills, the capture of an 82mm mortar, and the securing of Hòn Ngang.[76] With the PLAF attack on Hòn Ngang now thwarted and the hill firmly under RF control, the enemy no longer threatened the 53d RF headquarters and firebase. The fight on Hòn Ngang claimed the lives of twenty-eight PLAF and fourteen RF troopers. The remnants of the K-13 Local Force Battalion—now firmly on the defensive—took cover within Bắc Lý. The 96th Local Force Battalion instead disengaged itself from the battle and retreated from the area. American and South Vietnamese authorities could not confirm "hard contact" between the RF and the 96th.[77] In a scene repeated across the RVN throughout the war, including in Phú Yên, K-13's soldiers occupied buildings and waited for allied firepower to consume them and the hamlet. Typically a tactic of PAVN, in this instance PLAF troops kept pacification locked in the destruction-construction cycle—a process emblematic of the war in Phú Yên. PLAF's use of that tactic reflected Nông Trường 5's influence over the Communist war in Phú Yên, and it indicated at the very least the sharing of knowledge—if not personnel—between PAVN and PLAF. Regardless, despite the new approach to pacification in the APC, old, tested methods to contest the spread of Saigon's control remained effective.

On the offensive, South Vietnamese forces moved to encircle the remaining K-13 elements, with American gunships circling overhead. By 1100, all of RF Mobile Battalion 206's elements had arrived and assumed blocking positions. Thereafter, surviving soldiers of the K-13 Local Force Battalion found themselves surrounded in Bắc Lý. At 1200, Nguyễn Phú Hiếu and Thayer requested a PSYOP mission to encourage the civilians to evacuate. PLAF permitted the inhabitants to leave, knowing full well that the absence of noncombatants meant airstrikes, which would guarantee the destruction of property and a setback for pacification.[78]

Before airstrikes commenced, gunships engaged more enemy targets. Concurrently, a company of the RF Mobile Battalion 206 attempted to penetrate the K-13's line, but fell back in the face of intense enemy fire. "Our forces fought the enemy for every house and every rice-paddy dike," K-13's Sr. Col. Trần Văn Mười later recalled.[79] Therefore, another RF Mobile Battalion 206 company moved farther west to attack from that direction. Nevertheless, RF assaults between 1400 and 1500 hours did not break through K-13's wall of fire. Gunships, too, failed to dislodge the PLAF troops from the hamlet's buildings. Yet the gunships continued to fire and an RF company made one last assault, this time from the north. These attacks had also failed by 1630, at which point the FAC requested an airstrike. At 1715, an airstrike rocked Bắc Lý, with some K-13 elements attempting to break contact by moving northward. In doing so, however, PLAF quickly encountered fire from RF soldiers. Between 1745 and 2000 hours, the battle reached its apogee as an RF unit broke through and battled the remaining K-13 elements in a series of firefights. Nightfall ended the intense exchanges, with fighting resuming and the battle ending the next morning.[80]

For Thayer, the battle proved a momentous end to his service in the RVN. Thayer and Nguyễn Phú Hiếu coordinated the allied response throughout the battle without regard for their own safety. "After learning that a large force of the enemy had moved into the hamlets of Son Luong, Phuoc Hoa and Van Hoa, Capt. Thayer and the district chief, constantly exposing themselves to enemy fire, consolidated and placed the Popular and Territorial Forces around the three hamlets, allowing none of the enemy to escape," the accolades went. "Due to his presence and leadership, the enemy lost almost an entire Battalion"—a feat not seen in years in Phú Yên.[81] For such actions, the U.S. Army awarded Thayer the Bronze Star, with ARVN bestowing him with a Cross of Gallantry with Gold Star.[82] Nguyễn Phú Hiếu, too, proved himself a deft officer. Already well respected for his leadership, he now found himself requested by John Paul Vann, senior advisor for MR2, for a posting in Bình Định, a request that he graciously declined as he felt needed in Sơn Hòa District.[83]

The effects of the battle of Củng Sơn reverberated throughout the province and MR2. Nguyễn Văn Tố surmised that the RF won the day partially because the enemy's contempt for the South Vietnamese meant PLAF had not anticipated being outflanked by Saigon's forces.[84] For that, PLAF paid the price of between 127 and 187 of its solders, which "virtually annihilated" the K-13 Local Force Battalion. Meanwhile, the RF lost 16 dead.[85] Lt. Col. Charles S. Varnum, the deputy senior province advisor, wrote in the June province report, "a tenacious defense all night by the RF forces held until morning when gunships, airstrikes and a reaction force inflicted the heaviest losses upon the enemy since Tet 1968."[86] The combined power of the Americans and South Vietnamese overcame the Communist ploy to decapitate the GVN in Sơn Hòa District. For CORDS, at both the province and corps levels, the battle demonstrated that Phú Yên's defense forces could take on the enemy and win. The aggressive spirit on the part of the RF and local GVN leadership pleased the American advisors.[87] The firepower wrought by the American helicopters proved to be indispensable as the 134th Assault Helicopter demonstrated U.S. airpower's ability to neutralize enemy mobility. Equally significant was the RF's skillful maneuvering, which provided the coup de grâce. Events at Củng Sơn therefore unveiled a truth about the war in Phú Yên and the Vietnam War in general: the South Vietnamese could defeat a sizable enemy force, but with U.S. airpower. With Vietnamization nearing full realization, the likelihood of future battles having the same outcome as Củng Sơn seemed exceedingly unlikely.

Destruction after the Battle at Củng Sơn, Sơn Hòa
District, Phú Yên Province, circa 1971.
Courtesy of Hans J. Underwood, 134th Assault Helicopter Company.

The Battle of Củng Sơn best encapsulated destruction as pacification. PLAF losses fulfilled the destruction phase, while the devastation of entire hamlets meant more construction. Events at Củng Sơn kept pacification in stasis. As relayed by MR2, the battle begat "the destruction of 228 homes, many cattle and hogs and the deaths of 8 civilians. Nine hundred seventy people were made homeless."[88] GVN province authorities quickly released and flew supplies to Củng Sơn; nevertheless, such devastation meant rebuilding—not advancing—pacification. Inhibited advancement of the construction phase meant that MR2 categorized Củng Sơn as a pyrrhic victory. In its reporting, MR2 noted that "although a victory for the GVN," the Battle of Củng Sơn "demonstrates some similarity to the Phu Nhon battle in Pleiku in March in that there was occupation of hamlets from which the war was waged with the inevitable result of a setback in the pacification program for the district."[89] The destruction wrought by the battle left large portions of the district capital utterly devastated.[90] With Vietnamization well underway, the continuance of the destruction phase meant that pacification had not progressed as envisioned by the Americans. At this late stage of the war, the Americans needed pacification to enter—and remain in—the construction phase.

The Sông Đà Rằng Bridges

Although victorious at the Battle of Củng Sơn, the GVN and the American advisory effort faced embarrassment ten days later. As Meerdink later remarked, PLAF "dropped the goddamn bridge."[91] In fact, PLAF targeted two bridges on the night of 28 June, as "the VC blew both the railroad and newly constructed Da Rang river bridges."[92] By attacking the bridges, the enemy demonstrated that Phú Yên remained susceptible to terrorism and, thus, to the plans of PLAF in general. According to Varnum, PLAF attached charges to both bridges, detonating the one on the railroad bridge in the early morning hours. Spectators gathered to view the effects of the explosion, with an armored personnel carrier occupying a position on the highway bridge. The enemy then detonated the charges on the highway bridge, plummeting two spans and the armored personnel carrier to the river below. Vann flew down from MR2 headquarters in Pleiku and, upon seeing the damage, asked Varnum what he saw in the water. Varnum responded that he could see an armored personnel carrier, to which Vann said something to the effect of, "no Charlie, what you see down there is Colonel To's eagle, his full colonelcy."[93] In addition to destroying GVN infrastructure and setting back pacification, PLAF was equally adept at ruining the careers of those serving Saigon. The following morning, inhabitants resumed use of the railroad bridge. Yet Varnum estimated at least six weeks of reconstruction before the reopening of the highway bridge. Varnum noted that the destruction of the new highway bridge over the Sông Đà Rằng "was a great psychological victory for the enemy, particularly in view of the recent pomp and pageantry of the bridge dedication."[94] Varnum later recalled that, approximately two days prior to the bridge attacks, RVN President Nguyễn Văn Thiệu had attended the ceremony to open the highway bridge.[95] MR2 affirmed the dropping of the bridge as a significant PLAF feat, stating, "the enemy avenged his defeat at Son Hoa by destroying two spans of the new Da Rang highway bridge in Tuy Hoa; certainly a psychological victory."[96] The destruction of the bridges signaled that province security was still hostage to COSVN's cause.

Hanoi celebrated the Củng Sơn and Sông Đà Rằng bridge episodes as significant victories against Saigon. Hanoi's Liberation Press Agency heralded a litany of attacks against GVN assets in Phú Yên: "The liberation fighters leveled a series of important positions including Nui Sam, Nui Tranh, Han Sac, and Ca Lui strongholds, demolished one artillery site in Cung Son area, destroyed the Phu Lam and Cung Son towns and wrecked 142 military vehicles." Other claims included the destruction of "44 aircraft of various types, derailed 13 engines and

Aerial view of the damaged highway and railroad bridges
at Tuy Hòa City, Phú Yên Province. 7 July 1971.
Photographer unknown. Courtesy of National Archives, photo no. 111-CC-81103.

66 wagons, demolished 12 howitzers and 12 105mm artillery batteries, blew
up 96 pillboxes, 277 barracks and 12 bridges including the Da Rang bridge, set
afire 18 ammo 110 dumps and one fuel dump."[97] Of course, the Communists
embellished their gains and omitted certain details. For instance, the attacks
against GVN-controlled communities occurred at the expense of PLAF lives.
Exaggeration aside, there were kernels of truth to the propaganda as in the case
of the Sông Đà Rằng highway bridge. Out of those assertions, the simple fact
that the NLF demonstrated the limits of GVN security mattered most. The year
1971 was anything but a banner year for pacification in the province.

Phú Hiệp

The rapid drawdown of America's military presence in the RVN was nearing
full realization. The transfer of military facilities to the South Vietnamese was a
key part of Vietnamization. In Phú Yên, Vietnamization included the handover
of Phú Hiệp, the former epicenter of U.S. Army activity in the province. The
USAF ceased operating out of Tuy Hòa South Air Base in October 1970, with the
U.S. Army shifting assets to that location from Phú Hiệp. The U.S. Army then
renamed the base Tuy Hòa Army Airfield. Yet the transfer of the original Phú

Hiệp to the South Vietnamese in January 1971 revealed serious problems with American execution of Vietnamization and the relationship between American and South Vietnamese authorities. By July, the plundering of Phú Hiệp by South Vietnamese military personnel smothered much of the remaining faith that Phú Yên would survive Vietnamization.[98] As Meerdink emphasized in the monthly progress report for July, American authorities decided the fate of Phú Hiệp in a matter of weeks, with both AT28 and the province chief left out of the planning sessions. As much as GVN corruption stripped Phú Hiệp of every asset, poor U.S. decision-making prevented a proper handover of the base. Meerdink feared that a similar fate might befall the far more modern Tuy Hòa Army Airfield.[99] Fallout from the "Phu Hiep caper" entailed the reassignment of fifteen RF soldiers to the ARVN 1st Division at the demilitarized zone, and "the periodic unannounced absences of various sector officers who are known to be under interrogation in Saigon."[100] By July, GVN investigations found a total of eighteen ARVN officers guilty of participating in the plunder of Phú Hiệp. Most prominently, Lt. Col. Lê Văn Trọng, the district chief of Hiếu Xương (in which Phú Hiệp sat), found himself dismissed from his post.[101]

While the relationship between the Americans and the South Vietnamese in Phú Yên returned to the abysmal levels of the Advisory Crisis era, ROKA operations continued to focus on pacification. In July, ROKA executed operations to a degree not recently seen in the province. Rekindling progress through conventional warfare, ROKA targeted the Sui Lanh Valley and the border area between Sông Cầu and Đồng Xuân districts. In the Sui Lanh Valley, ROKA killed forty-two PLAF members; its efforts along the Sông Cầu–Đồng Xuân border resulted in 207 PLAF deaths.[102] As ROKA soldiers collected only eighty weapons, one might surmise that many of the PLAF killed were Phú Yên civilians pressed into service by the Communists to serve as support personnel.

Observations of the NLF's Presence in the Hamlets

Yet by far the most telling observations of the situation in Phú Yên were those of pacification at the hamlet level. At Hòa Trị village in Tuy Hòa District, Frobenius found a village tainted by PLAF influence. Despite the presence of the 2/29 RF Group Headquarters in the village, the enemy held noteworthy influence. Although three of the four hamlets experienced GVN control, a fourth hamlet existed under PLAF rule. Frobenius reported that "Viet Cong incidents are on the upswing in this Village, and there seems to be no counter moves by the GVN. The GVN is a reality in three of the 4 hamlets of this Village."[103] While most of the village benefited from quality GVN security efforts, the presence of one troublesome hamlet raised concerns.

In his 28 July inspection of Tuy Hòa District's village of Hoà Trị, Frobenius observed troubling signs of PLAF activity in village's hamlet of Lông Tường. He noted that, despite the presence of an RF company, the inhabitants were subject to frequent PLAF abductions and assassinations. This RF contingent made an appearance for four hours each day but conducted no military operations. Frobenius summed up the effects of hamlet's questionable security as follows: "7 people were abducted five days ago. 1 was killed 15 days ago, and 10 more previous to that. When the VC come to the Hamlet, they evidently use the school as a base of operations."[104] PLAF conducted business openly, as also indicated by the rundown state of the seemingly disused hamlet office—the supposed epicenter of GVN authority. Further demonstrating the enemy's control over Lông Tường was the population's daily abandonment of the hamlet between 0800 and 1600 hours; many inhabitants sought refuge away from the hamlet and the threat of PLAF violence. Clearly, those who remained had "made their peace with the Viet Cong."[105] Frobenius poignantly added, "the GVN does not govern here. If you sleep there and cooperate with the GVN, you'll find yourself looking into the barell [sic] of the gun."[106] Validating Frobenius's report, an undated AT28 report titled "Notes on Tuy Hoa District" added that "Long Tuong Hamlet has always had a very active VCI infrastructure . . . the VCI have started to operate more overtly both at night and during the daylight hours."[107] The lack of sound security that meant government offices were abandoned, and thus little to no means of fostering a positive relationship with the locals existed. It is no surprise that the inhabitants, seeing no alternative, worked with PLAF and against Saigon.

As covered in the "Notes on Tuy Hoa District" report, PLAF essentially governed Lông Tường hamlet, and "have been very successful in getting people to move from Long Tuong hamlet to old Phong Nguyen hamlet."[108] Alarmingly, the GVN had not recognized Phong Nguyên hamlet as a legal hamlet for over three years. Under PLAF pressure, roughly 150 people had already returned to Phong Nguyên, which existed "completely under the control of VC cadre." Consequently, "the VCI infrastructure in Hoa Tri Village is now rebuilding at a very fast rate. They currently have two action arrow teams working in the village combined strength approximately 15 people."[109] Hòa Trị village sat in the Tuy Hòa Valley to the west of Tuy Hòa City within relatively close proximity to other villages.[110] Why it inched closer to PLAF domination emerged from "the economic situation and because of the location."[111] According to the "Notes on Tuy Hoa District" report, starting in March, the security within Hòa Trị village had deteriorated "to the point that VC cadre and action arrow teams can move throughout these hamlets with relative freedom."[112] PLAF had turned Hòa Trị village into a nexus from which to expand their control.

A symptom of the nature of American assistance to the South Vietnamese, the lack of proactive leadership from Saigon plagued pacification efforts throughout the war. The very essence of the United States' relationship with the RVN made pacification exceedingly difficult in Phú Yên. Years of flooding the RVN with U.S. dollars and military hardware, now combined with Vietnamization, meant that Saigon found itself awash in responsibilities. In pressing the GVN to accept accelerated pacification, American authorities inadvertently created problems that reverberated to the hamlet level. When touring the three hamlets that comprised Hòa Định village, Frobenius found a community suffering from the lack of GVN interest. Situated in the southwest corner of Tuy Hòa District along LTL-7B, Hòa Định was the scene of heavy fighting during the 1968 Tết Offensive. The village's recovery seemed questionable, as Frobenius noted that he only came across the village chief and none of the government officials who ought to have been there. Holding nothing back, he wrote, "from all appearances, one might rightfully say that it is a progressing Village. Appearance lies."[113] Although Hòa Định lacked any clear trace of Communist influence, PLAF occupied positions in the surrounding hills. Frobenius surmised that PLAF lacked the troops necessary to mount an incursion into the village. Yet no officials slept in the hamlets, instead returning to the safety of Tuy Hòa City every night. Consequently, little coordination transpired between government officials and the RF.[114]

Frobenius's report on Hòa Định caught the attention of Maj. Myron K. Rice, DSA for Tuy Hòa District. Rice forwarded a copy of Frobenius's original report to Meerdink and Varnum, along with a letter outlining his opinions. The DSA wrote that Frobenius's "report is one among several that I have received within the last week that is indicative of the Security Situation in Tuy Hoa District. I feel that if something is not done in the very near future the overall situation of security and pacification will be in jeopardy."[115] Rice's comments went even deeper than Frobenius's observations: "The HES report ending on 30 June does not truly reflect the true security situation within Tuy Hoa District," he remarked.[116] The DSA specified that the villages of Hòa Định, Hòa Quang, Hòa Kiến, and An Chấn—which constituted most of the Tuy Hòa Valley outside of

Tuy Hòa City—all exhibited signs of poor security. Hòa Định and Hòa Quang specifically, he noted "have easy access routes which are currently being used by the enemy."[117] Hòa Kiến, too, had "easy access routes and virtual absence of security which is reflected by the mobile population."[118] As for An Chấn, Rice informed his superiors that "the situation is so bad that the hamlet chief's [*sic*] of Phu Thanh, Phu Quy, and Phu Phong rotate entering their hamlets. The population here is also mobile."[119] Frobenius later visited and confirmed the status of these other communities. For Rice, "the current security problem is partially attributed to the fact that there has been a rapid turnover of both District Senior Advisors and District Chiefs in Tuy Hoa District within the last 6 months."[120] In confirming Frobenius's report, Rice offered additional credibility. He placed some responsibility for the worsening security conditions on the routine personal changes to the advisory system. Yet Rice did not diminish the obvious—that PLAF established and continued to make inroads into strategically significant villages in Phú Yên's most vital district.

Conditions at Hòa Định proved most troubling. "Situation in Hoa Dinh Village is still very serious," began the description of the community in "Notes on Tuy Hoa District," the reasoning being that PLAF and VCI enjoyed unhindered movement "through the village both day and night with all kinds of freedom."[121] The presence of two RF companies and many pro-GVN officials did not improve the situation, as "the Hamlet Chief of Thanh Nghiep Hamlet, Hoa Dinh Village, is currently operating openly for the VC."[122] The proof was that the hamlet chief "has operated for the local action arrow team on two occasions during the month of April. He has also been seen attending local propaganda meetings which have been held in his hamlet for the local VC cadre."[123] The village's "VC cadre . . . have been instrumental in getting people from Phu Sen, and Cam Thach Hamlets to move back out to their old hamlet locations. . . . The VCI infrastructure currently working in and living in Hoa Dinh Village is one of the strongest in Tuy Hoa District. . . . The control of the VC over the Hoa Dinh population is to a point now where they can positively sway the people in any election either local or national."[124]

Aside from intense influence, PLAF operating from Hòa Định village actively engaged the local GVN. "On two occasions the VC have used 60mm mortars and M79 grenade launchers to fire CS gas into the security forces night locations. This has caused nothing but havoc."[125] As a result, the two RF companies stationed at Hòa Định retreated nightly to the safety of the more secure Hòa Thắng village. To the west of the village, PLAF operated "a rest haven, refurbishing area, and

R&R center for units not only located in Tuy Hoa District, but also through the province."[126] Over the past year, the "Notes on Tuy Hoa District" report recounted, "there have been three times as many sightings in the western part of Hoa Dinh Village," as numerous PLAF units from Hiếu Xương District passed through the village en route to Tuy Hòa District.[127] Ultimately, the unspecified author reported "that the VC plan is to make Hoa Dinh village a VC combat village."[128] With PLAF influence incubating at the hamlet level, the guerrillas remained a serious threat to the Saigon government's hold in Phú Yên.

For the GVN, August 1971 brought forth renewed PLAF activity. In spite of a campaign to expand GVN control over more territory, GVN forces in Phú Yên made little headway. "The Dong Khoi campaign must have sounded good to the VC since he immediately start[ed] pushing on all fronts," Meerdink wrote in AT28's monthly report.[129] The GVN's campaign to improve province security only encouraged further enemy activity. PLAF conducted sixty-two attacks in August—a sharp increase from the previous July's twenty-seven. "On the night of the 24–25 August, supposedly the start of the GVN Dong Khoi II campaign," noted the report, PLAF "initiated 13 contacts in province, climaxed by his mortar-sapper attack on Nui Son Company HQ in Hieu Xuong District."[130] Like at the Battle of Cùng Sơn, "only the prompt arrival of 17th Combat Aviation Group gunships which killed a known eight in the wire and a possible 20 more, averted another major disaster."[131] With the removal of all U.S. ground forces, American airpower remained an indispensable asset to pacification. Indeed, the reliance on U.S. airpower to halt enemy advances was an ever-apparent reality in Phú Yên throughout 1971.

ROKA, too, had an active August. A two-week-long operation in Base Area 236 netted the 28th Regiment 325 enemy kills. The 28th Regiment's commander, "privately confided, however, that productive workers made up the majority of the kills and the main force units avoided contact."[132] The killing of more PLAF laborers surely meant future abductions by PLAF. Thus, by August, ROKA had established a theme of conducting operations that looked beneficial on paper, but adversely affected the hamlets that its actions supposedly protected. Even exacting a human toll from PLAF occurred at a steep cost to the local population and did not necessarily improve security. In attacking rear-echelon PLAF, ROKA acquired easy kills, while ultimately guaranteeing PLAF infiltration of hamlets for personnel replacement abductions. At least ROKA's aggressiveness made pacification for the month look good on paper. Meerdink surmised, "were if not for the actions of the 28th ROK Regiment in Base Area 236, it would have been a very bad month in Phu Yen."[133] That comment furthered the notion on the American advisors' part that conventional operations, regardless of effectiveness, made the abstract concept of progress concrete: simply by maneuvering in the field, conventional forces fostered an aura of improvement.

Back at the hamlet level, Frobenius encountered more discouraging indicators of the war's direction. Control of people and their rice afforded PLAF a vital source to keep their movement very much alive. While touring Hiếu Xương District's Hòa Thành village on 10 August, Frobenius came across Phú Xuân, a hamlet he described as "among the worst that I have seen."[134] There, Frobenius found that PLAF taxed each family ten kilos of rice and $VN1,500 per month. With approximately 280 families in the hamlet, PLAF collected from them 2,800 kilos of rice and $VN420,000. Frobenius estimated that PLAF consumed 15 kilos per person—enough rice to feed about 187 guerrillas. Food and taxes made this hamlet nearly indispensable to PLAF operations.[135]

On Tuy Hòa District's western frontier sat another village that troubled Frobenius. Hòa Quang village and its eight hamlets were north of An Nghiệp, east of the mountains, south of Hòa Kiến village, and west of Hòa Trị and Núi Sam. "Being the Frontier, it suffers accordingly," Frobenius remarked in his notes on the village's security.[136] "Once the traveler crosses Nui Sam, the picture changes almost immediately. The sense of security leaves."[137] Despite the presence of a hilltop ROKA compound, the South Koreans overlooked a "'New Life' hamlet, that offers anything but new life." Frobenius explained that the hamlet in question, Ngọc Đồng, functioned more as a "way station" for people as they came only to work the fields, with all the young South Vietnamese vacating the area at dusk. In addition to Ngọc Đồng, the hamlets of Mậu Lâm and Phú Thạnh fell under ROKA area of operations.[138] Regardless of ROKA presence, the inhabitants of these hamlets left for the sanctuary of Tuy Hòa City every evening.

Further still, abductions were the most telling sign of the area's poor security conditions. "Within the past 15 days the following abductions have taken place: 3 women from Ngoc Dong, 8 men from Nho Lam, 1 killing in Long Tuong, and several abductions from Qui Hau," Frobenius reported.[139] Compounding matters, he noted that none of the officials assigned to the hamlets remained on-site at night. Instead, "the RD Cadre, the National Police, and in some cases the PSDF" moved to safe areas to sleep. Frobenius noted that the Nho Lâm hamlet's twenty PSDF personnel left before nightfall. Similarly, out of Hạnh

Lâm hamlet's eleven PSDF personnel, two left at dusk.[140] For Frobenius, such occurrences indicated clear security problems.

Hòa Quang's Phú Thạnh hamlet offered Frobenius another striking picture of a community untouched by pacification. Poor roads and questionable GVN oversight kept Phú Thạnh isolated. While visiting the hamlet on 3 August, Frobenius noted that access to the hamlet consisted of a narrow muddy trail on which a well-built roadblock obstructed entry into the hamlet. Frobenius wrote, "at the outskirts of the hamlet, I was unable to travel any further on the road for a barricade across it was a deterrent for my entering the hamlet (both physical and psychological!)."[141] Though he did not rule out the local population as being responsible for the barricade, the quality of its construction left him suspecting PLAF—who would have benefited the most from such an obstruction—as the likely builders. Quite literally, the route into Phú Thạnh afforded PLAF a means to restrict traffic into the area and thereby strengthen its hold over the hamlet. Moreover, the barricade "does give indication to the fact that the VC . . . can enter the hamlet and build something like this during the daylight (it would be difficult to build something like it at night)," Frobenius noted.[142]

Unable to access the hamlet, Frobenius sought information from a blind man he encountered. From him, Frobenius learned that the hamlet's chief was rarely present and that the hamlet lacked RD Cadre. With that, Frobenius left the vicinity. Later, when he returned with an unnamed member of the Tuy Hòa District team, Frobenius's interpreter stopped an old man as he passed by. The old man warned the interpreter that, "I think you better leave the area fast."[143] Such a warning gave further credence to PLAF as controlling the hamlet. Immediately thereafter, everyone, including the old man, vacated the area. At the end of his report to Varnum, Frobenius remarked, "I wouldn't be surprised if the NLF flag were raised any time now and the VC pledge of Allegiance was flowing from Phu Thanh's populace!"[144]

PLAF activity also posed a problem for Hòa Quang and its hamlets:

> The Village office of Xa Hoa Quang was destroyed by the Viet Cong recently. The Village Chief simply taxed the Village people that he knew had ties with the Viet Cong for money in order to rebuild it. The Village office is rebuilt, but the basic problem still remains . . . security. In all likelihood other Hamlet offices will continue to be destroyed unless security is brought to the area. The population

is in a transient status. There is a mass exit into the more secure
hamlets in the Valley and into Tuy Hoa City every night. And this
will continue until security becomes a reality.[145]

Frobenius hit on the security problem that had troubled Phú Yên throughout the
war. Yet by 1971, as American withdrawal neared completion, solving such a
dilemma was less likely than ever before. Years of pacification efforts yielded
only marginal improvements in Phú Yên's overall security; the safety of those
residing beyond Tuy Hòa City remained under threat of enemy encroachment.

At Mậu Lâm, PLAF's interaction with the local population confounded
Frobenius. Despite falling under ROKA AO, Hòa Quang village remained
largely untouched by security efforts. There, Frobenius reported, when PLAF
collected taxes, it took at least 2 kilos of rice per family—"that is enough to
feed 20 men a month for one month."[146] Frobenius concluded that the hamlet
"is nothing more than a Viet Cong way station at night."[147] For all intents and
purposes, Mậu Lâm further solidified Hòa Quang as a burgeoning PLAF village
and source of power in Tuy Hòa District.

ROKA's mere presence complicated matters for local defense forces. Like
Mậu Lâm, Ngọc Đồng sat in the ROKA AO. Yet the presence of an adjacent
ROKA firebase did not make this hamlet secure. In evaluating Ngọc Đồng—a
purportedly vibrant hamlet—on 3 August, Frobenius wrote, "it is the 'New
Life' hamlet that seems to be anything but new life."[148] A hamlet of mud huts
and no foliage, Ngọc Đồng experienced routine taxation by PLAF. "The VC
have a tax base and a support base out of this Hamlet," Frobenius reported to
his superiors. "Frequently the VC come into the [hamlet] (there is no one to
stop them!). Propaganda meetings, taxing, food collection, and abductions take
place in regular intervals in this hamlet."[149] Poor coordination among the allies
continued to harm pacification; Ngọc Đồng faced a security conundrum as it
fell under the ROKA AO, which meant that the GVN could not place its own
forces in the hamlet. As for the South Koreans, they "do not seem anxious to
execute their responsibility in the area. Possibly because the ROK's do not have
enough forces to do so."[150] Instead, the South Koreans focused on "securing the
area that is within their barb wire."[151] Consequently, because nothing challenged
PLAF, the hamlet remained anything but under GVN control.

Alliance problems at the hamlet level left pacification province-wide pock-
marked with blemishes for PLAF to exploit. Ultimately, his experiences in the
hamlets comprising Hòa Quang village left Frobenius frustrated and questioning

the purpose of pacification and, more generally, the war itself. He bemoaned the general situation befalling Phú Yên:

> My "war" ends in 24 days, these peoples war may not end for a long time yet, but that is thru their own choosing, not mine. Many American's have been killed here, some of them have been my friends and my soldiers. I see no reason that Americans should continue to risk their lives in any fashion at all, until some of these gross inequities are corrected by the South Vietnamese. Too many excuses have been offered to the listening American: these excuses should not be accepted any more. No more rapport needs to be made. For they have the arms, the ammunition, the organization, the knowledge, to do it themselves. I think that now is the time to tell them to get off their asses and start doing what so badly needs to be done. Some day we may be sitting back and watching our TV sets back in America and see the National Liberation Front Flag being raised over Saigon if these people don't start doing what they are supposed to do.[152]

Frobenius's remarks, however, placed the blame for pacification's failings on the South Vietnamese and not the Americans, who overburdened their allies with Vietnamization. With the protection afforded by U.S. Army forces long gone, Phú Yên's local defense forces found themselves in need everywhere all at once. On balance, the rapid expansion of territory for the Saigon government to pacify and administer alone overburdened the South Vietnamese tasked with providing security.

Substantiating the points raised by Frobenius, the "Notes on Tuy Hoa District" report revealed more about the troubled village of Hòa Quang. In that vein, the unnamed author perceived "Hoa Quang Village to be under the control of the VC at night and is debatable whose control it is under during the daylight hours."[153] Regardless of the security provided by two RF companies and five PF platoons, "the village administrative committee, the village council, and most hamlet administrative boards, all have people located in them which are currently actively working for the VCI."[154] An open arms initiative by Saigon to encourage defections from the NLF to the GVN—the Chiêu Hồi program—did not permanently secure loyalty. Ralliers could, and in the case of Hòa Quang, did return to NLF service: "the Village Chief, the Deputy for Security and the Village council Chairman for Ho Quang Village are ex Chieu Hoi's and are reoperating for the VC. Their current contact is Nguyen Lu who is the VC Village chief of Hoa Quang Village."[155] "Notes on Tuy Hoa District" confirmed Frobenius's earlier mention of the village's mass abandonment by all GVN officials, as well as the RD Cadre and the National Police.[156] The trend of leaving the village for safer places to sleep had been going on "for over a year," with emboldened PLAF, VCI, and Action Arrow groups "able to move about with real freedom with no fear of GVN forces."[157] Without any threat to their operations, PLAF had "the people completely under their control mainly out of fear."[158] With such power, "the VC themselves have set up and given monies to the Nho Lam Hamlet Chief's to build a rice mill in Nho Lam Hamlet. . . . They currently plan to buy two tractors and several water pumps which are to be used by the hamleteers located in Hoa Quang village."[159] The situation in Hòa Quang village turned out to be even worse than when Frobenius made his observations. In taking over Hòa Quang, PLAF gained a significant foothold in Tuy Hòa District, in turn exercising considerable control at the expense of the GVN.

A secure village did not mean that all of its hamlets existed outside of PLAF influence. When Frobenius visited Xuân Phước, a village in Đồng Xuân District, on 18 August, he saw that noteworthy security existed near the village. The Đồng Tre camp and its RF companies had the capability to keep the entire village secure, yet the troops instead opted to protect themselves.[160] The inaction of 2/54 RF Group and its three companies had essentially permitted the hamlet of Phú Xuân to fall under PLAF control. Indeed, Phú Xuân was "a VC dominated Hamlet entirely," not the "C"-rated hamlet as presented by HES/70.[161] "In this war the battleground is the 'people,' and therefore the places that they live," Frobenius stated—a reality amiss in much of Phú Yên.

Tuy Hòa District's Hòa Kiến village offered Frobenius considerable insight into the failure of pacification in Phú Yên. During his undated inspection of Minh Đức—the same hamlet near Núi Chấp Chài where the hilltop disaster of 1 April 1970 occurred—Frobenius found a community without dependable defenders and leadership. Despite the presence of "two platoons and the headquarters element of RF 947," the majority of the hamlet's inhabitants left the area for the safety of Tuy Hòa City every evening.[162] Included among those leaving before nightfall included all government officials. The RD Cadre assigned to the hamlet, Frobenius remarked, "does nothing except show up during the day to prevent being red-lined."[163] Void of reliable hamlet officials, the population lacked the leadership necessary to act against possible PLAF aggression. "Fear is paramount in this hamlet," began Frobenius in his analysis. His was an unsurprising statement, since Minh Đức was "reputed to be a 'Hideout' of the VCI" despite the presence of an RF company there. Frobenius added that "the ones that stay there must have made their peace with the Viet Cong."[164] Yet again, compromised security did not bode well for the pacification in the district nor province.

At Hòa Kiến's Tường Quang hamlet, Frobenius uncovered another community untouched by pacification efforts. In the middle of the afternoon, Frobenius noticed that the hamlet lacked a hamlet office and the hamlet chief was gone. The PSDF and RF troops who were meant to defend the population were not patrolling the hamlet. Moreover, the RD Cadre also did not operate in the hamlet. After sunset, only five out of 100 inhabitants remained in the hamlet. Clearly, this hamlet was "not a community of people at all."[165] Frobenius reported, "I believe that the people moved out of this hamlet to get away from the war, both the Viet Cong and the GVN soldiers who stole from there. Because this hamlet vanished indicates a failure on the part of the GVN to provide security for its people."[166] Continuing his damning report to Varnum, Frobenius gave the following assessment of Tường Quang as yet another hamlet suffering from inadequate government supervision and poor defense: "the PSDF—if indeed they do exist—should have all of their weapons taken away. The Hamlet should be taken off the HES," with whatever remains transferred to another hamlet. He added that "if, and only if, the GVN were to provide a certain degree of security would this hamlet be able to come back to life."[167]

The status of Hòa Kiến did not please AT28. Aside from Frobenius's observations, "Notes of Tuy Hoa District" described Hòa Kiến as a village teaming with PLAF activity. "There is very high increase of enemy activity which can be attributed to Pham Lu, Action Arrow Leader, Tuy Hoa City, responsible for Lien Tri, Ninh Tinh and Tuy Hoa City. He is the individual who heads the most wanted list in Tuy Hoa District," went the report.[168] Moreover, "abductions, increase in taxation, rice collection" typified PLAF activity.[169] PLAF also controlled the distribution of rice by prohibiting the passage of Lambrettas on roads in Hòa Kiến "to stop the people from taking the rice into more secure areas from Tuy Hoa District such as Ninh Tinh or into the hamlets of Tuy Hoa Village."[170] Village officials compounded issues since they dabbled in corruption with the "selling of hamlet positions," which "occurred four different times in Hoa Kien."[171] Moreover, "these particular positions are going for approximately 40 to 60,000 P per position. Individuals who are now filling these positions are X-RD Cadre."[172]

"X-RD Cadre" referred to former members of the entity created by the GVN to spread revolutionary zeal to those residing in the RVN's hamlets. The report went on to mention that the village hosted VCI, with the Communists having "action arrow meetings and VC cadre meetings" here.[173] Essentially, Hòa Kiến served PLAF and not the GVN.

Within Hòa Kiến's borders sat Núi Chấp Chài, the same mountain involved in the Minh Đức disaster of 1970. Over a year later, PLAF sanctuary there still provided a safe area for the Communists. The base at Núi Chấp Chài offered "action arrow leaders, VC cadre and VC" a haven as its "east side is known to have several bunkers, tunnels, and access routes running east and west all the way into Tuy Hoa village and back up the northwestern part of Hoa Kien (V)."[174] The presence of PLAF Action Arrows within Hòa Kiến provided a damning indicator of a war getting worse. According to the "Notes on Tuy Hoa District" report, "VCI action arrow teams are constantly in the village, operating overtly at night."[175] Worse, the scarcity of intelligence harmed the longevity of pacification. "In the western part of the village, there is a definite lack of information coming into district or American headquarters due to the fact that there are no hamlet officials, no village officials, RD cadre or National Police," read the report.[176] What assets remained operated briefly, thus undercutting security and actionable intelligence. Indeed, "the only GVN presence we have on occasions is RF and PF forces. These forces, especially PF platoons, have in the past and are still currently, pulling back to more secure areas or else linking up with other RF and PF units to secure themselves and not the hamleteers in the areas."[177] The presence of formidable PLAF infrastructure so close to Tuy Hòa City indicated that even so late in the war, pacification remained largely confined to the province capital. The lack of sufficient intelligence out of the village also hampered the GVN's influence in the area.

Attempts to inspect the village of An Chấn provided Frobenius with still more disheartening observations of security conditions. "Because of the situation in Xa An Chan and the deterioration of the PSDF," read his undated report, "I was not able to report solely upon the PSDF, as there would be nothing but hopelessness to report on."[178] Bordering Tuy An District, An Chấn was Tuy Hòa District's northernmost village. Nine hamlets comprised the village, three of which sat on Hòn Chùa Island.[179] Security on the island proved sufficient during Frobenius's travels. On the mainland at Xuân Dục and Long Thủy hamlets, however, security appeared to be in trouble. "Since the hamlet chiefs do not sleep in the hamlets, the fear is transmitted right down the line to the RD and the PSDF who also leave the area at night."[180] At Phú Phong, Phú Quí, and Phú Thạnh hamlets, too, the hamlet chiefs, like their counterparts at Xuân Dục and Long Thủy, slept in Tuy Hòa City and often remained away "for several days at a time."[181] This resulted in Phú Thạnh's RD "not doing anything, nor did they plan to do anything," according to an RF platoon leader. [182] Making matters worse, the one RF platoon and one PF platoon meant to defend Phú Phong refused to go there "out of fear"; when Frobenius requested that the RF platoon leader accompany him, "the answer was an emphatic 'no.'"[183] Frobenius concluded that "the VC influence undoubtedly is high in this hamlet. . . . The situation is such, that if something is not done in the near future, these three hamlets will drop to a D HES, if not a V HES, and worst yet, all that has been gained will be lost in a short time."[184] An Chấn appeared on the brink of existing outside of GVN control.

The GVN's position in An Chấn never improved. Rather, the "Notes on Tuy Hoa District" report deemed "VC control to be stronger than in other locations of the district."[185]

> The VC exert much control of the people and could actually force the people to vote their way either in a hamlet and village election or a national election. The people in An Chan village are like reeds in the wind. Depending on the current enemy and GVN situation, they would bend themselves to either side, depending on the current outlook or situation. Presently, 3/4ths of the village migrates to either Hon Chua island, Chin Nghia Hamlet or all the way into Tuy Hoa Village at night because of their fear of the VC because of fear of being abducted, taxed, or assassinated.[186]

As some South Vietnamese moved to Hòn Chùa Island, so too did PLAF. Although Frobenius perceived Hòn Chùa as secure, the "Notes on Tuy Hoa District" report relayed a different picture of the island. In the time after Frobenius's visit, the island's hamlets underwent "an upsurge of VCI activity."[187] Such happenings entailed PLAF having "dropped leaflets, conducted propaganda meetings, and destroyed 2 fishing boats on the island."[188] Moreover, the report noted "approximately 10 to 15 VCI" living on the island, with the inhabitants taxed by VC elements "in the form of rice, fish, and monies."[189] Transportation, too, felt the effects of PLAF influence as the VC charged boat owners a tax for ferrying people from the Long Thủy ferry site to Hòn Chùa Island.[190] Lastly, the report revealed that according to intelligence from the island, "the hamlet chief of Me Qunag Hamlet located on Hon Chua Island has been known to operate for the VCI in the past and on two occasions during the month of May has informed the VCI and the deserters located on Hon Chua Island of friendly operations which were to be conducted and were conducted by RF and PF units."[191] The deterioration of security on Hòn Chùa validated Frobenius's warning that the An Chấn village would fall farther away from GVN control without prompt countermeasures.

Even the village of Tuy Hòa appeared as anything but a haven. There, according to the "Notes on Tuy Hoa District" report, PLAF "targeted the hamlet office of Binh Tinh and Binh Hoa," and on "numerous occasions" set explosives inside both hamlet offices.[192] Efforts by the National Police and RF Mobile Battalion 206 to curtain enemy activity, revealed "45 category A and B VCI in Tuy Hoa Village" and "three 5-man sapper elements that are operating in Tuy Hoa Village. Their mission is to destroy GVN facilities and assassinate GVN and Free World Forces and officials located within Tuy Hoa Village."[193] Although attacks against such targets had not materialized, there were numerous instances of vehicles being damaged or blown up "which can possibly be attributed to the sapper elements or to the local cowboy or veteran elements."[194] Such harassment reinforced the sense that PLAF had indeed supplanted Saigon's authority in the village.

South Vietnamese security measures once again troubled Frobenius during an undated inspection of An Ninh village in Tuy An District. In an all-too-familiar scene for Frobenius, a dire political and security situation engulfed all of An Ninh's hamlets. With scant trace of GVN authority, PLAF controlled the area. Frobenius contended:

> In the Village of An Ninh it would be ridiculous to assume that the "insurgents" are the Viet Cong. The GVN is the "insurgent" in An Ninh from the eyes of the people. In the eyes of the people the GVN is the one that disrupts the Village by having its soldiers occasionally sweep thru on an operation to clear the area of the enemy! After the GVN's troops leave, all returns to normal and life goes on.[195]

An Ninh functioned as a source of PLAF power. Frobenius ascertained that the PLAF DK-7 Local Force Company called An Ninh home, and had operated from there as far back at 1940 as part of the Việt Minh. "The Village has given its sons and its store of food to the Viet Minh and to the Viet Cong more recently," Frobenius reported to Varnum. "It shares a heritage with the 'enemy' that cannot be overlooked, nor underscored enough to emphasize that it is a bastion of enemy strength."[196] According to Frobenius, GVN units were aware of An Ninh's history and of DK-7, fearing the unit so much that its troops avoided engaging it in battle.[197]

An Ninh and its focus on fishing and rice demonstrated the symbiotic relationship between Communist efforts in Bình Định and Phú Yên. Frobenius contended that the NLF government in An Ninh owned the nearby rice paddies. Thus, with complete control over rice production, the NLF harnessed that power while maximizing the village's location on the coast. Since An Ninh looked like the typical fishing village, the NLF used that appearance to mask its supplying of fish and rice via boat to PAVN and PLAF units operating north in Bình Định.[198]

Aside from the NLF's control of An Ninh, Frobenius reported on how the village, like all communities in Vietnam, served as the foundation for Vietnamese lives.[199] Frobenius had this to say about the centrality of the community not only to Vietnamese society but also to winning the war. Despite the ongoing conflict, he wrote to Varnum, "the elders are still respected and the ancestors are still worshiped. The village's function in Vietnam remains paramount."[200] His report underscored a critical truth—and oversight on the part of the Americans—that "if any war is to be fought in Vietnam, the Village must be paramount, for within its confines lies the 'key' to any guerrilla war: the people. If the people are controlled and loyal, the guerrilla is denied a source of food, shelter, labor, and intelligence."[201] Such insight never affected the decisions made by the higher echelons of American leadership. The Vietnamese people remained misunderstood, and the allies' hopes for victory stayed out of reach.

Frobenius's reports revealed pacification in Phú Yên as a seriously troubled endeavor. Although the communities he visited constituted only a small portion of the many villages and hamlets in Phú Yên, the problems in these locations affirmed that Phú Yên remained far from the pacified province the American authorities desired. In that vein, the poor security conditions Frobenius reported indicated PLAF's resilience and the limits of GVN power. More to the point, the presence of even a few failing hamlets demonstrated PLAF's resurgence on the eve of Vietnamization's completion. As for Frobenius, jaded over his findings, he requested and received an early dismissal from his duties in Phú Yên and the U.S. Army.

Vietnamization continued in Phú Yên, regardless of Frobenius's and the "Notes on Tuy Hoa District" reports. September began quietly: for the first half of the month, PLAF activity amounted to "a gathering of virtually all the Tuy

Hoa District VC apparatus in the Western Tuy Hoa. Other than that, silence!"[202] On the typically contested LTL-7B, the enemy "seemed satisfied with firing a B-40 at the convoy once each day as it passed."[203] The highway had finally opened, albeit because the enemy permitted it. On a more positive note, for ROKA, September entailed executing "two battalion sized and one regimental operation in the Kỳ Lộ Valley. The latter operation accounted for 174 KIA plus 74 weapons and virtually decimated the DK-9 Battalion."[204] Nonetheless, and as usual, the enemy ultimately dictated the tempo of the war. The province report for September noted that beginning on the 21st, PLAF mortared unspecified major installations in Phú Yên during a series of attacks.[205] Like many prior months in Phú Yên, September demonstrated the shortcomings of pacification in the province.

VCI clearly survived allied efforts to root it out. The Phoenix Program failed to thwart the takeover of key hamlets across Phú Yên, particularly those in the rice-producing heart of the province, Tuy Hòa District. Varnum recalled that his advisory team had held considerable intelligence on the PLAF chief in Phú Yên, obtained by a less conventional approach: they knew that his family lived in Sơn Hòa District and that he spent most of his time in the remote jungle with his fighters. On one occasion, Americans visited his home to gift a brand-new television to the PLAF chief's hysterical wife in an effort to discredit his reputation among other PLAF members.[206] Such an act is representative of the acceptance of PLAF's presence in Phú Yên that spread across the province as Vietnamization progressed—with, or usually without, lasting indicators of improved security.

Events in October produced mixed results for Phú Yên. The monthly progress report began with "October is spelled F-R-U-S-T-R-A-T-I-O-N."[207] Before delving into the month's disappointing events, the report noted that to the astonishment of both CORDS and GVN authorities, Capt. Nguyễn Hồng Long, the commander of the PLAF K-14 Battalion, rallied to the cause of the Saigon government. From him, American and South Vietnamese authorities confirmed that K-14 operated out of Hiếu Xương District's mountains.[208] As the base camp fell under ROKA's AO, they had first right to mount an attack against K-14's base camp; amid a change in command, ROKA deferred to ARVN. "The 22nd ARVN Division volunteered to conduct a two battalion operation in the area after numerous flaps over the type of ordnance to be used to blast the landing zones in the dense foliage," Meerdink wrote.[209] The weather ultimately thwarted attempts to exploit the intelligence: torrential downpours caused by the monsoon grounded all aircraft, and the soil, too wet for artillery shells, "rendered the vast planning academic."[210]

The rain, too, caused considerable flooding in Tuy Hòa City, with flood waters reaching 1.5 meters in some portions of the province capital. Much to Meerdink's chagrin, the local GVN failed to act on the PSA's earlier calls for improved flood prevention countermeasures. "The GVN made its annual promise to do so and following historic precedent, failed to follow through," Meerdink wrote.[211] His comment smacked of contempt for the GVN and foreshadowed his departure from Phú Yên later that month. Varnum remarked that his and Meerdink's departures stemmed from heated exchanges with Nguyễn Văn Tố over his political motives in handling province affairs. The province chief's complaints to Saigon resulted in CORDS's promoting Meerdink and Varnum out of the province. CORDS sent Meerdink to MR2 headquarters as the chief of operations under Vann. Varnum found himself in Quảng Đức Province as the PSA.[212] Lt. Col. Willard A. Holbrook III replaced Meerdink as the PSA, and Carroll L. Floyd replaced Varnum as the DPSA. Having arrived in the province in June, Holbrook was keenly aware of Phú Yên's suspect security conditions.[213]

As Holbrook took over as PSA, the monsoon continued to drench the province. Despite the torrential rains, significant security-related events did occur. Although resistant to the heavy rainfall, the railroad transiting the province was less resilient to enemy explosives. PLAF interdicted the railroad four times during the first two and a half weeks of November. "While this display provided a touchingly warm welcome for the new PSA, DPSA, and Sector Deputy for Security . . . the last incident was nothing short of insult added to injury: a repair train blown up on its way to clear the roadway of the previous day's wreckage," Holbrook stated in the November province report.[214]

After a brief hiatus, PLAF attacks against the railroad resumed in December. "The hapless train was attached twice on the 10th and again on the 17th, resulting in two friendly KIA, six cars derailed, and ten meters of track destroyed," Floyd reported.[215] In other news, between 18 and 25 December, the enemy assailed four hamlet offices in Tuy Hòa District and two in Hiếu Xương District.[216] These enemy actions paled in comparison to previous attacks during 1971, thus making December a relatively quiet month in Phú Yên. PLAF activity in December nonetheless suggested that Phú Yên was as far away from being secure in 1971 as ever before.

At the close of 1971, the general situation in Phú Yên grimly portrayed the future of pacification. Little of consequence had fundamentally changed between

1965 and 1971 as Saigon's power in the province remained largely within the bounds of Tuy Hòa City. Beyond the province capital, NLF efforts undercut the perceived gains of pacification at haste, with VCI firmly rooted in hamlets close to the city. Hanoi's units still maintained Base Area 236—the infamous Hub—a fact not lost on the Americans. Short on time because of Vietnamization, AT28 increasingly lacked the ability to sway the course. The most the Americans could do, and much to the benefit of future scholars, was to document the final sputtering of pacification during the American War.

9

"Consequently, no one knows"

Pacification's Permanence and the End of the Second Indochina War, 1972–1975

To disintegrate a major portion of the enemy ((FWMAF/RVNAF)) elite forces, and create a favorable situation for the friendly ((VC/NVA)) side in both the military and political fields, especially before and after the cease-fire, the enemy and military proselyting mission must be primarily executed by all subordinate units and agencies ((of the Phu Yen Province Party Committee)) in the immediate future," ordered the Phú Yên Province Party Committee in October 1972.[1] For the NLF in Phú Yên, the objective was clear—prepare the province for the inevitable cease-fire with the Americans and South Vietnamese. To that end, the NLF sought the solidification of liberated areas and the continued intrusion into the communities under Saigon's banner.[2]

As much as 1971 validated the disintegration of pacification suspected by American authorities in 1970, the complete absence of progress in 1972 revealed Phú Yên's return to its pre–American military intervention state. Expansion of Communist influence on the eve of the Paris Peace Accords posed serious problems that CORDS simply could not remedy. The final act of CORDS's mission in Phú Yên entailed the war's end with the province appearing much like it had in 1965. During 1972, PLAF retained base areas and probed contested spaces. Like in previous years, Communist forces directed their efforts at disrupting and reversing pacification. Although monitoring the upswing in enemy activity in the province, the principal task of AT28 was withdrawing the mission to complete Vietnamization. By the close of the year, and with the departure of the Americans, Phú Yên remained a province in the throes of war.

American Withdrawal: Leaving Phú Yên the Way They Found It

Socioeconomic repercussions caused by Vietnamization undercut quality of life and weakened security. In January, MR2 came to understand the effects of the American drawdown on Phú Yên's population. A study found that the prior closure of Tuy Hòa Army Airfield had left 3,000 South Vietnamese unemployed—most of whom remained jobless into 1972. The scarcity of jobs in the provincial capital and the lack of assistance from the GVN Social Welfare Service compounded matters. Unemployment also proved difficult if not impossible for many in Hiếu Xương District to overcome, as PLAF's presence in agricultural areas prevented many locals from returning to farming. The closure of the base, too, removed what they saw as the only barrier to PLAF activity in the area—U.S. airpower. Surveyed inhabitants asserted that USAF security measures were "the essential defensive force for the security of Tuy Hoa and Hieu Xuong."[3] Further proof existed in the interdiction of QL-1 by PLAF—an act only previously accomplished prior to the arrival of American and South Korean troops in 1965.[4]

The war remained intense as the Americans approached the full realization of withdrawal. IFFV's successor, the Second Regional Assistance Group, reported in its monthly MR2 overview that January seemed a relatively quiet month save for in two provinces: "long turbulent Binh Dinh and Phu Yen Provinces saw increased enemy activity in the form of harassing attacks, interdictions of lines of communication, and terrorist incidents."[5] PLAF overran an outpost in each province. ROKA executed twelve operations in Phú Yên, two of which sent Korean troops into the infamous Base Area 236.[6] Yet AT28's newsletter for 1972—which highlighted the year's major security occurrences—posited much of January and February as relatively calm as time was "spent preparing for a Tet offensive that never came."[7] Nevertheless, for some, February was anything but dull: a jeep traversing QL-1 hit a mine on 27 February, resulting in the medical evacuation of the driver, Sgt. John N. Crawford. Two unnamed South Vietnamese occupants were killed, and "Sgt. [David R.] Dalton was blown free of the vehicle."[8]

March ruined any positive outlook on Phú Yên's future, as Tuy Hòa District exemplified the issues thwarting pacification. Although the seven RF companies assigned to the district performed well in DSA Rice's eyes, those troops were the only "bright light" in an otherwise dark valley. Rice reported "an upsurge" in PLAF audacity—"95 different entries were recorded in our HES log for March."[9] Activity included abductions, proselytizing, and rice collection. In Tuy Hòa's western reaches, PLAF laid 23 mines and booby traps, while also completing "27 abductions of 149 people"; those abducted had relatives employed by the GVN. After two weeks of indoctrination, PLAF freed its captives to serve as part of the VCI. Through such abductees, PLAF sought to convince others to abandon the GVN and instead work for the NLF.[10]

The response of South Vietnamese forces and officials proved ephemeral. According to Rice, they "initiated contact with the enemy once."[11] Explaining why, he noted that many villages lacked government officials and security at night, and that some villages experienced "prolonged periods of time" without traces of Saigon's administrative apparatus or effectors of pacification.[12] At night, some PF units sought refuge in areas safer than the hamlets and villages the province assigned them to protect. Rice noted that these PF units relocated to Đông Phước hamlet in Hòa Thắng village, Ninh Tịnh hamlet in Tuy Hòa village, and Hòa Thành village on Hòn Chùa Island, where PF troops were "clustering up . . . to provide security for themselves and not the hamlet people."[13] The PSDF, too, neglected their duties at night. "They follow in the foot steps of their Village/Hamlet Chiefs," stated Rice.[14] A lack of support from the Saigon government ensured that the PSDF remained ineffective. The absence of support, however, resulted from the rapid spread of pacification in 1969 under the APC. Thus in 1972, as in 1970 and 1971, the effects of that experiment left GVN officials with more territory and responsibilities than it could manage.

The glaring security issues of 1970 and 1971 remained unsolved. PSA Holbrook informed CORDS' Reports and Analysis Directorate that the four district chiefs of Đồng Xuân, Hiếu Xương, Sông Cầu, and Tuy Hòa requested transfers. The allied situation did not appear any better, as "friendly military activity during the last part of the month was perfunctory at best."[15] Despite its operating in Hiếu Xương and Tuy An, Holbrook did not anticipate the ROKA achieving "the large kills they expected" in April.[16] Holbrook's comments turned out to be prophetic as pacification in Phú Yên remained as tenuous as ever into April: Hanoi commenced its 1972 Easter Offensive, or Nguyễn Huệ Offensive, on 30 March to complete what the offensive of 1968 had failed to achieve—the capitulation of the Saigon government.

The Nguyễn Huệ Offensive plunged much of MR2 into the throes of full-blown conventional warfare. By April, the offensive included Phú Yên. Intense fighting transpired in Phú Yên, albeit not as intensely as in other areas of the RVN; instead, a different brand of warfare transpired as PAVN and PLAF cells continued a harassment campaign across the province. Thus, as other parts of

MR2 experienced a mechanized invasion, comparatively lower-intensity enemy attacks typified the Nguyễn Huệ Offensive in Phú Yên.

Like past Aprils, the one of 1972 tormented Phú Yên. On 13 April, the relative quiet that hung over the province lifted as "the long awaited enemy high point got off with a bang."[17] The monthly province report for April began, "The province erupted with enemy activity in the early morning hours of the 13th."[18] In five of Phú Yên's six districts, PLAF fired on GVN targets. The 1972 offensive proved markedly different that those of the past, 1968 particularly. Instead of gambling all on another attempt on Tuy Hòa City, the Nguyễn Huệ Offensive saw PLAF strike multiple targets across the entire province.[19]

Two PLAF main force battalions—D-9 and K-13—made LTL-6B impassible to traffic and isolated the village of Xuân Sơn in Đồng Xuân District. On 13 April, those two battalions, with supporting PLAF local forces, successfully attacked the nearby 2/54 RF Group. Later, on 15 April, a company-sized unit from the aforementioned Communist forces ambushed a South Vietnamese convoy on LTL-6B as the vehicles passed through the border area between Đồng Xuân and Tuy An districts. PLAF destroyed all but two of the convoy vehicles. As AT28 and province officials investigated the incident, for AT28, the ambush served as an indicator of the poor security provided by the South Vietnamese.[20]

PLAF conducted assaults against military targets at four places. Two such attacks transpired in Tuy Hòa District and Đồng Xuân District. Accordingly, Carroll L. Floyd, acting PSA while Holbrook attended to matters outside the province, reported the following:

> [Twenty-]plus sappers penetrated the Nui Sam artillery location in Tuy Hoa under the cover of a mortar attack. In addition to 11 bunkers and ban coup equipment being destroyed; friendlies sustained heavy casualties. 4 enemy were killed. The same morning Dong Xuan District Headquarters was hit with 82mm and 60mm mortar fire, 75mm and 57mm recoilless rifle fire, B-40, B-41, automatic weapons, small arms and tear gas. 3 sappers were killed in the wire. This began a two week plus siege that well ventilated the team house and eventually resulted in the evacuation of Xuan Lanh Village and fall of the Dong Tre camp. Traveling 6B remains unhealthy.[21]

Floyd noted that these attacks were "the opening of two weeks of continued harassment, with district seats, RF/PF outposts, and LOC's all receiving their full share of VC attention."[22] Additionally, Holbrook reported that "three bridges on

QL-1 were dropped by enemy sappers but quickly repaired by local engineers."[23] As recounted in the AT28 newsletter for 1972, "the Chi Thanh pass ambush site saw a lot of activity and two spans of the Ngan Son bridge were dropped" in Tuy An District.[24] Presumably, the Ngân Sơn bridge bombing accounted for one of the three dropped bridges Floyd reported.

PLAF activity subsided toward the end of April. Instead of fighting, PLAF shifted its attention toward rice collection. April also saw allegations of collusion between GVN hamlet officials in the western tracts of the Tuy Hòa Valley and PLAF.[25] Considering Vietnamization's near-full realization and PLAF's continued presence, the South Vietnamese certainly understood the conflict as anything but over. Pacification had failed to make the GVN the sole arbiter in the province, leaving individuals to make difficult allegiance choices. Although many in Phú Yên were fearful that PAVN would return en masse, Floyd noted that despite numerous reports of PAVN movement in the province, no physical evidence validated such claims. Rather, "there has, as yet, been no actual evidence that we are dealing with enemy force other than those organic to the province."[26] As demonstrated throughout the Nguyễn Huệ Offensive, PLAF main force units posed a serious threat to the GVN's security apparatus in the province—even without direct PAVN involvement.

Deteriorating security in Phú Yên continued into July. "Territorial security continues as usual to be the name of the game in Phu Yen" began the monthly province report for July.[27] The situation befalling Đồng Xuân District demonstrated pacification's failure: "Effective GVN influence in beleaguered Dong Xuan remains limited to the area around the district capital of La Hai and a small section of the Song Cai river valley dominated by the headquarters of the ROKA 1/26 battalion," the report read. "Route 6B, the main LOC to Dong Xuan, is closed to military vehicles and is traversed only by intermittent civilian traffic."[28]

Elsewhere in the province, waning security conditions plagued the westernmost portions of Hiếu Xương and Tuy Hòa districts. Tuy Hòa District exhibited "disturbing signs of even further deterioration in security." In Tuy An District, "heavy VC military pressure" remained noticeable. In that vein, the PLAF's D-9 and K-13 Main Force battalions "occupied Phu My hamlet and failed in a plan to destroy the Ngan Son bridge," the July report read. Yet those actions cost PLAF 63 of its own. Security conditions continued to deteriorate. According to Holbrook, Phú Yên's "lackluster performance in both pacification and development is even more discouraging when viewed against the fact that the number of significant enemy incidents in July declined to the lowest level this year."[29] GVN presence in the province seemed to disintegrate in front of the PSA's eyes, and it did so with seemingly minimal Communist effort.

Enemy activity in September revealed that the back-and-forth nature of the war remained intact. PLAF mortars and rockets struck Tuy Hòa City, the National Police headquarters in the province, and the Tuy Hòa subsector compound, the latter of which, Holbrook reported, diverted attention away from K-96 Main Force Battalion's entrance into the western reaches of Tuy Hòa District: "By midday 28 September the K-96, supported by elements of the 204 Sapper Company, occupied almost all of the hamlets in the district west of grid line 13 and south of grid line 45."[30] The GVN responded to the enemy's assertiveness with heavy artillery fire and airstrikes, with battalions of troops slowly pushing K-96 back into the foothills of western Tuy Hòa District from which it came.[31] Although the GVN in Phú Yên quickly retaliated against overt enemy activity, the enemy's bold advance reaffirmed the Communists' ability to physically challenge the GVN despite years of conventional allied operations to break PAVN and PLAF power. Thus, the enemy still controlled the tempo of the war, with the GVN reacting to Communist activity.

Enemy activity for much of 1972 produced sobering problems for pacification. A September CORDS report on the Nguyễn Huệ Offensive revealed that enemy pressure on pacification continued to weaken Saigon's control. Maj. Larry D. Budge, a CORDS field evaluator, reported Phú Yên's as among the worst GVN population control loss statistics: "In MR 2 four of the northern province sustained moderate or serious regressions (Phu Bon—19%, Binh Dinh—34.8%, Phu Yen—36.3% and Kon Tum—96%) while the fifth province, Pleiku, regressed on 8.6%."[32] By October, Budge revised the numbers, with Phú Bổn decreasing to 10.4 percent and Phú Yên increasing to 40. The other provinces of MR 2 retained the same numbers from September.[33] "Progress is likely to continue in much of southern MR 2, but recovery remains tenuous in the northern provinces," Budge noted in both reports. For at least one of those northern MR 2 provinces—Phú Yên—such loses in population control aptly reflected its existence as a largely unpacified province. That distinction gained further credence throughout the ensuing months.

October saw a decrease in enemy activity as PLAF took its share of the rice harvest. "A sizable number of lower level enemy cadre have been occupied with completing the final stages of the September—October rice harvest," stated Holbrook in the monthly province report.[34] Arguably, the gains made by IFFV's maneuver battalions in 1966 and 1967 were now irrevocably reversed as PLAF infiltrated the province's rice harvest. "October was an unusually quiet month for Phu Yen," Holbrook reported.[35] "Enemy initiated incidents numbered 7 which is the lowest number since January 1970."[36] Monsoon weather, too, meant an expected halt in enemy movement. The report asserted that PLAF had shifted its attention toward preparing for after the Paris Peace Accords. In that vein, PLAF activity entailed preparations for attacks against GVN facilities and defenses as well as the production of propaganda materials.[37]

As the American War neared its end, the struggle between North and South Vietnamese forces remained intense. In the November monthly province report— Holbrook's last—the PSA described a war in Phú Yên that remained in flux. Successful operations conducted by RF units during November indicated a newfound resolve among the province's local defense forces: RF 221 fought-off "an ABF and three sapper attacks by elements of the D-9 Battalion [on] 6 November against the key Ngan Son Bridge on QL-1 in Tuy An District."[38] Similarly, RF 220 "administered a severe beating [on] 4–6 November to units of the D-96 battalion which had attempted to take over several hamlets in the western portion of Tuy Hoa District."[39] In doing so, RF 220 killed D-96's chief of staff and C-2 Company's commander and political officer.[40] Both instances demonstrated that RF units could fight well and that PLAF remained anything but invincible. These RF victories notwithstanding, November was a relatively quiet month; both the GVN and PLAF found themselves placing greater emphasis on propaganda as each side prepared for the cease-fire.

Regardless of the quiet that seemed to engulf the province, the final AT28 report for the year offered a telling if not damning summation of 1972 in Phú Yên—and the same ambiguity around pacification that had plagued the American advisory efforts since the early days of the war. The province's last PSA, Lt. Col. John M. McDonald, began the report as follows:

The GVN Community and Local Development effort the past six months has been characterized by only limited progress on the security front but more encouraging advances in the development field. . . . The end result is that the GVN finds itself pretty much in the same position at Year's end as it was at the beginning of the year. . . . This factor combined with slow but continual progress in the province's development program has enabled the GVN to contain the VC insurgency; however, the Province's pacification and development efforts still sorely lacks spirited leadership and decisive implementation required to forge into an effective weapon for getting at the roots of the enemy's insurgent system.[41]

Here, pacification is presented as separate from development. Even as the war ended for the Americans, pacification lacked a precise meaning. Moreover, its main concern—security—remained unachieved.

McDonald discussed PLAF activity as the report progressed. He reported that the enemy's failed spring offensive had resulted in resumed efforts to undermine GVN influence by other means in Hiếu Xương, Tuy An, and Tuy Hòa districts, with the Communists endeavoring to interdict QL-1 and occupy GVN facilities in those districts. Yet the "highpoint of enemy activity came during the three months of July, August, and September, when 148 terrorist incidents and 665 abductions were reported along with 76 significant enemy initiated military incidents."[42] Although the enemy lacked sufficient strength to capture Tuy Hòa City or any of the district capitals, "the enemy still posed at year's end a serious threat to the security of the province."[43] The report elaborated as follows:

> [There is] considerable influence in the rural villages and hamlets throughout the province, and especially in the western Tuy Hoa Valley and in the northeast and northwest section of Tuy An District. The enemy also still denies the GVN the use of Route 7B, effectively isolating Son Hoa District from the rest of the Province. Enemy pressure on Route 6B has practically closed it to regular military traffic and PLAF harassing tactics even makes QL-1 hazardous to travel at times.[44]

Although PLAF had failed at the Battle of Củng Sơn in 1971 to wrest control of Sơn Hòa District from the GVN, the Communists practically realized that objective in 1972 by cutting off the district's access to the rest of the province. PLAF posturing at the end of 1972 suggested grim prospects for the RVNs future.

The isolation of Sơn Hòa District revealed all that was wrong with pacification in Phú Yên. McDonald's senior debriefing report was emblematic of Phú Yên's security through the war. He specified PLAF's ability to cut off Sơn Hòa District from the rest of the province as one of three problems plaguing the province at the end of CORDS's mission, the other two being the enemy's interdiction of communication lines and, most alarmingly, that no one—save for maybe PLAF—knew how much territory fell under GVN control.[45] McDonald noted

PACIFICATION'S PERMANENCE 243

that, on the eve of the Paris Peace Accords, such an information vacuum posed serious problems for the province's long-term stability. The most damning commentary on Phú Yên, regardless of year, came from McDonald:

> Lack of knowledge as to just how much territory in Phu Yen is physically controlled by the VC-NVA. While the GVN has successfully controlled 80–90% of the population and the critical crop-lands (20–30% of Phu Yen's land), there has been little or no attempt to operate in the remaining landmasses. Consequently, no one knows just how much of Base Area 236, the Cay Vung (Ky Lo Valley), the Ha Roi and the Hon Cheng areas are, or have been under VC-NVA physical control. If claimed by the VC-NVA it will be difficult for the GVN to refute their claims.[46]

Such a revelation called into question the war's entire premise and execution. Despite the conventional allied forces' operations, noteworthy enemy influence—and possible extensive control of Phú Yên's interior—remained intact. Relatedly, uncertainty around just how much of the province the Communists controlled suggested that despite all the various measurement data CORDS collected, intelligence on territorial control remained spotty at best. McDonald's statement further encapsulated pacification as the folly it had become.

Doubts, too, persisted over the quality of Phú Yên's local defense forces and province leadership. Despite signs of improved performance, on the whole, AT28 found the province's RF companies still timid of battle and too dependent on artillery and aircraft support when engagements with the enemy arose.[47] Ironically, this reliance on fire support stemmed from how the Americans crafted the RVN's military forces in the first place.[48] McDonald perceived the province's local GVN leadership as largely unconcerned with the lives of those residing in the villages and hamlets. The PSA connected his view of a disinterested leadership with August HES/70 data that showed "an alarming 129 DEV hamlets in the province including 38 'V' rated hamlets."[49] McDonald noted that local GVN authorities did eventually take interest in village and hamlet affairs—a shift noticeable in more recent HES/70 data—but he qualified that observation by noting that because the enemy recognized the approaching cease-fire, it had curtailed its military operations in favor of focusing on political activity.[50] As in years prior, the enemy's choices controlled the war in Phú Yên. The security concerns at the end of 1972 exposed the fundamental flaws of American-influenced pacification in Phú Yên as truth and not simply anomaly. Ultimately, 1972 and the advisory mission as whole ended rife with doubt as to the accomplishments of pacification and Phú Yên's future.

By the end of America's war, the problems befalling Phú Yên were emblematic of pacification as a whole. Imbued with the determination to complete the rapid withdrawal from the RVN on schedule, senior American leadership appeared disinterested toward events that challenged the abandonment of the RVN. As much as the abductions that occurred after the Advisory Crisis and the continued erosion of GVN influence in the province exposed serious problems with American aims in the RVN, the refusal to reassess reflected the acceptance of the status quo that engulfed Phú Yên by the end of 1972. Just like the French before them, the Americans left the war in Phú Yên with pacification incomplete.

Saigon's Last Stand on the South China Sea

Even before the signing of the Paris Peace Accords on 27 January 1973 and the capitulation of Saigon on 30 April 1975, tranquility escaped Phú Yên. Excluded from the peace talks in Paris, the GVN had no say in the accords. With no regard for the RVN's security concerns, the United States did not demand the removal of North Vietnamese forces from South Vietnamese territory, which ultimately left Saigon with a security nightmare. Between 23 January and 3 February 1973, both Hanoi and Saigon participated in a massive escalation of violence—known alternately as the Battle of the Flags, the War of the Flags, and Landgrab 73—as both sought to extend their control over contested South Vietnamese territory before the accords were implemented. As demonstrated in Phú Yên, fighting continued after the signing on 27 January. Hanoi attempted to isolate the ARVN 22nd Division in Bình Định by cutting QL-1 at multiple points in Phú Yên; that effort failed, but the destruction of bridges nevertheless left the highway closed to civilian traffic. Communist forces did overrun several of Phú Yên's hamlets, but by 2 February, RF/PF troops retook all but two hamlets.[51]

The war came full circle in 1975 when, with the resumption of open hostilities between North and South Vietnam, conventional warfare returned to Phú Yên. By the beginning of 1975, the ARVN 47th Regiment still operated in Bình Định to defend the critical—and infamous—An Khê Pass. What began as PAVN probing efforts turned into a full-blown invasion of the RVN's north after defeating ARVN at Ban Mê Thuột. Thereafter, President Nguyễn Văn Thiệu decided to redeploy military assets in I and II Corps. As the fallback position for ARVN troops vacating the Central Highlands, Tuy Hòa City now anchored Nguyễn Văn Thiệu's ill-fated defense line: the South Vietnamese would defend everything south, while abandoning everything north. In practice, redeployment meant abandonment.[52] That placed 20,000 ARVN soldiers and thousands upon thousands of refugees on a hasty retreat from Pleiku in Pleiku Province to Tuy Hòa City in Phú Yên. That journey sent ARVN and accompanying civilians to Cheo Reo, the capital of Phú Bổn Province, before embarking on the most dangerous portion of LTL-7B from Cheo Reo to Tuy Hòa City. All the while, PAVN continued its efforts to clear II Corps of ARVN.[53]

Conventional warfare's return to Phú Yên decided the province's fate. As elements of the PAVN 320th Division pursued ARVN remnants toward Phú Yên, three understrength company-sized PLAF local force battalions blocked select portions of LTL-7B and LTL-436. Tasked with disrupting ARVN's movement at all costs, PLAF placed one battalion in a blocking position on LTL-7B at a bridge about sixteen kilometers outside of Tuy Hòa City; another battalion blocked a stretch of LTL-7B near Củng Sơn. PLAF knew that ROKA had extensively mined the roughly eighty kilometers of LTL-7B between Củng Sơn and Tuy Hòa City before departing Phú Yên. A third battalion dispersed, with its troops employing various fires to harass traffic on LTL-436. RF units could not dislodge PLAF from its blocking positions. With that stretch of LTL-7B impassible due to the ROKA landmines, ARVN needed to cross the Sông Ba and use the smaller LTL-436 on the opposite bank to reach the province capital. The war had left the bridge over the river destroyed, forcing ARVN to build a new crossing. With a pontoon flown in by helicopter from Tuy Hòa City and steel planking repurposed from the Củng Sơn airstrip, the ARVN 9th Rangers completed the bridge in the morning hours of 23 March. That same day, the PAVN 64th Regiment made contact with PLAF local forces outside of Củng Sơn. Noticing the movement of the last remaining ARVN Rangers from the district capital on 24 March, Communist forces commenced their attack. With the first salvo of 120mm mortars smashing into South Vietnamese convoy, PAVN and PLAF attackers made good use of the confusion, disabling ARVN tanks at close range. PLAF mortars hit the new bridge, destroying vehicles and making crossing by foot exceptionally dangerous. Hundreds of surviving civilians and soldiers died while attempting to swim across the fast-moving river. Củng Sơn, the scene of the RF's significant 1971 victory, now belonged to the Communists.[54]

The South Vietnamese convoy pressed on toward Tuy Hòa City. After ARVN and the refugees reached the other side of the Sông Ba at Củng Sơn, PLAF delayed the movement of the South Vietnamese forces and civilians on LTL-436 to Tuy Hòa City. The 34th Ranger Battalion's Thunder Tigers, or Lôi Hổ—the elite reconnaissance elements of ARVN Special Forces—along with napalm strikes from the Vietnamese Air Force 92nd Wing broke the roadblock on LTL-436. Next, the 34th Ranger Battalion and assisting M-113 armored personnel carriers destroyed—after multiple attempts—the last PLAF position obstructing LTL-436. The leading elements of the approximately thirty-two-kilometer-long convoy finally entered the province capital on 25 March.[55] The PAVN 64th Regiment remained at Củng Sơn while the other elements of the division arrived for the final push toward Tuy Hòa City. The U.S. Embassy in Saigon reported PAVN shelling of ARVN's bridge until at least 26 March: "river crossing was heavily shelled by communist mortar fire . . . over one thousand burning vehicles at the river crossing."[56]

For a brief period only, Phú Yên stood as the RVN's northernmost bastion against the rapidly spreading border of the DRVN.[57] Every province to the north and west of Phú Yên belonged to PAVN. South Vietnamese forces intended to make a final stand in II Corps at Tuy Hòa City. There, under the leadership of Lt. Gen. Đồng Văn Khuyên, ARVN and supporting forces prepared for the looming confrontation with the PAVN 320th Division. With the arrival of the convoy from Cheo Reo, Tuy Hòa City swelled with the addition of 40,000 refugees. Yet only one in three civilians survived the trek to Tuy Hòa City. What ARVN elements remained entered the city battered—approximately only 5,000 out of 20,000 ARVN soldiers arrived from Cheo Reo. Several RF battalions, the 96th Ranger Battalion, and a battery of 105mm howitzers remained to defend the doomed city.[58]

Once again, 1 April was a pivotal day in Phú Yên. Exactly five years after the disaster on Hill 40, PAVN and supporting PLAF elements prepared a three-pronged assault against Tuy Hòa City. Surviving ARVN elements confronted three infantry regiments, a tank battalion, and supporting artillery organized against the city by the PAVN 320th Division. PAVN artillery began shelling the city at 0530 hours, followed by an armor and infantry assault at 0630. ARVN resistance proved futile by 0730 as PAVN armor rattled along city streets toward ARVN's command center. Shortly thereafter, the city belonged to PAVN, with outlying villages and hamlets submitting by 1500. Remnants of the 34th Ranger Battalion held-out in the mountainous terrain of Hiếu Xương between the defunct Tuy Hòa Army Airfield and Vũng Rô until defeated by elements of the PAVN 320th Division on 2 April.[59] The destruction phase of pacification had finally ended for the GVN; so too did Saigon's control over the much-contested province. The capture of Phú Yên by PAVN destroyed the last major organized resistance between it and the northern approaches to Saigon.

Hanoi's seizure of Phú Yên was also highly symbolic. On 3 April, an editorial in the official Vietnamese Workers' Party newspaper *Nhân Dân* proclaimed that the province had "regained complete mastership."[60] It continued, "When we speak of stalwart and unsubmissive central Trung Bo, we speak proudly of Phu Yen."[61] Indeed, the message recalled that Phú Yên "was one of the first provinces to launch the general uprising movement."[62] Yet the propaganda piece emphasized the victory as one borne by the province itself, with no mention of outside conventional help from PAVN. While PLAF in Phú Yên had certainly "continuously frustrat[ed] the enemy's pacification scheme" as evidenced in the years after 1969, those efforts had not ejected the GVN from the province.[63] In framing what happened in Phú Yên as organic, *Nhân Dân* distorted the reality that the PAVN 320th Division had finished what the PAVN 95th Regiment had started in 1964. Conventional warfare had dictated pacification from beginning to end in Phú Yên.

Conclusion

Why Phú Yên Matters

The situation will be placed inevitably in the context of Vietnamization with the clear implication that the Vietnamese can't go it alone," CORDS's George D. Jacobson said to Prime Minister Trần Thiện Khiêm in April 1970, adding that "the worst of it all is that the stories are all true."[1] These words, spoken after security in Phú Yên essentially existed in name only, encapsulated the plight of pacification in that during the American War.

Pacification lay at the core of the United States' execution of the war. American diplomats and military authorities perceived and articulated pacification as the modus operandi of the entire war effort. Placed in the context of larger U.S. geopolitical goals, such as Vietnamization and the subordinate Accelerated Pacification Campaign, it becomes clear that superficial information drove the perception of pacification advancement and not the data that indicated otherwise. Although the revisionist consensus suggests that pacification succeeded by the war's end, events in Phú Yên contradict such a notion. The concentration on Phú Yên reveals the issues that challenged pacification.

Pacification was the means of executing the war in the RVN. As evidenced through the myriad of security issues raised in AT28 documents, pacification in Phú Yên lasted only as long as IFFV sustained numerous offensive maneuvers in the province. Events in Phú Yên effectively posited conventional military forces as the advancer of pacification. Despite the efforts of IFFV and AT28 to transform Phú Yên into a Saigon government stronghold in the region, processes such as Vietnamization and the APC ensured the disintegration of pacification gains and the return of the province to a state similar to that seen in 1965. In the end, the South Vietnamese could not maintain pacification in the face of America's dwindling military presence and geopolitical interest in the RVN.

Examining events between 1965 and 1972 reveals much about the war in Phú Yên. Pacification was entwined with conventional military units in a manner that blurred the lines between warfare and developmental efforts. Extensive and numerous offensive operations by IFFV's maneuver battalions, however, expanded the GVN's control in the province. IFFV's operations to secure Phú Yên's rice harvests—the second largest in the region—while expanding Saigon's control placed pacification firmly in the realm of conventional warfare. Later, elements of IFFV offered a veil of security behind which pacification expanded.

Conventional warfare and pacification remained wedded into 1967 and 1968. Yet by the close of 1967, conventional warfare had not transformed Phú Yên into a secure province. Although American officials correlated IFFV's operations with pacification advancement, allied maneuver battalions only furthered province security so long as those operations continued. Pacification in Phú Yên made Tuy Hòa City a GVN island awash in a sea of contested space. While Tuy Hòa City remained under Saigon's banner—despite multiple efforts by PAVN and PLAF units to capture that flag—the encompassing Tuy Hòa Valley remained unpacified. As the Tết Offensive demonstrated, allied forays into the valley did not prevent the Communist forces' use of that space. The Tết Offensive that unfolded in Phú Yên was devastating to long-term GVN pacification success. The events of 1967 and 1968 as whole reflected a war in which sustained pacification progress was fleeting.

The province's 1970 saga served as a preamble to the late war period across all of the RVN. The Advisory Crisis of 1970 unsurprisingly began after IFFV removed its maneuver battalions from Phú Yên. That relocation of assets left the province dangerously exposed to PLAF. The scaling back of U.S. Army forces occurred elsewhere in the RVN, further taxing the already thinly spread ARVN. That the removal of U.S. Army maneuver battalions lay at the center of Phú Yên's troubles neglects the role that American political objectives played. The manner in which the United States approached the war itself weakened efforts to build a stable and resilient Republic of Vietnam. Vietnamization and the APC hastened pacification—a process that made pacification appear successful. Yet the rapid acceleration of pacification merely created a false sense of a war being won. That, however, does not discount the efforts of those, both American and South Vietnamese, who sacrificed time, and perhaps themselves, for Washington and Saigon.

The APC lay at the center of Phú Yên's progress and problems. In the face of rapidly decreasing U.S. support for the ongoing ground war, or Vietnamization, the APC did more to advance the image of a GVN with vast inroads into the countryside than actually place people under its control. The troubles that persisted in the province highlighted the limitations of American and South Vietnamese power to the extent that, despite four years of war, province security displayed meager signs of improvement. Years of Americanization meant that local GVN authorities in Phú Yên could not seamlessly implement Vietnamization. Assuming the burden of increasing province security without the once-ever-present IFFV units damned the local GVN into a position of appearing recalcitrant—an easy scapegoat for Americans' increasing frustration with the direction of the war.

Phú Yên is a clarion for students and practitioners of pacification. The war there fused together conventional warfare and pacification. Without sustained IFFV conventional military operations, pacification lost momentum. The uncertainty that engulfed Phú Yên at the end of the U.S. advisory mission reflected pacification's questionable gains. With considerable tracks of the province under Communist control after nearly seven years of U.S.-backed pacification in Phú Yên, the continued existence of enemy base areas near Tuy Hòa City demonstrated that pacification amounted to naught, as it did not strengthen the GVN's position in Phú Yên. Largely unpacified, Phú Yên's war finally concluded in 1975 at the hands of PAVN and PLAF.

That scene of five dead American soldiers on a hill outside of Minh Đức matters over forty years later because Americans are still fighting battles in places about which other Americans know little. Americans wrangled with the United States' actions in Vietnam during and after the war. Yet that most ignominious military defeat up to that time in American history continues to offer lessons. Places like Phú Yên must matter to policymakers and the public alike. Until they do, the lessons of the CORDS experience in Phú Yên remain on paper, with no indicators of application in the current wars of the twenty-first century.

Notes

Introduction

1. "Núi Chấp Chài" appeared on the maps printed by the National Geographic Service Vietnam, instead of the current spelling "Núi Chóp Chài." Since this book is a work of history, the former spelling is used throughout.

2. AT28, report, "Action of US 173d Airborne Brigade and RF 112 Company at Minh Duc on 1 April 1970," pp. 1–2, folder 10, Phu Yen, U.S. Army Center of Military History, Fort McNair, Washington, D.C. (hereafter cited as CMH).

3. AT28, "Action of US 173d Airborne Brigade and RF 112 Company at Minh Duc on 1 April 1970," p. 2, CMH.

4. Ibid., 1–2.

5. AT28, report, "Phu Yen Province Chief's Month Meeting (April) with Allied Commanders," p. 3, RG 472, A1 690, box 297, National Archives and Records Administration, College Park, Md. (hereafter cited as NARA II).

6. Although the Việt Minh evolved into the Liên Việt (or Vietnamese National Popular Front) after 1951, Việt Minh remained the widely used term, as few, even in Vietnam, knew of the name change. For that, and for clarity's sake, this study uses the term Việt Minh. Pierre Asselin, *Hanoi's Road to the Vietnam War, 1954–1965* (Berkeley: University of California Press, 2013), xxii, xxiv, 61.

7. Jessica M. Chapman, *Cauldron of Resistance: Ngo Dinh Diem, the United States, and 1950s Southern Vietnam* (Ithaca, N.Y.: Cornell University Press, 2013), 189.

8. Douglas Pike, *PAVN: People's Army of Vietnam* (Novato, Calif.: Presidio, 1986), 217–22.

9. The release of Lewis Sorley's *A Better War: The Unexamined Victories and Final Tragedy of America's Last Years in Vietnam* (Orlando, Fla.: Harcourt Brace, 1999), and, later, Mark Moyar's *Triumph Forsaken: The Vietnam War, 1954–1965* (Cambridge: Cambridge University Press, 2006), ushered in a wave of critics, all eager

to debunk the myth of a winnable war in Southeast Asia. For the better part of the past two decades, orthodox and revisionist scholars have perpetuated a cyclical debate. That, however, is nearing its end, in part because of Gregory A. Daddis's *Withdrawal: Reassessing America's Final Years in Vietnam* (New York: Oxford University Press, 2017). In his most recent work, Daddis provided the best rebuke to date of Vietnam War revisionism, while encouraging new paths for historical inquiry into the conflict.

10. For proof that a study of Phú Yên is both necessary and timely, see Kevin M. Boylan, *Losing Binh Dinh: The Failure of Pacification and Vietnamization, 1969–1971* (Lawrence: University Press of Kansas, 2016). Boylan's examination of Bình Định Province, and his emphasis on Operation Washington Green, reveals flaws in accelerated pacification and Vietnamization. The theme of unprepared and stretched South Vietnamese security forces and the ensuing use of more IFFV resources is well established. With a larger population and arguably greater strategic value, Bình Định mattered more to IFFV. Naturally, IFFV pulled combat forces from Phú Yên to buttress the overburdened GVN forces in and after 1969. The scope of Boylan's superb work lies outside of the 1965–68 period—meaning the role of maneuver battalions in the initial expansion of pacification and the influence of such forces throughout the war remain unknown. Ergo, this study of Phú Yên is crucial.

11. For examples of arguments for two separate wars, see Lewis Sorley, "The Conduct of the War: Strategy, Doctrine, Tactics, and Policy," in *Rolling Thunder in a Gentle Land: The Vietnam War Revisited*, ed. Andrew Wiest (New York: Osprey Publishing, 2006); Sorley, *A Better War*; and Sorley, *Westmoreland: The General Who Lost Vietnam* (Boston: Houghton Mifflin Harcourt, 2011). Counters to Sorley include Andrew Birtle, *"Triumph Forsaken* as Military History," in *Triumph Revisited: Historians Battle for the Vietnam War*, eds. Andrew Wiest and Michael J. Doidge (New York: Routledge, 2010); Charles Hill, "Fighting Stories," in Wiest and Doidge, *Triumph Revisited*; Daddis, *Westmoreland's War: Reassessing American Strategy in Vietnam* (New York: Oxford University Press, 2014); and Gian Gentile, *Wrong Turn: America's Deadly Embrace of Counterinsurgency* (New York: New Press, 2013).

12. Andrew J. Gawthorpe, *To Build as Well as Destroy: American Nation Building in South Vietnam* (Ithaca, N.Y.: Cornell University Press, 2018). Gawthorpe provided a discussion of pacification, but preferred "nation building" as a more accurate term to explain pacification's more developmental aspects.

13. For examples, see Mark Neocleous and George S. Rigakos, eds., *Anti-Security* (Ottawa, Ont.: Red Quill Books, 2011); Mark Neocleous, George Rigakos, and Tyler Wall, "On Pacification: Introduction to the Special Issue," *Socialist Studies/Études Socialistes* 9, no. 2 (Winter 2013): 1–6; Stuart Schrader, "To Secure the Global Great Society: Participation in Pacification," *Humanity: An International Journal*

of Human Rights, Humanitarianism, and Development 7, no. 2 (Summer 2016): 225–53; and Schrader, *Badges Without Borders: How Global Counterinsurgency Transformed American Policing* (Oakland: University of California Press, 2019).

14. For example, see Richard A. Hunt, *Pacification: The American Struggle for Vietnam's Hearts and Minds* (Boulder, Colo.: Westview Press, 1995), 47, 49, 59–60. Such works of the so-called "other war," or pacification, downplay the connection between conventional warfare and pacification. Hunt's work typifies the contention that big-unit warfare and pacification are separate foci. In his macro study of pacification, Hunt argued that the military support for pacification is one of "semantics." Although military operations often dislodged PLAF units and brought humanitarian assistance to South Vietnamese peasants, these acts did not translate into improved relations between the countryside and Saigon. Those living in the countryside did not always equate American goodwill with the government in Saigon. Moreover, Hunt argued that although the U.S. Army sought both to engage the Communist forces and to assist in pacification efforts, the big-unit war always took precedence over pacification. Hunt ultimately decided that the U.S. Army's big-unit war did not help pacification; the problem with this tack is that pacification could not happen *without* the big-unit war. Hunt fails to appreciate the U.S. Army's ability to create the necessary physical space in which pacification initiatives could occur.

15. Following the works of Martin G. Clemis, T*he Control War: The Struggle for South Vietnam, 1968–1975* (Norman: University of Oklahoma Press, 2018) and Edward Miller, *Misalliance: Ngo Dinh Diem, the United States, and the Fate of South Vietnam* (Cambridge, Mass: Harvard University Press, 2013), this study accepts the contention that pacification sought to control the people, not to win their hearts and minds. The United States and the RVN never framed winning the hearts and minds of South Vietnamese civilians as an objective of pacification. Despite rhetoric about kindling a cozy friendship between the GVN and the common people, in practice, how the two nations kept the population under Saigon's banner mattered little if at all. To the contrary, the Vietnam War functioned as a control war rather than one of fostering warm relations between the Saigon government and the South Vietnamese peasants. Examining the war in Phú Yên yields a similar conclusion.

16. Military briefing at Pentagon, 22 November 1967, p. 5, box 09, folder 08, Douglas Pike Collection (hereafter cited as Pike Collection), unit 01, Vietnam Center and Sam Johnson Vietnam Archive, Texas Tech University (hereafter cited as TTUVA), accessed 14 July 2020, www.vietnam.ttu.edu/virtualarchive/items.php?item= 2120908026.

17. For critics of the war's execution, see Andrew F. Krepinevich, Jr., *The Army and Vietnam* (Baltimore: Johns Hopkins University Press, 1986); Sorley, "The Conduct of the War," in Wiest, *Rolling Thunder*; Sorley, *A Better War*; and Sorley, *Westmoreland*.

18. Daddis, *Westmoreland's War*, xx; Gentile, *Wrong Turn*, 68.
19. Daddis, *Westmoreland's War*, 12.
20. Daddis, *Westmoreland's War*, 66, 70.
21. On the link between conventional warfare and pacification, see Boylan, *Losing Binh Dinh*, and Thomas Richardson, *Destroy and Build: Pacification in Phuoc Tuy, 1966–72* (Cambridge: Cambridge University Press, 2017).
22. Maxwell D. Taylor, interview by Stanley Karnow, "America's Mandarin: 1954–1963," *Vietnam: A Television History*, part 3 of 4, January 1979, Open Vault (WGHB Media Library and Archives), accessed 13 July 2020, http://openvault.wgbh.org /catalog/V_B182E52F36DD4A64A65D5342CA3D69E3.
23. Christian G. Appy, *Working-Class War: American Combat Soldiers and Vietnam* (Chapel Hill: University of North Carolina Press, 1993), 22–25.
24. Province studies include David W. P. Elliott and W. A. Stewart, *Pacification and the Viet Cong System in Dinh Tuong, 1966–1967* (Santa Monica, Calif.: RAND Corporation, [1969] 1975); Jeffrey Race, *War Comes to Long An: Revolutionary Conflict in a Vietnamese Province* (Berkeley: University of California Press, 1972); Eric M. Bergerud, *The Dynamics of Defeat: The Vietnam War in Hau Nghia Province* (Boulder, Colo.: Westview Press, 1993); David W. P. Elliott, *The Vietnamese War: Revolution and Social Change in the Mekong Delta, 1930–1975* (New York: Routledge, 2006); Boylan, *Losing Binh Dinh*; and Richardson, *Destroy and Build*.
25. Civil Operations and Revolutionary Development Support later became Civil Operations and Rural Development Support—a change that addressed semantics rather than substance.
26. See also Stuart A. Herrington, *Silence Was a Weapon: The Vietnam War in the Villages* (Novato, Calif.: Presidio Press, 1982). Herrington provided a firsthand account of American-backed pacification efforts during Vietnamization. As an intelligence officer, he was privy to the finer details of the Phoenix Program. In discussing the program, Herrington contended that South Vietnamese officials cared little about the covert war. He presented a war undermined by a recalcitrant GVN.

Chapter 1

1. Richard Holbrooke to Political Section (POL), U.S. Embassy, Saigon, untitled, n.d., p. 1, box 34, Charles T. R. Bohannan Papers (hereafter cited as Bohannan Papers), Hoover Institution Library and Archives, Stanford University, Stanford, Calif. (hereafter cited as HIA).
2. See Andrew J. Birtle, *U.S. Army Counterinsurgency and Contingency Operations Doctrine, 1860–1941* (Washington, D.C.: U.S. Army Center of Military History, [1998], 2009), accessed 14 July 2020, https://history.army.mil/html/books/070/70 -66-1/CMH_Pub_70-66-1.pdf; Andrew J. Birtle, *U.S. Army Counterinsurgency*

and Contingency Operations Doctrine, 1942–1976 (Washington, D.C.: U.S. Army Center of Military History, 2006), accessed 14 July 2020, https://history .army.mil/html/books/us_army_counterinsurgency/CMH_70-98-1US%20Army _Counterinsurgency_WQ.pdf.

3. See Elliott and Stewart, *Pacification and the Viet Cong System in Dinh Tuong*; Race, *War Comes to Long An*; Bergerud, *Dynamics of Defeat*; and Hunt, *Pacification*.

4. Regarding the first assumption, see for example Hunt, *Pacification*; Sorley, "The Conduct of the War," in Wiest, *Rolling Thunder*; Sorley, *A Better War*; and Sorley, *Westmoreland*.

5. By this juncture of his career, Lansdale held little political clout yet remained a powerful symbol of the U.S. commitment to building democracies in Southeast Asia. See Jonathan Nashel, *Edward Lansdale's Cold War* (Amherst: University of Massachusetts Press, 2005), 8–10, 86–88, 124–25.

6. "Report of the Office of the Secretary of Defense Vietnam Task Force" (hereafter cited as Pentagon Papers), part IV.C: Evolution of the War, vol. 8, Re-emphasis on Pacification: 1965–1967, p. 12, RG 330, P 760, box 6, NARA II, accessed 14 July 2020, http://nara-media-001.s3.amazonaws.com/arcmedia/research/pentagon-papers /Pentagon-Papers-Part-IV-C-8.pdf.

7. Edward Lansdale, briefing for secretary of defense, 29 November 1965, p. 1, box 59, Edward Geary Lansdale Papers (hereafter cited as Lansdale Papers), HIA.

8. Andrew J. Gawthorpe makes such an argument in *To Build as Well as Destroy*.

9. Gawthorpe, *To Build as Well as Destroy*, i–ii.

10. Sir Robert Thompson, *Defeating Communist Insurgency: Experiences from Malaya and Vietnam* (London: Chatto and Windus, 1966), 51.

11. Thompson, *Defeating Communist Insurgency*, 62.

12. Thompson, *Defeating Communist Insurgency*, 50–55.

13. Thompson, *Make for the Hills: Memories of Far Eastern Wars* (London: Leo Cooper, 1989), 127, 158.

14. David Galula, *Pacification in Algeria, 1956–1958* (Santa Monica, Calif.: RAND Corporation, 1963).

15. Roger Trinquier, *Modern Warfare: A French View of Counterinsurgency* (London: Pall Mall Press, 1964), 49.

16. Ibid., 4.

17. Ibid., 29.

18. Bernard B. Fall, *Street without Joy* (Mechanicsburg, Pa.: Stackpole Books, 1994), 375.

19. Fall, *Street without Joy*, 20–21.

20. Bernard Fall, lecture, Far East Training Center, Hawaii, December 1966, p. 1, box 12, Lansdale Papers, HIA.

21. Ibid.

22. V. J. Croizat, trans., *A Translation from the French: Lessons of the War in Indochina, Volume 2*, (Santa Monica, Calif.: RAND Corporation, 1967), 2.

23. Croizat, *Translation from the French*.

24. Croizat, *Translation from the French*.

25. Pentagon Papers, part IV.C: Evolution of the War, vol. 8, Re-emphasis on Pacification: 1965–1967, pp. i–ii, RG 330, P 760, box 6, NARA II, accessed 14 July 2020, http://nara-media-001.s3.amazonaws.com/arcmedia/research/pentagon-papers/Pentagon-Papers-Part-IV-C-8.pdf.

26. Ibid., ii.

27. *U.S. Army Counterinsurgency Forces*, Field Manual 31-22 (Washington, D.C.: Department of the Army, November 1963), 106, accessed 14 July 2020, http://smallwarsjournal.com/documents/maxwell1963doctrine.pdf.

28. Ibid., 106–9.

29. Miller, *Misalliance*, 232–33; Trinquier, *Modern Warfare*, 4.

30. Pentagon Papers, part IV.B: Evolution of the War, vol. 2, Counterinsurgency: Strategic Hamlet Program, 1961–63, pp. i–ii, RG 330, P 760, box 6, NARA II, accessed 14 July 2020, https://nara-media-001.s3.amazonaws.com/arcmedia/research/pentagon-papers/Pentagon-Papers-Part-IV-B-2.pdf.

31. Ibid., iii.

32. Maxwell Taylor, "Definition of Pacification," 7 October 1964, box 34, folder 8, Bohannan Papers, HIA.

33. William N. Turpin to USAID, "Toward an Operational Definition of Pacification" (hereafter cited as TOAID A-822), 7 October 1964, p. 1, box 34, folder 8, Bohannan Papers, HIA.

34. Ibid.

35. Ibid.

36. Note from Dick Holbrooke forwarding comments by Ogden Williams to USAID A-822, "Definition of Pacification," 8 October 1964, p. 1, box 02, folder 03, Vladimir Lehovich Collection (hereafter cited as Lehovich Collection), TTUVA, accessed 14 July 2020, www.vietnam.ttu.edu/virtualarchive/items.php?item=12050203006.

37. Ibid.

38. Ibid.

39. Turpin, TOAID A-822, p. 2, Bohannan Papers, HIA.

40. Note from Dick Holbrooke, 8 October 1964, p. 1, box 02, folder 03, Lehovich Collection, TTUVA.

41. Ibid.

42. Turpin, TOAID A-822, p. 4, Bohannan Papers, HIA. Charles T. R. Bohannan noted his initial thoughts on his copy of Turpin's paper.

43. Ibid.

44. Ibid., 6.

45. Ibid. (emphasis added).

46. Ibid., 9.

47. Ibid.

48. Charles T. R. Bohannan, "Definition of Pacification," October 1964, p. 2, box 34, folder 8, Bohannan Papers, HIA.

49. U.S. MACV, "The Concept of Pacification and Certain Definitions and Procedures," 2 March 1965, p. 1, U.S. Army Military History Institute, Carlisle, Pa.

50. Ibid., 1–2.

51. Ibid., 3.

52. Memo on Pacification, n.d., p. 1, box 61, Lansdale Papers, HIA.

53. Ibid.

54. Richard Holbrooke to Political Section (POL), U.S. Embassy, Saigon, untitled, n.d., p. 1, box 34, Bohannan Papers, HIA.

55. Rufus Phillips to Edward Lansdale, "Thoughts on Rural Construction Concept and Organization," 25 September 1965, p. 1, box 55, Lansdale Papers, HIA.

56. Henry Cabot Lodge to Edward Lansdale, office memorandum, 4 October 1965, box 58, Lansdale Papers, HIA.

57. Ibid.

58. Edward Lansdale to Henry Cabot Lodge, "Pacification Meeting with Prime Minister Ky," 29 September, 30 September 1965, p. 2, box 55, Lansdale Papers, HIA.

59. Ibid.

60. Informal Discussion with Col. Lansdale, USAF, and Col. Valeriano, Philippines Military Attaché, 22 February 1957, 27 February 1957, ref. para. 2, box 80, Lansdale Papers, HIA.

61. Henry Cabot Lodge to William Bundy and Leonard Unger, telegram, 9 October 1965, pp. 3–4, box 55, Lansdale Papers, HIA.

62. Edward Lansdale, briefing for secretary of defense, 29 November 1965, p. 1, box 59, Lansdale Papers, HIA.

63. Ibid., 1–2.

64. Pentagon Papers, part IV.C: Evolution of the War, vol. 8, Re-emphasis on Pacification: 1965–1967, pp. 8–9, RG 330, P 760, box 6, NARA II, accessed 14 July 2020, https://nara-media-001.s3.amazonaws.com/arcmedia/research/pentagon-papers /Pentagon-Papers-Part-IV-C-8.pdf.

65. Henry Cabot Lodge to Edward Lansdale, memorandum, 7 December 1965, box 58, Lansdale Papers, HIA.

66. Henry Cabot Lodge to Edward Lansdale, "Roles of Different U.S. Agencies in the Three Phases of Rural Construction, that is, Military Clearing, Pacification and Development," 15 December 1965, box 58, Lansdale Papers, HIA.

67. Edward Lansdale to U.S. Mission Liaison Group, "GVN Doctrine," box 55, Lansdale Papers, HIA.

68. Daniel Ellsberg to SLO, "GVN Concepts of Rural Construction" [draft], 6 January 1966, p. 2, box 55, Lansdale Papers, HIA.

69. Nguyen Cao Ky quoted in Ellsberg to SLO, "GVN Concepts of Rural Construction" [draft], 6 January 1966, p. 2, box 55, Lansdale Papers, HIA.

70. Edward Lansdale to U.S. Mission Liaison Group, "GVN Doctrine," Lansdale Papers, HIA.

71. Nguyen Cao Ky quoted in Ellsberg to SLO, "GVN Concepts of Rural Construction" [draft], Lansdale Papers, HIA.

72. Samuel Karrick to SLO, "Background Paper—Revolutionary Development" [draft], 24 February 1966, p. 1, box 55, Lansdale Papers, HIA.

73. John C. F. Tillson, "II Corps Conference at Dalat," 21 September 1966, p. 2, box 62, Lansdale Papers, HIA. Tillson himself admitted that he was not directly quoting Thang, but instead the essences of Thang's comments.

74. Ibid.

75. Ibid.

76. Edward Lansdale to the Ambassador and U.S. Mission Council Members, "Vietnamese Needs," 21 March 1966, box 55, p. 2, Lansdale Papers, HIA.

77. After 1963, the RVN's civil guard consisted of the Regional Forces (RF) and Popular Forces (PF), collectively known as the Territorial Forces, which remained separate from ARVN until 1970. Jeffrey J. Clarke, *Advice and Support: The Final Years—The U.S. Army in Vietnam, 1965–1973* (Washington, D.C.: U.S. Army Center of Military History, 1998), 19n2. Territorial Forces saw less combat and operated closer to home. Bribes often constituted the means of securing a place with the Territorial Forces. However, operating closer to home meant recruits often went AWOL, leaving unit consistently understrength. Boylan, *Losing Binh Dinh*, 78.

78. Edward Lansdale to the Ambassador and U.S. Mission Council Members, "Vietnamese Needs," Lansdale Papers, HIA.

79. Edward Lansdale to U.S. Mission Council, "Vietnamese Needs," 21 March 1966, p. 1, box 55, Lansdale Papers, HIA.

80. Gen. Nguyen Duc Thang, "Thang's presentation at the Honolulu Conference," 7 February 1966, p. 1, box 62, Lansdale Papers, HIA.

81. Ingrid B. Kobrak, "Rural Pacification in South Viet Nam," *Editorial Research Reports*, vol. 1, 11 January 1967, p. 24, box 15, folder 18, Victoria Schuck Papers, HIA.

82. Pentagon Papers, part IV.C: Evolution of the War, vol. 8, Re-emphasis on Pacification: 1965–1967, p. 66, RG 330, P 760, box 6, NARA II, accessed 14 July 2020, https://nara-media-001.s3.amazonaws.com/arcmedia/research/pentagon-papers/Pentagon-Papers-Part-IV-C-8.pdf (emphasis in original). "Giving a New Thrust to Pacification" appears in the cited Pentagon Papers.

83. Ibid.

84. Ibid.

85. Ibid., 67.

86. Ibid.

87. Ibid.

88. Ibid. (emphasis in original).

89. Ibid., 65–66.

90. Ibid.

91. Lathram memo to Corps DEPCORDS, "1968 Pacification Planning; Definition of Terms," 12 November 1967, Komer-Leonhart Files, box 17, Lyndon Baines Johnson Presidential Library, Austin, Tex., quoted in James Hubert Embrey, "Reorienting Pacification: The Accelerated Pacification Campaign of 1968" (PhD diss., University of Kentucky), 1.

92. Sir Robert Thompson, *No Exit from Vietnam* (New York: David McKay Company, 1969), 55.

93. See, for example, "Monthly Report of Rural Pacification Progress and Population Control and Area Control for the Period 26 September to 25 October 1965," 8 November 1965, box 34, Bohannan Papers, HIA.

94. "Military Operations," n.d., box 34, p. 1, Bohannan Papers, HIA.

95. Ibid.

96. Ibid., 2.

97. "PSYOPS Policy, no. 53: PSYOP Support of Pacification," 22 January 1968, box 13, folder 16, Pike Collection, unit 03, TTUVA, accessed 14 July 2020, www.vietnam .ttu.edu/virtualarchive/items.php?item=2171316005.

98. Ibid.

99. Ibid.

100. Ibid.

101. Committee on Foreign Relations, United States Senate, *Vietnam: December 1969* (Washington, D.C.: United States Government Printing Office, 1970), p. 3, box 25, Allen E. Goodman Papers, HIA.

102. Robert W. Komer, "Clear, Hold and Rebuild," *Army* 10, no. 5 (May 1970): 16–17, box 24, Lansdale Papers, HIA.

103. *Handbook for District Senior Advisor*, MACCORDS, 20 August 1970, box 01, folder 04, Pike Collection, unit 03, TTUVA, accessed 14 July 2020, www.vietnam .ttu.edu/virtualarchive/items.php?item=2160104002.

104. Ibid.

105. For examples, see U.S. MACV, *RF-PF Handbook for Advisors*, January 1969 edition, 1 January 1969, box 03, folder 18, William Colby Collection hereafter cited as Colby Collection), TTUVA, accessed 14 July 2020, www.vietnam.ttu .edu/virtualarchive/items.php?item=0440318001; *RF-PF Handbook for Advisors*,

November 1969 edition, November 1969, box 03, folder 19, Colby Collection, TTUVA, accessed 14 July 2020, www.vietnam.ttu.edu/virtualarchive/items.php ?item=0440319001; *RF-PF Handbook for Advisors*, 1970 edition, 6 February 1970, box 18, folder 11, Pike Collection, unit 03, TTUVA, accessed 14 July 2020, www .vietnam.ttu.edu/virtualarchive/items.php?item=2171811001; and *RF/PF Advisors Handbook*, January 1971 edition, 1 January 1971, box 18, folder 11, Pike Collection, unit 03, TTUVA, accessed 14 July 2020, www.vietnam.ttu.edu/virtualarchive/items .php?item=2171811002.

106. CORDS, MACV, *The Vietnamese Village: A Handbook for Advisors*, 1971 edition, June 1971, box 01, folder 03, John Haseman Collection, TTUVA, accessed 14 July 2020, www.vietnam.ttu.edu/virtualarchive/items.php?item=14040103001.

107. Tran Dinh Tho, *Pacification* (Washington, D.C.: U.S. Army Center of Military History, 1980), v.

108. Selected Statements by DOD and Other Administration Officials on Vietnam, July 1–December 31, 1967, p. 211, box 01, folder 17, Glenn Helm Collection (hereafter cited as Helm Collection), TTUVA, accessed 14 July 2020, www.vietnam.ttu .edu/virtualarchive/items.php?item=1070117001.

109. Ibid., 108.

110. Ibid.

111. Hal Drake, "Pacification: Killing Viet Cong Is Not Enough," *Stars and Stripes*, July 13, 1969, accessed 14 July 2020, www.stripes.com/news/pacification-killing -viet-cong-is-not-enough-1.78700.

112. William Colby, *Lost Victory: A Firsthand Account of America's Sixteen-Year Involvement in Vietnam* (Chicago: Contemporary Books, 1989), 214.

113. Ibid.

114. See the historiographical discussion in this book's introduction for more on this debate.

115. Rose Kushner, "The War in Vietnam," 7 January 1967 (unpublished), box 60, Lansdale Papers, HIA (emphasis in original).

116. Thompson, *No Exit from Vietnam*, 55.

117. Ibid., 145.

118. Robert W. Komer to Edward Lansdale, 26 May 1971, box 4, Lansdale Papers, HIA.

119. Edward Lansdale to Robert W. Komer, 30 May 1971, box 4, Lansdale Papers, HIA.

120. Robert W. Komer to Edward Lansdale, 1 June 1971, box 4, Lansdale Papers, HIA.

Chapter 2

1. "Lao Dong Ninth Plenum Decision on War in South," December 1963, p. 15, box 03, folder 02, Pike Collection, unit 01, TTUVA, accessed 16 July 2020, www.vietnam .ttu.edu/virtualarchive/items.php?item=2120302009 (emphasis in original).

2. Ibid., 16–17.

3. Provincial briefing, folder 9: Phu-Yen Province, USAID Region II, Nha Trang, second printing, November 1966, pp. 2–3, CMH.

4. Ibid., 3.

5. Ibid., 5.

6. Operational Report on Lessons Learned (hereafter ORLL), quarterly period ending 30 April 1966, Department of the Army, Headquarters, I Field Force, Vietnam, 15 May 1966, p. 7, Defense Technical Information Center, Fort Belvoir, Va. (hereafter cited as DTIC), accessed 16 July 2020.

7. "Visit to Cochin China," *Maryland Gazette*, 21 November 1833, p. 2; Robert Lanigan, "Phu Yen Province Briefing Folder," 6 September 1971, p. 1, box 2, folder 6, Courtney L. Frobenius Papers (hereafter cited as Frobenius Papers), McCain Library and Archives, University of Southern Mississippi, Hattiesburg, Miss. (hereafter cited as MLA).

8. Ibid.

9. George Dutton, *The Tây Son Uprising: Society and Rebellion in Eighteenth-Century Vietnam* (Honolulu: University of Hawai'i Press, 2006), 2, 54–55.

10. Ibid.

11. "Visit to Cochin China."

12. Lanigan, "Phu Yen Province Briefing Folder," 6 September 1971, p. 2, Frobenius Papers, MLA.

13. David G. Marr, *Vietnam 1945: The Quest for Power* (Berkeley: University of California Press, 1995), 14, 25, 29.

14. Ibid., 42, 54–61.

15. Lanigan, "Phu Yen Province Briefing Folder," 6 September 1971, p. 2, Frobenius Papers, MLA.

16. Michel Grintchenko, "Operation Atlante (January–July 1954): The Last Pacification Operation in Indochina," *Doctrine* 12 (May 2007): 102–5.

17. Michel Grintchenko, *L'Opération Atlante: Les Dernières Illusions de la France en Indochine* (Paris: Economica, 2008), 22–23.

18. Fall, *Street without Joy*, 189.

19. Grintchenko, "Operation Atlante," 103; Grintchenko, *L'Opération Atlante*, 142–43.

20. Lanigan, "Phu Yen Province Briefing Folder," 6 September 1971, p. 2, Frobenius Papers, MLA.

21. Fall, *Street without Joy*, 189.

22. "Red Troops Wipe Out 200 Vietnamese," *Shreveport (La.) Times*, 4 June 1954, 1.

23. The end of Operation Atlante placed GM 100 on a course toward its own demise. GM 100's mission terminated as soon as it arrived at Tuy Hòa village as the task force then moved to Kon Tum to counter a burgeoning Việt Minh presence in

that province. Shortly thereafter, GM 100 received orders from the French high command to assist with the evacuation of French assets from An Khe to Pleiku. As GM 100 tried to rendezvous with other French units en route to Pleiku, the Việt Minh's 803rd Regiment ambushed and annihilated the task force at the Battle of Mang Yang Pass. See Kirk A. Luedeke, "Death on the Highway: The Destruction of Groupement Mobile 100," *Armor*, January–February 2001, 24–25; Fall, *Street without Joy*, 220–23.

24. Boylan, *Losing Binh Dinh*, 12.

25. William A. Dymsza to D. C. Lavergne, memo, "Refugee situation in Nhatrang and Phu Yen," 7 December 1954, p. 3, box 08, folder 19, Ronald B. Frankum, Jr. Collection (hereafter cited as Frankum Collection), TTUVA, accessed 16 July 2020, www.vietnam.ttu.edu/virtualarchive/items.php?item=10390819024.

26. Lanigan, "Phu Yen Province Briefing Folder," 6 September 1971, p. 2, Frobenius Papers, MLA.

27. William A. Dymsza to Charles A. Mann, "Report on Visit to Province of Phu-Yen," 3 January 1955, p. 3, box 08, folder 21, Frankum Collection, TTUVA, accessed 16 July 2020, www.vietnam.ttu.edu/virtualarchive/items.php?item=10390821007.

28. Ibid., 1.

29. Ibid.

30. Ibid., 2.

31. Ibid.

32. Ibid.

33. A. Terry Rambo, Jerry M. Tinker, and John D. LeNoir, *The Refugee Situation in Phu-Yen Province, Viet-Nam* (MacLean, Va.: Human Sciences Research, Inc., July 1967), p. 59, box 02, folder 02, Gary Larsen Collection (hereafter cited as Larsen Collection), TTUVA, accessed 16 July 2020, www.vietnam.ttu.edu/virtualarchive /items.php?item=19600202001.

34. "Organization of the NFLSVN Committee of Phu Yen Province," August 1967, pp. 2–7, box 08, folder 11, Pike Collection, unit 05, TTUVA, accessed 13 September 2020, https://www.vietnam.ttu.edu/virtualarchive/items.php?item=2310811011.

35. "332. Memorandum From the Director of the Bureau of Intelligence and Research (Hilsman) to the Assistant Secretary of State for Far Eastern Affairs (Harriman)," 19 December 1962, in John P. Glennon, David M. Baehler, and Charles S. Simpson, eds., *Foreign Relations of the United States, 1961–1963, Volume II, Vietnam, 1962* (Washington, D.C.: U.S. Government Printing Office, 1990), accessed 16 July 2020, https://history.state.gov/historicaldocuments/frus1961-63v02/d332.

36. Ibid.; Lanigan, "Phu Yen Province Briefing Folder," 6 September 1971, Frobenius Papers, MLA.

37. J. P. Harris, *Vietnam's High Ground: Armed Struggle for the Central Highlands, 1954–1965* (Lawrence: University Press of Kansas, 2016), 123, 135.

38. "203. Telegram From the Embassy in Vietnam to the Department of State," 23 May 1962, in Glennon, Baehler, and Simpson, eds., *Foreign Relations of the United States, 1961–1963, Volume II*, accessed 16 July 2020, https://history.state.gov /historicaldocuments/frus1961-63v02/d203.

39. Lanigan, "Phu Yen Province Briefing Folder," 6 September 1971, p. 2, Frobenius Papers, MLA.

40. "Weekly Report: The Situation in South Vietnam," CIA Research Report, 9 December 1964, p. 12, box 0004, folder 0464, Sam Johnson Vietnam Archive Collection (hereafter cited as Johnson Collection), TTUVA, accessed 16 July 2020, www .vietnam.ttu.edu/virtualarchive/items.php?item=F029100040464.

41. Rufus Phillips, *Why Vietnam Matters: An Eyewitness Account of Lessons Not Learned* (Annapolis, Md.: Naval Institute Press, 2008), 110–14.

42. Rufus Phillips to John M. Dunn, memo, "Proposed Ambassadorial Visit to Phu Yen Province," 2 October 1963, box 02, folder 01, Rufus Phillips Collection (hereafter cited as Phillips Collection), TTUVA, accessed 16 July 2020, www.vietnam.ttu .edu/virtualarchive/items.php?item=23970201047.

43. Ibid.

44. "320. Letter From the Ambassador in Vietnam (Nolting) to the Assistant Secretary of State for Far Eastern Affairs (Harriman)," 19 November 1962, in Glennon, Baehler, and Simpson, eds., *Foreign Relations of the United States, 1961–1963, Volume II*, accessed 16 July 2020, https://history.state.gov/historicaldocuments /frus1961-63v02/d320.

45. "319. Memorandum From the Director of the Bureau of Intelligence and Research (Hilsman) and Michael V. Forrestal of the National Security Council Staff to the President," 25 January 1963, in Glennon, Baehler, and Simpson, eds., *Foreign Relations of the United States, 1961–1963, Volume II*, accessed 16 July 2020, https:// history.state.gov/historicaldocuments/frus1961-63v03/d19.

46. "Weekly Report: The Situation in South Vietnam," CIA Research Report, 9 December 1964, p. 12, Johnson Collection, TTUVA, accessed 16 July 2020, www.vietnam .ttu.edu/virtualarchive/items.php?item=F029100040464.

47. Ibid.

48. Ibid.

49. Ibid.

50. Ibid.

51. Ibid.

52. Ibid., 12–13.

53. Ibid., 13.

54. Ibid.

55. Ibid.

56. Ibid., 12.

57. Mao Tse-tung, *Selected Military Writings of Mao Tse-tung* (Peking: Foreign Language Press, 1968), 210–15.

58. Lien-Hang T. Nguyen, *Hanoi's War: An International History of the War for Peace in Vietnam* (Chapel Hill: University of North Carolina Press, 2012), 10, 49, 64–65.

59. Ibid., 65–66.

60. Military History Institute of Vietnam, *Victory in Vietnam: The Official History of the People's Army of Vietnam, 1954–1975*, trans. Merle L. Pribbenow (Lawrence: University Press of Kansas, 2002), 127.

61. Lanigan, "Phu Yen Province Briefing Folder," 6 September 1971, p. 2, Frobenius Papers, MLA.

62. Rambo, Tinker, and LeNoir, *Refugee Situation in Phu-Yen Province*, p. 59, Larsen Collection, TTUVA.

63. Franklin Sawyer, "Decimated 95th N. Vietnam Regiment Hopes to Recoup Strength," 20 November 1967, p. 2, box 10, folder 01, Pike Collection, unit 02, TTUVA, accessed 16 July 2020, www.vietnam.ttu.edu/virtualarchive/items.php ?item=2131001052.

64. Rambo, Tinker, and LeNoir, *The Refugee Situation in Phu-Yen Province*, p. 60, Larsen Collection, TTUVA.

65. Bernard B. Fall, *Viet-Nam Witness, 1953–66* (New York: Frederick A. Praeger, 1966), 293.

66. Võ Nguyên and Lễ Tân Danh, "In the Liberated Zones of South Vietnam," *Vietnamese Studies* 8 (1966): 164, box 15, folder 12, Pike Collection, unit 05, TTUVA, accessed 16 July 2020, www.vietnam.ttu.edu/virtualarchive/items.php?item= 2311512018.

67. "Viet Cong Loss of Population Control: Evidence from Captured Documents," n.d., p. 3, box 07, folder 01, Pike Collection, unit 01, TTUVA, accessed 16 July 2020, www.vietnam.ttu.edu/virtualarchive/items.php?item=2120701002.

68. Douglas Pike, *Viet Cong: The Organization and Techniques of the National Liberation Front of South Vietnam* (Cambridge, Mass.: MIT Press, 1966), 269–74.

69. Provincial briefing, folder 9, Phú Yên Province, USAID Region II, November 1966, pp. 2–3, CMH.

70. "Aggression from the North: The Record of North Viet-Nam's Campaign To Conquer South Viet-Nam," Department of State, Washington, D.C., February 1965, pp. 15–16, box 23, Lansdale Papers, HIA.

71. Ibid., 19.

72. Ibid., 16.

73. Ibid., 19.

74. Ibid., 17.

75. Combined Documentation Exploitation Center, "Translation Report of Guerrilla Warfare in Phu Yen Province, Military Region V," 15 July 1967, p. 1, box 0163,

folder 2522, Vietnam Archive Collection, TTUVA, accessed 16 July 2020, www
.vietnam.ttu.edu/virtualarchive/items.php?item=F034601632522.

76. Pike, *Viet Cong*, 239.

77. Combined Documentation Exploitation Center, "Translation Report of Guerrilla
Warfare in Phu Yen Province," p. 1, Vietnam Archive Collection, TTUVA.

78. Ibid., 1.

79. Combined Documentation Exploitation Center, "Study of the 1964 Guerrilla
Movement in Tuy Hoa I District," 29 April 1966, p. 2, box 0036, folder 0666,
Vietnam Archive Collection, TTUVA, accessed 16 July 2020, www.vietnam.ttu
.edu/virtualarchive/items.php?item=F034600360666.

80. Department of External Affairs, Canberra, "Situation in Central Vietnam," 3 March
1965, box 02, folder 30, Frankum Collection, TTUVA, accessed 16 July 2020, www
.vietnam.ttu.edu/virtualarchive/items.php?item=10390230010.

81. Ibid.

82. John M. Carland, *Combat Operations: Stemming the Tide, May 1965 to October
1966* (Washington, D.C.: U.S. Army Center of Military History, 2000), 201.

83. U.S. Embassy Saigon to Department of State, "Provincial Reporting: Improved
Security in Phu Yen," 27 January 1967, p. 1, CMH.

84. Combined Documentation Exploitation Center, "Translation report of 95th Regiment, Nong Truong 5 North Vietnamese Army Division, Military Region V,"
19 July 1967, box 0163, folder 1906, Vietnam Archive Collection, TTUVA, accessed
16 July 2020, www.vietnam.ttu.edu/virtualarchive/items.php?item=F034601631906;
Translation of Certificates, 4th Battalion, 95th Regiment, Nong Truong 5 North
Vietnamese Army Division, Military Region V, 19 July 1967, box 0165, folder 0810,
Vietnam Archive Collection, TTUVA, accessed 16 July 2020, www.vietnam.ttu
.edu/virtualarchive/items.php?item=F034601650810; Combined Documentation
Exploitation Center, "Translation of Certificates, 4th Battalion, 95th Regiment,
Nong Truong 5 North Vietnamese Army Division, Military Region V," 19 July
1967, box 0165, folder 0828, Vietnam Archive Collection, TTUVA, accessed 16 July
2020, www.vietnam.ttu.edu/virtualarchive/items.php?item=F034601650828.

85. Stanley Robert Larsen and James Lawton Collins Jr., *Vietnam Studies: Allied
Participation in Vietnam* (Washington, D.C.: Department of the Army, 1975),
123, accessed 27 November 2020, https://history.army.mil/html/books/090/90-5
-1/CMH_Pub_90-5-1.pdf.

86. Pentagon Papers, part IV.C: Evolution of the War, vol. 8, Re-emphasis on Pacification: 1965–1967, p. 1, RG 330, P 760, box 6, NARA II, accessed 16 July 2020,
http://nara-media-001.s3.amazonaws.com/arcmedia/research/pentagon-papers
/Pentagon-Papers-Part-IV-C-8.pdf>.

87. Pentagon Papers, part IV.C: Evolution of the War, vol. 5, Phase I in the Build-up
of U.S. Forces: March–July 1965, p. 54, RG 330, P 760, box 4, NARA II, accessed

16 July 2020, https://nara-media-001.s3.amazonaws.com/arcmedia/research/pentagon-papers/Pentagon-Papers-Part-IV-C-5.pdf.

88. Ibid., 117.

89. Reports of USOM provincial representatives, month ending 31 August 1965, box 01, folder 01, Phillips Collection, TTUVA, accessed 16 July 2020, www.vietnam.ttu.edu/virtualarchive/items.php?item=23970101001.

90. Ibid.

91. ORLL, quarterly period ending 31 December 1965, Department of the Army, Headquarters, Field Force, Vietnam, 14 January 1966, DTIC, p. 7. For context, on 1 August 1965, MACV activated Task Force Alpha, which became Field Force, Vietnam on 25 September, which in turn became I Field Force, Vietnam on 15 March 1966. All three were corps-level commands headquartered in the city of Nha Trang. See Maj. Gen. George S. Eckhardt, *Vietnam Studies: Command and Control, 1950–1969* (Washington, D.C.: Department of the Army, 2004), 53–54, 64, accessed 29 August 2020, https://history.army.mil/html/books/090/90-8-1/CMH_Pub_90-8-1.pdf.

92. ORLL, quarterly period ending 31 December 1965, Department of the Army, 14 January 1966, DTIC, p. 9.

93. Ibid., 44.

94. Ibid., 50.

95. Trinquier, *Modern Warfare*, 4; Miller, *Misalliance*, 232–33.

96. Reports of JUSPAO provincial representatives, month ending 30 November 1965, box 01, folder 03, Phillips Collection, TTUVA, accessed 17 July 2020, www.vietnam.ttu.edu/virtualarchive/items.php?item=23970103001. Despite the title provided by the archive, this document is a series of reports from Joint United States Public Affairs Office (JUSPAO) field representatives.

97. Henry Cabot Lodge to Edward Lansdale, "Roles of Different U.S. Agencies in the Three Phases of Rural Construction, that is, Military Clearing, Pacification and Development," 15 December 1965, box 58, Lansdale Papers, HIA.

98. "A Brief Narrative Report on the Status and Progress of Activities Planned under the 1965 Rural Construction Program in Phu-Yen Covering the Period from May 1965 through September 1965," n.d., p. 1, box 03, folder 08, Phillips Collection, TTUVA, accessed 17 July 2020, www.vietnam.ttu.edu/virtualarchive/items.php?item=23970308001.

99. Pentagon Papers, part IV.C: Evolution of the War, vol. 6a, U.S. Grand Strategy and Force Deployments: 1965–1967, p. 62, RG 330, P 760, box 5, NARA II, accessed 17 July 2020, https://nara-media-001.s3.amazonaws.com/arcmedia/research/pentagon-papers/Pentagon-Papers-Part-IV-C-6-a.pdf. In this instance, LOC meant lines of communication. I CTZ (I Corps Tactical Zone), or I Corps, referred to the northern region of South Vietnam directly opposite North Vietnam.

100. 322d Military History Detachment, *The First Brigade in the Republic of Vietnam, July 1956–January 1968* (Tuscaloosa, Ala.: U.S. Army Reserve, n.d.), 27.

101. Lanigan, "Phu Yen Province Briefing Folder," 6 September 1971, p. 2, Frobenius Papers, MLA.

102. Reports of JUSPAO provincial representatives, month ending 30 December 1965, p. 1, box 01, folder 04, Phillips Collection, TTUVA, accessed July 2020, www.vietnam.ttu.edu/virtualarchive/items.php?item=23970104001. Despite the title provided by the archive, this document is a series of reports from JUSPAO field representatives.

103. Ibid.

Chapter 3

1. Lt. Gen. Stanley Larsen, press conference, White House, Washington, D.C., 25 August 1967, p. 8, *The War in Vietnam: Papers of William C. Westmoreland, Part 1: History, Statements, and Clipping Files*, box 907, folder 10, CMH.

2. Edward G. Lansdale, "Civic Action," lecture, Counter-Guerilla School, Special Warfare Center, Fort Bragg, North Carolina, 24 February 1961, p. 3, box 45, Lansdale Papers, HIA.

3. War History Compilation Committee, *Pictorial War History of ROK Forces to Vietnam, 1964.6–1970.6* (Seoul, Korea: Ministry of National Defense, 1970), 11, accessed 14 September 2020, http://www.vietvet.or.kr/hwabo/pawol1/vnb001.htm.

4. ORLL, period of 1 January to 30 April 1966, Department of the Army, Headquarters, 5th Howitzer Battalion, 27th Artillery, 12 May 1966, p. 3, DTIC.

5. ORLL, quarterly period ending 30 April 1966, Department of the Army, Headquarters, I Field Force, Vietnam, 15 May 1966, p. 2, DTIC.

6. Ibid., 3.

7. Rambo, Tinker, and LeNoir, *The Refugee Situation in Phu-Yen Province, Viet-Nam*, p. 60, box 02, folder 02, Larsen Collection, TTUVA, accessed 21 July 2020, www.vietnam.ttu.edu/virtualarchive/items.php?item=19600202001.

8. Ibid.

9. Jack Foisie, "U.S., Korea, and Viet Forces Join in Drive on Red Units," *Los Angeles Times*, January 26, 1966.

10. Carland, *Combat Operations*, 186.

11. Combined Documentation Exploitation Center, "Translation report of elements of Nong Truong 5 North Vietnamese Army Division, Military Region V," 22 July 1967, box 0163, folder 1897, Vietnam Archive Collection, TTUVA, accessed 21 July 2020, www.vietnam.ttu.edu/virtualarchive/items.php?item=F034601631897.

12. Carland, *Combat Operations*, 186–87.

13. Ibid., 187.

14. For more on the war crimes committed by Tiger Force members, see Michael Sallah and Mitch Weiss, *Tiger Force: A True Story of Men and War* (New York: Back Bay Books, 2007).

15. David H. Hackworth and Julie Sherman, *About Face: The Odyssey of an American Warrior* (New York: Simon and Schuster, 1989), 502.

16. Ibid., 504.

17. Ibid., 505; Carland, *Combat Operations*, 188.

18. Hackworth and Sherman, *About Face*, 506.

19. Carland, *Combat Operations*, 188.

20. ORLL, period of 1 January to 30 April 1966, Department of the Army, 12 May 1966, p. 3, DTIC.

21. "U.S. Military Assistance Command Vietnam Weekly Summaries: Summary of USMACV News Events 1966," 14 January 1967, p. 4, box 02, folder 03, Helm Collection, TTUVA, accessed 21 July 2020, www.vietnam.ttu.edu/virtualarchive /items.php?item=1070203003.

22. John J. Falbo and Leslie J. Hepler, *Unit History: Vagabonds of Vietnam—Tenth Combat Aviation Battalion, 1965–1966*, n.d., pp. IV–3, box 03, folder 04, Vietnam Helicopter Pilots Association Collection: Unit Histories—1st Aviation Brigade (hereafter cited as VHPA Collection), TTUVA, accessed 21 July 2020, www.vietnam .ttu.edu/virtualarchive/items.php?item=3030304003.

23. Rambo, Tinker, and LeNoir, *The Refugee Situation in Phu-Yen Province, Viet-Nam*, p. 60, Larsen Collection, TTUVA.

24. Ibid.

25. Falbo and Hepler, *Unit History: Vagabonds of Vietnam*, pp. iv–4, VHPA Collection: Unit Histories, TTUVA.

26. Carland, *Combat Operations*, 191–92.

27. John D. Howard, *First In, Last Out: An American Paratrooper in Vietnam with the 101st and Vietnamese Airborne* (Guilford, Conn.: Stackpole Books, 2017), 88.

28. Ibid., 88–90; Hackworth and Sherman, *About Face*, 517–19; Carland, *Combat Operations*, 191–92.

29. Combined Documentation Exploitation Center, "Study of the 1964 Guerrilla Movement in Tuy Hoa I District," 29 April 1966, pp. 2–3, box 0036, folder 0666, Vietnam Archive Collection, TTUVA, accessed 21 July 2020, www.vietnam.ttu .edu/virtualarchive/items.php?item=F034600360666.

30. Ibid., 3.

31. Ibid.

32. Ibid.

33. Ibid.

34. Ibid.
35. War History Compilation Committee, *Pictorial War History of ROK Forces to Vietnam*, 122.
36. Combat Operations AAR, Operation Fillmore, Department of the Army, Headquarters, 1st Brigade, 101st Airborne Division, 17 August 1966, p. 2, DTIC.
37. Ibid.
38. Ibid.
39. Ibid.
40. Ibid., 3.
41. Ibid.
42. Ibid.
43. Ibid.
44. ORLL, quarterly period ending 30 April 1966, Department of the Army, 15 May 1966, p. 7, DTIC.
45. Combat Operations AAR, Operation Fillmore, Department of the Army, Headquarters, 1st Brigade, 101st Airborne Division, 17 August 1966, p. 22, DTIC.
46. Ibid.
47. Phú Yên Province Report, period ending 30 April 1966, "II Corps Special Joint Report on Revolutionary Development," 31 October 1966, p. 1, CMH. In South Vietnam, the CIA operated under the name Office of the Special Assistant.
48. MACV, "Upgrading of Viet Cong Forces," part 2, 29 April 1967, p. 4, box 0024, folder 0589, TTUVA, accessed 21 July 2020, www.vietnam.ttu.edu/virtualarchive /items.php?item=F015900240589 (emphasis in original).
49. Ibid., 4–5.
50. Ibid., 5.
51. "Operations of U.S. Marine Forces, Vietnam," 1 June 1966, p. 18, box n.a., folder 001, U.S. Marine Corps History Division, Vietnam War Documents Collection, TTUVA, accessed 21 July 2020, www.vietnam.ttu.edu/virtualarchive/items.php ?item=1201001060.
52. Ibid.; Jack Shulimson, *U.S. Marines in Vietnam: An Expanding War, 1966* (Washington, D.C.: History and Museums Division, Headquarters, U.S. Marine Corps, 1982), 304, 357.
53. Combat Operations AAR, Operation Nathan Hale, Headquarters 1st Battalion (Airborne), 8th Cavalry, 1st Cavalry Division (Airmobile), 20 June–1 July 1966, 14 July 1966, p. 1, box 01, folder 03, Levin B. Broughton Collection, TTUVA, accessed 21 July 2020, www.vietnam.ttu.edu/virtualarchive/items.php?item=6910103005.
54. Ibid., 4.
55. Ibid.
56. Carland, *Combat Operations*, 198.

57. "MACV Weekly Summaries: Summary of USMACV News Events 1966," 14 January 1967, p. 2, box 02, folder 03, Helm Collection, TTUVA, accessed 21 July 2020, www.vietnam.ttu.edu/virtualarchive/items.php?item=1070203003.

58. Carland, *Combat Operations*, 198.

59. Combat Operations AAR, Operation John Paul Jones, Department of the Army, Headquarters, 1st Brigade, 101st Airborne Division, 28 September 1966, p. 2, DTIC.

60. Arc Light raids featured the use of strategic bombers in a tactical role: a flight of B-52s dropped thousands of tons of bombs on an area suspected of harboring a sizable enemy force, transferring lush terrain into moonscape.

61. Ibid., 3.

62. Ibid.

63. Combat Operations AAR, Operation John Paul Jones, Department of the Army, 28 September 1966, p. 26, DTIC.

64. Ibid.

65. Ibid.

66. Ibid.

67. Ibid.

68. "The Status of the North Vietnamese Divisions in Central II Corps," intelligence memorandum, Directorate of Intelligence, Central Intelligence Agency, 25 November 1967, p. 12, CMH.

69. Ibid.

70. Ibid.

71. Ibid.

72. Combat Operations AAR, Operation Seward, Department of the Army, Headquarters, 1st Brigade, 101st Airborne Division, 6 November 1966, pp. 1–2, DTIC. For this reference in the footnotes below and others like it, the numerals indicate page numbers, not page ranges.

73. Ibid., 2-3.

74. Ibid., 3.

75. Ibid.

76. Ibid.

77. Ibid.

78. Ibid.

79. Ibid. American and South Vietnamese authorities organized minority ethnic groups into armed defense forces under the CIDG program.

80. Ibid.

81. Ibid.

82. Ibid.

83. Ibid., 3-4.

84. Ibid., 4.

85. Ibid., 6-1.

86. Ibid., 1-1.

87. Ibid.

88. Ibid., 1-4–2-1.

89. Ibid., 6-1.

90. ORLL, quarterly period ending 31 October 1966, Department of the Army, Headquarters, I Field Force, Vietnam, 30 November 1966, p. 27, DTIC.

91. Operation Adams Narrative, p. 1, folder: 4th Inf Div (Adams), CMH; Historian's Notes and Working Papers, p. 4, folder: 4th Inf Div (Adams), CMH.

92. ORLL, quarterly period ending 31 October 1966, Department of the Army, 30 November 1966, p. 12, DTIC.

93. 322d Military History Detachment, *First Brigade*, 44.

94. Ibid.

95. ORLL, quarterly period ending 31 January 1967, Department of the Army, Headquarters, 1st Brigade, 4th Infantry Division, 1 February 1967, p. 10, DTIC (emphasis in original).

96. Ibid. (emphasis in original).

97. Ibid.

98. 322d Military History Department, *First Brigade*, 44.

99. Ibid.

100. Hackworth and Sherman, *About Face*, 566.

101. Ibid.

102. Ibid., 571.

103. Phú Yên Province Report, "II Corps Special Joint Report on Revolutionary Development," October 1966, p. 1, CMH.

104. Ibid., 2.

105. Ibid., 2–3.

106. Ibid., 3.

107. "The Status of the North Vietnamese Divisions in Central II Corps," intelligence memorandum, Directorate of Intelligence, Central Intelligence Agency, 25 November 1967, p. 8, CMH.

Chapter 4

1. Selected statements on Vietnam by DOD and other administration officials, 1 July–31 December 1967, 11 January 1967, box 01, folder 18, Helm Collection, TTUVA, p. 211, accessed 29 August 2020, https://www.vietnam.ttu.edu/reports/images.php?img=/images/107/1070118001E.pdf.

2. American Embassy Saigon to Department of State, memo, "Province Reporting: Improve Security in Phú Yên," 27 January 1967, p.1, CMH.

3. Ibid.

4. Ibid.

5. Ibid., 2.

6. Ibid.

7. Ibid., 3.

8. Gen. William C. Westmoreland quoted in Erik B. Villard, *Combat Operations: Staying the Course—October 1967 to September 1968* (Washington, D.C.: U.S. Army Center of Military History, 2017), 190, accessed 21 July 2020, https://history.army.mil/html/books/091/91-15-1/cmhPub_91-15-1.pdf.

9. Memo to President Lyndon B. Johnson, "Review of Robert McNamara's Draft Memo," 20 May 1967, p. 3, box 06, folder 20, Larry Berman Collection (Presidential Archives Research; hereafter cited as Berman Collection), TTUVA, accessed 21 July 2020, www.vietnam.ttu.edu/virtualarchive/items.php?item=0240620008. Although sections of the document are redacted, the quoted portion above appears lined out, possibly by Walt Rostow.

10. Ibid.

11. General 1967 MACV monthly summary, February 1967, p. 8, folder 01, Bud Harton Collection (hereafter Harton Collection), TTUVA, accessed 21 July 2020, www.vietnam.ttu.edu/virtualarchive/items.php?item=168300010726.

12. ORLL, quarterly period ending 31 January 1967, Department of the Army, Headquarters, 1st Brigade, 4th Infantry Division, 1 February 1967, p. 9, DTIC.

13. General 1967 MACV monthly summary, February 1967, p. 8, folder 01, Harton Collection, TTUVA.

14. Ibid.

15. MACV, "Targeting Branch Revised VC/NVA Base and Operations Areas," part 2, 1 March 1967, p. A-26, box 0023, folder 0924, TTUVA, accessed 21 July 2020, www.vietnam.ttu.edu/virtualarchive/items.php?item=F015900230924.

16. Ibid.

17. Ibid.

18. Ibid.

19. Ibid., A-14.

20. Ibid.

21. Ibid., A-24.

22. Ibid.

23. Ibid.

24. Ibid., A-25.

25. Ibid.

26. Ibid.

27. Warren K. Wilkins, *Nine Days in May: The Battles of the 4th Infantry Division on the Cambodian Border, 1967* (Norman: University of Oklahoma Press, 2017), 172; MACV History Operational Summary, Operation Adams Narrative, 26 October 1966–2 April 1967, p. 1, folder: 4th Inf Div (Adams), CMH.

28. MACV History Operational Summary, Operation Adams Narrative, p. 2.

29. Ibid.

30. MACV report, 95th Regiment, 325th Division, 1 May 1968, p. 2, box 16, folder 13, Helm Collection, TTUVA, accessed 21 July 2020, www.vietnam.ttu .edu/virtualarchive/items.php?item=1071613004.

31. "Memo to President Lyndon B. Johnson from W. W. Rostow: Ambassador Lodge's Weekly Telegram," 6 April 1967, p. 9, box 06, folder 14, Berman Collection, TTUVA, accessed 21 July 2020, www.vietnam.ttu.edu/virtualarchive/items.php ?item=0240614011.

32. Gian Gentile, *Wrong Turn: America's Deadly Embrace of Counterinsurgency.* (New York: The New Press, 2013), 69–70.

33. Rambo, Tinker, and LeNoir, *The Refugee Situation in Phu-Yen Province, Viet-Nam,* p. xii-xiii, box 02, folder 02, Larsen Collection, TTUVA, accessed 21 July 2020, www.vietnam.ttu.edu/virtualarchive/items.php?item=19600202001.

34. Provincial briefing, folder number 9: Phú Yên Province, USAID Region II, Nha Trang, second printing, November 1966, pp. 2–3, CMH.

35. Rambo, Tinker, and LeNoir, *The Refugee Situation in Phu-Yen Province, Viet-Nam,* p. xv, box 02, folder 02, Larsen Collection, TTUVA, accessed 21 July 2020, www .vietnam.ttu.edu/virtualarchive/items.php?item=19600202001.

36. Combined Documentation Exploitation Center, "95th Regiment, Nong Truong 5 North Vietnamese Army Division, Military Region V," 15 July 1967, box 0163, folder 2015, Vietnam Archive Collection, TTUVA, accessed 21 July 2020, www .vietnam.ttu.edu/virtualarchive/items.php?item=F034601632015.

37. Edwin E. Moïse, *The Myths of Tet: The Most Misunderstood Event of the Vietnam War* (Lawrence: University Press of Kansas, 2017), 94; George L. MacGarrigle, *Combat Operations: Taking the Offensive, October 1966 to October 1967* (Washington, D.C.: U.S. Army Center of Military History, 1998), 313–14, accessed 21 July 2020, https://history.army.mil/html/books/091/91-4/CMH_Pub_91-4-B.pdf.

38. Ibid., 314; MACV report, 95th Regiment, 325th Division, 1 May 1968, p. 4, box 16, folder 13, Helm Collection, TTUVA.

39. Lt. Gen. Stanley Larsen, press conference, White House, 25 August 1967, p. 2, *The War in Vietnam: Papers of William C. Westmoreland, Part 1: History, Statements, and Clipping Files,* 10:907, CMH.

40. Ibid., 4.

41. Ibid.

42. Ibid.

43. MACV Monthly Assessment—August, September 1967, p. 5, folder 01, Harton Collection, TTUVA, accessed 21 July 220, www.vietnam.ttu.edu/virtualarchive /items.php?item=168300010730.

44. Ibid.

45. Phú Yên Province Report, period ending 30 September 1967, 14 February 1968, p. 2, CMH.

46. Combat Operations AAR, Operation Bolling, Department of the Army, Headquarters, 3rd Battalion (Airborne), 503rd Infantry, 173rd Airborne Brigade (Separate), 14 February 1968, p. 1, DTIC (emphasis in original).

47. Phú Yên Province Report, period ending 30 September 1967, p. 2, CMH.

48. Villard, *Combat Operations*, 16; Combat Operations AAR, Operation Bolling, Department of the Army, 14 February 1968, p. 1, DTIC.

49. ORLL, quarterly period ending 31 October 1967, Department of the Army, Headquarters, I Field Force, Vietnam, 15 November 1967, p. 11, DTIC.

50. Phú Yên province report, period ending 30 September 1967, p. 2, CMH.

51. Ibid.

52. Ibid., 1.

53. Ibid.

54. Ibid.

55. Ibid.

56. Ibid., 2.

57. Ibid., 2–3.

58. Ibid.

59. Ibid.

60. ORLL, period 1 August to 31 October 1968, Department of the Army, Headquarters, 173rd Airborne Brigade, 15 November 1968, p. 39, DTIC.

61. Ibid., 40.

62. II Corps, Phú Yên Province Report, period ending 31 October 1967, Special Joint Narrative Report on Revolutionary Development, October 1967, p. 1, CMH.

63. Ibid., 2.

64. Ibid.

65. Ibid.

66. Quarterly historical report, 1 January to 31 December 1967, Company D, 16th Armor, 173rd Airborne Brigade, p. 31, RG 472, A1 1647, box 2, NARA II, accessed 2 August 2020, https://www.d16armor173rd.org/uploads/2/6/4/0/26400706/d16th _historical_report_1967_pt.2.pdf.

67. Ibid.

68. Ibid.

69. Ibid.

70. Ibid., 32.

71. Ibid.

72. Hunt, *Pacification*, 99–100.

73. II Corps MACCORDS, provincial reports, Phú Yên, period ending 30 November 1967, p. 1, CMH.

74. Ibid.

75. Villard, *Combat Operations*, 17.

76. ORLL, period 1 February to 30 April 1968, Department of the Army, Headquarters, 173rd Airborne Brigade, 15 May 1968, p. 59, DTIC.

77. Combat Operations AAR, Operation Bolling, Department of the Army, 14 February 1968, p. 5, DTIC.

78. Combat Operations AAR, Department of the Army, Headquarters, I Field Force, Vietnam, 1968 Tet Offensive II Corps Tactical Zone, "Battle for Tuy Hoa," 9 April 1968, p. 2, RG 472, UD 42196, box 268, folder: Operations: Tet Offensive—II Corps Tactical Zone (part 2 of 3), NARA II.

79. Combat Operations AAR, Operation Bolling, Department of the Army, 14 February 1968, p. 5, DTIC.

80. Quarterly historical report, 1 January to 31 December 1967, Company D, 16th Armor, 173rd Airborne Brigade, p. 33, NARA II.

81. II Corps MACCORDS, provincial reports, Phú Yên, period ending 28 December 1968, p. 1, CMH.

82. Quarterly historical report, 1 January to 31 December 1967, Company D, 16th Armor, 173rd Airborne Brigade, p. 34, NARA II.

83. Ibid. A Chiêu Hồi member was an individual who had once served the Communist cause but had accepted Saigon's offer of amnesty.

84. Villard, *Combat Operations*, 206.

85. MACV, "Targeting Branch Revised VC/NVA Base and Operations Areas," part 2, 1 March 1967, p. A-14, box 0023, folder 0924, TTUVA.

86. Villard, *Combat Operations*, 206; Combat Operations AAR, Operation Bolling, Department of the Army, 14 February 1968, p. 22, DTIC.

87. Lt. Col. William A. Donald to MACCORDS, Reports and Evaluation Division, Evaluation Report Working Draft, 3rd Battalion, ARVN 47th Regiment, 22nd Division in Support of RD, 28–31 December 1967, p. 1, CMH.

88. Ibid.

89. Ibid.

90. Ibid.

91. Ibid.

92. Ted G. Arthurs, *Land with No Sun: A Year in Vietnam with the 173rd Airborne* (Mechanicsburg, PA: Stackpole Books, 2006), 28.

93. Donald to MACCORDS, 28–31 December 1967, p. 3, CMH. Although the report identifies the PAVN 95th Regiment as the 95B, it is certainly the former and not the latter.

94. Ibid.

95. Ibid., 4.

96. Ibid.

97. Ibid.

98. Ibid.

99. "MORD Review of RD Plans in Phu Yen and Phu Bon Provinces," n.d., p. 1, CMH. Curiously, the GVN adopted the term *Ap Binh Dinh* (pacification hamlet), perhaps because upon conquering the province from the Champa, the Vietnamese named their new territory "Pacified Settlement," or Bình Định. Pacification was synonymous with that province. Incidentally, as noted by Edward G. Lansdale, the first large-scale pacification efforts in the Republic of Vietnam transpired in Bình Định Province. Lansdale also claimed that PLAF units even shouted "Bình Định" when challenging the GVN's RD cadre near Hue in 1967—a direct reference to pacification in Bình Định Province. See Ed Lansdale to Ambassador Porter and Mr. Hart, War Cry, 21 April 1967, box 57, Lansdale Papers, HIA. The GVN likely derived the term *Nuôi Dưỡng* from *Chính phủ nuôi dưỡng dân* ("the government nurtures the people").

100. Villard, *Combat Operations*, 206.

Chapter 5

1. "Hanoi Papers Underline Great Significance of South Viet Nam General Offensive," Hanoi VNA (Vietnam News Agency), 23 March 1968, p. 2, box 11, folder 09, Pike Collection, unit 02, TTUVA, accessed 21 July 2020, www.vietnam.ttu.edu/virtualarchive/items.php?item=2131109018.

2. Nguyen, *Hanoi's War*, 89, 98–99.

3. Nguyễn Văn Minh, ed., *History of the Resistance War Against the Americans to Save the Nation, 1954–1975*, vol. 5: *The 1968 General Offensive and Uprising* [*Lịch Sử Kháng Chiến Chống Mỹ Cứu Nước, 1954–1975*, Tạp V: *Tổng Tiến Công Và Nổi Dậy 1968*], trans. Merle Pribbenow (Hanoi: National Political Publishing House, 2001), 63.

4. Press briefing, 1968 Tet Offensive in II CTZ, 17 April 1968, p. 3, box 11, folder 10, Pike Collection, unit 02, TTUVA, accessed 21 July 2020, www.vietnam.ttu.edu/virtualarchive/items.php?item=2131110019.

5. Ibid.

6. Combat Operations AAR, Department of the Army, Headquarters, I Field Force, Vietnam, 1968 Tet Offensive II Corps Tactical Zone, "Battle for Tuy Hoa," 9 April 1968, p. 2, RG 472, UD 42196, box 268, folder: Operations: Tet Offensive—II Corps Tactical Zone (part 2 of 3), NARA II.

7. Combat Operations AAR, Department of the Army, Headquarters I Field Force Vietnam, 1968 Tet Offensive II Corps Tactical Zone, "Historical Document: 1968 Tet Offensive Actions in the II Corps Tactical Zone," 9 April 1968, p. 2, RG 472, UD 42196, box 268, folder: Operations: Tet Offensive—II Corps Tactical Zone (part 2 of 3), NARA II.

8. Ibid.

9. Combat operations AAR, Department of the Army, Headquarters I Field Force Vietnam, 1968 Tet Offensive II Corps Tactical Zone, "Battle for Tuy Hoa," 9 April 1968, p. 2, NARA II.

10. AT28, province report, period ending 31 January 1968, incl. 3-2, RG 472, A1 690, box 274, September 1967 to June 1968, NARA II.

11. Villard, *Combat Operations*, 205.

12. AT28, province report, period ending 31 January 1968, incl. 3-2, NARA II.

13. Ibid.

14. AT28, province report, period ending 31 January 1968, incl. 3–2, NARA II. Long Tuong might be Lông Trường.

15. "Employment of Revolutionary Development Cadre," 1 November 1966, pp. 1–2, box 03, folder 01, John Donnell Collection, TTUVA, accessed 21 July 2020, https://www.vietnam.ttu.edu/virtualarchive/items.php?item=0720301009 (emphasis in original).

16. AT28, province report, period ending 31 January 1968, incl. 2, NARA II.

17. Ibid.

18. AT28, province report, period ending 31 January 1968, incl. 1, NARA II.

19. Ibid.

20. AT28, province report, period ending 31 January 1968, incl. 4, NARA II.

21. Ibid.

22. Bernard Fall, lecture, Far East Training Center, Hawaii, December 1966, p. 1, box 12, folder: Subject File: Insurgency and Counterinsurgency, Lansdale Papers, HIA.

23. AT28, province report, period ending 31 January 1968, incl. 4, NARA II.

24. AT28, province report, period ending 31 January 1968, Incl. 5, NARA II.

25. Frank C. Foster, "Summary of the Taped Combat After Action Interview with D Company 16th Armor, 173rd Airborne Brigade on 4 March 1968," 15 May 1968, 24th Military History Detachment, p. 1, CMH; Frank C. Foster, "Additional Information for CAAI with D Co. 16th Armor (4 March 1968)," 24th Military History Detachment, CMH.

26. Villard, *Combat Operations*, 281–82, 287.

27. James H. Willbanks, *The Tet Offensive: A Concise History* (New York: Columbia University Press, 2006), 29–30; Moïse, *The Myths of Tet*, 134–35.

28. Villard, *Combat Operations*, 287.

29. "Status of Pacification—Phu Yen (10) Province (Tet Offensive)," 25 March 1968, p. 1, CMH.

30. ORLL, 1 February to 30 April 1968, Department of the Army, Headquarters, 173rd Airborne Brigade, 15 May 1968, p. 59, DTIC (emphasis in original).

31. Villard, *Combat Operations*, 288.

32. ORLL, 1 February to 30 April 1968, Department of the Army, 15 May 1968, p. 60, DTIC (emphasis in original).

33. Ibid.

34. Combat Operations AAR, Department of the Army, Headquarters, I Field Force, Vietnam, 1968 Tet Offensive II Corps Tactical Zone, "Battle for Tuy Hoa," 9 April 1968, p. 3, NARA II; Villard, *Combat Operations*, 288.

35. ORLL, 1 February to 30 April 1968, Department of the Army, 15 May 1968, p. 60, DTIC.

36. Villard, *Combat Operations*, 288.

37. Ibid.; ORLL, 1 February to 30 April 1968, Department of the Army, 15 May 1968, p. 60, DTIC.

38. Ibid., 61.

39. Ibid.

40. Arthurs, *Land with No Sun*, 34–35.

41. Ibid., 36.

42. ORLL, 1 February to 30 April 1968, Department of the Army, 15 May 1968, p. 61, DTIC.

43. Ibid.

44. Ibid., 62–63.

45. Ibid., 63.

46. Ibid., 61.

47. Ibid., 62; Arthurs, *Land with No Sun*, 37.

48. ORLL, 1 February to 30 April 1968, Department of the Army, 15 May 1968, p. 63, DTIC. Neither Bình Tín nor Binh Tin—as rendered by CORDS—appear on any official maps from the war. Therefore, Bình Tín is, at worst, an approximation.

49. Ibid.

50. Ibid., 64.

51. Ibid., 69.

52. Antoine Edward Roy, interview by Richard B. Verrone, 8 January 2003, p. 188, Antoine Edward Roy Collection, TTUVA, accessed 21 July 2020, www.vietnam .ttu.edu/virtualarchive/items.php?item=OH0255.

53. Ibid.; Villard, *Combat Operations*, 290.

54. ORLL, 1 February to 30 April 1968, Department of the Army, 15 May 1968, p. 71, DTIC.

55. Ibid.; press briefing, 1968 Tet Offensive in II CTZ, 17 April 1968, p. 4, Pike Collection, TTUVA.

56. ORLL, 1 February to 30 April 1968, Department of the Army, 15 May 1968, p. 61; Villard, *Combat Operations*, 290.

57. ORLL, 1 February to 30 April 1968, Department of the Army, 15 May 1968, p. 59, DTIC.

58. Ibid., 14.

59. Ibid.

60. Combat Operations AAR, Department of the Army, Headquarters, I Field Force, Vietnam, 1968 Tet Offensive II Corps Tactical Zone, "Battle for Tuy Hoa," 9 April 1968, p. 3, NARA II.

61. Ibid., 3–4.

62. Ibid.

63. "Status of Pacification—Phu Yen (10) Province (Tet Offensive)," 25 March 1968, p. 1, CMH.

64. Quarterly historical report, January to April 1968, Company D, 16th Armor, 173rd Airborne Brigade, p. 7, RG 472, A1 1647, box 2, NARA II (emphasis in original).

65. Ibid.

66. Ibid., 8.

67. ORLL, 1 November 1967 to 31 January 1968, Department of the Army, Headquarters, 173rd Airborne Brigade, 15 February 1968, p. 4, DTIC.

68. Ibid.

69. Ibid.

70. "Status of Pacification—Phu Yen (10) Province (Tet Offensive)," 25 March 1968, p. 1, CMH.

71. Frank C. Foster, "Summary of the Taped Combat After Action Interview with D Company 16th Armor, 173rd Airborne Brigade on 4 March 1968," 15 May 1968, p. 1, CMH; Status of Pacification—Phu Yen (10) Province (Tet Offensive), 25 March 1968, p. 1, CMH.

72. "Combat After Action Interview with Members of Company D (Airborne), 16th Armor, 173rd Airborne Brigade," interviewed by Capt. Frank C. Foster, 4 March 1968, Phu Hiep Army Base, Phu Yen Province, Republic of Vietnam, transcribed by David Curtis, January 2016, p. 10, personal collection of David Curtis. Curtis's transcript is a more complete version of the CAAI found at CMH (see footnote 26).

73. Ibid., 4, 10.

74. Ibid., 2; D/16th Armor earned a Bronze Star unit citation for their heroic actions at Ninh Tinh.

75. "Status of Pacification—Phu Yen (10) Province (Tet Offensive)," 25 March 1968, p. 3, CMH.

76. Ibid., 2.

77. Ibid.

78. AT28, province report, period ending 31 March 1968, p. 1, RG 472, A1 690, box 274, folder 211-03, OPN Program, Progress Reports, September 1967 to June 1968, NARA II.

79. Ibid., 1.

80. Combat Operations AAR, Department of the Army, Headquarters, I Field Force, Vietnam, 1968 Tet Offensive II Corps Tactical Zone, "Historical Document 1968 Tet Offensive Actions in the II Corps Tactical Zone," 9 April 1968, p. 3, NARA II.

81. Combat Operations AAR, Department of the Army, Headquarters, I Field Force, Vietnam, 1968 Tet Offensive II Corps Tactical Zone, "Battle for Tuy Hoa," 9 April 1968, p. 3, NARA II.

82. Ibid.

83. AT28, province report, period ending 31 March 1968, p. 2, NARA II.

84. CORDS field overview, March 1968, 13 April 1968, p. 5, CMH.

85. Ibid.

86. Ibid.

87. Ibid.

88. Gen. Westmoreland to Adm. Sharp, "Post-Tet Pacification Assessment," 29 March 1968, p. 8, CMH (report drafted by Robert Komer).

89. II Corps MACCORDS, provincial reports, "District Senior Advisor's Report—Tuy Hoa District, Phu Yen Province," period ending 30 April 1968, CMH.

90. Ibid.

91. Hamlet Chief Nguyễn Thi, "Danh Sach Phu Ban Dong Bao Ap My Thanh Bi Tai Nan Vi Chien Cuoc Xay Ra [List of Supplement (to) Citizens (of) Mỹ Thành Hamlet Affected Due to the War Situation Occurring]," 1968, pp. 1–6, in Ellis Wisner's possession.

92. ORLL, 1 November 1967 to 31 January 1968, Department of the Army, 15 February 1968, p. 15, DTIC.

93. II Corps MACCORDS, provincial reports, Phú Yên, period ending 30 April 1968, p. 1, CMH.

94. Quarterly historical report, January to April 1968, Company D, 16th Armor, 173rd Airborne Brigade, p. 11, NARA II.

95. Quarterly historical report, April–June 1968, Company D, 16th Armor, 173rd Airborne Brigade, p. 1, NARA II.

96. Ibid.

97. R. W. Komer to Daniel L. Leaty, memo, "Evaluation of Pacification in Phu Yen," 7 May 1968, CMH.

98. Ibid.

99. II Corps MACCORDS, provincial reports, Phú Yên, period ending 31 May 1968, p. 1, CMH.

100. Ibid.

101. II Corps MACCORDS, provincial reports, Phú Yên, period ending 30 June 1968, p. 1, CMH.

102. Ibid.

103. Ibid., 6.

104. Ibid.

105. Ibid.

106. Ibid., 1.

107. ORLL, 1 May to 31 July 1968, Department of the Army, Headquarters, 173rd Airborne Brigade, 15 August 1968, p. 34, DTIC.

108. Ibid.

109. Ibid.

110. Combat Operations AAR, Operation Bolling-Dan Hoa, 19 September 1967–31 January 1969, Department of the Army, Headquarters, 173rd Airborne Brigade, 2 March 1969, p. 8, accessed 22 July 2020, www.d16armor173rd.org/uploads/2/6 /4/0/26400706/5aar_bolling-dan_hoa19_sep_67-31jan_69.pdf.

111. Ibid., 35.

112. Ibid. (emphasis in original).

113. Phạm Thành Công, "Danh Noi Bat Kha Xam Pham" ["Attacking an 'Impenetrable' Position"], *Quan Doi Nhan Dan* (People's Army newspaper), 3 May 2008, translated by Merle Pribbenow, accessed 22 July 2020, http://archive.is/zwiGQ#selection-869 .0–869.15; William D. Donald, "Unit History, 545th Transportation Company, 54th Transportation Battalion, USA Support Command, Qui Nhon, 1 January 1968–31 December 1968," 11 March 1969, pp. 3–4, United States Army Transportation Corps, accessed 22 July 2020, https://transportation.army.mil/Historian /Vietnam%20Unit%20History%20Reports/545th%20Trans%20Co%201968.pdf.

114. Abner M. Aust, Jr., "End of Tour Report," 31st Tactical Fighter Wing, Tuy Hoa Air Base, Vietnam, 3 May 1968–8 February 1969, accessed 22 July 2020, www.vspa .com/tuy-larsen-dick-end-of-tour-report-3-may-1968-8-feb-1969.htm.

115. CORDS field overview, July 1968, 14 August 1968, Headquarters I Field Force, p. 11, CMH.

116. Ibid.

117. Ibid.

118. Robert Barron, interview by Stephen Maxner, 21 April 2001, p. 35, Robert Barron Collection, TTUVA, accessed 22 July 2020, www.vietnam.ttu.edu/virtualarchive /items.php?item=OH0163. Đại Úy was ARVN's equivalent of captain in the U.S. Army.

119. Ellis Wisner, interview by author, e-mail conversation, 11 November 2019.

120. Ibid.

121. For a detailed analysis of this contemporary and academic discussion, see Thomas C. Thayer, *War Without Fronts: The American Experience in Vietnam* (Annapolis, Md.: Naval Institute Press, 2016), 30; and Willbanks, *The Tet Offensive*, 79–81.

122. II Corps MACCORDS, provincial reports, Phú Yên, period ending 31 August 1968, p. 1, CMH.

123. II Corps MACCORDS, provincial reports, Phú Yên, period ending 30 September 1968, p. 1, CMH.

124. Ibid., 1–2.

125. Ibid., 2.

126. Ibid.

127. Combat Operations AAR, Operation Bolling-Dan Hoa, 19 September 1967–31 January 1969, Department of the Army, 2 March 1969, p. 8.

128. II Corps MACCORDS, provincial reports, Phú Yên, period ending 31 October 1968, p. 1, CMH.

129. Ibid., 2.

130. Hunt, *Pacification*, 156–57.

131. Gregory A. Daddis, *No Sure Victory: Measuring U.S. Army Effectiveness and Progress in the Vietnam War* (New York: Oxford University Press, 2011), 150.

132. II Corps MACCORDS, provincial reports, Phú Yên, period ending 30 November 1968, p. 1, CMH; AT28, province report, period ending 30 December 1968, p. 1, RG 472, A1 690, box 1, folder: 101–07 Phu Yen, NARA II.

133. II Corps MACCORDS, provincial reports, Phú Yên, period ending 30 November 1968, p. 1, CMH.

134. Donald, "Unit History," 4.

135. Phạm Thành Công, "Danh Noi Bat Kha Xam Pham" ["Attacking an 'Impenetrable' Position"].

136. George C. Jacobson to Edward G. Lansdale, 11 February 1969, p. 1, box 23, folder: Vietnamese Conflict, Pacification and land reform / General, 1964–1969, Lansdale Papers, HIA.

137. Ibid.

138. II Corps MACCORDS, provincial reports, Phú Yên, period ending 30 November 1968, p. 1, CMH.

139. Ibid.

140. Ibid.

141. Quarterly historical report, October–December 1968, Company D, 16th Armor, 173rd Airborne Brigade, p. 3, RG 472, A1 1647, box 2, NARA II.

142. Ibid.
143. Ibid.
144. Ibid.
145. Ibid.

Chapter 6

1. "PLAF Political Indoctrination Course: Summer 1969," 1 May 1969, p. 7, box 17, folder 09, Pike Collection, Unit 05, TTUVA, accessed 2 August 2020, www.vietnam.ttu.edu/virtualarchive/items.php?item=2311709012.

2. James H. Willbanks, *Abandoning Vietnam: How America Left and South Vietnam Lost Its War* (Lawrence: University Press of Kansas, 2004), 15–20; Andrew L. Johns, *Vietnam's Second Front: Domestic Politics, the Republican Party, and the War* (Lexington: University Press of Kentucky, 2010), 244, 276–77.

3. Frank Leith Jones, *Blowtorch: Robert Komer, Vietnam, and American Cold War Strategy* (Annapolis: Naval Institute Press, 2013), 200–201.

4. Thayer, *War Without Fronts*, 139–40; Gawthorpe, *To Build as Well as Destroy*, 112–13.

5. Lt. Gen. Charles A. Corcoran, interview by Lt. Col. Joseph A. Langer Jr., 1975, Senior Officer Oral History Program, 1988, U.S. Army Military History Institute, p. 136, http://usahec.contentdm.oclc.org/cdm/ref/collection/p16635coll26/id/177/ (no longer accessible).

6. Sp4. Paul Sheehan, "D/15 Outfights NVA Company," in *Fire Base 173* (173rd Airborne Brigade), vol. 2, no. 5 (1 March 1969):1. Excerpt provided by Dave Curtin.

7. AT28, province report, period ending 31 January 1969, p. 2, CMH.

8. Ibid.

9. Ibid., 7.

10. Ibid.

11. AT28, province report, period ending 31 January 1969, p. 1, CMH.

12. Ibid.

13. AT28, province report, period ending 28 February 1969, p. 1, CMH.

14. Ibid.

15. Ibid., 6–7.

16. Ibid., 1.

17. Ibid.

18. Ibid., 2.

19. Robert A. Doughty, *Leavenworth Papers: The Evolution of US Army Tactical Doctrine, 1946–76* (Fort Leavenworth, KS: Combat Studies Institute, U.S. Army Command and General Staff College, 1979), 31.

20. Ibid., 32.

21. ORLL, 1 February 1969 to 30 April 1969, Department of the Army, Headquarters, 173rd Airborne Brigade, 15 May 1969, p. 22, accessed 2 August 2020, https://www.d16armor173rd.org/uploads/2/6/4/0/26400706/110rll_feb_69_-_apr_69.pdf (emphasis in original).

22. Ibid.

23. Ibid.

24. AT28, province report, period ending 28 February 1969, p. 3, CMH.

25. ORLL,1 February 1969 to 30 April 1969, Department of the Army, 15 May 1969, p. 22.

26. Ibid.

27. Ibid., 6.

28. Lt. Gen. Charles A. Corcoran, senior officer debriefing report, 23 February 1970, Department of the Army, Office of the Adjutant General, Washington, D.C., p. 3, DTIC.

29. ORLL, quarterly period ending 30 April 1969, Department of the Army, 15 May 1969, p. 10, DTIC (emphasis in original).

30. Ibid.

31. ORLL, 1 February 1969 to 30 April 1969, Department of the Army, 15 May 1969, p. 22.

32. Ibid.

33. Ibid.

34. Ibid., 23.

35. Ibid.

36. Ibid., 32.

37. Ibid., 24.

38. Ibid., 24–25.

39. Ibid., 24.

40. Ibid.

41. Ibid., 25.

42. AT28, province report, period ending 28 February 1969, p. 3, CMH.

43. Ibid., 1.

44. Ibid.

45. ADEPCORDS, HES Data Summary, "II CTZ HES DATA SUMMARY—BASED ON SECURITY/DEVELOPMENT (AS OF 31 MAR 69)," 26 April 1969, RG 472, A1 690, box 284, folder: HES Data, NARA II.

46. AT28, province report, period ending 31 March 1969, incl. 1, CMH.

47. Ibid., incl. 2.

48. Ibid.

49. Ibid., incl. 3.

50. Ibid.

51. Ibid., incl. 5.

52. "Pacification," memo, Department of the Army, Headquarters, 173rd Airborne Brigade, 12 April 1969, p. 1, accessed 2 August 2020, www.d16armor173rd.org /uploads/2/6/4/0/26400706/13_pacification_12_april_1969.pdf.

53. ORLL, 1 February 1969 to 30 April 1969, Department of the Army, 15 May 1969, p. 4. The Tuy Hòa Provisional Tank Company had no tanks.

54. Ibid., 25.

55. Ibid., 26.

56. Headquarters, I Field Force, Vietnam, "HES Evaluation of Phu Yen Province Based on Security as of 30 April 1969," 30 April 1969, p. 1, RG 472, A1 690, box 284, folder: HES Data, NARA II.

57. Ibid., 2.

58. Ibid., 1.

59. Headquarters, I Field Force, Vietnam, "HES Evaluation of Phu Yen Province Based on Security as of 31 May 1969," 31 May 1969, RG 472, A1 690, box 284, folder: HES Data, NARA II.

60. ORLL, quarterly period ending 30 April 1969, Department of the Army, 15 May 1969, p. 5, DTIC.

61. Ibid.

62. AT28, province report, period ending on 31 May 1969, p. 2, CMH.

63. Ibid.

64. AT28, province report, period ending 30 June 1969, p. 2, RG 472, A1 690, box 2, NARA II. PAVN units changed designations often, some so frequently that even Hanoi had trouble keeping track of which was which. While often called the PAVN 95th Regiment, that unit also existed as the PAVN 10th Regiment.

65. Ibid.

66. "Những trận đánh nổi tiếng của Trung đoàn 10 trên đất Phú Yên [Famous Battles Fought by the 10th Regiment in Phu Yen]," Báo Phú Yên, 5 July 2013, accessed 8 October 2020, http://www.baophuyen.com.vn/94/100265/nhung-tran -danh-noi-tieng-cua-trung-doan-10-tren-dat-phu-yen.html. Translated by Merle Pribbenow.

67. AT28, province report, period ending 30 June 1969, p. 2, CMH.

68. Ibid.

69. AT28, report, "Response to Current Enemy Activity," RG 472, A1 690, box 283, folder: Enemy Activity Reports/AT #28, NARA II.

70. AT28, province report, period ending on 31 May 1969, p. 1, CMH.

71. Ibid.

72. AT28, province report, period ending 31 May 1969, p. 1, CMH.

73. AT28, "HES Evaluation of Phu Yen Province Based on Security as of 31 May 69," n.d., RG 472, A1 690, box 284, folder: HES Data, NARA II.

74. "PLAF Political Indoctrination Course: Summer 1969," 1 May 1969, p. 8, box 17, folder 09, Pike Collection, unit 05, TTUVA, accessed 2 August 2020, www.vietnam.ttu.edu/virtualarchive/items.php?item=2311709012.

75. COSVN's Resolution 9 should not be confused with the Central Committee of the Communist Party of North Vietnam's Resolution 9 of January 1964.

76. AT28, province report, period ending 30 June 1969, p. 2, CMH.

77. Ibid.

78. Translation of COSVN Resolution 9, 31 July 1969, p. 13, box 01, folder 05, Ronald Bruce St. John Collection, TTUVA, accessed 2 August 2020, www.vietnam.ttu.edu/virtualarchive/items.php?item=16710105003.

79. Ibid., 27.

80. Ibid., 28.

81. For more on Bình Định during this period, see Boylan, *Losing Binh Dinh*.

82. ORLL, period of 1 May 1969 to 31 July 1969, Department of the Army, Headquarters, 173rd Airborne Brigade, 15 August 1969, p. 2, accessed 2 August 2020, www.d16armor173rd.org/uploads/2/6/4/0/26400706/12_orll_1may_69-31july_69.pdf.

83. Ibid., 9.

84. AT28, province report, period ending 31 August 1969, p. 1, CMH.

85. AT28, note affixed to "HES Evaluation of Phú Yên Province Based on Security as of 31 Aug 69," 25 September 1969, RG 472, A1 690, box 284, folder: HES Data, NARA II.

86. AT28, margin comment on "HES Evaluation of Phú Yên Province Based on Security as of 31 Aug 69," 25 September 1969, p. 2, RG 472, A1 690, box 284, folder: HES Data, NARA II.

87. AT28, memo, "attached," 25 September 1969, RG 472, A1 690, box 284, folder: HES Data, NARA II.

88. Ibid.

89. Maj. Stanley W. Lamonte, Pacification Studies Group, "Village Security," 15 September 1969, pp. 8–9, CORDS Historical Working Group Files, RG 472, A1 690, box 9, folder: Village Security, NARA II.

90. Ibid., 5.

91. Ibid.

92. William E. Colby, CORDS, memo, 3 October 1969, p. 1, CORDS Historical Working Group Files, RG 472, A1 690, box 9, folder: Village Security, NARA II.

93. Ibid.; Maj. Gen. Elias C. Townsend, MACV HQ, "Village Security," 23 October 1969, p. 1, CORDS Historical Working Group Files, RG 472, A1 690, box 9, folder: Village Security, NARA II.

94. AT28, province report, period ending on 30 September 1969, p. 1, 9, CMH.

95. Ibid., 2.

96. AT28, district report, Tuy Hoa, 26 September 1969, p. 1, RG 472, A1 690, box 275, folder: District Senior Advisor's Monthly Reports, 05/1969–12/1970, NARA II.

97. Ibid.

98. Ibid., 1–2.

99. AT28, district semimonthly report, Tuy Hòa, 10–25 October 1969, p. 1, RG 472, A1 690, box 275, folder: District Senior Advisor's Monthly Reports, 05/1969–12/1970, NARA II.

100. Ibid., 1–2. "Quan Triều" could be the hamlet "Quang Triều" that appears in chapter 8.

101. AT28, district semimonthly report, Tuy Hòa, 10–25 October 1969, p. 2, RG 472, A1 690, box 275, folder: District Senior Advisor's Monthly Reports, 05/1969–12/1970, NARA II.

102. MACV, report, Summary of VCI Activities 1–31 May 1971, 30 June 1971, p. 32, box 29, folder 01, Dale W. Andrade Collection, TTUVA, accessed 2 August 2020, www.vietnam.ttu.edu/virtualarchive/items.php?item=2499290101I.

103. AT28, district semimonthly report, Tuy Hòa, 10–25 October 1969, p. 1, RG 472, A1 690, box 275, folder: District Senior Advisor's Monthly Reports, 05/1969–12/1970, NARA II.

104. Remarks Form, Tuy Hòa District, 31 October 1969, RG 472, A1 690, box 284, folder: HES Data, NARA II.

105. Memorandum, "HES Evaluation of Phu Yen Province Based on Security as of 31 Oct 1969," 31 October 1969, RG 472, A1 690, box 284, folder: HES Data, NARA II.

106. AT28, district semimonthly report, Tuy Hòa, October 25–November 10, 1969, 11 November 1969, p. 1, RG 472, A1 690, box 275, folder: District Senior Advisor's Monthly Reports, 05/1969–12/1970, NARA II.

107. Ibid., 1–2.

108. AT28, province report, period ending 30 November 1969, p. 1, CMH.

109. Fact Sheet, "Summary of Pacification Status, November 1969," 11 December 1969, p. 4, RG 472, A1 690, box 284, folder: HES Data, NARA II.

110. Chart, "II Corps HES Data Summary Based On Security Only As Of 30 November 1969," 30 November 1969, p. 2, RG 472, A1 690, box 284, folder: HES Data, NARA II.

111. Ibid.

112. AT28, province report, period ending 30 November 1969, p. 1, CMH.

113. AT28, memo, "Phu Yen Son Hoa," 30 November 1969, RG 472, A1 690, box 284, folder: HES Data, NARA II. This document contains two pieces of commentary:

the top portion is from Tarbet and is dated 29 November 1969; the bottom half
is from Engle and is dated 30 November 1969. Both men addressed the status of
pacification in Sơn Hòa District.

114. Ibid.

115. AT28, province report, period ending 31 December 1969, p. 1, CMH.

116. Ibid.

117. Ibid.

118. Ibid.

119. Ibid.

Chapter 7

1. Robert G. Kaiser, "New VC Tactics Turn Optimism to Bitterness in Phuyen,"
Washington Post, 18 March 1970, A14.

2. Ibid.

3. Robert W. Komer, *Impact of Pacification on Insurgency in South Vietnam* (Santa
Monica, Calif: RAND Corporation, 1970), 5, accessed 2 August 2020, www.rand
.org/content/dam/rand/pubs/papers/2008/P4443.pdf.

4. Ibid., 14 (emphasis in original).

5. Ibid.

6. Report, Intelligence: DIP—Bi-Weekly Summary of VCI Activities—Record of
MACV Part 1, 4–17 January 1970, p. 8, box 0019, folder 0675, TTUVA, accessed
2 August 2020, www.vietnam.ttu.edu/virtualarchive/items.php?item=F015800190675.

7. Ibid., 8–9.

8. Ibid., 8.

9. Ibid.

10. AT28, progress report, period ending 31 January 1970, p. 1, CMH.

11. Ibid.

12. Ibid., 2.

13. Ibid.

14. Ibid., 1.

15. AT28, biweekly district report, Tuy Hòa, 10 January 1970, p. 1, RG 472, A1 690,
box 275, folder: District Senior Advisor's Monthly Reports, 05/1969–12/1970,
NARA II.

16. AT28, province feeder report, Đồng Xuân District, period ending 10 January 1970,
p. 1, RG 472, A1 690, box 275, folder: District Senior Advisor's Monthly Reports,
05/1969–12/1970, NARA II.

17. AT28, district semimonthly report, Tuy Hòa, 25 January–10 February 1970, p. 1,
RG 472, A1 690, box 275, folder: District Senior Advisor's Monthly Reports,
05/1969–12/1970, NARA II.

18. AT28, district semimonthly report, Tuy Hòa, 10–25 February 1970, p. 1, RG 472, A1 690, box 275, folder: District Senior Advisor's Monthly Reports, 05/1969–12/1970, NARA II.

19. AT28, district semimonthly feeder report, Sơn Hòa, period ending 11 February 1970, p. 1, RG 472, A1 690, box 275, folder: District Senior Advisor's Monthly Reports, 05/1969–12/1970, NARA II.

20. Ibid.

21. Ibid.

22. Ibid.

23. Ibid.

24. Ibid.

25. Ibid.

26. "They Went to the Mountains," *Washington Post*, 18 March 1970, A14. It is possible that the *Washington Post* used inaccurate or misspelled names for the two abductees.

27. Ibid.

28. Ibid.

29. Ibid.; AT28, district semimonthly feeder report, Sông Cầu, period ending 11 February 1970, p. 1, NARA II.

30. Ibid.

31. Ibid.

32. Ibid., 2.

33. Ibid., 1.

34. AT28, district report, Sông Cầu, period ending 12 February 1970, p. 1, RG 472, A1 690, box 275, folder: District Senior Advisor's Monthly Reports, 05/1969–12/1970, NARA II.

35. AT28, district report, Sông Cầu, period ending 25 February 1970, p. 1, RG 472, A1 690, box 275, folder: District Senior Advisor's Monthly Reports, 05/1969–12/1970, NARA II.

36. AT28, province feeder report, Đồng Xuân District, period ending 14 February 1970, p. 1, RG 472, A1 690, box 275, folder: District Senior Advisor's Monthly Reports, 05/1969–12/1970, NARA II.

37. Ibid.

38. AT28, district report, Tuy An, period of 26 February to 11 March 1970, pp. 1–2, RG 472, A1 690, box 275, folder: District Senior Advisor's Monthly Reports, 05/1969–12/1970, NARA II.

39. AT28, memo, James B. Engle to Senior Advisor—II CTZ, "Operational Techniques—Unnecessary Use of Helicopters by Troops on Operations," 31 March 1970, p. 2, RG 472, A1 690, box 296, folder: 1601–11A/CORRES. W/SA/OUTGOING JAN–APR '70, NARA II.

40. AT28, memo, James B. Engle to William Yancey, "Ordnance Jettison Zone," 28 February 1970, RG 472, A1 690, box 296, folder: 1601–11A/CORRES. (GENERAL) '70, NARA II.

41. Ibid.

42. AT28, semimonthly district report, Tuy Hòa, 12–25 March [1970], p. 1, RG 472, A1 690, box 275, folder: District Senior Advisor's Monthly Reports, 05/1969–12/1970, NARA II.

43. AT28, semimonthly district report, Tuy Hòa, 1–25 February 1970, p. 2, RG 472, A1 690, box 275, folder: District Senior Advisor's Monthly Reports, 05/1969–12/1970, NARA II.

44. Lt. Gen. Arthur S. Collins, I FFORCEV to Gen. Creighton Abrams, COMUMACV, Message #5416, 26 February 1970, p. 1, General Abrams Message Files, CMH.

45. Ibid., 1–2.

46. Ibid., 2.

47. AT28, semimonthly district report, Tuy Hòa, 25 February to 12 March 1970, p. 1, RG 472, A1 690, box 275, folder: District Senior Advisor's Monthly Reports, 05/1969–12/1970, NARA II.

48. Ibid.

49. AT28, semimonthly district report, Hiếu Xương, 12 March 1970, p. 1, RG 472, A1 690, box 275, folder: District Senior Advisor's Monthly Reports, 05/1969–12/1970, NARA II.

50. AT28, semimonthly district report, Hiếu Xương, 25 March 1970, p. 1, RG 472, A1 690, box 275, folder: District Senior Advisor's Monthly Reports, 05/1969–12/1970, NARA II.

51. Ibid.

52. Combat After Action Report, Task Force 22, 12–20 March 1970, p. 2, RG 472, A1 690, box 296, folder: 1601–11A/CORRES. W/SA/OUTGOING JAN–APR '70, NARA II.

53. Lt. Gen. Arthur S. Collins, I FFORCEV to Gen. Creighton Abrams, COMUMACV, Message #5524, 10 March 1970, pp. 1–2, General Abrams Message Files, CMH.

54. Combat after action report, Task Force 22, 12–20 March 1970, pp. 1–2, RG 472, A1 690, box 296, folder: 1601–11A/CORRES. W/SA/OUTGOING JAN–APR '70, NARA II.

55. Lt. Gen. Arthur S. Collins, I FFORCEV to Gen. Creighton Abrams, COMUMACV, Message #5524, 10 March 1970, pp. 1–2, General Abrams Message Files, CMH.

56. Ibid.; U.S. Embassy Saigon, report, Theodore G. Shackley to Gen. Creighton W. Abrams, "Situation in Phu Yen Province," 6 April 1970, p. 5, CORDS Historical

Working Group Files, 1967–1973, RG 472, A1 462, box 14, folder: Memos & Messages/Mr. Jacobson/Visits, NARA II.

57. AT28, newspaper article, George McArthur, "Reds Making Inroads In 'Secure' Viet Province," *Los Angeles Times*, 22 March 1970, p. 3, RG 472, A1 690, box 285, folder: Advisory Crisis in Tuy Hoa District '70, NARA II.

58. AT28, report, James B. Engle to Willard E. Chambers, 16 March 1970, p. 1, RG 472, A1 690, box 296, folder: 1601-11A/CORRES. W/SA/OUTGOING JAN–APR '70, NARA II.

59. Ibid., 2.

60. AT28, semimonthly district report, Tuy Hòa, 12–25 March 1970, p. 1, RG 472, A1 690, box 275, folder: District Senior Advisor's Monthly Reports, 05/1969–12/1970, NARA II; U.S. Embassy Saigon, report, Shackley to Abrams, "Situation in Phu Yen Province," 6 April 1970, p. 5, NARA II.

61. AT28, report, James B. Engle to Willard E. Chambers, 16 March 1970, p. 2, NARA II.

62. Ibid.

63. AT28, semimonthly district report, Tuy Hòa, 12–25 March 1970, p. 1, NARA II.

64. Ibid.

65. AT28, report, "Major William H. Pretto's After-Action Report of March 25 on Task Force 22 from March 12 to 20, 1970," p. 1, RG 472, A1 690, box 297, folder: ARVN 4th Regiment/Phú Yên, NARA II.

66. Ibid.

67. Ibid., 2 (emphasis in original).

68. Ibid.

69. Ibid., 1.

70. AT28, *Los Angeles Times* newspaper article, George McArthur, "Reds Making Inroads In 'Secure' Viet Province," *Los Angeles Times*, Sunday March 22, 1970, p. 1, NARA II. *The Pacific Stars and Stripes* reprinted McArthur's article as "Phu Yen—Province that 'Went to Sleep,'" 10 April 1970.

71. Ibid., 1.

72. Ibid.

73. Ibid.

74. Ibid., 3.

75. Ibid.

76. Ibid., 2.

77. Ibid.

78. AT28, report, Douglas McCollum to CORDS II CTZ, "Abductions in Tuy Hoa District," 23 March 1970, p. 1, RG 472, A1 690, box 285, folder: Advisory Crisis in Tuy Hoa District '70, NARA II.

79. Ibid.

80. See AT28, newspaper article, "Terrorist-Hit Village Wants ROKs to Return," *Pacific Stars and Stripes*, February 1970, James B. Engle to Senior Advisor—II CTZ, "Phu Yen Political Report No. 21: Comments on slanted ROK press stories and the public attitude in Phu Yen Province towards ROK forces," 25 April 1970, enclosure no. 1, RG 472, A1 690, box 296, folder: 1601–11A/CORRES. W/SA/OUTGOING JAN–APR '70, NARA II; Vietnam Bureau, "Villagers Demonstrate—And Get ROKs Back," *Pacific Stars and Stripes*, 26 March 1970, enclosure no. 2, RG 472, A1 690, box 296, folder: 1601–11A/CORRES. W/SA/OUTGOING JAN–APR '70, NARA II.

81. AT28, memo, James B. Engle to Senior Advisor—II CTZ, "Phu Yen Political Report No. 21," p. 2, NARA II.

82. Ibid.

83. Ibid., 2–3.

84. AT28, semimonthly district report, Tuy Hòa, 12–25 March 1970, p. 1, NARA II.

85. Task Force Talon, Headquarters, 3D Battalion (ABN), 503rd Infantry, 173rd Airborne Brigade, Combat Operations AAR, 27 April 1970, enclosure 2, "Report of Task Force Contact on 1 April 1970," 2 April 1970, p. 201, in Thomas Kaulukukui private collection (henceforth Kaulukukui collection).

86. AT28, semimonthly district report, Tuy Hòa, 12–25 March 1970, pp. 5–6, NARA II.; AT28, report, "Visit to Phu Yen of MG Quang, DCG II Corps—20 April 1970," 22 April 1970, pp. 1–2, folder 10, CMH; AT28, report, "Action of US 173d Airborne Brigade and RF 112 Company at Minh Duc on 1 April 1970," pp. 1–2, folder 10, CMH; Task Force Talon, Headquarters, 3D Battalion (ABN), 503rd Infantry, 173rd Airborne Brigade, Combat Operations AAR, 27 April 1970, enclosure 2, "Report of Task Force Contact on 1 April 1970," 2 April 1970, p. 201, Kaulukukui collection. Task Force Talon reports reside in NARA II's RG 472.

87. AT28, report, "Visit to Phu Yen of MG Quang, DCG II Corps," pp. 1–2, CMH; AT28, "Action of US 173d Airborne Brigade and RF 112 Company at Minh Duc on 1 April 1970," pp. 1–2, CMH; Task Force Talon, Combat Operations AAR, enclosure 2, p. 3, Kaulukukui collection.

88. Eugene Fluke, telephone interview with author, 25 September 2015 (hereafter cited as Fluke interview).

89. AT28, semimonthly district report, Tuy Hòa, 25 March to 12 April 1970, p. 1, RG 472, A1 690, box 275, folder: District Senior Advisor's Monthly Reports, 05/1969–12/1970, NARA II.

90. AT28, report, "Phu Yen Province Chief's Month Meeting (April [1970]) with Allied Commanders," 16 April 1970, p. 3, RG 472, A1 690, box 297, folder: PC's Monthly Commanders Meeting, NARA II.

91. Ibid.

92. Ibid., 3.

93. Ibid., 4.

94. Bruce W. Clark, interview by Charles Stuart Kennedy, Association for Diplomatic Studies and Training Foreign Affairs Oral History Project, 4 June 2002, accessed 3 August 2020, www.adst.org/OH%20TOCs/Clark,%20Bruce%20W.toc.pdf.

95. U.S. Embassy Saigon, Shackley to Abrams, "Situation in Phu Yen Province," p. 3, NARA II.

96. AT28, report, "COL Ba, Province Chief, Phu Yen, and the situation in Tuy Hoa District," p. 1, RG 472, A1 690, box 285, folder: Advisory Crisis in Tuy Hoa District '70, NARA II.

97. Ibid., 1.

98. Ibid., 2.

99. Ibid., 3.

100. Nguyễn Thái Lâm to Nguyễn Văn Ba, "Request to transfer DSA at Tuy-Hoa Subsector," 4 April 1970, RG 472, A1 690, box 285, folder: Advisory Crisis in Tuy Hoa District '70, NARA II.

101. AT28, report, "COL Ba, Province Chief, Phú Yên, and the situation in Tuy Hoa District," p. 1, NARA II.

102. Fluke interview.

103. DEPCORDS I Field Force, Vietnam, Memo, Willard E. Chambers to James B. Engle, "My talk with Colonel Ba this evening," 6 April 1970, RG 472, A1 690, box 296, folder: 1601–11A/CORRES. W/SA/OUTGOING JAN–APR '70, NARA II.

104. U.S. Embassy Saigon, Shackley to Abrams, "Situation in Phu Yen Province," p. 1, NARA II.

105. Ibid., 1.

106. Ibid., 2.

107. Ibid.

108. Ibid.

109. Ibid.

110. Ibid.

111. Ibid., 2–3.

112. Ibid., 3.

113. Ibid., 4.

114. Ibid., 5.

115. Ibid., 5–6.

116. Letter from Gen. Abrams to Mr. Shackley, COMUSMACV—re: Situation in Phu Yen Province—Record of MACV Part 1, 10 April 1970, box 0001, folder 0480, Vietnam Archive Collection, TTUVA, accessed 3 August 2020, www.vietnam.ttu .edu/virtualarchive/items.php?item=F015800010480.

117. Gen. Abrams COMUSMACV Saigon to Lt. Gen. Collins CCV IFFORCEV, Nha Trang, "Phu Yen Province Situation," 10 April 1970, p. 5942, box: Abrams Messages: 28 Dec 1969–27 Apr 1970: 4992–6260, folder: 5462–5779, CMH.

118. Ibid.

119. DEPCORDS I Field Force, Vietnam, Memo, Willard E. Chambers to William Colby, "Col. Ba, Province Chief, Phu Yen, and the situation in Tuy Hoa District," 11 April 1970, p. 1, RG 472, A1 690, box 285, folder: Advisory Crisis in Tuy Hoa District '70, NARA II.

120. Ibid., 1–2.

121. Ibid., 2.

122. MACCORDS, memo, "Meeting between Mr. Jacobson and Mr. McManaway and the Prime Minister," 12 April 1970, p. 1, CORDS Historical Working Group Files, 1967–1973, RG 472, A1 462, box 14, folder: Memos and Messages/Mr. Jacobson/ Visits, NARA II.

123. Ibid.

124. Ibid.

125. Ibid.

126. Ibid.

127. AT28, memo, John T. Hayes, "Visit of General Hon," 14 April 1970, pp. 1–2, RG 472, A1 690, box 296, folder: 1601-11A/CORRES. W/SA/OUTGOING JAN–APR '70, NARA II.

128. AT28, memo, James B. Engle to Senior Advisor—II CTZ, "Political Report No. 16—Phu Yen Province Chief stung by critical U.S. press articles," 10 April 1970, p. 1, RG 472, A1 690, box 296, folder: 1601-11A/CORRES. W/SA/OUTGOING JAN–APR '70, NARA II.

129. AT28, memo, John T. Hayes, "Visit of General Hon," 14 April 1970, p. 2, NARA II.

130. Ibid.

131. Ibid., 3 (emphasis in original).

132. Ibid., 4.

133. Ibid., 5.

134. Ibid. (emphasis in original).

135. Ibid.

136. Ibid.

137. Fluke interview.

138. AT28, progress report, period ending 30 April 1970, p. 1, CMH.

139. Robert Shaplen, "Letter From Indo-China," *New Yorker*, 16 May 1970, p. 132.

140. Ibid.

141. Ibid., 133; AT28, memo, James B. Engle to Senior Advisor—II CTZ, "Political Report No. 16—Phu Yen Province Chief stung by critical U.S. press articles," 10

April 1970, p. 2, NARA II. The AT28 report misspelled Thạnh Nghiệp as Thanh Nhiep.

142. Shaplen, "Letter From Indo-China," 133–34.

143. "Letter From Indochina," *Congressional Record*, Senate, 91st U.S. Cong., 2nd sess., 22 May 1970, p. 16759, accessed 3 August 2020, www.gpo.gov/fdsys/pkg /GPO-CRECB-1970-pt12/pdf/GPO-CRECB-1970-pt12-7-1.pdf.

144. AT28, biweekly district report, Tuy Hòa, 25 April to 12 May 1970, p. 1, RG 472, A1 690, box 275, folder: District Senior Advisor's Monthly Reports, 05/1969–12/1970, NARA II.

145. AT28, report, Russell Meerdink to Willard E. Chambers, "GVN Initiative to Thwart VC Abductions," 27 May 1970, p. 1, RG 472, A1 690, box 296, folder: 1601–110/ CORRES. W/SA—OUTGOING MAY–AUG '70, NARA II.

146. Ibid., 1–2.

147. AT28, biweekly district report, Tuy Hòa, 25 April to 12 May 1970, p. 1, NARA II.

148. AT28, biweekly district report, Tuy Hòa, 13–27 May 1970, p. 1, RG 472, A1 690, box 275, folder: District Senior Advisor's Monthly Reports, 05/1969–12/1970, NARA II.

149. Ibid.

150. Ibid.

151. AT28, biweekly district report, Tuy Hòa, 13–25 April 1970, p. 1, RG 472, A1 690, box 275, folder: District Senior Advisor's Monthly Reports, 05/1969–12/1970, NARA II.

152. Boylan, *Losing Binh Dinh*, 7–8.

153. AT28, semimonthly district report, Hiếu Xương, 1 May 1970, p. 1, RG 472, A1 690, box 275, folder: District Senior Advisor's Monthly Reports, 05/1969–12/1970, NARA II.

154. Ibid.

155. Ibid.

156. Ibid.

157. AT28, semimonthly district report, Hiếu Xương, 26 May 1970, p. 1, RG 472, A1 690, box 275, folder: District Senior Advisor's Monthly Reports, 05/1969–12/1970, NARA II.

158. Russell L. Meerdink, telephone interview with author, 9 December 2012.

159. AT28, district report, Sông Cầu, period ending 12 May 1970, p. 1, RG 472, A1 690, box 275, folder: District Senior Advisor's Monthly Reports, 05/1969–12/1970, NARA II.

160. AT28, biweekly district report, Tuy Hòa, 28 May to 14 June 1970, p. 3, RG 472, A1 690, box 275, folder: District Senior Advisor's Monthly Reports, 05/1969– 12/1970, NARA II.

161. Ibid., 1.
162. AT28, province feeder report, Đồng Xuân District, period ending 25 September 1970, p. 1, RG 472, A1 690, box 275, folder: District Senior Advisor's Monthly Reports, 05/1969–12/1970, NARA II.
163. Ibid.
164. Ibid.
165. Ibid.
166. AT28, district report, Tuy An, 27 September to 26 October 1970, p. 1, RG 472, A1 690, box 275, folder: District Senior Advisor's Monthly Reports, 05/1969–12/1970, NARA II.
167. AT28, province report, period ending 30 September 1970, p. 1, CMH.
168. Ibid.
169. Ibid.
170. Ibid.
171. Ibid.
172. AT28, monthly district report, Tuy Hòa, period ending 27 September 1970, p. 1, RG 472, A1 690, box 275, folder: District Senior Advisor's Monthly Reports, 05/1969–12/1970, NARA II.
173. Ibid.
174. Ibid.
175. Ibid.
176. AT28, province report, period ending 30 September 1970, p. 1, CMH.
177. Ibid., 1–2.
178. Ibid., 1.
179. Radio transcription, "Former VC Province Leader Boasts of People's Ardour" (recorded statement by Võ Học, former chairman of the Phu Yen Resistance and Administrative Committee), 1 August 1970, p. 9, box 17, folder 08, Pike Collection, unit 01, TTUVA, accessed 3 August 2020, www.vietnam.ttu.edu/reports/images.php?img=/images/212/2121708009.pdf.
180. Ibid., 10.
181. Ibid.
182. Combat Operations AAR, Operation Wayne Force, Department of the Army, Headquarters 2d Battalion 35th Infantry Regiment, accessed 3 August 2020, www.cacti35th.com/history/1968-70/70%208%20Sep-1%20Oct%20Wayne%20Force.pdf. This copy mistakenly refers to Operation Wayne Forge as Operation Wayne Force.
183. Ibid.
184. MACV, "VC/NVA Base Area Study," part 2, 5 January 1971, pp. 15–16, box 0027, folder 0185, TTUVA, accessed 3 August 2020, www.vietnam.ttu.edu/virtualarchive/items.php?item=F015900270185.
185. Ibid., 16.

186. AT28, monthly district report, Hiếu Xương, period ending 26 September 1970, p. 1, RG 472, A1 690, box 275, folder: District Senior Advisor's Monthly Reports, 05/1969–12/1970, NARA II.

187. AT28, monthly district report, Hiếu Xương, period ending 26 November 1970, p. 1, RG 472, A1 690, box 275, folder: District Senior Advisor's Monthly Reports, 05/1969–12/1970, NARA II.

188. Ibid.

189. AT28, letter, Walter F. Kyle to Russell Meerdink, 15 November 1970, RG 472, A1 690, box 296, folder: Corres W/DSA—Incoming, NARA II.

190. Ibid.

191. Ibid.

192. Ibid.

193. Ibid.

194. Ibid.

195. AT28, province report, period ending 20 November 1970, p. 5, CMH.

196. "Terror in South Vietnam—The Pulping of a People—III," Congressional Record, House of Representatives, 91st U.S. Cong., 2nd sess., 30 December 1970, p. 1, box 16, folder 13, Pike Collection, unit 02, TTUVA, accessed 3 August 2020, www .vietnam.ttu.edu/virtualarchive/items.php?item=2131613156.

197. Ibid., 2.

198. Ibid., 1.

199. AT28, district report, Sông Cầu, period ending 26 November 1970, p. 1, RG 472, A1 690, box 275, folder: District Senior Advisor's Monthly Reports, 05/1969– 12/1970, NARA II.

200. "Terror in South Vietnam—The Pulping of a People," p. E10875, Pike Collection, TTUVA.

201. Ibid.

202. Ibid.

203. Ibid., E10876.

204. Ibid., E10875.

205. Ibid., E10877.

206. Ibid., E10876

207. AT28, province report, period ending 30 December 1970, p. 1, CMH.

208. Ibid., 2.

209. Ibid.

210. Ibid.

211. AT28, district report, Sông Cầu, period ending 26 December 1970, p.1, RG 472, A1 690, box 275, folder: District Senior Advisor's Monthly Reports, 05/1969– 12/1970, NARA II.

212. Ibid. (emphasis in original).

213. Ibid. (emphasis in original).
214. AT28, province report, period ending 30 December 1970, p. 2, CMH.
215. Ibid.
216. AT28, district report, Sông Cầu, period ending 26 December 1970, p. 1, NARA II.
217. Ibid.
218. AT28, province report, period ending 30 December 1970, p. 2, CMH.
219. Viện Lịch Sử Quân Sự Việt Nam [Military History Institute of Vietnam], *Lịch Sử Kháng Chiến Chống Mỹ Cứu Nước, 1954–1975, Tập VI: Thắng Mỹ Trên Chiến Trường Ba Nước Đông Dươn* [History of the Resistance War Against the Americans to Save the Nation, 1954–1975, vol. VI: Defeating the Americans in the Three Nations of Indochina] (Hanoi: Nhà Xuất Bản Chính Trị Quốc Gi, 2003), 136. Translated by Merle Pribbenow.

Chapter 8

1. Rowland Evans and Robert Novak, "Red Stronghold a Testing Ground of Saigon's Control in the Provinces," *Los Angeles Times*, 16 September 1971, D6.
2. Ibid.
3. Evans and Novak, "Red Stronghold a Testing Ground of Saigon's Control of the Provinces."
4. For more on Bình Định Province during this period, see Boylan, *Losing Bình Dinh*.
5. AT28, province report, period ending 31 January 1971, p. 1, CMH.
6. Ibid., 2.
7. Ibid.
8. Ibid.
9. Ibid.
10. Ibid., 3.
11. Ibid., 1.
12. Ibid.
13. Ibid.
14. Ibid.
15. Russell L. Meerdink, telephone interview with author, 12 September 2012 (hereafter cited as Meerdink interview).
16. AT28, province report, period ending 31 January 1971, p. 2, CMH.
17. "Six G.I.'s Reported Killed in Attacks by Enemy," *New York Times*, 2 February 1971.
18. AT28, province report, period ending 28 February 1971, p. 1, CMH.
19. Ibid.
20. Annual Supplement History of 134th Aviation Company (Assault Helicopter), 268th Combat Aviation Battalion, 1st Aviation Brigade, 1 January

1971–31 December 1971, p. 14, n.d., box 04, folder 19, Vietnam Helicopter Pilots Association (VHPA) Collection: Unit Histories—1st Aviation Brigade, TTUVA, accessed 3 August 2020, www.vietnam.ttu.edu/virtualarchive/items.php?item= 3030419002.

21. Thayer, *War Without Fronts*, 207.
22. Ibid.
23. AT28, province report, period ending 31 March 1971, p. 1, CMH.
24. Ibid., 2.
25. Ibid., 1.
26. Ibid., 2.
27. Ibid.
28. Ibid., 3.
29. Ibid.
30. AT28, province report, period ending 30 April 1971, p. 1, CMH.
31. Ibid., 2.
32. Ibid., 1.
33. Ibid.
34. Ibid., 2.
35. Ibid., 1.
36. Ibid., 2.
37. Ibid., 1.
38. AT28, province report, period ending 31 May 1971, p. 1, CMH.
39. Ibid.
40. Capt. Courtney L. Frobenius, "Dong Xuan District Highway 6B," n.d., p. 1, box 2, folder 21, Frobenius Papers, MLA.
41. Ibid.
42. Ibid.
43. Ibid.
44. Ibid.
45. Ibid.
46. Ibid.
47. Ibid.
48. Ibid.
49. Ibid.
50. Ibid., 2.
51. Ibid.
52. Ibid.
53. Ibid.
54. Ibid.
55. AT28, province report, period ending 31 May 1971, p. 2, CMH.

56. Ibid.

57. Senior Colonel Trần Văn Mười, former Commander of the K-13 Local Force Battalion, "Bac Ly Hamlet and Its Mass Grave," *Bao Phú Yên* (Phu Yen Newspaper), 6 June 2017, translated by Merle Pribbenow, accessed 10 January 2018, www .baophuyen.com.vn/94/175845/ap-bac-ly-va-ngoi-mo-tap-the.html.

58. Lt. Col. Nguyễn Văn Tố to Brigadier General II CTZ, MR2 Commander, "Report VC Attack Hon-Ngang Fire Base at CQ 801435 of Son Hoa and Operation of 206th RF Battalion on 18 June 1971," n.d., p. 1, box 2, folder 25, Frobenius Papers, MLA. Note: this document is the GVN after action report for the battle.

59. Sơn Hòa after action report, 18 June 1971, p. 1, box 2, folder 24, Frobenius Papers, MLA.

60. "Reds, South Vietnamese Clashing Day-Long Battle," *Star Tribune* (Minneapolis, MN), 19 June 1971, 2A.

61. Sơn Hòa after action report, 18 June 1971, p. 1, box 2, folder 24, Frobenius Papers, MLA.

62. "Report VC Attack Hon-Ngang Fire Base at CQ 801435 of Son Hoa and Operation of 206th RF Battalion on 18 June 1971," p. 1, Frobenius Papers, MLA.

63. Thayer interview.

64. Sơn Hòa after action report, 18 June 1971, p. 1, Frobenius Papers, MLA.

65. Senior Colonel Trần Văn Mười, "Bac Ly Hamlet and Its Mass Grave."

66. Sơn Hòa after action report, 18 June 1971, p. 1, Frobenius Papers, MLA.

67. Senior Colonel Trần Văn Mười, "Bac Ly Hamlet and Its Mass Grave."

68. Award of the Bronze Star, 29 December 1971, in Ronald Thayer's possession.

69. Thayer interview.

70. Hans J. Underwood, "The Battle for Cung Son," accessed 31 October 2020, http:// 134thahc.com/Storiesof134.htm#the_battle_for_cung_son.

71. Sơn Hòa after action report, 18 June 1971, p. 2, Frobenius Papers, MLA.

72. Ibid., 1.

73. Ibid.

74. Ibid., 2.

75. Ibid.

76. Ibid.

77. "Report VC Attack Hon-Ngang Fire Base at CQ 801435 of Son Hoa and Operation of 206th RF Battalion on 18 June 1971," p. 2, Frobenius Papers, MLA; Sơn Hòa after action report, 18 June 1971, p. 3, Frobenius Papers, MLA.

78. Thayer interview.

79. Senior Colonel Trần Văn Mười, "Bac Ly Hamlet and Its Mass Grave."

80. Sơn Hòa after action report, 18 June 1971, p. 3, Frobenius Papers, MLA.

81. Ibid.

82. Award of the Bronze Star, 27 December 1971, and RVN Cross of Gallantry with Gold Star, 16 July 1971, both in Ronald Thayer's possession.

83. AT28, Meerdink to Maj. Alfred W. Baker, 27 September 1971, RG 472, A1 690, box 3002, folder: Bio / Reports Son Hoa, NARA II.

84. "Report VC Attack Hon-Ngang Fire Base at CQ 801435 of Son Hoa and Operation of 206th RF Battalion on 18 June 1971," p. 2, Frobenius Papers, MLA.

85. Sơn Hòa after action report, 18 June 1971, p. 3, Frobenius Papers, MLA; "Report VC Attack Hon-Ngang Fire Base at CQ 801435 of Son Hoa and Operation of 206th RF Battalion on 18 June 1971," p. 2, Frobenius Papers, MLA. Note: the American and South Vietnamese AARs differ on the number of PLAF and RF killed. The Americans placed the enemy KIAs at 127; the South Vietnamese put the number at 186. In terms of RF killed, the Americans recorded sixteen as opposed to the two claimed by the South Vietnamese. See: Military Region 2, military region overview, period ending 30 June 1971, p. 3, CMH.

86. AT28, province report, period ending 31 June 1971, p. 1, CMH.

87. AT28, province report, period ending 30 June 1971, p. 2, CMH.

88. Ibid., 4.

89. Military Region 2, military region overview, period ending 30 June 1971, p. 1, CMH.

90. Hans-Jürgen Underwood, "Cung Sun the Morning After!," 19 June 1971, accessed 3 August 2020, http://134thahc.com/CungSon.html.

91. Meerdink interview.

92. AT28, province report, period ending 30 June 1971, p. 2, CMH.

93. Charles S. Varnum, telephone interview with author, 29 November 2012 (hereafter cited as Varnum interview).

94. AT28, province report, period ending 30 June 1971, p. 1, CMH.

95. Varnum interview.

96. Military Region 2, military region overview, period ending 30 June 1971, p. 3, CMH.

97. "LPA reviews 1971 victories in two provinces," 18 January 1972, box 19, folder 04, Pike Collection: Unit 02—Military Operations, TTUVA, accessed 3 August 2020, www.vietnam.ttu.edu/virtualarchive/items.php?item=2131904116.

98. AT28, province report, period ending 31 July 1971, p. 1, CMH.

99. Ibid., 4.

100. Ibid.

101. Ibid., 2.

102. Ibid.

103. Frobenius to Varnum, "Status of Security at Hoa Tri Hamlet," 28 July 1971, p. 2, box 2, folder 8, Frobenius Papers, MLA. Note: Frobenius misidentified Hoa Tri as a hamlet.

104. Ibid., 3.

105. Ibid.
106. Ibid.
107. Ibid.
108. AT28, "Notes on Tuy Hoa District," n.d., p. 12, Folder: Phu Yen 210, CMH. CMH has both the rough draft and the final copy of the notes; citations in this chapter reference the final copy of the notes.
109. Ibid., 12–13. Phong Nguyên is an approximation since it does not appear on ARVN maps, which raises the possibility of ARVN never recognizing the hamlet as being legal.
110. Frobenius to Varnum, "Status of Security at Hoa Tri Hamlet," p. 2, Frobenius Papers, MLA.
111. AT28, "Notes on Tuy Hoa District," n.d., pp. 12–13, Folder: Phu Yen 210, CMH.
112. Ibid., 13.
113. Frobenius to Varnum, "Security in Xa Hoa Dinh," 26 July 1971, p. 2, box 2, folder 10, Frobenius Papers, MLA.
114. Ibid.
115. AT28, Myron K. Rice to Russell L. Meerdink, "Status of Security in Hoa Dinh Village," 27 July 1971, RG 472, A1 690, box 300, folder: Eval Reps—PSA I, NARA II.
116. Ibid.
117. Ibid.
118. Ibid.
119. Ibid.
120. Ibid.
121. AT28, "Notes on Tuy Hoa District," p. 9, CMH.
122. Ibid.
123. Ibid.
124. Ibid., 9–10.
125. Ibid.
126. Ibid.
127. Ibid.
128. Ibid., 11.
129. AT28, province report, period ending 31 August 1971, p. 2, CMH.
130. Ibid.
131. Ibid.
132. Ibid.
133. Ibid.
134. Frobenius to Varnum, "Status of Security of Xa Hon Thanh Hieu Xuong District," n.d., p. 4, box 2, folder 12, Frobenius Papers, MLA. Frobenius does not specify

which Phu Xuan hamlet he visited (i.e., Phu Xuan 1, Phu Xuan 2, Phu Xuan 3, or Phu Xuan 4). Nevertheless, the hamlet in question is most likely Phu Xuan 4 as it was the most remote of the Xuan Phuoc village's hamlets.

135. Ibid.
136. Frobenius, "Xa Hoa Quang," n.d., p. 1, box 2, folder 16, Frobenius Papers, MLA.
137. Ibid.
138. Ibid.
139. Ibid.
140. Ibid.
141. Ibid.
142. Ibid.
143. Ibid.
144. Ibid.
145. Ibid.
146. Frobenius to Varnum, "Status of Security of the Hamlets of Mau Lam, Ngoc Dong, and Phu Thanh," 3 August 1971, p. 4, box 2, folder 11, Frobenius Papers, MLA
147. Ibid.
148. Ibid., 2.
149. Ibid.
150. Ibid.
151. Ibid.
152. Ibid., 5.
153. AT28, "Notes on Tuy Hoa District," p. 5, CMH.
154. Ibid.
155. Ibid., 6.
156. Ibid.
157. Ibid.
158. Ibid.
159. Ibid.
160. Frobenius, "Xa Xuan Phuoc," 18 August 1971, p. 4, box 2, folder 15, Frobenius Papers, MLA.
161. Ibid., 3, 6.
162. Frobenius to Varnum, "Xa Hoa Kien," n.d., p. 3, box 2, folder 13, Frobenius Papers, MLA.
163. Ibid.
164. Ibid., 4.
165. Ibid., 6.
166. Ibid.
167. Ibid.

168. AT28, "Notes on Tuy Hoa District," p. 1, CMH.
169. Ibid.
170. Ibid.
171. Ibid.
172. Ibid.
173. Ibid.
174. Ibid., 2.
175. Ibid.
176. Ibid.
177. Ibid.
178. Frobenius to Varnum, "Security in Xa An Chan," n.d., p. 1, box 2, folder 14, Frobenius Papers, MLA.
179. Ibid., 2.
180. Ibid., 4.
181. Ibid.
182. Ibid.
183. Ibid.
184. Ibid.
185. AT28, "Notes on Tuy Hoa District," p. 5, CMH.
186. Ibid.
187. Ibid., 4.
188. Ibid.
189. Ibid.
190. Ibid.
191. Ibid., 4–5.
192. Ibid., 14.
193. Ibid.
194. Ibid.
195. Frobenius to Varnum, "An Ninh Village," n.d., p. 3, box 2, folder 18, Frobenius Papers, MLA.
196. Ibid., 1.
197. Ibid., 2.
198. Ibid., 3.
199. Ibid., 2.
200. Ibid.
201. Ibid.
202. AT28, province report, period ending 30 September 1971, p. 2, CMH.
203. Ibid.
204. Ibid., 3.
205. Ibid., 2.

206. Varnum interview.

207. AT28, province report, period ending 31 October 1971, p. 1, CMH (emphasis in original).

208. Ibid.

209. Ibid.

210. Ibid.

211. Ibid.

212. Varnum interview.

213. AT28, province report, period ending 30 November 1971, p. 1, CMH.

214. Ibid.

215. AT28, province report, period ending 31 December 1971, p. 1, CMH. Note: this is the first province report that mentions Carroll L. Floyd by name (he signed the report).

216. Ibid.

Chapter 9

1. "Military Proselyting Activities of Agencies of the Phu Yen Province Party Committee, VC Region 5," 23 October 1972, box 15, folder 09, Pike Collection, unit 05, TTUVA, accessed 13 September 2020, https://www.vietnam.ttu.edu/virtualarchive/items.php?item=2311509046. Perhaps because of typewriter limitations, the original translation used double parentheses instead of square brackets.

2. "Cease Fire Plans of Phu Yen PRP CC," October 1972, 1 October 1972, p. 7, box 25, folder 04, Pike Collection: Unit 01—Assessment and Strategy, TTUVA, accessed 3 August 2020, www.vietnam.ttu.edu/virtualarchive/items.php?item=2122504044. U.S. intelligence surmised that this message emanated from the Phú Yên Province Party Committee.

3. Pacification Research Report, "Survey of the people's attitude concerning the effect of the closing of Tuy Hoa AB on social, economic and security conditions," Office of the Deputy for CORDS, Pacification Research Program, MR2, 17–25 January 1972, p. 1, RG 472, A1 462, box 103, folder: Phu Yen prov, 1972, NARA II.

4. Ibid., 5.

5. Second Regional Assistance Group, military region overview for the month ending 31 January 1972, p. 1, folder: Corps Overviews—January–June 1972, CMH.

6. Ibid., 2–3.

7. Advisory Team 28 Newsletter, August 1972, p. 2, box 2, folder 42, Frobenius Papers, MLA.

8. Ibid.

9. Myron K. Rice Jr., Comments by the Senior District Advisor, n.d., p. 1, CMH. Information in the document places Rice having wrote it at the end of March or early April.

10. Ibid., 2.

11. Ibid., 1.

12. Ibid.

13. Ibid.

14. Ibid.

15. AT28, memorandum, Ltc. William A. Holbrook III to James Green, Reports and Analysis Directorate, "PSA HES Comments—March 1972," 3 April 1972, CMH.

16. Ibid.

17. "Advisory Team 28 Newsletter," August 1972, p. 2, Frobenius Papers, MLA.

18. AT28, province report, period ending 30 April 1972, p. 1, CMH.

19. Ibid.

20. AT28, report, "Convoy Ambush in Dong Xuan District, Phu Yen Province," enclosure 1, 11 May 1972, RG 472, A1 551, box 35, folder: 1601–09A Prov. Corr. Phu Yen, NARA II; Lt. Col. Nguyen Van To to Lt. Col. W. A. Holbrook, "Report of VC Ambush on Highway 6B, 15 April 1972," 27 April 1972, RG 472, A1 551, box 35, folder: 1601–09A Prov. Corr. Phu Yen, NARA II.

21. "Advisory Team 28 Newsletter," August 1972, pp. 2–3, folder 42, box 2, Frobenius Papers, MLA.

22. AT28, province report, period ending 30 April 1972, p. 1, CMH.

23. Ibid.

24. Ibid., 3.

25. Ibid., 2.

26. Ibid.

27. AT28, province report, period ending 31 July 1972, p. 1, CMH.

28. Ibid.

29. "Advisory Team 28 Newsletter," August 1972, p. 3, folder 42, box 2, Frobenius Papers, MLA.

30. AT28, province report, period ending 30 September 1972, p. 1, CMH.

31. Ibid.

32. Evaluation, "Impact of the Enemy Offensive on Pacification," 16 September 1972, p. 2, RG 472, A1 462, box 42, folder: 1601–10A/Study/Evaluation/Enemy Offensive Impact on Pacification/1972, NARA II.

33. Evaluation, "Impact of the Enemy Offensive on Pacification," 5 October 1972, p. 4, RG 472, A1 462, box 42, folder: 1601–10A/Study/Evaluation/Enemy Offensive Impact on Pacification/1972, NARA II.

34. AT28, province report, period ending 31 October 1972, p. 1, CMH.

35. Ibid.

36. Ibid.

37. Ibid.

38. AT28, province report, period ending 30 November 1972, p. 2, CMH.
39. Ibid.
40. Ibid.
41. AT28, province report, period ending 31 December 1972, p. 1, CMH.
42. Ibid.
43. Ibid.
44. Ibid., 1–2.
45. Lt. Col. John M. McDonald, "Province Advisor's Completion of Tour Report," 19 February 1973, p. 6, Department of the Army, Office of the Adjutant General, Washington, D.C., DTIC.
46. Ibid.
47. AT28, province report, period ending 31 December 1972, p. 2, CMH.
48. See Krepinevich, *The Army and Vietnam*, for a more detailed appraisal of how the U.S. brought the RVNAF to the point of utmost dependence on American support.
49. AT28, province report, period ending 31 December 1972, p. 2, CMH.
50. Ibid.
51. Asselin, *Hanoi's Road to the Vietnam War*, 210; William E. Le Gro, *Vietnam from Cease-Fire to Capitulation* (Washington, D.C.: U.S. Army Center of Military History, 1985), 24.
52. Cao Van Vien, *The Final Collapse* (Washington, D.C.: U.S. Army Center of Military History, 1985), 78–79.
53. Ibid., 86, 93.
54. George J. Veith, *Black April: The Fall of South Vietnam, 1973–75* (New York: Encounter Books, 2012), 229–33.
55. Veith, *Black April*, 136–37, 179–80, 229, 232; "Quarter-Million Viets Flee Abandoned Provinces," *Arizona Republic* (Phoenix), 21 March 1975, A2.
56. "Phu Yen Convoy Reaches Highway 1," American Embassy Saigon to Secretary of State, no. 3513, 26 March 1975, quoted in Veith, *Black April*, 234.
57. "Communist forces are gobbling up S. Vietnam," *Capital Journal* (Pierre, S.D.), 1 April 1975, 2.
58. Veith, *Black April*, 222, 348–49.
59. Ibid.; Cao Van Vien, *Final Collapse*, 118.
60. "Media Acclaim Liberation of Phu Yen Province," 4 April 1975, p. 2, box 25, folder 14, Pike Collection, unit 02, TTUVA, accessed 11 September 2020, https://www.vietnam.ttu.edu/virtualarchive/items.php?item=2132514072.
61. Ibid.
62. Ibid.
63. Ibid.

Conclusion

1. MACCORDS, memo, "Meeting between Mr. Jacobson and Mr. McManaway and the Prime Minister," 12 April 1970, p. 1, CORDS Historical Working Group Files, 1967–1973, RG 472, A1 462, box 14, folder: Memos & Messages / Mr. Jacobson / Visits, NARA II.

Bibliography

Primary Sources

Archives

Defense Technical Information Center, Fort Belvoir, Va.

Hoover Institution Library and Archives (cited as HIA), Stanford, Calif.

Edward Geary Lansdale Papers. Collection no. 80116.

Charles T. R. Bohannan Papers. Collection no. 78063.

Victoria Schuck Papers. Collection no. 98064.

Allen E. Goodman Papers. Collection no. 75001.

McCain Library and Archives (cited as MLA), University of Southern Mississippi, Hattiesburg, Miss.

Courtney L. Frobenius Papers. Collection no. M396.

National Archives and Records Administration (cited as NARA II), College Park, Md.

Records of the U.S. Forces in Southeast Asia. Record group 472.

The Pentagon papers. Record group 330.

Office of the Historian, Washington, D.C.

Foreign Relations of the United States, 1961–1963. Vol. II, *Vietnam, 1962.* Edited by Glenn W. LaFantasie. Washington, D.C.: U.S. Government Printing Office, 1990.

U.S. Army Center of Military History (cited as CMH), Fort Leslie J. McNair, Washington, D.C.

United States Military History Institute, Carlisle, Pa.

The Vietnam Center and Sam Johnson Vietnam Archive, Texas Tech University (cited as TTUVA), Lubbock, Tex.

Dale W. Andrade Collection

Larry Berman Collection

Levin B. Broughton Collection

William Colby Collection

John Donnell Collection
Ronald B. Frankum Jr. Collection
Bud Harton Collection
John Haseman Collection
Glenn Helm Collection
Gary Larsen Collection
Vladimir Lehovich Collection
Rufus Phillips Collection
Douglas Pike Collection
Antoine Edward Roy Collection
Ronald Bruce St. John Collection
Thomas C. Thayer Collection
Vietnam Archive Collection
Vietnam Helicopter Pilots Association (VHPA) Collection

Interviews by the Author
Robert Barron, 7 May 2015. Email and phone.
Eugene Fluke, 25 September 2015. Email and phone.
Russell L. Meerdink, 9 December 2012. Email and phone.
Ronald Thayer, 8, 15 December 2015. Email and phone.
Charles S. Varnum, 29 November 2012. Email and phone.

Interviews by Others
Robert Barron. Interview by Stephen Maxner, 21 April 2001. Robert Barron Collection, TTUVA. Accessed 22 July 2020. http://www.vietnam.ttu.edu/virtualarchive/items .php?item=OH0163.
Bruce W. Clark. Interview by Charles Stuart Kennedy, 4 June 2002. Association for Diplomatic Studies and Training Foreign Affairs Oral History Project. Accessed 13 July 2020. www.adst.org/OH%20TOCs/Clark,%20Bruce%20W.toc.pdf.
Lt. Gen. Charles A. Corcoran. Interview by Lt. Col. Joseph A. Langer, Jr., 1975. Senior Officer Oral History Program, 1988, U.S. Army Military History Institute. http:// usahec.contentdm.oclc.org/cdm/ref/collection/p16635coll26/id/177. (No longer accessible.)
Antoine Edward Roy. Interview by Richard B. Verrone, 8 January 2003. Antoine Edward Roy Collection, TTUVA. Accessed 21 July 2020. www.vietnam.ttu.edu/virtualarchive /items.php?item=OH0255.
Maxwell D. Taylor. Interviewed by Stanley Karnow. "America's Mandarin: 1954–1963." *Vietnam: A Television History,* part 3 of 4, 30 January 1979. Open Vault (WGBH Media Library and Archives). Accessed 13 July 2020. http://openvault.wgbh.org /catalog/V_B182E52F36DD4A64A65D5342CA3D69E3.

Personal Collections

David Curtin

Thomas Kaulukukui

Merle Pribbenow

Ellis Wisner

Hans-Jürgen Underwood

Published Memoirs and Firsthand Accounts

Colby, William. *Lost Victory: A Firsthand Account of America's Sixteen-Year Involvement in Vietnam*. Chicago: Contemporary Books, 1989.

Hackworth, David H. and Julie Sherman. *About Face: The Odyssey of an American Warrior*. New York: Simon and Schuster, 1989.

Hagan, Edward A. *To Vietnam in Vain: Memoir of an Irish-American Intelligence Advisor, 1969–1970*. Jefferson, N.C.: McFarland & Company, 2016.

Herrington, Stuart A. *Silence Was a Weapon: The Vietnam War in the Villages*. Novato, Calif.: Presidio Press, 1982.

Lansdale, Edward Geary. *In The Midst of Wars: An American's Mission to Southeast Asia*. New York: Harper & Row, 1972.

Marshall, S. L. A. *The Fields of Bamboo: Three Battles Just Beyond the South China Sea*. New York: Dial Press, 1971.

Phillips, Rufus. *Why Vietnam Matters: An Eyewitness Account of Lessons Not Learned*. Annapolis, Md.: Naval Institute Press, 2008.

Sorley, Lewis, ed. *Vietnam Chronicles: The Abrams Tapes, 1968–1972*. Lubbock: Texas Tech University Press, 2004.

Tho, Tran Dinh. *Pacification*. Washington, D.C.: U.S. Army Center of Military History, 1980.

Tse-tung, Mao. *Selected Military Writings of Mao Tse-tung*. Peking: Foreign Language Press, 1968.

Westmoreland, William C. *A Soldier Reports*. New York: Doubleday, 1976.

Manuals, Reports, and Studies

Croizat, V. J., trans. *A Translation from the French: Lessons of the War in Indochina, Volume 2*. Santa Monica, Calif.: RAND Corporation, May 1967.

Elliott, David W. P. and W. A. Stewart. *Pacification and the Viet Cong System in Dinh Tuong: 1966–1967*. Santa Monica, Calif.: RAND Corporation, January [1969] 1975.

Komer, Robert W. *Impact of Pacification on Insurgency in South Vietnam*. Santa Monica, Calif.: RAND Corporation, August 1970.

U.S. Army Counterinsurgency Forces. Field Manual 31-22. Washington, D.C.: Department of the Army, November 1963. Accessed 14 July 2020. http://smallwarsjournal.com /documents/maxwell1963doctrine.pdf

Vietnam Task Force. *United States–Vietnam Relations, 1945–1967.* Washington, D.C.: Office of the Secretary of Defense, 2011. (Cited as Pentagon Papers.)

Westmoreland, William. "Military Briefing." Paper presented at the Pentagon, Washington, D.C., 22 November 1967.

Periodicals

Arizona Republic

Báo Phú Yên

Capital Journal

Los Angeles Times

Maryland Gazette

New York Times

New Yorker

Pacific Stars and Stripes

Star Tribune

Washington Post

Books and Articles

Anderson, David L. and John Ernst, eds. *The War That Never Ends: New Perspectives on the Vietnam War.* Lexington: University Press of Kentucky, 2007.

Andradé, Dale. *America's Last Vietnam Battle: Halting Hanoi's 1972 Easter Offensive.* Lawrence: University Press of Kansas, 2001.

———. *Ashes to Ashes: The Phoenix Program and the Vietnam War.* Lexington, Mass.: Lexington Books, 1990.

Appy, Christian G. *Working-Class War: American Combat Soldiers and Vietnam.* Chapel Hill: University of North Carolina Press, 1993.

Arthurs, Ted G. *Land with No Sun: A Year in Vietnam with the 173rd Airborne.* Mechanicsburg, Pa.: Stackpole Books, 2006.

Asselin, Pierre. *Hanoi's Road to the Vietnam War, 1954–1965.* Berkeley: University of California Press, 2013.

———. *Vietnam's American War: A History.* Cambridge: Cambridge University Press, 2018.

Bergerud, Eric M. *The Dynamics of Defeat: the Vietnam War in Hau Nghia Province.* Boulder, Colo.: Westview Press, 1993.

Birtle, Andrew J. *U.S. Army Counterinsurgency and Contingency Operations Doctrine, 1860–1941.* Washington, D.C.: U.S. Army Center of Military History, [1998] 2009.

———. *U.S. Army Counterinsurgency and Contingency Operations Doctrine, 1942–1976.* Washington, D.C.: U.S. Army Center of Military History, 2006.

———. "Triumph Forsaken as Military History." In *Triumph Revisited: Historians Battle for the Vietnam War,* edited by Andrew Wiest and Michael J. Doidge, 120–35. New York: Routledge, 2010.

Boylan, Kevin M. "The Red Queen's Race: Operation Washington Green and Pacification in Binh Dinh Province, 1969–1970." *Journal of Military History* 73, no. 4 (October 2009): 1195–1230.

———. *Losing Binh Dinh: The Failure of Pacification and Vietnamization, 1969–1971.* Lawrence: University Press of Kansas, 2016.

Bradley, Mark Philip. *Imagining Vietnam and America: The Making of Postcolonial Vietnam, 1919–1950.* Chapel Hill: University of North Carolina Press, 2000.

Carland, John M. *Combat Operations: Stemming the Tide, May 1965 to October 1966.* Washington, D.C.: U.S. Army Center of Military History, 2000.

Catton, Philip E. *Diem's Final Failure: Prelude to America's War in Vietnam.* Lawrence: University Press of Kansas, 2002.

———. "Refighting Vietnam in the History Books: The Historiography of the War." *Magazine of History* 18, no. 5 (October 2004): 7–11.

Chapman, Jessica M. *Cauldron of Resistance: Ngo Dinh Diem, the United States, and 1950s Southern Vietnam.* Ithaca, N.Y.: Cornell University Press, 2013.

Clarke, Jeffrey J. *Advice and Support: The Final Years—The U.S. Army in Vietnam, 1965–1973.* Washington, D.C.: U.S. Army Center of Military History, 1998.

Clemis, Martin G. *The Control War: The Struggle for South Vietnam, 1968–1975.* Norman: University of Oklahoma Press, 2018.

Daddis, Gregory A. *No Sure Victory: Measuring U.S. Army Effectiveness and Progress in the Vietnam War.* New York: Oxford University Press, 2011.

———. *Westmoreland's War: Reassessing American Strategy in Vietnam.* New York: Oxford University Press, 2014.

———. *Withdrawal: Reassessing America's Final Years in Vietnam.* New York: Oxford University Press, 2017.

Doughty, Robert A. *Leavenworth Papers: The Evolution of US Army Tactical Doctrine, 1946–76.* Fort Leavenworth, KS: Combat Studies Institute, U.S. Army Command and General Staff College, 1979.

Dutton, George. *The Tây Sơn Uprising: Society and Rebellion in Eighteenth-Century Vietnam.* Honolulu: University of Hawai'i Press, 2006.

Elliott, David W. P. *The Vietnamese War: Revolution and Social Change in the Mekong Delta, 1930–1975.* New York: Routledge, 2006.

Embrey, James H. "Reorienting Pacification: The Accelerated Pacification Campaign of 1968." PhD Diss., University of Kentucky, 1997.

Fall, Bernard B. *Viet-Nam Witness, 1953–66.* New York: Frederick A. Praeger, 1966.

———. *Street Without Joy.* Mechanicsburg, Pa.: Stackpole Books, [1961] 1994.

Fitzgerald, Francis. *Fire in the Lake: The Vietnamese and the Americans in Vietnam.* Boston: Little, Brown and Company, 1972.

Galula, David. *Pacification in Algeria, 1956–1958.* Santa Monica, Calif.: RAND Corporation, 1963.

————. *Counterinsurgency Warfare: Theory and Practice.* Westport, Conn.: Praeger, 1964.

Gawthorpe, Andrew J. *To Build as Well as Destroy: American Nation Building in South Vietnam.* Ithaca, N.Y.: Cornell University Press, 2018.

Gentile, Gian. *Wrong Turn: America's Deadly Embrace of Counterinsurgency.* New York: The New Press, 2013.

Grintchenko, Michel. *L'Opération Atlante: Les Dernières Illusions de la France en Indochine.* Paris: Economica, 2008.

————. "Operation Atlante (January–July 1954): The Last Pacification Operation in Indochina." *Doctrine* 12 (May 2007): 102–5.

Harris, J. P. *Vietnam's High Ground: Armed Struggle for the Central Highlands, 1954–1965.* Lawrence: University Press of Kansas, 2016.

Hennessy, Michael A. *Strategy in Vietnam: The Marines and Revolutionary Warfare in I Corps, 1965–1975.* Westport, Conn.: Praeger, 1997.

Herring, George C. "American Strategy in Vietnam: The Postwar Debate." *Military Affairs* 46, no. 2 (April 1982): 57–63.

————. *America's Longest War: The United States and Vietnam, 1950–1975.* New York: McGraw Hill, 2002.

Hill, Charles. "Fighting Stories." In *Triumph Revisited: Historians Battle for the Vietnam War,* edited by Andrew Wiest and Michael J. Doidge, 79–89. New York: Routledge, 2010.

Howard, John D. *First In, Last Out: An American Paratrooper in Vietnam with the 101st and Vietnamese Airborne.* Guilford, Conn.: Stackpole Books, 2017.

Hunt, Richard A. *Pacification: The American Struggle for Vietnam's Hearts and Minds.* Boulder, Colo.: Westview Press, 1995.

Jacobsen, Kurt. *Pacification and Its Discontents.* Chicago: Prickly Paradigm Press, 2009.

Johns, Andrew L. *Vietnam's Second Front: Domestic Politics, the Republican Party, and the War.* Lexington: University Press of Kentucky, 2010.

Jones, Frank Leith. *Blowtorch: Robert Komer, Vietnam, and American Cold War Strategy.* Annapolis, Md.: Naval Institute Press, 2013.

Karnow, Stanley. *Vietnam: A History.* New York: Viking, 1983.

Kolko, Gabriel. *Anatomy of a War: Vietnam, the United States, and the Modern Historical Experience.* New York: Pantheon, 1985.

Krepinevich, Andrew F. Jr. *The Army and Vietnam.* Baltimore: Johns Hopkins University Press, 1986.

Larsen, Stanley Robert, and James Lawton Collins Jr. *Vietnam Studies: Allied Participation in Vietnam.* Washington, D.C.: Department of the Army, 1975.

Le Gro, William E. *Vietnam from Cease-Fire to Capitulation.* Washington, D.C.: U.S. Army Center of Military History, 1985.

Lewy, Guenter. *America in Vietnam*. New York: Oxford University Press, 1978.

Luedeke, Kirk A. "Death on the Highway: The Destruction of Groupement Mobile 100." *Armor*, January–February 2001, 22–29.

MacGarrigle, George L. *Combat Operations: Taking the Offensive, October 1966 to October 1967*. Washington, D.C.: U.S. Army Center of Military History, 1998.

Maclear, Michael. *The Ten Thousand Day War: Vietnam: 1945–1975*. New York: St. Martin's Press, 1981.

Marr, David D. *Vietnam 1945: The Quest for Power*. Berkeley: University of California Press, 1995.

Military History Institute of Vietnam. *Victory in Vietnam: The Official History of the People's Army of Vietnam, 1954–1975*. Translated by Merle L. Pribbenow. Lawrence: University Press of Kansas, 2002.

Miller, Edward. *Misalliance: Ngo Dinh Diem, the United States, and the Fate of South Vietnam*. Cambridge, Mass.: Harvard University Press, 2013.

Moïse, Edwin E. *The Myths of Tet: The Most Misunderstood Event of the Vietnam War*. Lawrence: University Press of Kansas, 2017.

Moyar, Mark. *Phoenix and the Birds of Prey: The CIA's Secret Campaign to Destroy the Viet Cong*. Annapolis, Md.: Naval Institute Press, 1997.

———. *Triumph Forsaken: The Vietnam War, 1954–1965*. Cambridge: Cambridge University Press, 2006.

Nagl, John A. *Learning to Eat Soup with a Knife: Counterinsurgency Lessons from Malaya and Vietnam*. Chicago: University of Chicago Press, 2002.

Nashel, Jonathan. *Edward Lansdale's Cold War*. Amherst: University of Massachusetts Press, 2005.

Neocleous, Mark, and George S. Rigakos, eds. *Anti-Security*. Ottawa, Ont.: Red Quill Books, 2011.

Neocleous, Mark, George Rigakos, and Tyler Wall, "On Pacification: Introduction to the Special Issue." *Socialist Studies/Études Socialistes* 9, no. 2 (Winter 2013): 1–6.

Nguyen, Lien-Hang T. *Hanoi's War: An International History of the War for Peace in Vietnam*. Chapel Hill: University of North Caroline Press, 2012.

Packer, George. *Our Man: Richard Holbrooke and the End of the American Century*. New York: Alfred A. Knopf, 2019.

Peterson, Michael E. *The Combined Action Platoons: The U.S. Marines' Other War in Vietnam*. Westport, Conn.: Praeger, 1989.

Pike, Douglas. *Viet Cong: The Organization and Technique of the National Liberation Front of South Vietnam*. Cambridge, Mass.: MIT Press, 1966.

———. *War, Peace, and the Viet Cong*. Cambridge, Mass.: MIT Press, 1969.

———. *PAVN: People's Army of Vietnam*. Novato, Calif.: Presidio Press, 1986.

Porch, Douglas. *Counterinsurgency: Exposing the Myths of the New Way of War*. Cambridge: Cambridge University Press, 2013.

Race, Jeffrey. *War Comes to Long An: Revolutionary Conflict in a Vietnamese Province.* Berkeley: University of California Press, 1972.

Richardson, Thomas. *Destroy and Build: Pacification in Phuoc Tuy, 1966–72.* Cambridge: Cambridge University Press, 2017.

Sallah, Michael and Mitch Weiss. *Tiger Force: A True Story of Men and War.* New York: Back Bay Books, 2007.

Schlesinger, Arthur M. Jr. *The Bitter Heritage: Vietnam and American Democracy, 1941–1968.* New York: Fawcett Premier, 1967.

Schrader, Stuart. "To Secure the Global Great Society: Participation in Pacification." *Humanity: An International Journal of Human Rights, Humanitarianism, and Development* 7, no. 2 (Summer 2016): 225–53.

———. *Badges Without Borders: How Global Counterinsurgency Transformed American Policing.* Oakland: University of California Press, 2019.

Sheehan, Neil. *A Bright Shining Lie: John Paul Vann and America in Vietnam.* New York: Vintage Books, 1989.

Shulimson, Jack. *U.S. Marines in Vietnam: An Expanding War, 1966.* Washington, D.C.: History and Museums Division, Headquarters, U.S. Marine Corps, 1982.

Sorley, Lewis. *A Better War: The Unexamined Victories and Final Tragedy of America's Last Years in Vietnam.* Orlando, Fla.: Harcourt Brace, 1999.

———. "The Conduct of the War: Strategy, Doctrine, Tactics, and Policy." In *Rolling Thunder in a Gentle Land: The Vietnam War Revisited,* edited by Andrew Wiest, 174–91. New York: Osprey Publishing, 2006.

———. *Westmoreland: The General Who Lost Vietnam.* Boston: Houghton Mifflin Harcourt, 2011.

Spector, Ronald H. *After Tet: The Bloodiest Year in Vietnam.* New York: Vintage Books, 1993.

Stanton, Shelby L. *The Rise and Fall of an American Army: U.S. Ground Forces in Vietnam, 1965–1973.* Novato, Calif.: Presidio Press, 1985.

Summers, Harry G. Jr. *On Strategy: A Critical Analysis of the Vietnam War.* Novato, Calif.: Presidio Press, 1982.

Thayer, Thomas C. *War Without Fronts: The American Experience in Vietnam.* Annapolis, Md.: Naval Institute Press, 2016.

Thompson, Sir Robert. *Defeating Communist Insurgency: Experiences from Malaya and Vietnam.* London: Chatto and Windus, 1966.

———. *Make For The Hills: Memories of Far Eastern Wars.* London: Leo Cooper, 1989.

———. *No Exit from Vietnam.* New York: David McKay Company, 1969.

———. *Peace Is Not At Hand.* London: Chatto and Windus, 1974.

322d Military History Detachment. *The First Brigade in the Republic of Vietnam July 1956–January 1968.* Tuscaloosa, Ala.: U.S. Army Reserve, n.d.

Trinquier, Roger. *Modern Warfare: A French View of Counterinsurgency.* London: Pall Mall Press, 1964.

Trullinger, James W. *Village at War: An Account of Revolution in Vietnam.* New York: Longman, 1980.

Veith, George J. *Black April: The Fall of South Vietnam, 1973–75.* New York: Encounter Books, 2012.

Viện Lịch Sử Quân Sự Việt Nam [Military History Institute of Vietnam]. *Lịch Sử Kháng Chiến Chống Mỹ Cứu Nước, 1954–1975, Tập VI: Thắng Mỹ Trên Chiến Trường Ba Nước Đông Dươn* [History of the Resistance War Against the Americans to Save the Nation, 1954–1975, volume VI: Defeating the Americans in the Three Nations of Indochina]. Hanoi: Nhà Xuất Bản Chính Trị Quốc Gi, 2003.

Vien, Cao Van. *The Final Collapse.* Washington, D.C.: U.S. Army Center of Military History, 1985.

Villard, Erik B. *Combat Operations: Staying the Course—October 1967 to September 1968.* Washington, D.C.: U.S. Army Center of Military History, 2017.

War History Compilation Committee. *Pictorial War History of ROK Forces to Vietnam, 1964.6–1970.6.* Seoul, Korea: Ministry of National Defense, 1970.

Wiest, Andrew, ed. *Rolling Thunder in a Gentle Land: The Vietnam War Revisited.* New York: Osprey Publishing, 2006.

———. *Vietnam's Forgotten Army: Heroism and Betrayal in the ARVN.* New York: New York University Press, 2008.

Wiest, Andrew and Michael J. Doidge, eds. *Triumph Revisited: Historians Battle for the Vietnam War.* New York: Routledge, 2010.

Wilkins, Warren K. *Nine Days In May: The Battles of the 4th Infantry Division on the Cambodian Border, 1967.* Norman: University of Oklahoma Press, 2017.

Willbanks, James H. *Abandoning Vietnam: How America Left and South Vietnam Lost Its War.* Lawrence: University Press of Kansas, 2004.

———. *The Tet Offensive: A Concise History.* New York: Columbia University Press, 2006.

Index

CPSIA information can be obtained
at www.ICGtesting.com
Printed in the USA
LVHW091932290621
691478LV00001B/115

9 780806 168692